NANDA DEVI

Exploration and Ascent

Eric Shipton and H. W. Tilman leaving England for Nanda Devi in 1934.

ERIC SHIPTON & H.W.TILMAN

NANDA DEVI
Exploration and Ascent

A compilation of the two mountain-exploration books
Nanda Devi and *The Ascent of Nanda Devi*,
plus Shipton's account of his later explorations.

with a new introductory memoir by
CHARLES HOUSTON

BÂTON WICKS · LONDON
THE MOUNTAINEERS · SEATTLE

Nanda Devi was first published in Great Britain in 1936 (Hodder and Stoughton, London) and is collected in *Eric Shipton - The Six Mountain-Travel Books* (Bâton Wicks, London; The Mountaineers, Seattle. 1985/1999)   Copyright © by Nick Shipton.
The Ascent of Nanda Devi was first published in Great Britain and the United States in 1937 (Cambridge University Press, London; Macmillan, New York) and is collected in *H.W.Tilman - The Seven Mountain-Travel Books* (Diadem, London; The Mountaineers, Seattle. 1983/1997) Copyright © by Joan A. Mullins and Pamela H. Davis.
Surveying Trips Around Nanda Devi in 1936 was published in the *Alpine Journal* Vol. 49, 1937 as "Survey in the Nanda Devi District".   Copyright © by Nick Shipton.

Nanda Devi - Exploration and Ascent
is published in Great Britain and America in 1999 and 2000
by Bâton Wicks, London and The Mountaineers, Seattle.
Copyright © by Nick Shipton, Joan A.Mullins and Pamela H.Davis

All trade enquiries in Great Britain, Europe and the Commonwealth (except Canada) to
Bâton Wicks Publications, c/o Cordee, 3a De Montfort Street, Leicester LE1 7HD

All trade enquiries in U.S.A. and Canada to
The Mountaineers · Books, 1001 SW Klickitat Way, Suite 201, Seattle, WA 98134

British Library Cataloguing in Publication Data
ISBN 1-898573-43-3 A catalogue record of this book is available in the British Library

United States Library of Congress Catalog Data
ISBN 0-89886-721-5   A catalog record of this book is available at the Library of Congress

Printed and bound in Great Britain by Butler and Tanner, Frome.

Contents

Photographs in the Text

between pages 96 and 97

Shipton and Tilman leaving Wallasey in 1934;   the 1934 team;
in the Rishi Gorge;   peaks in the Sanctuary;   crossing Satopanth Col;
in the "Bamboo Valley";   the northern rim of the Sanctuary;
the lower part of Nanda Devi's South Ridge.

between pages 224 and 225

The 1936 team;   views of the southern side of Nanda Devi;
on the South Ridge of Nanda Devi;   Longstaff's Col;
Tilman, Kikuli and Houston;   Nanda Devi veterans at Plas y Brenin in 1975;
The Osmaston survey party;   Dunagiri and Changabang;
Angtharkay, Kusang and Pasang;   Shipton and Tilman in 1937;
Pamela Freston and Elizabeth Cowles.

Maps in the Text

ACKNOWLEDGEMENTS The copyright holders and the Publisher wish to acknowledge and thank the following for their help in producing this book: Dr Charles Houston for his entertaining, and historically valuable, introductory memoir; John Shipton, John Harvey and Ben Lovett for photos of the Satopanth Col crossing and Nanda Devi from the south; Hamish Brown for photos of peaks from within the Sanctuary; Commander A. St John Armitage and Celia Armitage for a picture of Pamela Freston (her mother) and other editorial material; the late Joe Tasker for pictures of Dunagiri and Changabang; Major Gordon Osmaston for pictures of the 1936 Survey team, Doug Scott for the pictures of Nanda Devi that introduce the two books, Chris Bonington for the cover photograph; Audrey Salkeld and Frances Daltrey for other photographic assistance; Margaret Body, Margaret Ecclestone, Dorothy Boardman, John Shipton, and Gloria Wilson for sundry editorial and research assistance; Terry King, Martin Moran, George Dvorsky, Dr David Hopkins, Andrew Wielochowski and Lindsay Griffin for mountaineering advice. Books and journals used for reference are noted in the Chronology on pages 283-287 and particular note should be made of the reliable reporting of the *American Alpine Journal* under the editorship of H.Adams Carter, and the thorough coverage of Nanda Devi events in 1934 and 1936 in the *Alpine Journal* under the editorship of Edward Strutt. Other books referred to are *The Last Hero* by Tim Madge (Hodder and Stoughton, London 1995), *Elizabeth Cowles Partridge: Mountaineer* by Janet Robertson (University Press of Colorado Denver, 1999), *Eric Shipton: Everest and Beyond* by Peter Steele Constable, London / The Mountaineers, Seattle 1998).

INTRODUCTION

by Charles Houston

'The Americans and ourselves do not always see eye to eye, but on those rare occasions when we come together – as for example in war, or in the more serious matter of climbing a mountain, we seem to pull together rather well.' So wrote H.W. Tilman in his book *The Ascent of Nanda Devi*. But Tilman didn't tell all, and I welcome this invitation to add some tales to his.

Combined in this book are two stories about a great mountain, by two gifted authors. Not only do they describe great adventures, but, even better – they demonstrate a fascinating contrast in styles. Tilman, taciturn yet witty and explicit in writing. Shipton, loquacious, free-ranging and eloquent, skilled and inspirational in his description of the landscape. Other expedition accounts have been written, but few compare, in style and spirit, with these.

But how four young exuberant Americans and four reserved British veterans were able to harmoniously climb a big mountain which many others had not even been able to reach is the stuff of legend, and surprisingly much is true.

A trace of xenophobia tints Tilman's account of how our expedition began, and glosses over the fact that our 1936 trip did not originate in Britain but in that other Cambridge, in Massachusetts. There in the spring of 1935 some of us undergraduates were captivated by Terry Moore's account of his 1934 ascent of Minya Konka. He, Art Emmons and Dick Burdsall had travelled across China to a virtually unknown and very high mountain and had climbed it. Emmons sustained frostbite injuries to his feet, but the expedition was otherwise a smashing success. Listening spellbound, we thought we too should go to Asia, although we had only vague ideas of where.

The four of us were members of the fledgling Harvard Mountaineering Club which had been revitalised by Brad Washburn and a few of the leading climbers of the day. Ad Carter had done some of the usual alpine climbs and was an expert downhill skier. He was strong, irrepressibly cheerful and outgoing, qualities which later made him a splendid editor of the *American Alpine Journal* for thirty years. He and I had both been on Brad Washburn's expedition to Mount Crillon in Alaska and were good friends. Farnie Loomis had less climbing experience but was strong, enthusiastic, and agile on New England rock. He intended a career in medical research. Art Emmons was just back from Minya Konka and would surely know a lot about the Himalayas; we didn't realise how different his Minya Konka was from the Himalayas we aspired to. Art had spent six months in hospital in Tatsien-lu near the mountain, where he had lost half of each foot to his frostbite. No problem, he said: the excellent care had given him tough skin (complete with hair he claimed) on the remains of his feet and he would have special climbing boots made. Art was headed for a career in the State Department and took life more seriously than some of us did.

As for myself, when I was twelve my parents and I had walked from Lake Geneva to Chamonix where I first read *On High Hills*, and was so excited that my father engaged a guide to take me up a small aiguille. Later I qualified for the Harvard Mountaineering Club and fell under the spell of Brad Washburn who invited me to join his second attempt on Mount Crillon in Alaska. Brad had climbed a lot in the Alps, but his forte was in Alaska. He has had a profound influence on dozens of aspiring climbers. After this I returned to Chamonix where I met and climbed with Graham Brown. In 1934 he joined my father's party to make the first ascent of Mount Foraker, neighbour to McKinley.

Thus, with no touch of humility, the four of us were sure we could do anything! Why not teach the equally cocky Germans a lesson? Perhaps we could show them a thing or two by climbing the Bavarian ridge on Kangchenjunga, where Paul Bauer's strong parties had failed.

Late in 1935 we got serious, read about Kanch and began planning. We soon recognised that we would need different equipment than we used in Alaska, and Loomis went to England to buy this. Graham Brown showed him around and introduced him to the Alpine Club. Loomis was enchanted and cabled me asking if we could invite a few Brits to join us on Kangchenjunga; Emmons and Carter, my co-conspirators, agreed.

Senior Brits delicately suggested that Kanch might be a bit much and perhaps we should try something just a touch less severe. Loomis asked around and either Shipton or Tilman suggested Nanda Devi. It's embarrassing to admit that we didn't appreciate what an extraordinarily generous offer this was. Only later did we learn that among their many adventures they had been the first to find a way through the famous Rishi Gorge in 1934 and certainly planned to return and make the climb. It seemed more than fitting to invite them to join our party, but in 1936 Shipton would be on Everest so, Tilman only could come.

Then Loomis invited Noel Odell, Graham Brown, and Peter Lloyd. We knew all about Odell and Everest, and he had taught at Harvard for several years and been active in the mountaineering club. I had climbed with Graham Brown, but we knew nothing of Tilman and Lloyd. Loomis liked them all, and they seemed to like each other! So it began. What cheek! We tempered this by naming ours the British-American Himalayan Expedition!

Loomis bought gear in England while Carter, Emmons and I, still planning for Kangchenjunga, packed the food. Tilman too, his heart really set on Kanch, where he had never been, went out to India in May hoping to get permission from the Government of India for us to enter Sikkim. But that bureaucracy proved more difficult to penetrate than the Rishi Gorge. So, fortunately for all of us, he gave up Kanch and, to pass the time, trekked in Sikkim for a fortnight, then collected eight Sherpas in Darjeeling, and met Loomis in Ranikhet in late May. The rest of us would arrive at Bombay by ship in early July, and Carter would be coming a bit later from China.

My father planned to go with us at least to the Sanctuary, and he, my mother and sister, and I would meet the Brits in Marseilles and take the P&O steamship to Bombay together. Travelling on the great steamers was in itself a wonderful pleasure, especially on the Pacific and Orient line, flourishing in the great days of the British Raj. For all of us the heady departure from the sights of Marseilles, the even more exotic Port Said and the Suez Canal transported us not only eastward but into a different world.

As we came to know each other better, it slowly appeared to the Brits that my father was not up to the rigours of the Rishi Gorge, and gentle tactful Odell was deputed to break the news. My father took it hard: he considered himself in good shape, had been to Foraker and Mount Hayes and, after all, Graham Brown was his age. He said little but afterward I felt he never forgave Odell.

Meanwhile, disappointed about Kanch, Tilman and Loomis met in Ranikhet and hired porters to carry food to the Nanda Devi Sanctuary. Typically for Tilman they pushed forward, and were not slowed by a falling rock which cracked Tilman's rib, or by Loomis' multiple tropical ulcers. They made it through the Rishi Gorge and left a cache of tsamba (parched barley), rice, and ata (flour) on the rim of the Sanctuary. Thinner and tired, they made double marches back to meet us in Ranikhet.

Our first test came when Tilman approached the mound of supplies which we had, with great difficulty, cleared through customs in Calcutta. With few words (none were needed) he began 'bagging and scrapping', a euphemism we would become more familiar with as time passed. Cowed by this taciturn stranger, Loomis and Emmons could voice only pitiful pleas. About half of the pile, mostly our favourite foods, had been set aside. Then Tilman repeated the process with the equipment which we had so carefully selected. My protests were futile.

Somehow this early neo-confrontation did much to foster our togetherness; at least it showed us something about Tilman. He was careless of creature comforts, scornful of processed foods and seemed to believe bamboo shoots and barley an adequate diet. The Brits didn't know what to make of us Yanks and had some difficulty understanding our form of the language we were supposed to share. True to form, Tilman said nothing, but looked wary. Our celebration of the Fourth of July was viewed with tolerant amusement.

Our eight Sherpas, recruited by Tilman, arrived and each was assigned to one of us. For us Americans the idea of a 'personal' Sherpa was a new and at first an embarrassing experience. We were accustomed to carrying and doing everything ourselves. But we were quickly seduced by the pleasure of waking to hot tea presented at our tent by a smiling Sherpa, who also packed our gear, broke camp, and laid out our bedding again each evening.

Pasang Kikuli, the sirdar, was assigned to me and we soon became good friends. He had survived the awful 1934 tragedy on Nanga Parbat where three Germans and six Sherpas had died in a shameful retreat during a storm. Pasang would go with me to K2 in 1938 where he was magnificent. In 1939, while assisting the next American K2 bid, he died in a heroic attempt to rescue Dudley Wolfe. He was one of the all time great Sherpas,

After giving away, bartering, or leaving for our return a great pile of scrapped goodies, we made up eighty pound loads for thirty-seven Dotial porters who would meet us and our eight Sherpas at the roadhead in Garul. It was raining, as it would for most of the next three weeks, but for some of us with the optimism of youth and ignorance rain made the occasional sunlight doubly sweet.

We were marching through Jim Corbett's country and we saw man-eaters in every thicket. It was Kipling country too, the stage for the Great Game, played for a century by Russians and British for control of India. We believed that Kim had sat on the rim of the Nanda Devi Sanctuary. All the world was ours. I specially remember Odell striding beneath fragrant deodars along a ridge to Gwaldam repeating over and over: 'Gad, it's good to be back.' It had been twelve years since his remarkable feats on Everest and he was ecstatic. On one momentous day we soaked in a hot spring watched by a naked saddhu. It was all too good to be true. The paths were good, our pace steady and spirits high. Rain, lice and the leeches waiting on every leaf didn't matter. We had brought Logan tents, standard for Alaska, but their weakness soon became apparent. Tilman said in short unmistakable words that it was drier outside than in; we cut holes in the floor to drain out the water. He insisted that leeches went through the fabric as easily as the rain did. Not till deep snow on the mountain did he concede their value. We religiously drank only tea or boiled or iodinized water; even so, most of us were introduced to 'squitters'. Saving out special foods for later, we ate mostly what we could buy in the villages and soon came to love chupattis (unleavened flat bread baked over the fire).

I'm dwelling on the approach march not only because it was so exciting for us, but because such a 175-mile walk is unusual today when most parties fly or travel by jeep almost to Base Camp, missing the shared joys and sorrows and chances to learn about their companions. We believed whatever the Brits said because we knew so little about them or the Himalayas. All we could offer were stories from Alaska. Despite what Tilman wrote later, we never claimed the mosquitoes there were as big as birds, nor the bears like elephants, though we might have made a few slightly misleading statements. Tilman smoked his pipe and said little. It was impossible to be sure what he was thinking of this strange group to which he had been invited, but he did not seem overjoyed.

Odell was determined to 'do some geology', and despite Tilman's scowls, we (that is the porters) carried a long and heavy glacier drill all the way to Base Camp; it was never unpacked and brought home virginal. I was eager to collect some data about how we tolerated altitude and distributed small diaries to be completed every day; that plan didn't last long. Emmons now had to concentrate on his first long trek since his months in hospital. Loomis was trying to regain weight and strength and heal his painful tropical ulcers which I treated with the ignorant enthusiasm of a first year medical student.

We were about to enter the true Himalayas at last. Leaving good paths, we dropped down into the Rishi Gorge that had foiled so many others. Fortunately Tilman knew the way and led us into the gorge where half the porters refused to cross a raging torrent, leaving us to double carry our gear.

Under a huge overhang beside the Rishi we inevitably faced more 'bagging and scrapping'. Our few remaining special foods were abandoned – 'bloody chemicals,' snorted Tilman. 'Might as well eat a boiled shirt' was his verdict on our special rice. The last canned foods were banned, except those which Tilman said 'gave good value for weight'.

Even slimmed down we had to make two carries with heavy packs over rain-slick rock. The most difficult and dangerous passages were along wet, narrow, down-sloping grassy ledges with precious little purchase, trying not to look down thousands of feet to the Rishi, whose thunder we could barely hear.

Finally we climbed a wider ledge we called Pisgah – and looked down and out over the rolling Sanctuary at our mountain which was even more awesome in the real. The supplies Tilman and Loomis had left were untouched and we camped on a rugged slope above the valley floor.

After the drama of the Gorge the Sanctuary seemed a trifle disappointing – thousands of acres of grass with only scattered fields of flowers, and little wildlife except the ubiquitous Himalayan partridge. A number of deep gullies slowed us and we camped halfway along. Back in those days few if any humans had been there, but soon shepherds and climbers would so crowd the area that government felt it important to close the Sanctuary for twenty years.

Above a flat outwash from one of the glaciers falling from the mountain we set up our Base Camp. Next day we climbed a thousand feet of scree and examined the route which Shipton and Tilman had thought feasible.

We looked up at a very steep wall of rock and ice, but to the left was a nice ridge, the obvious choice. We would travel light with only enough supplies to stock a few camps high enough to make a bid for the top. Each day one pair would be out ahead to recce, while the rest did donkey service, repeating this higher and higher. Emmons would not go on the mountain, fearing further frost-bite injury, but would take care of Base Camp and map parts of the Sanctuary.

The route was steep, and quite dangerous here and there, but it had little technical climbing until the last few thousand feet. We suffered a nearly disastrous blow at Camp One when the entire supply of tea fell down the steep snow slope; frantic search was unproductive and the Brits were devastated. There was serious talk of going home, but we were quite happy with our Ovaltine and insisted on continuing. Some Sherpas came down sick. Pasang Kikuli developed snow-blindness from climbing in dense snow and fog without sunglasses. They went down to Base and we carried everything ourselves, finally settling in a comfortable site at about 21,800 feet.

We had gained height slowly and were well-acclimatised, except for Graham Brown who was bluer and more short of breath than the others. More disturbing was how unaware of his condition he was and, indeed, rather paranoid. It was obvious he could not go higher, but not till years later, when I knew more about altitude, did I recognise that he had had a severe case of altitude illness.

To this point we hadn't really had a leader because things just seemed to work themselves out. Looking back it's clear that Tilman, saying nothing, guided our progress. In the process he became more amiable, his barbs less sharp, even smiling now and then. One memorable evening, lubricated by a celebratory bottle of Apricot Brandy, he had even talked about his travels; our stories about Alaska dwindled to dust, and we listened spell-bound. Odell said little about Everest after his happy recollections on the march in; Graham Brown described in detail the routes he had pioneered on the Italian face of Mont Blanc.

That night by a secret ballot we chose Tilman as leader and asked him to name a summit team. He did, and next day in promising weather, the party moved Odell and me up to a microscopic ledge and left us at dusk to scratch out a tent 'platform' at 23,400 feet. Next morning we started for the top, making slow going over deep snow and steep rock. By mid-afternoon we clearly would not summit, although there seemed to be little difficulty above us. We went back to camp where we celebrated with a rare tin of meat. But my half, the bottom, was spoiled and within an hour I was wishing myself dead. All night I crawled in and out of the tent.

In the clear still morning Odell shouted down a few thousand feet to the others,

'Charlie is ill', a great semantic error which led Carter to believe me 'killed'. The others rushed up in six hours and seemed rather annoyed to find me alive. Tilman had brought his kit; I was trundled down, and next day Odell and Tilman moved camp a little higher and then went to the summit. After narrowly escaping an avalanche they stood on the top where, as Tilman's classic quotation implies, British reserve was momentarily relaxed. 'I believe we so far forgot ourselves as to shake hands on it.'

Earlier we had agreed never to tell who made the top, and later dispatched a telegram to Dr Tom Longstaff, who had seen our mountain from a pass on the rim of the Sanctuary, saying only 'Two reached summit August 30.' The secret could not be kept of course, but we all knew that success belonged to all. All of us regarded Nanda Devi as an adventure, not the path to fame and fortune. It had been a great journey and a gallant crew.

How then did we get along so happily, coming from different countries and with such different temperaments? Attitude and motivation were partly responsible. We climbed during the era of amateurism and in 1936 our expedition cost a fraction of what such a trip would cost today. Fortunately we could afford this with a little help from friends and a few small lecture fees. We were there for fun, adventure in a new region. We Americans had career plans ahead, and our climbs were pure vacation. Tilman had no ambition to be famous and had enough money from his Kenya days for his ascetic life style. Odell and Graham Brown had made their names and were university professors. Lloyd had his own career and showed no sign of wanting to be a mountain hero. All of us could afford Nanda Devi as an adventure, not a path to fame or fortune. The climate today is quite different.

Our route had been quite difficult and occasionally dangerous, but it was the logical way. We did it safely (most of the time) and without accident.

We all got down safely too but sadly at Base Camp we found that Kitar had died of dysentery. Emmons did not know how to cope with him, since our medical kit was very small and we had no medicine to give him. This was a sad blow to all of us but the only blemish on a happy time. After a small ceremony we marked his grave with a cairn and a great slab with his name.

Then it was time to go. Tilman from the start had wanted to leave by crossing a high pass on the eastern rim of the Sanctuary which we later named for Tom Longstaff who had reached it from the other side. He asked me and Pasang Kikuli to go with him and I was delighted. We planned to cross the col and then Traill's Pass down into the Gori Ganga valley. This was thought to be shorter, and with luck would get me to Ranikhet and Delhi in time for the twice weekly flight to London. The others would return the way we had come – down the Rishi. We parted sadly but well pleased with the effort.

Crossing the col turned out to be the most dangerous part of the whole trip, with wet sloppy snow on loose rock and steep ice. We fumbled a way over in the dusk, bivouacked, abandoned Traill's Pass which we couldn't see, and slid down twenty miles to Martoli. It was a hard hundred miles to the roadhead where we commandeered a nabob's car and rode to Ranikhet and I flew home to medical school.

Nanda Devi was an extraordinary experience. We knew that Tilman had steered the ship and we all had rowed. There may have been some bad times but they've been forgotten. We certainly wanted to reach the top, and two of us did. But the top was only the icing on a delicious cake. Peter Lloyd and I are the only ones left but when we join the others we'll have a bottle of Apricot Brandy with us. We had lived and worked together unbelievably well, and Tilman's book ends with a better comment than I can:

It was but a short three months that we had met, many of us as strangers, but inspired by a single hope and bound by a common purpose. This purpose was only achieved by team-work, team-work the more remarkable on account of the two different nationalities; and though these two nations have a common origin they are for that reason more critical of each other's shortcomings – as relationship leads proverbially to ill-feeling ...

Where each man pulled his weight each must share the credit; for though it is natural for each man to have his own aspirations, it is in mountaineering more than in most things, that we try to believe:

'The game is more than the players of the game, and the ship is more than the crew.'

EPILOGUE

Bill Tilman, curiously, was the one I came closest to over the next thirty years. He had been decorated for bravery in the Great War, and had been wounded several times – once it was rumoured, by a broken romance. Did this send him to plant coffee in Kenya? He never said. In 1950, by a wonderful chance in Kathmandu, he met my father who invited him to join his small party and walk across Nepal to be the first westerners ever to visit the Khumbu and south side of Everest. Hearing I would be in the party he accepted. Not until we began the walk did he know that Elizabeth Cowles, a well-travelled American climber, would be with us. Betsy had been amicably divorced from a wealthy businessman and was one of the few outstanding American women mountaineers. She was charming and strong and enthusiastic and one of my close friends. For four days Tilman sulked, walking ahead or behind us, eating separately, shunning all of us. But then his allegedly misogynist barriers crumbled, and he and Betsy became friends. Walking together they were quite sweet, if such a word could ever apply to Tilman, and later exchanged letters, even rare visits, leading me to ask Betsy what the future might hold. She laughed it off but the platonic affair lasted until she died. Tilman and I met twice and wrote often until he was lost at sea in 1977.

Odell, older and famous, was gentle, courtly but warm, and a joy to be with. He and Emmons shared interests in geology, and they too corresponded. Years later Odell came to visit me in Vermont, and I managed to see him in his rooms at Cambridge University shortly before he died, at ninety-six, little changed by the years. Lloyd went on to distinguish himself on Everest in 1938, married, built a career and moved to Australia; we still correspond.

Graham Brown didn't fully recover even at Base Camp from his altitude-related paranoia. This was my first experience with what today would be called high-altitude cerebral oedema (RACE). There had been no sign of this when we had climbed together in Alaska or the Alps, but he had told me about his quarrel with another partner, Frank Smythe, which I didn't give much weight at the time, but later recognised as probably a symptom of disorder. His behaviour in our high camp did not end with the expedition. When I did not invite him to K2 in 1938 he went to Masherbrum instead where a similar episode developed, ending in failure and bad frostbite for him and some of the party. As we returned from K2,

I visited him in hospital in Srinagar, but we did not fully re-establish our friendship until 1975 when I dined with him in London. By then he had been editor of the *Alpine Journal* for several years and was criticised for his dictatorial decisions. His diary, which I saw much later, showed several harsh comments about all of us, but these had obviously been added later, in better handwriting, and in ink. In retrospect I suspect his exposure to altitude had triggered a fundamental emotional problem which surfaced again on Masherbrum and may have recurred.*

In describing our experience and my love for our party, I have barely mentioned the two books. Of course we did not see them until a year after our trip, and only then began to appreciate how warmly Tilman felt towards us.

I did not get to know Shipton until years later. Actually, while Tilman and I were crossing Longstaff's Col, the rest of the party in the Rishi Gorge met Shipton hurrying in on his surveying trip.

Since then many other expeditions have been to the Sanctuary and climbed on Nanda Devi and several new routes have been found (see Appendix I). Ad Carter returned with a larger party in 1976, but the group was incompatible and Nanda Devi Unsoeld, the daughter of the co-leader Willi Unsoeld, died of an abdominal catastrophe high on the route – a tragedy of particular poignancy as her father had named her after 'the most beautiful mountain I have seen.' Another expedition had a political-military mission whose details remain secret. Its failure led to at least two follow-up attempts, and it may have contributed to the decisions to close the Sanctuary at various times.

Shipton and I tried several times to meet, but on each occasion we missed each other by days or hours. Finally, in 1974 or 1975 we were in California at the same time my wife and I spent the whole day with him and his then partner Phyllis Wint. As others had predicted, I found him a great and wonderful contrast to Tilman: talkative, candid, full of eloquent reminiscences of beautiful scenes and hair-raising experiences. It was hard to believe he and Tilman had been so compatible and successful for so many years. Yet of the two, I found Tilman closer to my heart, but of course we had shared great days together.

What of the future? Certainly others will go to this blessed mountain, approaching it from over the rim rather than through the Sanctuary. The twin summits can be reached over the rim without trespassing on the Sanctuary, which hopefully will be protected, perhaps closed to all, because it has been so often littered since our stay. Though this is sad and would anger climbers, there are so many other lovely valleys and peaks that are not so fragile and more easily accessed, and these should satisfy those who truly love the mountains. How true was Oscar Wilde's statement: 'Each man kills the thing he loves' – only now are we beginning to revere and protect the mountains we love.

Charles S. Houston MD
Burlington, Vermont 1999

*After Nanda Devi, Arthur Emmons joined the State Department. Just before Pearl Harbor he was posted to Korea, where he was interned for a period. He also did consular work in Spain (where his wife took up bull-fighting), China, Ireland, Portugal and Australia. He rose to the rank of Ambassador just before he died in 1962.

William Farnsworth Loomis was recruited into the OSS just before WW2 and served in China with Ilya Tolstoi for several years. After the war he took his medical degree, married, and set up a laboratory to study cancer-like growths in a species of microscopic plants. He also taught Chemistry at Brandeis University and authored several books on philosophy and religion. He died in 1973.

NANDA DEVI

NANDA DEVI

by ERIC SHIPTON

First published by Hodder and Stoughton, 1936

Contents

FOREWORD

Hugh Ruttledge

WHEN Mr. Shipton honoured me by an invitation to write a foreword to his book, I accepted with a particular sense of both privilege and opportunity; of privilege because the book is an epic of mountaineering exploration, of opportunity because so little is yet known of three aspects of Himalayan travel: the comparatively easy and inexpensive access to some of the wildest regions, the almost unlimited scope for small but thoroughly competent parties, and the amazing strength and capacity of the Sherpa porter.

I had the good fortune to serve for nearly five years in the section of the Central Himalayan chain with which this book deals. I climbed there with Sherpa, Gurkha, Bhotia and Kumaoni – as well as British – companions; and we made four attempts to enter the great Nanda Devi Basin, as better mountaineers had done before us. It is therefore with some knowledge of the facts that I acclaim the success gained by Messrs. Shipton and Tilman and their three Sherpa comrades as one of the greatest feats in mountaineering history. Not only that: it has proved beyond doubt that, in these regions at any rate, a small homogeneous party, self-contained, able to live off the country, with no weak links and ably led, can go further and do more than the elaborate expeditions which have been thought necessary for the Himalaya. What a field of adventure and enter-prise this throws open to young mountaineers, now that most of the other great mountain ranges of the world are but too well known.

One word of warning is perhaps necessary: work of this kind should be undertaken only by those who have attained the highest degree of mountaineering skill, judgment and endurance. Those who read this book with understanding will realise the number of tight places this party got into, where nothing but the most brilliant technical competence could have got them out alive. It is not a game for the beginner, or for the lover of flesh-pots.

The greatest feat was the successful entry into, and departure from, the "inner sanctuary" of the Nanda Devi Basin – a place only about seventy-five miles from Almora, yet hitherto more inaccessible than the North Pole. At last men have set foot upon the slopes of the greatest mountain in the British Empire; and to them will be extended the admiration of those who have struggled and fought for it – notably Dr. T. G. Longstaff, who so nearly succeeded in 1907.

Less spectacular perhaps, but hardly less exacting, were the two great traverses of the Badrinath-Gangotri and the Badrinath-Kedarnath watershed, along lines famous in Hindu mythology. These were replete with all the misery that mountaineering in the monsoon season can entail, but the climbers have their reward in the completion of a task that was well worth accomplishment, and in the regard of good Hindus, in whose eyes this would be a pilgrimage of superabundant merit.

Mr. Shipton has paid generous and well-deserved tribute to the three Sherpa porters who accompanied him. It is no exaggeration to say that, without men of this type, climbing the higher Himalaya would be impossible. On them are based our hopes of climbing Mount Everest, and for years to come there will be none among the Himalayan peoples to equal them as mountaineers, porters, and loyal, unselfish companions. They are well on their way to become a corps of guides as famous as the men of the Alps. In time there may be others as good – there is splendid material in Kumaon, in Hunza or in Baltistan, to name a few Himalayan regions; and the humble Nepalese Dotials who served Mr. Shipton so faithfully in the Rishiganga are worth their salt. At present the Sherpa holds pride of place, and his morale and *esprit-de-corps* are tremendous assets. Given the right leaders – and they must be of the best – he is unbeatable. The description of him in this book is the most understanding and delightful that has ever been written.

The lists are now set for great deeds in the Himalayan snow-fields. Messrs. Shipton and Tilman have shown the way; let us hope that many will follow.

HUGH RUTTLEDGE

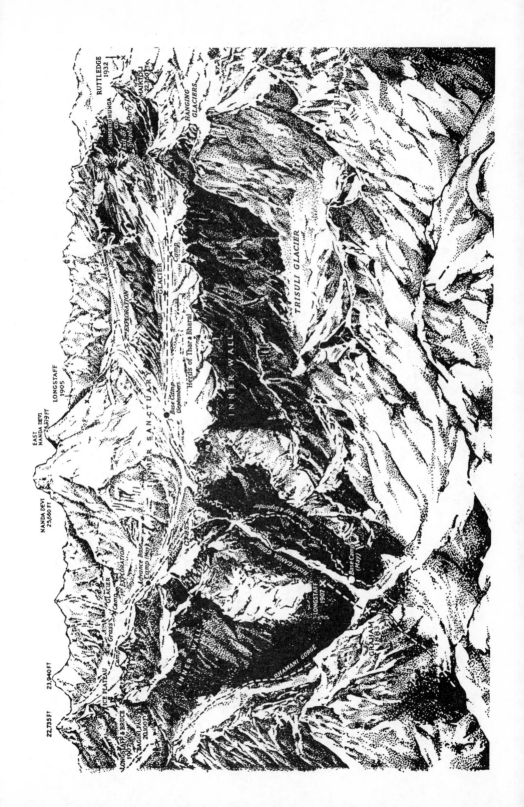

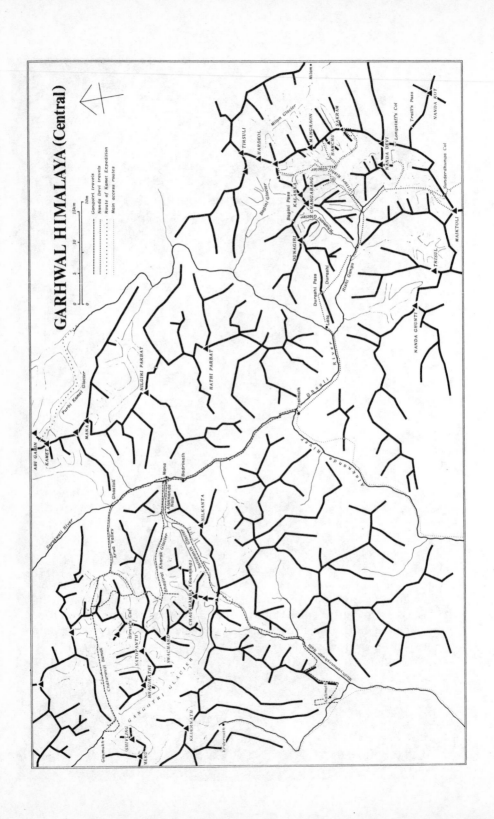

Part 1

Innocents from Nepal
– and London

CHAPTER ONE

IN the exploration of a continent the mountainous areas are generally the last strongholds of mystery to fall before the onslaught of man, be that onslaught brutal, scientific or merely inquisitive. The difficulties of transport are so great; the physical hardships so heavy; the reward so small – for glacier regions are materially useless. For these reasons then the high places of the earth remain remote and inaccessible until man, having explored all fertile regions of a particular country, finds himself dwelling under the very shadow of the mountains and becomes aware of an overwhelming desire to conquer them. This feeling doubtless owes its force partly to the attraction of the unknown and partly to the natural beauty and sublime grandeur of mountainous districts; but I like to think that it goes deeper; that the wish to explore springs from a delight in the purely æsthetic nature of the quest.

When man is conscious of the urge to explore, not all the arduous journeyings, the troubles that will beset him and the lack of material gain from his investigations will stop him. As a famous Arctic explorer remarked many years ago: "The great majority of men who visit the Arctic *do so because they want to*, a large number do so for publicity, while it is possible that one or two have gone there for purely scientific purposes."

The italics are mine. What was true of the Arctic then is equally true of the little-known mountain country of today, and of the Alps before they became "the playground of Europe". To the early explorer fighting his way across the passes of *Haute Savoie* and to people who, like myself, have come under the spell of the high Himalaya the reason for exploration remains the same – *we do so because we want to*.

It was my good fortune to visit the mighty ranges of South Central Asia, which stretch from east to west without a break for over fifteen hundred miles, as a member of F. S. Smythe's Kamet expedition in 1931. Then, for the first time, I saw mountains whose rugged splendour baffles description and whose complex structure probably renders them inaccessible even to the most advanced mountaineering technique. With this vision before me, surpassing all the wildest dreams of my early mountaineering apprenticeship, I welcomed the opportunity, some two years later, of joining the fourth expedition to Mount Everest, where I saw the harsher and less lovely aspect of the Tibetan side of the range.

The Kamet and Everest expeditions had, as their main objective, the climbing of a single lofty peak. In the one case we succeeded: in the other we failed. But on each occasion I had a mighty longing to detach myself from the big and cumbersome organisation which for some reason had been thought to be necessary for an attack on the more lofty summits of the earth, and to wander with a small, self-contained party through the labyrinth of unexplored valleys, forming our plans to suit the circumstances, climbing peaks when opportunity occurred, following up our own topographical clues and crossing passes into unknown territory. This desire held me captive even before I left the Everest Base Camp in July, 1933, and I resolved to carry out some such scheme before age, marriage or other considerations made it impossible of accomplishment.

During the winter of 1933–34 I began to form plans. The primary choice of district was not difficult. There can be few regions of the Himalaya providing topographical problems of more absorbing interest than that lying in the Almora and Garhwal districts of the United Provinces. Here there are no political obstacles (the bugbear of the Asiatic explorer) to be overcome as the region lies almost entirely in British India. Moreover, the transport of supplies and equipment to a suitable base is a simple matter, the organisation of which does not require any vast experience of the country or knowledge of the language. Brief acquaintance, while with the Kamet expedition, had given me some first-hand information on a number of problems and I felt confident that, with the modest resources at my disposal, I should be able to carry out my proposed campaign with some fair chance of achieving useful results. Therefore I plumped for Almora and Garhwal.

The question of companionship did not worry me. There were a number of people who would be quite prepared – and suitably qualified – to take part in such an enterprise, and my association with the Nepalese and Tibetan porters of the 1933 Everest expedition had convinced me that their natural, if undeveloped, mountaineering ability, their constant cheerfulness and their wonderful sense of loyalty, would make them ideal comrades. So I got into touch with Karma Paul, the Tibetan interpreter to the Everest expeditions, and requested him to send word to Angtharkay, Pasang Bhotia, and Rinzing, three men for whom I felt particular liking since they were among the eight porters who had placed our Camp VI at the enormous altitude of 27,400 feet the previous summer. Rinzing, however, was not available, and at the last moment Angtharkay brought forward his cousin, Kusang Namgir, a man of extraordinary toughness and ability.

In January '34 I had my best stroke of luck, in a letter from my old friend H. W. Tilman, who had been my companion on three expeditions to the mountains of East and Central Africa. This letter announced that, since he had long leave from Kenya, he had bought a second-hand bicycle and had ridden it across the continent alone, through Uganda, Belgian Congo and French Equatorial Territory, finally emerging on the West Coast where he sold the bicycle and boarded a cargo steamer bound for England. The letter said further that this had proved a most cheap and efficacious method of reaching home and that the writer, during his cycling travels, had existed entirely on native food, keeping pretty fit except for a few bouts of fever.

Here indeed was a kindred spirit. When I told him of my plans he at once offered to put up his share of the expenses. This, I estimated, would amount to £150 all told: that is, the whole expedition would not cost more than £300. Actually, we managed on less than that.

Our party was now complete and numbered four besides myself: Tilman, Angtharkay, Pasang and Kusang. Nobody could have had four more loyal, determined and unselfish comrades and there remained now only the choice of a main objective.

Now, nobody attempting mountain exploration in the Himalaya (or anywhere else, for that matter) can afford to miss an opportunity of discussing his plans with Dr. T. G. Longstaff. When he gave me that opportunity, therefore, I accepted with alacrity and, as a result of long discussions with him, I determined to make an attempt to force the hitherto inviolate sanctuary of the Nanda Devi Basin.

At first this seemed as if we were flying too high. Here was a mountain whose summit was the highest in the British Empire. For centuries it had inspired worship and propitiatory sacrifice as the "Blessed Goddess" of Hindu philosophers and scribes. For more than fifty years it had been the inaccessible goal of explorers who, attracted by the impregnability of its surroundings, had failed in repeated attempts to reach even its foot, the reason being that around the 25,660 foot mountain itself stretched a huge ring of peaks, more than thirty of them over 21,000 feet high, that constituted themselves unrelenting guardians of the great mountain and defeated any penetration.

And we, with light equipment, few stores, and a joint capital of £300, were setting forth to reach this goal. That we eventually succeeded was largely due to the unremitting labour of those who preceded us. To explorers in general and to mountaineers in particular, it is a well-known fact that each successive attempt at the solving of a problem makes that problem easier of solution. Few great mountains have been climbed, and few passes crossed, at first, second or even third essay. The man who eventually reaches the summit of Mount Everest will have done so, not by his own efforts alone, but over the shoulders of the pioneers – Mallory, Norton, Somervell – without whose hard-won experience he would have stood no chance. So with our own – seemingly fantastic – expedition. That measure of success met with in our enterprise, we owe primarily to those who went before us.

The days went on, passed swiftly in discussion of our base, our transport, our food – enthralling, this business of arranging an expedition that might well have been formulated on that classic statement of the great Duke of Wellington when comparing the organisation of the French tactical scheme in the

Peninsular War with that of his own. Of Napoleon's Generals he said that their plans were laid with such thoroughness that, at a single slight hitch, their whole structure was liable to collapse; whereas, if anything went wrong with his (Wellington's) less complex arrangements, all he had to do was "to tie it up with string" and so carry on . . . a moral that applies to exploration as well as to war, and is probably the reason why a small expedition, such as our own, almost invariably achieves far more than does a large and elaborate one when proportionate costs are taken into consideration.

So, on April 6th, 1934, after a short period of preparation we left Liverpool for Calcutta in the Brocklebank cargo ship *Mahsud*.

CHAPTER TWO

DURING the long hot days of the four weeks' voyage we discussed and re-discussed our plans, and made ourselves familiar with the history and geography of Garhwal; and in order to present the reader with a simple picture of the country, I cannot do better than to revert for the moment to geographical data.

"The Himalaya" is the rather loose name given to those mountains which extend, in an unbroken chain, for some fifteen hundred miles across the north of India. The word itself is a combination of two Sanskrit words, *him* meaning snow, and *alaya* abode. Modern geographers restrict the name to the range enclosed within the arms of the Indus River on the north-west, and the Brahmaputra on the south-east; but one must remember that the Karakoram and Hindu Kush ranges north and west of the Indus, and the mountains of northern Burmah and western China are all part of the same system.

Behind the chain to the north lies the plateau of Tibet at a general altitude of 15,000 feet. Here, at a point almost opposite the centre of the chain and within one hundred miles of each other, rise those two great rivers, Indus and Brahmaputra, which flow, in opposite directions to each other and parallel to the Himalaya, until they bend south and cut a way through the mountain barrier practically at its two extremities.

It might be expected, therefore, that the highest part of the Himalaya would form a watershed, but this is not so, and the Ganges, the Sutlej and numerous tributaries which between them constitute the system, rise on the north side of the axes of highest elevation. Two explanations are given of this: (a) that the rivers are gradually "cutting back" (that is, that the heads of the streams are eating their way northwards owing to the greater rainfall on the southern rather than the northern slopes); (b) that the line of drainage was formed antecedent to the elevation and has, by erosion, maintained its original course during a slow process of upheaval which is supposed to be still going on at the rate of a fraction of an inch a year.

Such geographical explanation may be dull, but it is intensely difficult to appreciate the Himalaya as it now is without indulging in these lofty speculations as to how or why. The extent of such a vast range is not easily realised, and many picture to themselves an area about the size of that of the Alps, with Everest towering in the centre and all the lesser satellites grouped round him. Some better notion may be gained if we visualise a mountain chain running from London to the Black Sea with Everest somewhere near Belgrade and Nanga Parbat somewhere near London.

Having these relative distances in mind it may be of further assistance to consider the range in its artificial or political divisions. Starting from the Indus Valley, over which looms the Nanga Parbat massif, the chain runs for two hundred miles through Kashmir, and in the same State, but across the Indus to the north, lies the parallel range of the Karakoram and Mount Godwin Austin (K2), second in height only to Everest.

Continuing south-east for another two hundred miles through a number of small States known collectively as the Simla Hill States, the range enters Garhwal. East of this it runs for nearly six hundred miles through the independent State of Nepal which contains the highest crest-line, all the southern slopes and, in its extreme north-east corner, Everest itself, the main watershed following the Nepal-Tibet border.

Two more independent States follow, Sikkim and Bhutan, which together account for another two hundred miles of the Himalaya. These States approximate in language, religion and custom to Tibet, and have both a spiritual and a temporal ruler. Finally, between Bhutan and the Brahmaputra are three hundred miles of wild and mountainous country, nominally Chinese, about which even now our knowledge is very imperfect.

The districts of British Garhwal and Almora, with which Tilman and I were chiefly concerned, lie almost in the centre of the Himalayan range and are, moreover, the only place where our border marches with that of Tibet. Garhwal has had a chequered history. In early days it was divided amongst no less than fifty-two petty chieftains, each with his own fortress, a state of affairs to which the name itself is a description, since the word *garh* means castle. Five hundred years ago the strongest chieftain brought the other fifty-one under his dominion and ruled as Prince of Garhwal, and from then down to the close of the eighteenth century there was constant warfare between his descendants and the rulers of the neigbouring State of Kumaon. But the Gurkhas of Nepal (it is worthy of note that even now Nepal, which contains at least forty-eight peaks known to exceed 25,000 feet, is strictly closed to European exploration), failing to extend their conquests in the direction of China, turned their attention to the west and overran both Garhwal and Kumaon as far west as the Sutlej. Garhwal they ruled with a rod of iron, and from this mountain stronghold they began to make raids into the plains – at the expense of subjects of the British Raj. As a consequence there followed the Nepalese War of 1814–15, which, after the usual disastrous start, finally resulted in the Gurkhas being driven back within their present boundaries. Western Garhwal was restored to its native ruler, and the rest of the State, plus its neighbour, Almora, became part of British India.

The first Commissioner was G. W. Traill, who reduced the country to order and laid a secure foundation for its future peace and prosperity. A worthy memorial to his work and the goodwill he earned as heritage for his successors, is the well-known Pass which he was the first to cross and which is named after him.

Garhwal covers about one hundred miles from east to west and some fifty from north to south. The natives are short and sturdy, and fairer in colour than the inhabitants of the plains. Blue eyes and cheeks tinged with red are not uncommon and some of the women are very beautiful although here, as in most mountainous regions, goitre is very prevalent. Approaching the Tibetan border the people are Bhotias of Tibetan origin speaking a Tibetan-Burman dialect. They have few traces of Buddhism and profess to be Hindus, but not of a strictly orthodox type. For instance, they are quite ready to eat with Tibetans, a fact which helps them considerably in their trade with that country. Indeed, they hold a monopoly of such trade and use goats and sheep to carry rice and wheat over the high passes, returning with borax, salt, and yaks' tails.

A broad outline of the topography of Garhwal is best understood by looking at the three or, if the Tehri State is included, the four great river valleys which run right up into the heart of the country, forming the trade routes and attracting populous centres. These valleys are of great depth and within ten miles of 20,000 feet snow peaks the valley floor may be but 4,000 feet above sea level and clothed in tropical vegetation.

All these rivers rise to the north of the main axis of elevation and have cut their way through the east-west range almost at right angles so that the containing walls of the valleys, on which are grouped the highest peaks, run roughly north and south. There are three such main ridges, each possessing many minor features of distinction: on the east that on which stands Nanda Devi, 25,660 feet, the highest peak in Garhwal; in the middle that of Kamet, 25,447, the second highest peak; and on the west that of the Badrinath-Kedernath group of peaks, in formation much more complex than that of the other two.

The Gori River, rising on the Tibetan border in the depression which forms the Untadhura Pass, for the first twenty miles of its course separates the eastern (or Nanda Devi) group from the tangle of snow peaks in western Nepal. Beyond this point the Gori bends away to the south-east to fix the political boundary of Nepal and concerns us no more, but its place is taken by the Pindar River which rises on the south-eastern extremities of the Nanda Devi group and, curling round it to the west, marks the termination of the regions of ice and snow in the south.

Before passing on to mention of the third river there are some interesting features to note about the valley of the Gori River, known as the Milam Valley. It forms the main highway between India and western Tibet and from it three routes lead to the Tibetan market of Gyanima and Taklakot. All involve the crossing of several high passes, the easiest of which is 16,750 feet high and can only be negotiated eight months of the year. The Bhotias have an amusing legend of the way these routes were pioneered: it seems that the first inhabitants of the Milam Valley were, like Esau, hairy – even to their tongues – and on the Gori Glacier there lived a bird of prey whose sole diet was these hairy ones. To free the people from this predatory fowl a Tibetan Lama sent his servant to kill it, and gave him as guide a man who was for ever changing his form, first into a dog at the Pass which is now called Kingribingri, then into a stag, which gave the name to the Dol Dunga Pass, then into a bear at the Topi Dunga Pass, a camel at the Unta Dhura, a tiger at the Dung Udiyar, and finally a hare at Samgoan. Thus the route to India was first shown and the bird of prey eventually killed – but not before it had eaten all the hairy ones. And the servant liked the valley so much that he expressed a desire to live in it but complained that there was no salt, so the kindly Lama took salt and sowed it like grain, with the result that there is today a salty grass on which the Bhotia flocks feed, and even yet Buddhist priests entering the valley ask for alms in the name of the Lama who sowed the salt, and Tibetans bring their herds over the border for the sake of the salty grass.

I digress. It is high time we followed the Pindar River westwards to where it flows into the Alaknanda some thirty miles away. Above this junction the Alaknanda bends to the north and receives from the north-east a large tributary, the Dhauli, whose valley lies between the Nanda Devi and the Kamet groups. At the head of this valley thirty miles further to the north is the Niti Pass, also leading to Tibet, and the river itself rises from the glaciers to the east and slightly north of Kamet. From this mountain near the Tibetan border the massif runs almost due south very nearly to the Dhauli-Alaknanda junction.

The main Alaknanda Valley which, as we saw, continues due north, separates the Kamet range from the Badrinath-Kedarnath group. The river rises near the Mana Pass and, passing under the western flanks of Kamet, receives large tributaries from the Badrinath peaks. This latter range does not extend so far south as its companion ranges but turns sharply back to the north-west, forming an acute angle in which lies the Gangotri Glacier, the largest in these parts and the source of the Bhagirathi River, the main tributary of the Ganges.

The Nanda Devi group itself, around which the interest of Tilman and myself gyrated throughout our voyage to Calcutta, presents unusual features. Imagine a main ridge running from north to south and in the southern half three arms projecting to the west. At the southern extremity a long one leads up to Trisul, 23,360 feet, and terminates ten miles to the west in Nandakna, 20,700 feet. Several miles north is a shorter arm on which is Dunagiri, 23,184 feet, and between the two lies the shortest arm of all which ends abruptly at Nanda Devi itself. From Trisul and from Dunagiri two spurs project towards each other to form the fourth side of the wall, nowhere less than 18,000 feet high, which surrounds Nanda Devi. The only breach in this formidable barrier is between these spurs where the Rishi Ganga, the river which drains the glaciers around Nanda Devi, breaks through by way of a deep gorge.

And it was by following the Rishi Ganga that we hoped to reach the shrine of the "Blessed Goddess".

CHAPTER THREE

HIMALAYAN travel is of course full of complexities. The shortness of the season during which expeditions are possible, the uncertainty of the monsoon, the danger of land-slips, endemic cholera and other diseases of the lower valleys, leeches and insect pests, extremes of heat and cold, altitude, local superstitions and the consequent difficulty in obtaining help from the natives – these are but a few of the obstacles to be overcome by the traveller.

And in the case of Nanda Devi one tremendous problem was added, the fact that the peak is encircled by a huge amphitheatre that must surely be unique. It is hard for anyone who has not studied this phenomenon at close quarters to form an adequate conception of a gigantic rampart, in places over 23,000 feet high, enclosing a bit of country itself not above the limits of dwarf trees, from the centre of which rises a stupendous peak 25,600 feet in height. Small wonder that this grim seventy mile ring of mountains had repulsed all assaults, and that the sanctuary of the inner basin had remained inviolate.

Mr. Hugh Ruttledge wrote in an article published in *The Times* of August 22nd, 1932, soon after his attempt of that year: "Nanda Devi imposes upon her votaries an admission test as yet beyond their skill and endurance; a seventy-mile barrier ring, on which stand twelve *measured* peaks over 21,000 feet high, which has no depression lower than 17,000 feet – except in the west, where the Rishi Ganga River, rising at the foot of Nanda Devi, and draining an area of some two hundred and fifty square miles of snow and ice has carved for itself what must be one of the most terrific gorges in the world. Two internal ridges, converging from north and south respectively upon this river form, as it were, the curtains of an inner sanctuary, within which the great mountain soars up to 25,600 feet. So tremendous is the aspect of the Rishi Ganga gorge that Hindu mythology described it as the last earthly home of the Seven Rishis. Here, if anywhere, their meditations might be undisturbed."

As I mentioned earlier, it was our intention to attempt to force our way up this gorge into the basin beyond. Naturally, therefore, we made an intensive study of all previous exploits of mountaineers and explorers who had tried to gain access to what Mr. Hugh Ruttledge calls, so aptly, "the inner sanctuary".

Most of the early explorers of the Nanda Devi group approached it from the east. As long ago as 1830 G. W. Traill, who was first Commissioner of Garhwal and Kumaon, ascended the Pindari Glacier and crossed a pass at its head into the Milam Valley. The object of this exploit was probably rather to find a short cut to Milam than to explore mountains. The fact that Traill suffered severely from snow-blindness was regarded by the natives as a sign that the Goddess had visited her wrath upon him and this belief had such effect that in 1855, when Adolf Schlagintweit, that remarkable Himalayan traveller, attempted to cross the range by the same route he took the precaution of making a handsome offering at the temple of Nanda Devi in Almora before he started. This inspired his coolies with much confidence and even when, on the glaciers, two of his strongest men were seized with epileptic fits, he was able to point out to the rest that it could be none of the goddess's doing and so persuade them to carry on. Later he was joined by his brother Robert, and together they explored the great Milam Glacier and crossed another pass which led them into Tibet. Travelling to the west they reached Kamet and climbed to an altitude of 22,239 feet on its Tibetan side, thus reaching the greatest height which had been so far attained.

In 1861 Traill's pass was again crossed by Colonel Edmund Smyth in the course of a memorable journey in those parts, while in 1883 Mr. T. S. Kennedy, the celebrated Alpine climber, carried out some further work on the Milam side of the range.

In that same year, on the western side of the group, was undertaken a portion of what Dr. T. G. Longstaff in 1906 described as "the greatest Himalayan expedition that has yet been made". The party was a small one and consisted of that redoubtable Himalayan explorer, W. W. Graham; the famous Swiss guide, Emil Boss, of whom Graham wrote: "One of the best mountaineers living, extremely well-educated, speaking seven languages equally fluently; a captain in the Swiss Army he is a splendid companion and I deemed myself fortunate to have his company." And lastly another first-rate guide, Ulrich Kauffmann, of Grindelwald. (Boss and Kauffmann are well remembered for their work on the Southern Alps of New Zealand for which, in conjunction with his Indian achievements, Boss received the Black Grant from the Royal Geographical Society.)

Dr. Longstaff writes (*Alpine Journal*, 1906, Vol. XXIII, pp. 203–204): "No one who reads the short and modest description of his (Graham's) Garhwal trip can fail to be fired with longing to revisit the scenes of his struggles, and no one who has not been lucky enough to have been there can realise what he went through, and what a strenuous pioneer and splendid climber he must have been. We can only lament that he did not give us as detailed an account we have since come to expect from the returning wanderer."

Graham's principal objective was to force a route up the Rishi Ganga gorge to the western base of Nanda Devi. Travel among the foothills must have been a very different proposition from what it is now, and only after several weeks of hard going did his little party reach the tiny hamlet of Rini, where the Rishi Ganga, issuing from the mouth of its lower gorge, bursts into the Dhaoli River.

"On the next day, July 6th," (he writes in *Good Words*, January, 1885) "we wished to start for Nanda Devi. As the crow flies, it was some twenty miles but, seeing the nature of the ground, we decided to allow at least a week to reach the foot of the peak. On inquiring for a guide we were told that the valley was impassable, that no sahib had ever been up it . . . etcetera, etcetera. We took most of this *cum grano*, but found, alas, that it was only too true! After getting up four miles we came to an unexpected obstacle. A glacier had once run due north from Trisul to the river; it had now retreated, leaving a bed with sheer perpendicular walls some four hundred feet in depth. We tried up and down to find a place where we could cross. Below, it fell sheer some fifteen hundred feet into the river: above, it only got deeper and deeper. It was a mighty moat of

nature's own digging to guard her virgin fortresses. We gave it up and returned
rather disconsolately to Rini."

After this the party moved round to the north and continued their
explorations in that direction. In the course of this journey they made a
determined but unsuccessful attempt to climb the giant peak of Dunagiri,
which stands on the outer rim of the Nanda Devi Basin. Later they learnt from
the shepherds of the Dhaoli Valley that a way was known across the ridge that
formed the northern retaining wall of the Rishi Nala.

Once more they started for Nanda Devi. "On July 15th," so the record goes,
"we began to make our way up the northern side of the Rishi Ganga. The climb
was sufficiently steep, there being no path, and we having pouring rain the
whole time. On the evening of the second day we reached a lovely little
tableland called Dunassau (Durashi). The last day's route had been extremely
wild, running along the southern face of the ridge, sometimes with a sheer drop
to the river below – some 7,000 to 8,000 feet. Such wild rocks and broken gullies
I had never met with before."

At Durashi, Graham and his companions were held up by heavy falls of snow
and were deserted by most of their terror-stricken coolies. These men had been
recruited from the Dhaoli Valley and shared the local superstition that their
route was infested with devils. Carrying double loads, the three Europeans and
the few local people who remained faithful to them, struggled on. "Our
progress," writes Graham, "was very slow, partly because we had to carry
fifteen loads between nine of us, partly owing to the nature of the ground,
which was not only very broken and precipitous but quite *terra incognita* to the
whole party . . . Guiding in its strict Alpine sense was wanted here; sharp rocky
ridges ran down from the peaks on our north, and fell, with high precipices,
sheer into the stream some 5,000 feet below. Occasionally we had to hang on by
a tuft of grass, or a bunch of Alpine roses, and I do not exaggerate when I say
that for half the total day's work hand-hold was as necessary as foot-hold. By
nightfall, after twelve hours' work, we had gained some three miles in absolute
distance, and this, perhaps, better than anything will give an idea of the labour
involved in working along these slopes."

And after several days of this sort of work Graham writes further:

"We camped on a little space, the only one we could find which was not so
steep as the rest and, after building a wall of stones to prevent us from rolling
into the river, we turned in. I found, however, that sleeping at an angle of 30
degrees is not conducive to comfort. Time after time did I dream that I was
rolling over the edge, and woke to find myself at the bottom of the tent on top of
Boss, or *vice versa*. (We took it in turns in a most impartial manner to roll down
first and made a bed for the other, who speedily followed.) On the morrow
Kauffmann took the coolies back to bring up the other loads, and Boss went
forward to explore the route. I lay, an interesting invalid in the tent, my foot
giving me great pain, and being quite unable to wear a boot.

"Next day we worked along the spur, following Boss, who had seen a place
where he thought we could cross the river. When above this we descended to it,
the hill being very steep and covered with thorny jungle. Rain began again and
we found ourselves on the bank of the stream shivering and waiting for Boss,

who had gone after some pheasants. This little delay effectually settled our chances of crossing. The stream rose several feet in an hour, and though we tried very hard to bridge the flood, everything was washed away as soon as laid in position. Boss stood up to his knees on a slippery rock, with the water rushing by at some twenty miles an hour and worked like a horse, but it was of no avail. Once, indeed, I thought that he was gone as he slipped and nearly fell. Needless to say, to fall into that torrent would have been certain death, battered to pieces against the tremendous rocks that blocked the way. At last, soaked to the skin and very tired, we gave it up and pitched camp under an overhanging boulder.

"Next day, Kauffmann and the coolies returned to fetch up the rest of the provisions, while Boss and I worked along the river to see if we could find a crossing. About half a mile up we came to a most magnificent gorge, one of the finest specimens of water erosion ever seen. Two hundred feet above, the rocks nearly met, their smooth, black, shiny sides overhanging considerably. Through this tunnel roared and raved the torrent, here pent within very narrow limits, raging with a sound as of thunder. Yet in this fearful din and turmoil we saw a curious thing. On a tiny ledge, just above the dashing waves, a pigeon had built her nest and therein lay the two white shining eggs in perfect security: no enemy could touch them there. We carefully examined the stream up to the point where it descended the cliff in a grand fall, and found that nowhere in its present state could a crossing be effected.

"It was provoking: we were halted high under the great cliffs of Nanda Devi, which rose almost perpendicularly above us, and we could see, so near and yet so far, the spur by which we had hoped to climb. To cross, however, was out of the question with our limited appliances, and we relucantly decided to return."

They camped where they were: "Suddenly there entered Kauffmann and the shikari (hunter).

"Well, Kauffmann, when are the others coming?"

"*Hélas, Monsieur, ils sont tous partis!*"

That remark, uttered under the very shadow of the mountain for which these few men had dared so much, was the death-knell to the expedition. Yet Graham's reaction to it was wholly admirable. "It was only too true," he writes. "The coolies had evidently planned the affair and, as soon as they had got out of sight of camp, had fairly bolted. Kauffmann's face was so lugubrious that, serious as the matter was, I couldn't help bursting out into laughter. However, this settled what we had previously almost decided."

To go on without native help was impossible. Graham and his party abandoned everything that was not absolutely necessary and fought their way back down the gorge. A heart-breaking journey that must have been, unrelieved by knowledge of happenings yet in the future which were to show the true value of Graham's achievement, since further attempts to penetrate the upper gorge of the Rishi Ganga met with but small success and it was not until 1907 that any other noteworthy exploration was carried out on this side of the range.

In July, 1893, Dr. Kurt Boeckh attacked the eastern side of the range and made his way up the Milam Glacier with the idea of forcing a passage across the eastern portion of the barrier wall surrounding the Nanda Devi Basin. He had with him the Austrian guide, Hans Kerer, but when the coolies realised his intention they refused to advance and Boeckh was obliged to abandon his project before he had got very far. (Even if the coolies had agreed to accompany him it is doubtful if he would ever have been able to lead them safely over the range; such a route entailing work of a tremendously high standard of mountaineering.) Unwilling to return by the way he had come Boeckh carried out a fine journey to the north, crossing the Untadhura Pass in the middle of September and descending the very difficult gorge of the Girthi to Malari in the Dhaoli Valley.

But early in the present century, the district attracted the attention of Dr. T. G. Longstaff, whose record as a mountain explorer is assuredly in a class by itself. In 1905 he came out with the Italian guides, Alexis and Henri Brocherel, with the intention of continuing the work which Graham had started on the western side of the group. The opportunity of accompanying Mr. C. A. Sherring on a political mission into western Tibet, however, caused him to alter his plans and to spend the period before the breaking of the monsoon in exploring the valleys east of Nanda Devi. After several marches through the fern-clad cliff country of the Gori defile and up into the bare, wind-swept valley of Milam, they pitched camp on May 27th, near the hamlet of Ganaghar, on the right bank of the Gori, at a height of 11,100 feet. From here they pushed their way up the Panchu Glacier and eventually crossed a difficult snow-pass at its head. This brought them on to the Lwanl Glacier, running parallel with the Panchu and not into the Nanda Devi Basin as their map had led them to expect. They descended to the main valley for supplies and shortly afterwards returned to the Lwanl. After three days climbing they gained the Almora-Garhwal water-parting which forms at this point part of the rim of the Nanda Devi Basin and from here, for the first time in history, did man gaze down upon the glaciers at the southern foot of the great mountain.

A descent on the other side of the ridge was found to be impracticable and after an unsuccessful attempt to climb the great peak of Nanda Kot the party continued their explorations to the south and succeeded before they were overtaken by the monsoon, in crossing a pass from the head of the Salung Gadh to Baughdiar, a remarkable piece of mountaineering.

But the lure of Nanda Devi stayed and 1907 again found Dr. Longstaff in the vicinity, this time concentrating on his old plan of continuing Graham's work on the country around the Rishi Ganga. He brought with him a very strong mountaineering party, including Major (now Brigadier-General) the Hon. C. G. Bruce – the most experienced Himalayan mountaineer of his time – Mr. A. L. Mumm, and three Alpine guides, the two brothers Brocherel again and Moritz Inderbinnen of Zermatt, who had been Mumm's companion for over twenty years.

Their first objective was the Rishi Valley and examination of the lower gorge decided them to attempt Graham's route, the first part of which was known to the Tolma and Lata shepherds of the Dhaoli Valley. But they were too early in the year and found too much snow to allow them to make the passage of the Durashi Pass so they moved round to the Bagini Glacier, in the hope that if they were able to cross a certain pass at its head they would find themselves in the

Nanda Devi Basin. They made their way up the glacier on May 20th, came in sight of a gap ahead of them. "All who were bound for the pass," writes Dr. Longstaff (*Alpine Journal*, Vol. XXIV), "were heavily loaded as we had to carry Primus stoves, petroleum, cooking pots, tents, sleeping-bags, instruments, rifles and ammunition, a large supply of ropes, and provisions sufficient to last our party of eight for ten days. For, having got into the Rishi Valley, we intended to get out of it some time. In the interval we must be self-supporting. The sun was so oppressive that after tramping over the snow for five hours, we stopped, at 11 a.m. (May 21st), under the shade of some huge blocks, which formed part of an irregular medial moraine (18,300 feet).

"Instead of making for the pass directly under Changabang, we had now decided to go right up to the head of this arm of the glacier, more directly under the great easterly spur of Dunagiri. Mumm, who was not very fit, did not intend to cross the pass with us, and returned to the camp above Dunagiri (grazing ground) with Inderbinnen and Damar Sing, leaving us a party of four Europeans and four Gurkhas. He rejoined us later at Surai Thota.

"On May 22nd, we started at 4.30 a.m., but Bruce and I had very soon to stop with cold feet; and it was probable at this time that Karbir got his frost-bite. We had to rope over the last slopes, and the guides cut many steps. Our loads seemed to grow inordinately heavy, but at 10 a.m. we stood on the crest of the pass. Its height comes out at 20,100 feet, and the name Bagini Pass would most naturally belong to it. From the pass we looked down to a vast firn (snow-field), shut in by snow-clad peaks, while 3,000 feet above us on the west towered the icy crest of Dunagiri. But the descent of the south side looked so bad that we had to set about it at once. The Brocherels had brought a good supply of pitons (iron stakes) from Courmayeur, and by means of these we were able to lower our loads down the snow-draped cliffs below us. It really was a difficult bit of mountaineering, the descent of about 1,000 feet occupying over five hours; and the two Brocherels were in their element. This was a very fine performance on the part of the Gurkhas, and a striking testimony both to their inherently resolute character, and to the excellence of their military training. Remember that they were called upon to perform a feat which was quite beyond the powers of any of the local men . . . We were very glad to camp about 4 p.m. on the snow-field directly at the southern foot of the pass (18,800 feet) . . . We had fondly hoped to find ourselves on the great glaciers at the foot of Nanda Devi itself."

But on descending from the snow-field they were on, they found themselves in the Rishi Nala, at a point below that which Graham had reached in 1883. They were able to shoot some bharal (wild sheep), which provided them with sufficient food to enable them to force their way down the valley to Durashi, and so to reach their main base at Surai Thota, in the Dhaoli Valley, after nearly a fortnight of very difficult mountaineering.

Later the party came back up the Rishi Valley, and it was then that Dr. Longstaff made his famous ascent of Trisul (23,406 feet), which for twenty-three years remained the highest summit reached by man. After this he and two of the Gurkhas pushed their way further up the valley. "With considerable difficulty we reached the junction of the Rhamani torrent with the Rishi Ganga, where we crossed the latter to the northern bank by a snow-bridge (11,790 feet), as we could get no further along the southern bank, and the current was too strong for wading. Here we camped under an overhanging rock amongst the birch trees. That morning we climbed straight up to about 13,500 feet, and in the intervening 1,700 feet of cliffs between this and the Rishi Ganga, saw no practicable route up the valley, though we obtained a most wonderful view of Nanda Devi, the 'Blessed Goddess', that queen of mountains fit to rank with the Matterhorn and Ushba. I think that we were just beyond Graham's furthest point in this direction . . ." "Though no one, native or European, has yet succeeded in forcing his way up the gorge to the western base of Nanda Devi, yet I feel convinced that it is possible to do so. I can think of no more interesting or arduous task for a party composed of mountaineers, than to follow up the great glacier under the southern face of Nanda Devi, and to cross the ridge on which I camped in 1905, over into the Milam Valley. The height of the pass is about 19,000 feet, and as we stood on its crest it appeared quite possible to climb up to it from the Nanda Devi Glacier on the west. But this expedition would involve the abandonment of the base camp and all impedimenta in the Dhaoli Valley, for at least a month. The return could be made most quickly by the Untadhura Pass, and the difficult Girthi Valley to Malari, for I do not think anyone would be likely to return by the same route."

Since then, until last year, 1934, the upper gorge of the Rishi Valley was left severely alone.

During the monsoon of 1907, Dr. Longstaff proceeded to explore the Nandagini and Sunderdhunga Valleys, both of which lead up to the wall of the basin from the south. Only those who have travelled amongst the unexplored valleys of those parts in the monsoon can appreciate the appalling conditions which rendered these two reconnaissances inconclusive.

No fewer than twenty years later Dr. Longstaff returned to the Nandagini with Mr. Hugh Ruttledge, and reached the crest of the wall at its lowest point, 17,000 feet. Bad weather prevented further progress, but in any case this approach would have led them down to a point in the Rishi Nala below that reached in 1907.

In 1926 a further attempt was made to reach the great mountain from the east by a strong party, consisting of Mr. Hugh Ruttledge, Dr. Howard Somervell, who accompanied Mallory and Norton on the two highest climbs on Everest in the years 1922 and 1924, and Colonel Commandant (now Major-General) R. C. Wilson. Though the attack was not pushed home, enough was done to warrant a conclusion that the defences on this side are even more elaborate than on the south or west.

May 1932 saw Mr. Ruttledge coming again to the attack, this time with the Italian guide, Emil Rey, of Courmayeur, grandson of his famous namesake, and six of the Everest Sherpas. His plan was to attempt to cross a gap at the head of the Sunderdhunga Valley, which had been tentatively reconnoitred by Dr. Longstaff in 1907. If the gap could be crossed it must lead into the inner sanctuary of Nanda Devi.

In an article published in *The Times* (August 22nd, 1932), Mr. Ruttledge writes: "In a mood of hopeful anticipation our party, on May 25th, trudged up the narrow glacier which leads from Sunderhunga itself to the base of the wall, of which the greater part is invisible from a distance. The Sherpas cheered derisively as a little avalanche had an ineffective shot at us from the cliffs above; and raced round the last corner. One step round it, and we were brought up all standing by a sight which almost took our remaining breath away. Six thousand feet of the steepest rock and ice. '*Nom de nom!*' said Emil, while Nima* exclaimed that this looked as bad as the north-west face of Kangchenjunga in 1930. However we had come a long way to see this, so we advanced across the stony slopes to a point from which we hoped, by detailed examination, to reduce terrific appearances to milder reality. But the first impressions were accurate. Near the top of the wall, for about a mile and a half, runs a terrace of ice some 200 feet thick; in fact the lower edge of a hanging glacier. Under the pull of gravity large masses constantly break off from this terrace, and thunder down to the valley below, polishing in their fall the successive bands of limestone precipice of which the face is composed. Even supposing the precipice to be climbable, an intelligent mountaineer may be acquitted on a charge of lack of enterprise if he declines to spend at least three days and two nights under fire from this artillery. As alternative, there is a choice of three knife-edge arêtes, excessively steep, sometimes over-hanging in the middle and lower sections, on which even the eye of faith, assisted by binoculars, fails to see one single platform large enough to accommodate the most modest of climbing tents.

"The jury's verdict was unanimous; and so, with a homely vernacular *non possumus* from Emil, vanished the last hope of a straightforward approach to Nanda Devi; and the goddess keeps her secret."

Would the goddess, who had so protected herself from human intrusion throughout the centuries, reveal her secret to us, with an expedition absurd in its smallness? As we neared Calcutta both Tilman and I realised more and more the size of our task and the unlikelihood of success. But if our resources were small, we had at least the "eyes of faith" and the knowledge of the experience of our predecessors to help us to reach our goal.

*Nima Dorji, a Sherpa Porter, who had been on Everest, Kangchenjunga and Kamet.

CHAPTER FOUR

BEFORE leaving England we had arranged to send a wire to Karma Paul in Darjeeling as soon as we knew the date of our arrival in Calcutta and he was then to send our porters to meet us there, but, as Tilman and I rehearsed for the fiftieth time the programme we had so carefully mapped out and we steamed ever nearer to our goal, we grew impatient and debated the advisability of disembarking at Visagapatam, the last port of call before Calcutta, which lies three days ahead. By taking the train from Visagapatam we could save two precious days. This idea, however, had to be turned down on the score of expense and we went ashore there merely to send a wire requesting that the three Sherpas should be sent down to Calcutta, to arrive there the same day as ourselves. Although the homes of these men lay far from Darjeeling, it was there that they spent most of their time working as rickshaw coolies, and the hill-station was all they knew of civilisation. To our knowledge they had never even travelled by train before and to avoid the risk of their wandering alone in Calcutta, Karma Paul was instructed to impress upon them most strongly the necessity of not stirring a yard from the station until met by us.

These arrangements made we had a further three days in which to ponder the mischances that might befall our innocents before we met them. Another problem was whether, on the day of our arrival, we could possibly do some shopping, dispatch business at a bank, interview several people and transport half a ton of stores from the ship to the Howrah Station in time for the nine o'clock train that night. Such was our impatience to reach the mountains that the possibility of an enforced week-end in Calcutta seemed to jeopardise the success of the whole expedition.

We landed in good time on a Saturday, got the most important jobs done and then hastened to our hotel, expecting to find a telegram advising us of the dispatch of the Sherpas. Sure enough, there was the wire, but it merely said that on receipt of journey-money and an advance of pay, the men would be put in the train.

We were annoyed, to say the least! Our invective must surely have made Karma Paul's ears tingle up in Darjeeling but a little reflection showed us that the demand was perfectly reasonable and that we had been exceedingly stupid not to think of its necessity earlier. I smile even now to think of the unnecessary stew into which we worked ourselves.

Well, the money had to be sent, and quickly, or the post office would be closed until Monday, so off we raced only to find that there exists in Calcutta the most exasperating arrangement whereby the wire is handed in at one office and the money paid over at another about half a mile away. To our harassed minds it seemed that the greater part of India's three hundred million inhabitants were assembled for the purpose of sending telegrams – and that five minutes before closing time – but eventually we got the money off.

This delay was a severe blow but it was softened when we obtained permission to live on the ship over the week-end, so that our somewhat slender financial resources were not depleted by extra hotel bills. We were now "sweating" on getting away by Monday and this war-time expression most adequately describes our condition, physical and mental. Even departure on Monday was expecting a lot, because were Karma Paul on the spot to receive the wire, he would have but Sunday morning in which to round up the men, give them time to make their arrangements, and shepherd them to the train.

No further news arrived and, assuming all was well, we made our way to the Sealdah Station at seven on the Monday morning. We reached the platform when the train was already in and disgorging its passengers. I, from my previous acquaintance with the Sherpas, knew the men we were looking for, and Tilman, who had never seen a Sherpa, observed that "Three men from the wilds of Nepal, shrinking from the noise and bustle and wearing a sort of 'Bing Boys on Broadway' air, should be easy enough to spot".

When most of the crowd had passed the barriers with no sign of our men, we began to search the platform, and soon our choice was reduced to some station coolies fast asleep, a sweetmeat seller, and a one-legged beggar – whom even Tilman, inexperienced as he was, rejected as a candidate. Doubtful now, we cast our net wider, taking in all eight platforms, the booking-hall, the first, second and third-class waiting-rooms for men and women, the refreshment-rooms for Europeans, Hindus, and Mohammedans, and all other likely and unlikely places in which three affrighted innocents abroad might seek refuge from the confusion around them.

Doubt became fear. Tilman was convinced they had not come: I had more faith in Karma Paul and our luck, and began to cross-question every official I could persuade to listen to our story. It was a shade too early to get hold of any of the Directors or the General Manager, but having catechised the higher ranks – as personified by Traffic Manager and Station-Master, we descended grade by grade to humble ticket-collectors. One of these proved more observant than seemed possible – or else something passing strange had arrived by the Darjeeling Mail – for his attention had been excited by "three exotic figures", apparently from the remoter parts of Asia. Here was a gleam of light, but, on thinking matters over we realised that the exotic three (whoever they might be) were now at large in the City of Calcutta and probably untraceable.

Before enlisting the aid of the Police we decided that it would be as well to ring up our hotel to see if there were any news from Darjeeling.

"There is no telegram," came the reply, "but can you throw any light on three very rum-looking birds who drove up here in a taxi an hour ago?"

"Are they from Darjeeling?" I asked excitedly.

"Well, they seem to talk Chinese," was the answer, "and I don't know enough of the language to ask them where they come from but they are in search of two sahibs, so you had better come along and see them – and the sooner the better. They're no advertisement for my hotel!"

We drove back in silence, conflicting emotions rendering us speechless.

Swift decision followed by swift action seemed to be the habit of these three and we wondered if they would wait or set off on a wild goose-chase around the city looking for us.

They *had* waited. Not in the lounge (as we had been half afraid they would do) and they *were* our Sherpas! We found them sitting patiently in the back regions and realised immediately the true meaning of the ticket-collector's description. Indeed, "exotic" was a mild adjective. Clad in shirts and shorts, and crowned with billycock hats from under which glossy black pig-tails descended, the three were distinctive enough, but when one took into consideration that their shirts were a blinding purple in colour and that this crude shade was matched in their lips and teeth (the result of much betel-chewing) one understood how even the most myopic ticket-collector would notice them.

They greeted us gravely, apparently completely unconcerned. In the face of such oriental calm Tilman and I restrained ourselves, although our relief at finding them after our mad chase had induced a mild form of hysteria in us both, and we carefully avoided mention of the events at the station. Soon we were all down at the docks, hard at work getting our gear on shore. The astonishment of the ship's company was considerable, but the Sherpas went about their work in a matter-of-fact way, as little impressed by an eleven thousand ton ship and the busy traffic of the Hooghly as with a bullock-cart in the Darjeeling bazaar.

This attitude should not have been a surprise to either of us who were both well acquainted with African natives. When the savage sees a train or a motor car for the first time in his life he does not, as one would expect, show either excitement or fear; nor does he behave like the old lady, who, when confronted for the first time with a giraffe, said that she didn't believe it. Tilman has told me that in East Africa the inauguration of the Air Mail caused no sensation whatever. An aeroplane passing overhead was regarded merely as an excuse to stop work for a moment – if the native was not working he simply did not bother to look up! Similarly, a native boy who accompanied a friend of his to England was impressed only by the meat hanging in the English butchers' shops, and although the Sherpas have little in common with the African native they are certainly alike on this one point – their attitude to the modern amenities of civilisation.

Having somehow got all our baggage to Howrah Station we sent the Sherpas off to see the sights of Calcutta in charge of a friend's servant, a man well fitted to be their cicerone since he acted in the same capacity to the seventy porters of the German Nanga Parbat expedition. Afterwards he informed us that the Zoo alone had excited any interest!

Meantime Tilman and I went off to arrange for seats on the train and met with an unexpected difficulty. The 9 p.m. train was the Bombay Mail, which took no third-class passengers but allowed other passengers one bearer apiece; at 10 p.m. there was another train which boasted third-class accommodation but on this we could not go since all second-class seats had been reserved. Very unwillingly we decided to split our party, taking one man with us and leaving the other two to follow on the later train. Their morning's work had shown us they were not quite the simpletons we had imagined – but it was tempting providence to let them travel to an unknown destination with but a smattering of Hindustani between them. Still, the only alternative was to wait yet another day – and another day of Calcutta would have worn what small patience we had left to tatters.

As it was we did not depart without further strain on our frayed nerves, for the friend with whom we had a farewell dinner insisted that ten minutes was ample time in which to weigh, book and load our 1,000 lbs. of luggage. Personally I felt that a full hour would be all too short and endured torment (with both eyes on the clock) while he ordered beer – and yet more beer. In the end we only reached our carriage with a second or two to spare, followed by the two Sherpas who were to take the later train loudly bemoaning their lot until our friend, who was thoroughly enjoying the whirl of our departure, forcibly restrained them from climbing in beside us and promised to see them off safely at 10 o'clock.

With us travelled Angtharkay, short, sturdy and self-possessed, and despite all our arguments he flatly refused to occupy the small cupboard thoughtfully provided by the railway for bearers, and insisted upon sleeping on the floor of our compartment – much to the disgust of our fellow passengers. It was a stifling night and Angtharkay, who felt the heat, recklessly squandered his money on beakers of tea at one anna a time. Tilman and I fumed and fretted about our abandoned Sherpas, whom we were to pick up some twenty-four hours later at Bareilly so that we could all take the Kathgodam train together.

At last we steamed into Bareilly Station, ill-tempered, dusty and exhausted. Fortunately we had time to wash off the outer layer of dust, stow our baggage in the Kathgodam train and have some food before meeting the Calcutta train bearing our precious freight. We were not feeling too happy – remembering our hectic time in Calcutta. True, our friend had had the strictest instructions to tell the Sherpas to sit tight until pulled out by us, since the name Bareilly conveyed no more to them than did Bombay, but twenty-four hours of sweltering heat might well have exhausted their patience and, if they thought we had missed them, they were perfectly capable of getting out where they thought fit. Moreover, the train only stopped for ten minutes, the platform was abominably lit, and most third-class passengers were certain to be asleep.

When the train arrived our hearts descended into our boots. It seemed twice as long as any train ought to be, its carriages were of vast size, very dark and over-crowded with natives lying asleep on top of each other, all with their faces covered. Packed like sardines is a poor simile, for packing denotes order and here was chaos. To search thirty-odd "black holes of Calcutta" in a few moments was an impossible task, so I shouted orders to Tilman and Angtharkay and we all began to dash frenziedly up and down, bawling the names of our two men through the open windows. Yells of "Kusang!!" . . . "Pasang!!" rose above the hiss of the engine and the few passengers who were sufficiently awake to take any notice scrambled to their feet and eyed us askance. But all our clamour utterly failed to upset traffic arrangements and after its alloted time the train pulled out, several occupants shaking their heads from the windows as though in relief that the three madmen were being left behind.

Here was a pretty mess. Blank-faced and sore-throated we stood miserably and debated our next move. Should we go or should we camp out on Bareilly platform, giving a rendering of our bawling performance to every train from Calcutta? Just as we began to debate this dismal question a warning toot sounded from the Kathgodam train and we sprinted towards it, fearful of losing luggage as well as men.

As we ran we glanced rapidly into each carriage trying to spot our gear and, of a sudden, Tilman gripped me by the arm. There, comfortably established among their possessions and eating oranges with every evidence of serene enjoyment, were Kusang and Pasang! It seemed a pity to disturb them. We crept quietly past to our own carriage, horribly conscious that Angtharkay's account of our antics would lose nothing in the telling.

But far into the night we argued about the mystery. The most experienced traveller who had to effect a change of trains at midnight in a country whose language he did not know, might be very pleased with himself if he managed without mishap. Yet two Sherpas, neither of whom had ever travelled by rail, neither of whom even knew the name of their destination, had contrived to get out at the right station and into the right train.

Part 2

The Secret Shrine

CHAPTER FIVE

THE remainder of our journey to Kathgodam was a peaceful one. The Sherpas were (presumably) behaving themselves in their compartment and the countless irritations of the past few days faded from our minds. Our spirits rose as we left the train at last and packed ourselves and our belongings into a somewhat decrepit lorry and began the last fifty-mile stage of our road to Ranikhet, one of the loveliest of Indian hill-stations. Jolting along the broad motor-road that winds its way amongst the steep, forest-clad foothills rising abruptly from the plains, we took great gulps of the cool, pine-scented air, deliciously sweet after two days of travel in the appalling heat and dust of pre-monsoon India.

Up and up the lorry circled to Ranikhet, from the crest of whose pine-clad ridge there is to be seen a vast panorama of the Snows. The place was full of troops and all the usual pleasures of a hill-station were in full swing but these, however, were not for us, as we hoped to get away on our first march to Joshimath in two days time if all necessary arrangements could be completed.

We were lucky to find ourselves sole occupants of a spacious rest-house, where we could spread ourselves as much as we liked. We arrived at midday on May 9th, and straightaway before lunch we went down to recruit coolies. We only required a dozen men and within an hour all was settled and twelve lusty Dotials had promised to leave at once and meet us two days later at Baijnath, a little village fifty miles to the north at the end of the motor-road. These coolies were not beautiful, but they were a likely looking lot and inspired us with confidence, for we gave them a substantial advance of pay and never had the slightest doubts about their failing to keep the rendezvous!

The next thirty-six hours were very fully occupied in making preparations for departure. A ration of kit was allotted to each member of the party, and all the surplus clothing which convention had thus far imposed upon us had to be packed away and handed over for safe custody. Each man was issued with a suit of light, wind-proof material, under which he might wear quite a quantity of garments. (I may say that this "underclothing" consisted of a heterogeneous mixture collected from various friends and included long-forgotten shirts, pyjamas, tail-coats, etcetera, which I had unearthed when turning out a box-room before leaving home. Later, Kusang became firmly attached to a pair of my dress trousers, while Pasang, considering that an ancient dinner-jacket I gave him would be wasted in Garhwal, proudly carried it back to his native Tibet when the expedition was over.) Then boots – the most important item of all – had to be attended to; and finally a careful estimate of the cash which would be required over the next five months had to be worked out and the amount obtained, almost entirely in coin, from the local native bank. Since this was not a correspondent of our Calcutta bank we had been compelled to draw all our money from there in notes and travel up with them in our pockets, a proceeding we had found very wearing indeed, and we now discovered that the process of exchanging these for silver was a lengthy one owing to the many spurious rupees in circulation in India. The Sherpas willingly assisted at this business, and were far quicker at spotting duds than we were, rejecting all doubtful ones without ado. At first our feelings were hurt at seeing any money we tendered being scrutinised, rung on a stone, bitten or otherwise tested, but we soon found it paid us to do the same.

We took one large Meade tent for the Sherpas and a smaller one for ourselves. We also had a very small tent weighing about 6 lbs. in all, but we soon realised that the weight saved in carrying it was not worth the discomfort of sleeping in it! We had the usual down sleeping bags – though real eiderdown ones would have been worth the extra expense; and for the purposes of cooking above the limits of firewood, we took a small Primus stove and about four dozen "Tommy's Cookers" for use when Tilman and I were separated from the Sherpas. We had brought with us about 250 lbs. of foodstuffs to help us out while we were getting accustomed to local food (which consisted almost entirely of coarse flour) and for use at high camps. Various last-minute purchases were made in the Ranikhet bazaar and then everything had to be packed in one-man loads, 80 lbs. each, for the first stage of our journey.

In the early hours of the morning of May 11th we piled our stuff on to the waiting lorry, starting off at 7 a.m. Passing through the bazaar we suddenly remembered vegetables, lemons and eggs – and well it was that we did so. As I have mentioned before it was our aim to live on the country as far as possible, not only to save transport but because any fresh food, plain or dull though it may be, is preferable to things embalmed in tins be they ever so skilfully disguised; but though, throughout our travels, we were to find ourselves able to obtain staple foods, flour, potatoes and occasionally milk, how succulent were additional fruits, vegetables and eggs. And of these last the three dozen we bought in Ranikhet were, with one exception, the only eggs we tasted until our return.

Our lorry rolled into Baijnath at 1 o'clock and there we found our Dotials, who lost no time in making up their loads and starting for Gwaldam, the first stage of our ten-day march to Joshimath. "March," with its associations of discipline, time-tables and the hard, high road, is scarcely applicable to the next lazy, carefree days. Beyond setting a time-limit we had no set plan, and pace had, fortunately for me, to conform to that of the heavily-laden Dotials. I say fortunately, because I was, at the moment, far from fit. Besides a heavy cold and an inside the reverse of happy, I had broken a toe on the voyage out soon after leaving Aden which had not yet mended and which caused much pain. In consequence I was obliged to walk in a tennis shoe with a piece cut out of the side. On the ship this had not mattered, but in Calcutta it had looked a bit odd until we had joined forces with the Sherpas, who looked so amazing that had I gone about barefoot nobody would have noticed *me*. Even now a boot was out of the question and we discussed the hire of a pony, but in the end my journey to Joshimath was done in a pair of tennis shoes – or rather in one and a half.

So we ambled leisurely through a world of exquisite beauty. We rested when we felt inclined (which was frequently), bathed if the opportunity offered, and slept wherever seemed good to us. Until Ranikhet, Tilman and I had flattered ourselves upon our astuteness in steering three timid followers amidst the manifold difficulties and dangers of modern travel. But now that we had cast off the trammels of civilisation the boot was on the other leg, and in camp or on the march they devoted all their care to our welfare without a thought for themselves.

For the next five months we were to live and climb together, and the more we saw of the Sherpas the more we grew to like them. Porters all the time, they were also fellow mountaineers and companions, in turn playing the parts of housekeeper, cook, butler, pantryman, valet, interpreter and, on occasion, entertainer. Angtharkay was the eldest, a more sophisticated man than his brethren and possessed of Hindustani which could be understood by us and by other natives. When we had to employ them, he acted as buffer between us and the local coolies, and could generally tell us what they were thinking or feeling before they knew themselves. We could also delegate to him the very unpleasant business of bargaining, for he was a Hotspur who would "cavil on the ninth part of a hair," sometimes carrying this to excess and depriving us of a thing we really wanted rather than let us be "done." He was the soundest, too, on a mountain, both in movement and judgment, and as a route-finder we had many occasions on which to bless him.

Pasang was the most presentable of the party, taller than the other two and a bit of a dandy. He was a most graceful mover and quite brilliant on rocks, but he was exceedingly temperamental and required tactful handling. He acted as my batman – and a full-time job that was – I being the most careless of men and wont to drop my belongings all over the place. Poor Pasang was then expected to retrieve anything I suddenly asked for. Worse, he had to cope with a very bad habit of mine which was disconcerting, to say the least. No sooner was everything packed up than I would discover I *must* have something for the march, a spare woollie, a film, or a pencil. Whatever I wanted was sure to be at the very bottom of the great sack which was Pasang's load and the wretched man would have to turn it all out again. But he never seemed flustered or angered and the more work I gave him the better he liked it.

He was more Tibetan than the others and more religious. He carried a private stock of prayer-flags on which was printed the usual formula: *"Om Mane Padme Hung"* . . . "Hail, the Jewel in the Lotus Flower!" . . . and one of these would be left fluttering on the top of a pass or to mark some camp site. In addition he hoarded mysterious little squares of adhesive yellow cloth which he stuck on his face just behind the corner of each eye, (after the manner of the patches of the eighteenth-century ladies of fashion), but the meaning of these we never discovered. Another of his customs was to throw a little of his food into the air before eating in order to propitiate the spirits; a rite which I regret to say was sometimes neglected, either through stress of hunger or dissatisfaction with the way the gods were treating us in the matter of weather. He was also an inveterate builder of cairns, as were his companions, particularly Kusang, in whom this building amounted to a passion. I believe this stone-posing is a favourite devotion of all Buddhists, and they like to choose the most difficult stones and perform remarkable feats of equilibrium with them. Long practice has made them very quick and skilful, and before we had found a suitable foundation stone for our cairn, they would have built one four or five feet high, surmounted by a long slab cleverly balanced on end.

Kusang was the youngest and least experienced of the three, and I fear he was rather put upon in the way of work, just as a recruit must do the chores for an old soldier. But Kusang was a lad who thrived on work, and from the time we got into camp until the time we left, he willingly became a sort of general servant. Almost before we had our loads off, if there was any firewood to be had he would stagger in half-hidden under a great load of it, and would then trot off again to fetch water or to collect snow for melting. By the time he returned the fire would be started but if, as usually happened, it was stubborn, his were the powerful lungs that supplied most of the forced draught. This bellows business became a kind of subconscious habit, for except when his mouth was full (and he ate in the wholehearted way he did everything) he directed a gentle but persistent zephyr towards the fire from wherever he happened to be sitting, with remarkable results. Indeed, when he got his head down and blew in earnest, an almost extinct fire became a holocaust, and on a wet morning the first thing of which one became aware was the blast of Kusang's bellows and a comforting sound it was since it meant that tea would not long be delayed.

Washing-up, that bugbear of camp-life, was to Kusang a pet hobby, second only to cairn-building in his affections. To save time and trouble Tilman and I preferred to use a single plate with no washing between courses, but this Kusang seldom allowed and if, as was often the case, we were dependent on snow and the Primus for our water, his misguided enthusiasm for cleanliness in the home had to be restrained.

On the march he had a singular habit of crooning a mournful dirge, a repetition of three words and two notes, at all times and seasons. The stiffest slope or the most perilous place had no power to still him, but if we had to ford some swift, ice-cold torrent the voice would gradually die away. The habit was maddening at times and I confess to having suffered many moments when my one desire was to silence Kusang forever with an ice-axe, but in places of difficulty one liked to hear him and thus be assured that the equanimity of at least one of the party was undisturbed.

We boasted no cook, and since the food we ate called for no vast display of culinary achievement, all took a hand at preparing it in turn. If more advanced treatment than boiling was required, Angtharkay, who had a light hand with a frying pan, would take charge, and we deferred to his judgment in the all-important matter of food and its cooking, for he was something of a gourmet. Further he had an extensive knowledge of edible plants which, as will appear later, proved of great value.

The Sherpas always used a very hot sauce of some kind to help down their rice, satu, or chupatties, and carried numerous condiments tied up in bits of rag, of which chillies was the most important. They assumed our tastes were similar, and to avoid blistered mouths we kept in our own hands the delicate business of seasoning our "hoosh".

They had an ingenious system of allotting the food when divided into three approximately equal parts; two of them would take three different-sized bits of twig or grass and name one of each of them; these were then handed to the third, who did not know to whom the pieces belonged, and he placed one on each of the three portions. But they were very unselfish about food, and even when it was short were always pressing bits on each other and on us.

The making of edible chupatties is supposed to require some skill, but it is also a fairly laborious process. It devolved therefore on Kusang, and his results were not much more leathery than the professional article. It is fine exercise for the arms, and sometimes Tilman and I would take a hand, to warm ourselves and to afford the Sherpas a little harmless amusement; the sight of a chupattie in the making, curling itself round our wrists or disintegrating through too vigorous smacking, never failed to convulse them.

Their readiness to laugh was characteristic, but they had an odd sense of humour. Any minor misfortune, such as breaking a pipe or burning a hole in drying socks, would bring the house down, and once when I sat on my snow glasses and held up the result for Pasang's inspection, I thought he would have hysterics.

At one mishap which they, no doubt, considered the cream of all, they exercised commendable restraint. We were moving on very steep rock and had sat down on a narrow ledge for a rest, and taken off our sacks. Mine was put down with inexcusable carelessness and on getting up to go on, I happened to touch it with my foot, and 30 lbs. of rice, lentils, and cheese went over the edge to burst like a bomb 200 feet below. The dismay on my face, great though it was, might not have restrained them, but the fact that it was food lent gravity to the affair, and they managed to control themselves. I recovered the sack, but not the contents, and the mangled remains, spilt in all directions, proved too much for them; for a month afterwards, while it yet hung together, the sight of it always fetched a laugh.

The extent of cultivation near the villages seemed out of proportion to the few people, and herds of cows and water-buffaloes, and flocks of goats and sheep, gave promise of a fruitful land. Nevertheless flour was dispensed, if at all, by the cupful, and the livestock was apparently non-milk-producing; the hen and its product a legend; and fruit and vegetables unknown.

In these circumstances there was small scope for Angtharkay's talent for haggling, and on the rare occasions that an egg or a cup of milk appeared on the market, we were too eager to have it to worry about the price.

The scarcity of eggs was to be expected, because hens were seldom kept, but the milk shortage we never understood; the cows, so the story went, had just gone dry, the goats were all in a distant pasture, or there might be some milk tomorrow, if we did not leave too early. Flour was never on hand, each family grinding enough for the next meal and no more, and the promise of fruit was represented by a few unhappy apricot trees. With these last, I am willing to admit, the owners were generous and allowed the Sherpas to climb all over them, taking what they would without thought of payment. True, they were not giving away much, for I never saw a ripe one, but ripe or raw was of no importance to our hungry followers, and after they had finished, the trees appeared to have been attacked by a swarm of locusts.

The willingness of the villagers to supply us with anything they did happen to possess varied from place to place in a puzzling way. Sex seemed to have something to do with success or failure; if all the men were out in the fields and the village fort was held by a few old dames, stony indifference or harsh words were usually our portion. On these occasions we used to arm Angtharkay with some rupees and send him to bell the cat, and as he had pertinacity and a thick skin he seldom came away empty-handed. Kusang, though possessing a more ingratiating manner, would have wilted under the first torrent of abuse, while Pasang might have started throwing things. Most of these villages were on, or near, a "Pilgrim Route" and my theory was that the traditional hospitality ascribed to mountain villages had been soured by the importunities of the many beggars, and doubtless our appearance justified them in placing us in the same category!

CHAPTER SIX

THE first march of our ten-day programme, an afternoon one to Gwaldam, was certainly the least pleasant of any. The road had dropped perversely, as such things do, 4,000 feet since Ranikhet, and now most of this had to be made good by untrained legs on a desperately hot day. Our Dotials must have been out of work for some time as they seemed no happier than we were, and it was late in the evening before a procession of cripples crawled painfully up the last steep rise to the Forest Bungalow. This was beautifully situated on the slopes overlooking the valley of the Pindar and surrounded by abandoned tea-gardens, and once we had established ourselves on the veranda in long cane chairs and procured a vast bowl of milk, our toils were soon forgotten. Tonight we felt we had really started, and though still under a roof the link with civilisation was wearing thin.

The view beyond the Pindar which we had hoped morning would reveal, was hidden in mist and cloud which later turned to rain. Our way lay first down to the valley of the Pindar River, past many villages and well-cultivated fields. The flats near the river were irrigated and were used for growing rice, and great skill and industry was shown in the extensive terracing of the hillsides, a crop of winter wheat already being reaped. Later we left this smiling valley and turned north up a lateral branch, camping amongst some oaks on a high col in a drizzle of rain. At sundown the clouds lifted and from our vantage point 9,000 feet up we had a brief but satisfying vision of Nanda Ghunti.

We were now travelling across higher country between two main valleys, and villages were few and far between, a matter of indifference to us but of much interest to the porters who had to buy their daily rations from the hamlets we did pass. It was not always easy to find 30 or 40 lbs. of rice or of wheat flour; near the larger villages there was usually a mill turned by water, but in most of the smaller the flour was ground by hand on a flat stone, and no more done at a time than would suffice for the next meal – a really literal hand-to-mouth existence. At last, at a village called Wan, the porters got what they needed and we camped here on a little plateau above the village, under some huge Deodars.

We were now about to cross the watershed between the Pindar and Nandakganga Rivers, a long ridge, here 11,000 feet high, which leads up to the mighty Trisul ten miles away to the south-east. Our start was delayed while we waited for the Sherpas who, having only breakfasted lightly off several double-handfuls of satu, now proceeded to fill up with three of the biggest mountains of rice, plates have ever held. Two hours steady climb through shady forests of oak and chestnut brought us to the col, and from there we climbed for another 2,000 feet up a hill west of it, for the sake of the view. The lower slopes were clothed in rhododendron forest, at this altitude still in flower and presenting a beautifully varied show of colour from white to pink and deep crimson. As we gained height, passing from forest to springy turf and then to rock, the mountains which we had been glimpsing through gaps in the trees now rose before us as a distant and broken wall of dazzling whiteness. Nearly all the giants of the Central Himalaya were there to welcome us, from the Kedarnath peaks and Kamet in the north round to Trisul in the east.

Despite a fierce sun it was very cold and snow was still lying in the gullies, so we tore ourselves away from the feast of beauty and hurried back to the col, and so down into the valley to Kanol. Against this name in my diary there is the laconic entry "flies and bulls," nor is more needed, for the recollection of being driven out of the camp by the one and flying naked before the other, which attacked us as we were about to bathe, is still very vivid. But Kanol is also memorable for the opening of the first of four big "Farmhouse" Cheddars we had brought with us; this somewhat premature attack on our luxuries being brought about partly by the difficulty of buying anything, already noted, and by some concern for its health. It had somehow got into my rucksack and so drew attention to itself, and we were anxious to know what effect the damp heat of Calcutta had had on it. Great was our relief to find it had suffered no serious harm. Certainly it had wilted a little but now the cool mountain air was having as bracing an effect upon the cheese as upon us.

Next day the Nandakganga was crossed and we embarked upon a succession of ups and downs over a country almost bare of trees, in the full glare of a hot sun. Plodding up the dusty bridle-path, we met coming down a portentous cavalcade of over twenty mules, a like number of coolies, and a cloud of followers and servants, no doubt the advance-guard of some Great Personage, and we felt uneasy at the threatened meeting, because we had given up shaving since leaving Ranikhet. However it proved to be only a Forest Officer making a tour of his district, the last European we were to meet for another three months.

The magnificent forests which are such a feature of the foothills are at present safe from exploitation for timber or for paper owing to transport difficulties, the rivers being quite useless for that purpose. There is something to be said for illiteracy, and for some time India's three hundred and fifty millions and these noble forests are safe from the devastating effects of a Daily Press. The only product at present is resin, the collection of which is under the Forest Department.

We had barely recovered from the apprehension aroused by the cavalcade and the subsequent reaction, when another passing wayfarer stretched our minds once more upon the rack of anticipation. This time the trouble was caused by an old chap who sported a row of War decorations, as many of these Garhwalis do since the Garhwal Rifles, which greatly distinguished itself in Flanders and Mesopotamia, is recruited solely from them. He saluted us with vigour and we propounded our usual question about eggs and chickens, a question we now put by way of a conversational gambit rather than as a serious inquiry, but the veteran startled us by hinting that he knew where a chicken might be got. He accompanied us to the next village talking all the time, but our replies were short as we were busy arguing the respective merits of roast and boiled chicken, finally deciding in favour of the latter because we wanted to eat it that night. Arrived at the village our friend disappeared into a house to find the victim. Returning presently with an air of self-satisfaction which told us he had been successful, he proudly produced, with the flourish of a conjurer, a rather ill-nourished fledgeling whose feathers were barely visible. As a joke we thought it in rather bad taste, but we had to acquit him of that intention for when we refused to treat he became quite indignant.

The weather was now so fine and settled that every night we abandoned our stuffy tent in favour of the open, and that night we had a glorious camp on a smooth grass terrace under some pines. Shaken though we had been by the affair of the chicken, our peace and content was almost perfect as we lay round a fire of pinewood which blazed like a torch and gave off an oily smoke smelling pleasantly of turpentine. The only discordant note was provided by the Sherpas who industriously held their caps in the smoke and then suddenly clapped them on their heads, an operation which suggested, quite wrongly I believe, a very disturbing train of thought. The true explanation of this curious rite we never discovered.

In front of us now was another high ridge projecting far to the west from the slopes of Nanda Ghunti. We started early for the ascent of this, and the freshness of the morning, the oaks, the hollies, and the chestnuts, the tapping of woodpeckers and the distant note of a cuckoo, made it seem like a spring morning in England. From the col at 10,000 feet Trisul and Nanda Ghunti again showed up prominently, and then we dropped quickly down to the valley of the Bireh Ganga, and camped in a pretty dell, carpeted with big white flowers which smelt like lilies. Pleasant enough it was, but no longer reminiscent of spring at home, plagued as we were by myriads of flies and amused by a school of grey monkeys who were equally interested in us.

Early next day we crossed the river with that thirst-provoking name, the Bireh Ganga, a name, alas! and nothing more for we bathed in it in order to make quite sure. The northern slopes were steep bare hillsides up which the track wound in narrow zig-zags, and at the steepest and narrowest part we were almost swept away by a flood of goats, all carrying little saddle-bags of grain. The photo I tried to take was not a success, and several goats were nearly frightened over the cliff much to the wrath of their owner. We experienced the same difficulty in taking pictures of some of the very picturesque-looking women we passed, festooned with necklaces and strings of coins, and wearing handsome jewelled nose-rings. They either fled at sight, turned their backs on us, or covered their heads.

Looking down the Bireh Ganga, a very prominent landmark is a great scar on the hillside and below it a lake of some size. This is the mark left by the great landslip of 1893 which dammed the river and formed the Gohna Lake beneath. The lake has dwindled now; at first it was much larger and the breaking of the dam caused great havoc lower down. Still mounting we finally camped amongst some large boulders near the village of Khaliaghat. By now we should have become indifferent to rebuffs in the matter of eggs and milk, annoying as it was to go without the second-named when one could hardly throw a stone without hitting a cow, a water buffalo, or a goat. But at Khaliaghat it seems to have rankled for there is something malicious about the entry in my diary, to the effect that the peasants here were of a very low type. So far as I remember we made no anthropological investigations to establish this; certainly cases of goitre were very frequent but so they were in all the higher valleys.

Next day's march, which was to bring us to the foot of the Kuari Pass, was a long one for which we made an early start on a raw, wet morning. It was so cold that at the first halt we lit a fire and sat round it for some time, baking and eating potatoes. Later it faired up and became hot enough to make a bathe in the Kuari glen a pleasant interlude.

The approach to the Kuari was up a steep, wooded glen down which a stream rushed, by gorge and waterfall, from near the pass. After a very long and steep grind the slope began to ease off, and crossing the glen we emerged on to grass downs, bare of trees but brilliant with dwarf iris and potentillas (or red buttercups, if that is not a contradiction in terms). The tinkle of sheep bells and the plaintive notes of a shepherd's pipe drew us towards a shepherd encampment, and here we spent the night, a thousand feet below the pass. There was not the savoury pot of goat's meat and the capacious goat-skin-bag full of wine which readers of Cervantes will remember almost reconciled Sancho to a shepherd's life, but for all that we were hospitably received. Like ourselves they were bound for the pass and the little bags carried by their flocks were full of grain. This is not such a contemptible form of transport as it may sound, as each animal will carry some twenty pounds, so that a flock of a hundred, which is a small one for these parts, can move a ton of stuff. When in camp the shepherds build these bags into a wall forming an admirable wind-break and as the tree-line was not too far below to get fuel, we enjoyed a very snug billet.

The Kuari Pass was known to be a remarkably fine view point so we prayed for a fine morning and made a resolution to be up there early. Before turning in it began to rain, thus offering an excellent excuse for reconsidering this rash resolve, but we hardened our hearts and were duly rewarded. The top of the pass was reached by 7 o'clock of a clear, cold morning and we were privileged to see what must be one of the grandest mountain views in the world. As we raised our heads above the top of the pass a gigantic sweep of icy peaks confronted us, and it was difficult to refrain from gasping at the vastness of the scene. The serrated line of the Kedarnath and Badrinath peaks, Kamet, Hathi Parbat, and the great cleft of the Dhauli Valley were easily recognised, but the glittering array of snowy peaks of all shapes and sizes which filled the gaps were easier to admire and wonder at than to identify. South of the Dhauli towered the graceful Dunagiri, but a sight of Nanda Devi, so soon to be our lodestone, was denied us.

There was some snow on the pass but not enough to trouble the porters, and presently we were down again amongst pines and grassy meadows. Here we had to stop repeatedly as fresh visions of mountain beauty, framed in vistas of pines, delighted our eyes, and film after film was exposed as we endeavoured to capture them. At the first village we came to, still high above the Dhauli, we were directed along a high level route leading over the southern slopes to Joshimath. The porters who were behind followed the more usual route straight down to Tapoban in the valley, and then by the main track which ran close to the river. For them it was a long day and they did not get in till late and one, who subsequently quitted, not until the next day. We had reason to bless our high level route in spite of the temporary separation from our porters, for happening to look back at a bend in the path, we found we were looking up part of the Rishi Ganga Valley and at the pyramid-like summit of Nanda Devi floating serenely in the background. It did not look to be ten miles away but was in fact at least thirty.

We ourselves reached Joshimath at 3 o'clock and the same evening opened negotiations for porters, and porters' food, to accompany us on our attempt on the Rishi Gorge. We wanted twenty porters and about four hundred pounds of food for them, but luckily flour was not ground by hand at Joshimath or we might be there still. Some of it, however, was wanted in the form of "satu" which takes a day or two to prepare, being made by first slightly roasting the wheat or barley (or a mixture of both) in iron pans and then grinding it. The advantage of "satu" is that it requires no cooking and can be eaten dry (not recommended), moistened with cold water, or as a porridge; we found it went down best in tea with plenty of sugar, and was then very good.

The problem of porters was unexpectedly alleviated by the Dotials who, though only engaged as far as Joshimath, were now eager to remain with us. This enthusiasm was the more surprising as most of them had only just arrived after a twelve hour day, and although we painted a gloomy picture of the perils and hardships awaiting them in the Rishi (not inaccurately as it happened) nothing would shake them.

Next day was a Sunday but there was no rest for us. We began work at 6 a.m. nor did Tilman need to have his first job, the killing of a scorpion, pointed out to him. It was curled up in his bedding and very gratifying it was to see the "early bird" and the sluggard for once receiving their respective dues – it might so easily have been the other way round. Curiously enough later in the day we killed a snake close by, but these two specimens must not be taken as typical Joshimath fauna, which consists almost entirely of the more homely but equally venomous fly.

Before getting down to sorting and weighing loads we sent off one of the Sherpas to scour the surrounding country for eggs. We reasoned that as Joshimath was a considerable village on the very populous Pilgrim Route such things ought not to be beyond the bounds of possibility. It is a place of some antiquity and lies 1,500 feet above the deep gorge where the Dhauli and Alaknanda Rivers unite. The junction is called Vishnuprayag and has many sacred associations but there is nothing there save a shrine and a few huts. Joshimath itself is a long straggling village built on a projecting spur, and besides two bazaars, nearly half a mile apart, there is a hospital, a school, a post office, and one or two large houses. One of these belongs to the Rawal of the Badrinath temple who passes the winter here. The villagers' houses are solidly built of stone, with two stories and a stone roof. The living-room is on the first floor which opens out in front on to a wooden balcony, the ground floor being used as a stable, store, or shop. The timber for the houses is all cut by hand and is very massive, and on the lintels and balcony there is sometimes elaborate carving.

For all its two bazaars no one living in Joshimath could have made much of a hole in his pocket or wasted his substance on riotous living. Once or twice we succumbed to the temptations of the sweetmeat sellers, but we always found sickness intervened before a whole rupee had been spent. Nevertheless, the cost of the few things we wanted and which were obtainable was quite high enough, and the bazaar fraternity had the fine independent air assumed by the owners of seaside lodgings at the height of a good summer season.

Towards evening the scattered debris of the loads had at least begun to resolve itself into two piles, one to go with us and one to remain, and the first was even shaping itself into approximate loads. But the strain was telling, the spring balance was now, through overwork, registering several pounds with nothing on it, and we were not sorry when an interruption came.

It was the Sherpa, faint but triumphant, accompanied by the owner of three eggs. We were too pleased to argue about the very stiff price, but put them straight into a bucket of water where, to our dismay, they bobbed about merrily on the surface, obviously, by all the laws, in a fairly advanced state. Wiser men would have called the deal off but second thoughts suggested that after all eggs were eggs, and the water test, infallible as we knew in Africa, might not apply to

Indian eggs. Further than that Joshimath was 6,000 feet above the sea, and though neither of us was a physicist, we knew that altitude had queer effects on boiling water and why not on the buoyancy factor? Anyway, for better or for worse, we decided to take them, but unfortunately three into two won't go so, in a spirit worthy of Mrs. Beeton, we recklessly sank all three in an omelette, telling Angtharkay not to spare the ghee in the frying, for it has a powerful taste of its own. The result was as excellent as it was surprising and worthy of more than our somewhat sententious remarks, I observing that "the highest wisdom is not to be too wise," while all Tilman could find to say was: "*De l'audace, toujours de l'audace.*" Had our heads not been in a whirl of figures relating to rations, days, and rupees (we had just counted the contents of our bag of rupees for the tenth time, to make sure we really had lost some), we might have worked out a learned thesis on "Altitude and the Specific Gravity of the Egg;" as it was we had one more unsuccessful count and turned in.

I am afraid that night we were unfeignedly glad that this delightful ten day prelude was over and that the morrow would see the beginning of more serious work, and our impatience was no doubt the reason why we did not enjoy the preliminary march to the full. At the back of our minds was regret at the apparent waste of time, regret which became more poignant as fine day succeeded fine day, for we well knew that this pre-monsoon weather was the best we should ever have. But for that we might have been content to put no limit to our wanderings in a country of such loveliness, where the air and the rivers, the flowers and the trees filled one with the joy of living.

Now, however, impatience was to be satisfied and though we should find nature in a sterner mood, there would be no carking care to prevent us echoing Petulengro's "Life is very sweet . . ."

CHAPTER SEVEN

LIGHT rain had fallen during the morning and the air was fresh and invigorating as we marched out of Joshimath along the well-made path that runs high up along the south side of the Dhaoli Valley. To the north dark precipices rose from the water's edge in a continuous sweep, to lose themselves in the clouds some thousands of feet above us. At irregular intervals these walls were cleft by narrow, ravine-like valleys, cut in the rock by streams descending from the glaciers of the great peaks above. I can never see such configuration without experiencing an almost irrepressible desire to select a valley at random and wander up into its mysterious recesses, and on such a day as this, when the clouds, darkening the upper reaches of the gorge, accentuated its apparent depth, it was hard to resist the temptation to make a drastic change of plan.

Our path, which started at Joshimath some 1,500 feet above the river, remained fairly level throughout the short day's march, and at the village of

Tapoban ran only a few feet above the floor of the valley. Here we caught up the Dotials, who had left some hours ahead of us, and a mile beyond the village, in a pleasantly wooded side-valley, we camped.

The evening was a fine one. Four miles upstream we could see the junction-point between the Rishi Nala and the main Dhaoli Valley. In the corner formed by these two valleys is a prominent forest-clad knoll called Lata afer the village at its foot. It really forms the butt end of the great western ridge of Dunagiri, and we could see at a glance that the summit of this hill must command a fine view up the Rishi Nala, a view which might well prove invaluable to us later on. It was decided, therefore, that Kusang and Angtharkay should go with the Dotials on the following day, and that Pasang, Tilman and I should climb Lata and join the others in the evening at Surai Tota, where we had made arrangements with the Bania to pick up our supplies of satu and ata.

Five a.m. saw the three of us again striding along the path by the side of the river. We moved at a good speed as we had a long day's work before us: five miles along the path, 6,500 feet of ascent and descent over the rough wooded hillside, and then some more miles of path to be accomplished before nightfall.

The morning was one of exquisite beauty. The air, cleansed and purified by the rain of the previous day, was filled with the delicate scents of the pine-woods. From behind the great ice-peaks came the beams of the newly-risen sun, in magnificent contrast to the sombre, heavily forested country about us. The trees with their drowsy limbs still wet with the dew, the song of the birds sharing with us the exaltation of the new-born day, the streams splashing down in silver waterfalls or lying dormant in deep-blue pools, all played their part in this – the second act of Nature's pageantry of dawn. A fine morning, when all consideration of time and distance was eclipsed by the pure delight in one's sur-roundings.

We had been going for an hour and a half when we came to a northward bend in the Dhaoli River, which marked the point where the Rishi Ganga joins it. There we paused for a moment to look into that section of the gorge up which Graham had made an attempt to force a route as far back as 1883: a gorge which has never yet been penetrated by anyone. As our object was to get into the Nanda Devi Basin, we could not afford to spend any time trying to explore this section of the Rishi Ganga. We knew of a practicable route into the middle section, and a failure to get up this lower section would cost us valuable time.

But it was interesting to have a close view of the river which, in its higher reaches, was going to play such an important part in our adventures of the next few weeks. There was less water in it than I had expected, and we became hopeful of being able to wade up it in parts where there was no other route – poor innocents that we were. I had an idea too that once the winter snows had gone from the lower mountain sides, the volume of water in the rivers would decrease considerably, and never regain its present proportions for the rest of the year. In this I was entirely wrong. In actual fact, as soon as the melting of the glacier ice sets in, after the departure of the winter snow, the rivers increase enormously in size. This I think is an impressive indication of the immense area of the glaciers in the district.

A mile beyond the mouth of the Rishi, we turned to the right and started mounting the steep slope of Lata, finding the going more complicated and strenuous than we had expected. The hillside was covered with dense undergrowth, through which it was hard work to make our way. The ground was steep, and every now and then we were faced by a little cliff which had been masked by the undergrowth. Moreover we had had no chance to make a selection of a suitable route from afar, and now we could not see far enough ahead to choose out the best line. Our pace was slow, the day waxed hot, and our throats became unpleasantly dry. Sometimes we were forced to descend a considerable way in order to avoid some overhanging cliff, which tried our tempers sorely. At 11 o'clock we arrived at the foot of a cliff of larger proportions than usual. This we saw would demand a long descent before we would be able to outflank it. Like the rawest novices we elected to try and climb the crag direct, though the upper section was screened from view. After an hour of stiff rock-climbing, we succeeded in getting down again to the spot from which we had started. More heated than ever, we started on the outflanking movement. This accomplished, we toiled upwards once more, feeling not a little humbled by the heavy weather we were making of this little knoll. Clinging on to mossy roots, which not infrequently came away from the hillside, showering earth into our mouths and down our backs, we reached at 2.30 p.m. a little bald rocky patch, which formed the summit of Lata.

A glance at the view changed our gloomy outlook on life to one of thrilling exultation. The afternoon was clear and still. All round us were scenes of grandeur, the scale of which was too vast for human conception. To the north, across the Dhaoli Valley, rose the grim turrets and delicate spires of the Hathi Parbat group, so complex in structure that we could not begin to understand its tangled topography. Eastwards was the lovely cone of Dunagiri, displaying to full advantage its beautifully proportioned curves. West of us was the Trisul range, its vast ice plateaux dazzlingly white in the torrid rays of the afternoon sun. And to the south Nanda Devi, queen of them all, held aloft her proud shapely head, her slender shoulders draped with snow-white braid.

Coming down to earth, we erected the plane-table, and worked with it for an hour. The views we had obtained of the Rishi Nala provided food for much thought.

Soon after 4 o'clock we started to descend. We got into a steep leaf-filled gully in the forest, and down this we plunged at a fine speed. I was still wearing my tennis shoes, and gave my bad toe several cracks which nearly sent me head first down the steep slope.

Since leaving the valley in the early morning, we had not come across a drop of water, nor did we find any now. The day was hot, we had been working hard, and by now were unpleasantly parched in tongue and throat. For my part this was accountable for the turn of speed which landed us on the shore of the Dhaoli River at 6 o'clock – a descent of six thousand odd feet in under two hours. To the infinite astonishment of a company of Bhotias who were camping on the shore close by, Tilman stripped and plunged into the turbulent waters of the river. I was more circumspect and performed my ablutions from a convenient boulder. Pasang, a true Tibetan, merely drank.

In the cool of the evening we marched silently up the valley. A fresh breeze blowing down from the peaks, and limbs just pleasantly tired, put me in sympathy with the subdued colouring of dusk, while I mused over the glimpse we had had into the mysterious country beyond the Rishi Ganga.

It was quite dark before we reached Surai Tota. Our camp was pitched on a flat stretch of grassland above the river, and a fine fire was blazing outside the tents. A large dish of lentils, followed by inexhaustible supplies of tea put us at peace with the world, and quite incapable of coping with a voluble flow of Hindustani from Kesar Singh,* who had awaited our arrival in the village. The night was warm, and we fell into luxurious slumber by the fireside, knowing nothing more until roused by the first beams of the morning sun.

Kesar Singh had arranged for eight Surai Tota men to come with us up the Rishi. They were to be paid at the same rate as the Dotials and receive the same rations, i.e., tea, salt, cigarettes and ata. Kesar Singh said he knew the men well, and according to him they were sure-footed, brave, strong, and absolutely reliable: in fact, it appeared that they were very paragons of virtue. The ata, it appeared, was bagged and ready; but the satu would not be ready until later in the morning. However, it was arranged that we should start on with three of the "locals" who knew the route, and the other five would follow on with the satu when it was ready. Our destination that day was a little alp known as Hyetui Kharak, situated near the upper limit of the forest, at an altitude of about 11,700 feet. The men who were coming with us assured us that they all knew the way well and, completing a touching farewell ceremony with Kesar Singh, we made our departure with his assurances that we would have no trouble from *his* men at least.

A rough track led steeply up through the forest which covered the southern side of the Dhaoli Valley, the floor of which at this point is about 7,500 feet. An hour's steady going along this track took us to the tiny village of Tolma, a charming spot built high on the steep mountain side under the shade of some gigantic conifers.

Life in these little mountain villages is delightfully simple, and the inhabitants are almost entirely self-supporting. A few stony fields, terraced out of the steep hillside by their ancestors, supply all the food they require. A flock of sheep and goats, tended in summer by the youth of the community on the high mountain pastures, provides them with wool for their clothing. This wool is spun into yarn by the men, who carry their simple apparatus about with them wherever they go, so that they can be constantly spinning, while carrying loads, tending sheep, or performing any job that does not involve the use of their hands. The yarn is then woven into cloth by the women, who sit outside their houses, manipulating complicated machines with astonishing skill. Thus all are busily employed, all are well-fed and clothed, and all are happy. Any surplus farm produce is exchanged with itinerant traders for such luxuries as salt, tobacco, etcetera.

We paused awhile to converse with some of the weavers, and to try and puzzle out how their machines worked, then continued on our ascent. Our newly enrolled Surai Tota men already seemed a bit doubtful of the way and we inquired of some ploughmen, whether or not the path to Hyetui Kharak was well

*Kesar Singh had accompanied us on the Kamet expedition and lived hereabouts.

defined. We gathered from them that we could not possibly miss it if we kept our eyes open. Nevertheless we were no sooner clear of the fields than we were floundering in dense forest, trying in vain to find the least vestige of a track. The "locals" assured us that we had just got to keep on up and we would be all right. But only when, after wading for some hours through the forest, we reached the brink of a 1,500 foot precipice, did they admit that the only two of the eight who knew the way were among those who had waited at Surai Tota for the satu! They thought that we had come too high and that the alp was somewhere below us.

It was obvious to us from Dr. Longstaff's descriptions of the country that it was still *above* us, and taking the matter of route finding into our own hands we reached the "kharak" in the middle of the afternoon. (Kharak, by the way, is a word used in these parts to mean a summer grazing ground. As the winter snows depart from the lowest of their pastures, so the shepherds and their flocks come up into occupation; later in the year they move to a still higher alp.)

The highest of these kharaks are about 14,000 feet in altitude, and are occupied for a bare two months each year. Hyetui Kharak was not yet occupied, as a quantity of snow still lingered on its higher slopes. It was a pleasant spot – a wide stretch of meadowland bordered on three sides by the forest, and we spent the remainder of the afternoon lying stretched out on the grass, dozing in the warm sunshine.

Towards dusk we began to get anxious about the non-arrival of the five satu men. Now that we had left the Dhaoli Valley, we could not afford to waste a day; for with such a large company of porters, each day spent in getting to our base in the Rishi Nala meant a large amount less food with which to carry out our work beyond. When night fell and there was still no sign of the missing five, we began to curse our folly in starting without them. We fully expected that they, like their fellows, had not the least idea of the way. However, at 8 o'clock our anxiety was relieved by their arrival.

We slept out in the open again, and were up as soon as it was light, for we knew that we were in for a hard day's work. Not far above us, at an altitude of about 12,500 feet, the forest zone ended abruptly. Above this line the snow was lying deep on the ground. This winter snow in the process of melting is vile stuff to get through. Soft and sodden, it allows one to sink in to the extent of its depth, but is sufficiently heavy to put up a formidable resistance against any forward progress.

The porters knew this as well as we did, and, as we were getting ready for an early start, the Surai Tota men came to us to say that they must have a ration of ghee before they could consent to go any further. Except for a small quantity of ghee intended for the use of the Sherpas high up, we had none to give them. But it was obvious that they had little intention of going any further, and I told them that they could do as they liked; to which they replied that they would go down and leave us! Indeed, I suspect that that had been their idea all along: to come with us as far as Hyetui Kharak, a very easy day's march from Surai Tota, to collect their pay, and clear off before they were involved in any hard work. In this they were disappointed, as of course we refused to pay them unless they fulfilled their agreement to come with us into the Rishi Nala. I would like to say here, however, that this was the only time in all our dealings with the people of this district that we were let down in any way.

The desertion of the Surai Tota men put us in a serious predicament, and threatened to wreck at the very outset our plans for the exploration of the Nanda Devi Basin. We summoned the Dotials, who were camped a hundred yards away, and explained the situation to them. Without a moment's hesitation they volunteered to carry as much as they could manage of the abandoned loads. We warned them that the going would be extremely bad, but they held to their offer, and added so much of the satu and ata to the loads which they had been carrying on the previous day, that only two loads of ata remained. These were dragged off to the forest and hidden, to be picked up on their return. Staggering under loads weighing more than eighty pounds each they cheerfully faced the steep slopes above the alp. Thus did these low-caste Dotials by their loyalty make it possible for us to go through with our plans.

These negotiations delayed our start, and it was 7.40 a.m. before we were on the move. We were making for the crest of that same ridge running down from the Dunagiri massif, whose westerly end culminated in the little peak of Lata, which we had climbed two days before. We knew that our route lay across a gap in this ridge, some 14,700 feet in height, to a grazing ground used in summer by the shepherds of Tolma and Lata, and known to them as Durashi. This kharak was not generally visited until the beginning of July, owing to the winter snow which makes the pass impossible for the transit of sheep. It was now May 24th, and the track was still buried under deep snow.

From the summit of a spur above Hyetui we got a good view of the ridge above us, and saw that there were no less than three gaps to choose from, each just as promising as the other. Moreover the ridge was serrated, and the condition of the snow made it impossible to get from one gap to another by following the crest. The only thing to do was to make a guess at which was the right one, and trust to luck.

Soon after leaving the forest we plunged into a morass of soft snow, through which we had to flog a track. At first it was not particularly deep and, keeping to the crest of a spur, the first gap was reached in a couple of hours. From here we looked down a sheer precipice of several thousand feet. We were obviously in the wrong gap, and a traverse had to be made round to the next one. Once off the spur our difficulties began. We sank first up to our knees, then up to our waists; sometimes we were floundering up to our armpits in the sodden snow. The day was fine, without a breath of wind. The blazing sun and the torrid glare from the snow produced a feeling of lassitude such as I have never experienced elsewhere except on enclosed glaciers at great altitudes.

Tilman and I took turns of twenty minutes each at the task of track making, while the others remained behind to assist the porters, whose cruel loads frequently caused them to overbalance. It was terribly hard work for them; but they stuck to it wonderfully, cheerfully chiding one another as they fell into some deep drift, from which they had to be extricated. The ground too was steep and very rough, and they avoided an accident only by their surprising skill.

It was a weary struggle and our progress seemed painfully slow. Beating with

our ice-axes, kicking and stamping, we continued without pause until
2.30 p.m., when we reached the second gap, only to find that the third was the
true pass. We made an attempt to get along the ridge towards it, but after some
hard work we had to give this up on account of the difficulty of the climbing
which made even the Dotials lose their cheerfulness. Descending a few
hundred feet we reached a small rocky ledge sticking out of the snow. It was
now 5 o'clock, and we decided to bivouac here for the night. We melted some
snow and brewed tea; never was a drink more welcome.

The outcrop we were on was sloping steeply downwards, so we built up
platforms on which to sleep. It was a commanding position, 6,000 feet above
the Dhaoli River, and one from which the surrounding peaks could be seen to
their best advantage.

It was a perfect evening. As I lay on my little platform, the multi-coloured
afterglow of sunset spreading over the vast mountain world about me, I was
filled with a deep content, untroubled either by the memory of the failures of
that day, or by the prospect of further trials on the morrow. A vision of such
beauty was worth a world of striving.

The last tint of sunset died, and a young moon, hanging over the ice-
buttresses of the giant peak of Dunagiri, held undisputed right to shed her pale
light over an enchanted world. The snowy crests stood now in superb contrast
to the abysmal gloom of the valleys. Interwoven with my dreams, I was vaguely
conscious of these sublime impressions throughout the night, until a new day
was heralded by the first faint flush of dawn.

We made full use of the cold of the early morning, in resuming our toil
through the snow, and with this ally we made more rapid progress. Now at last
we were on the right route, and at 10.30 a.m. we reached the true pass. There
we found a well-defined track running along the face of a steep precipice. The
rocks still held a good deal of ice and snow, especially in the gullies, and much
step cutting was required in order to get along the track. It was a remarkable
place. The cliffs were exceedingly steep and dropped in an almost unbroken
plunge for some 8,000 feet, and yet there was this narrow ledge, along which it
was possible for the shepherds to take their sheep in the summer time. The
length of the cliff was about half a mile.

My heart was in my mouth as I watched the Dotials coming along the track,
for the ice made the passage of certain sections exceedingly delicate work. But
we soon discovered that they were as sure-footed as cats, and needed very little
assistance, in spite of their formidable loads. Cutting steps for prolonged
periods is tiring work, but it was infinitely preferable to the heart-breaking toil
of the previous day. At the further end of the terrace was a deep gully into
which we had to descend for several hundred feet; when a climb up a boulder-
strewn slope took us to a small gap, from which we looked down gentle grassy
slopes to Durashi. The contrast could not have been more sudden and
unexpected. There at our feet lay a little stretch of country, enclosed by gently
rolling hills, for all the world like some quiet corner of the English Lake
District. There was about it not the least suggestion of the vast ruggedness of
the land from which we had just come.

The little vale of Durashi is really a hanging valley, lying high up on the northern side of the Rishi Nala. On three sides it is enclosed by these grassy hills, and on the fourth it opens out above the precipice which forms the side of the main valley. It seems to be entirely cut off from the outside world. Indeed if it were not for the cliff track, its luxuriant pastures would be inaccessible to the shepherds and their flocks. We found several stone shelters there, which were gladly occupied by the Dotials. Water and firewood were scarce and difficult of access.

In the evening we wandered down to the lower end of the valley, and looked straight down a 5,000 foot precipice into what must be one of the most fantastic gorges in the world. It has never yet been penetrated by any human being, and is believed by the locals to be the abode of demons – a superstition we were quite ready to share. The precipice was far too steep for us to be able to examine the near side of the valley, but the other side was almost grotesque in its structure. It was built up of tier upon tier of gigantic steeply inclined slabs, which culminated 10,000 feet above the river in a multitude of sharp rocky peaks set at a rakish angle. The river itself, only just visible in the depths below us, sent up a roar like that of Niagara. What a subject for an artist illustrating an old-fashioned travel book! No conception, even of Gustave Doré, could appear exaggerated beside the cliffs and turrets towering above that amazing canyon. To us the view was anything but encouraging.

The evening was overcast and we began to fear that our spell of fine weather was coming to an end. A little rain fell in the night, but we awoke to another cloudless morning. We started at 7 o'clock and climbed up to a saddle in the ridge which enclosed the head of the little Durashi glen. This ridge has been aptly named "the curtain" by Dr. Longstaff, for it is an offshoot of the main Dunagiri-Lata ridge which we had crossed the day before, and runs down at right angles into the Rishi Ganga, completely screening the upper part of that valley from Durashi. Before starting on its final plunge into the Rishi Ganga, the ridge rises to a little peak, which we called for want of a better name Durashi Peak. This was only about 600 feet above our saddle and, leaving the porters to rest awhile, Tilman and I ascended the peak with the plane-table, and spent two hours on top, studying the geography of the upper gorge and its surroundings, of which we commanded a fairly comprehensive view.

We could identify the furthest points reached by the Graham and Longstaff parties, just beyond the junction of the Rhamani Valley with the Rishi Nala, and it was about there that we proposed to put our base camp. Beyond was the untrodden section of the gorge, the key to the sanctuary of the Nanda Devi Basin. The view we got of it from here proved of the greatest value to us later.

Clouds soon began to form on the peaks around, but Nanda Devi remained clear. Indeed, this was a peculiarity of the mountain, which we came to recognise. Often when all the other peaks were obscured from view, wrapped in a dense mantle of cloud, the summit of Nanda Devi would remain clear. (This is directly contrary to general rule, for it is nearly always the big isolated rock mountains which first attract cloud, especially when they happen to be the highest in their particular district.) Now we obtained an uninterrupted view of the great southern ridge of the mountain. It was by this ridge that we entertained some slight hope of finding a practicable route to the summit, although we were not sufficiently equipped to make the attempt that year. But as we looked at the mighty upward sweep of the ridge all hope died, for the thing appeared utterly unclimbable, as indeed I still think it is.

At 10.30 a.m. we rejoined the porters on the saddle. From here we looked down some three thousand feet into a thickly wooded nala, descending from a glacier-covered south-westerly spur of Dunagiri. The nala was cut into two parts by streams which united further down. Between them, completely surrounded by a forest of tall pines, lay a beautiful strip of pasture land, known to the locals as Dibrughita. This too was used as a summer grazing ground. We were told later that nowadays it is very seldom visited by shepherds, presumably because of the difficulty of access, for the grazing must be very valuable.

The descent was steep and, owing to the loads, took a long time, but it was devoid of difficulties. Unluckily we crossed the stream in a bad place, and had considerable difficulty in getting up the other side. Later, however, we found an easy crossing, which was obviously the one used by the shepherds. It will have been noted by now that many of our difficulties at this early stage were due to our lack of local knowledge. This we had thought to provide against, by engaging Kesar Singh's friends at Surai Tota, some of whom I have no doubt knew the route well. Their desertion put us at a bad disadvantage. We had expected to have no difficulties in the matter of route-finding, at least until one march beyond Dibrughita. We were too pressed for time and food to employ any time in reconnaissance, and a false move meant hours of extra toil for ourselves and the unfortunate Dotials.

We had intended to camp on the alp, but we could not find any water there, and we were forced to go on beyond. This was disappointing, as it was undoubtedly one of the most lovely spots it had ever been my good fortune to behold. Dr. Longstaff had described it to me when I was staying with him in England, but even *his* well-known enthusiasm could not provide me with a picture to compare with the reality. Lying on the soft grass, surrounded by a luxuriant growth of wild flowers, the forest of tall stately pines bordering the alp on every side, and with only a glimpse here and there of some icy peak, it was impossible to imagine the grimly terrifying aspect of the main valley so close at hand. Tilman's remark that it was like "a horizontal oasis in a vertical desert" was one whose aptness we were afterwards to appreciate more fully.

Our camp that night was in the nala beyond Dibrughita. Close beside, a clear stream splashed its joyous way through the forest. Here the vegetation was neither dense nor oppressive, and the trees, great gnarled veterans, each possessed a striking individuality, as in a wood at home.

We had a long climb through the forest next morning to get out of the nala, and when we did so we found ourselves for the first time in the main valley of the Rishi Ganga. Looking back across the Dibrughita Nala we saw to full advantage the huge mass of "the curtain". We saw that it too was composed of gigantic steeply sloping slabs such as we had seen from Durashi on the other side of the valley. And very different it looked now from those gentle grassy slopes on which we had camped two nights before.

We now had our first taste of what moving about in the Rishi Nala was like. Having no local knowledge to guide us, we did not know whether to keep high up on the mountain side or low down, or which was the best route to take. We were then about 2,000 feet above the river, and decided to take a line at about that level. The valley-side was steep, and cut by innumerable deep gullies and cliffs. We could rarely get a clear view of the ground for more than a hundred yards ahead, and we were constantly toiling up some steep slope only to find that we had arrived at some impassable cut-off, which could only be avoided by making a long detour above or below. Tilman and I would go ahead taking different routes, and signal to the others behind to follow the better line. But even so we were continually making big mistakes, which cost us hours of needless toil. Some months later, when we came this way again with a party of porters, we had no difficulty whatever in picking out a good line, simply because we had already been over the country twice and knew it well. But on our first journey it was a worrying job, more particularly as we were in a hurry, and were relying entirely upon the good nature and steadiness of the Dotials.

At about 1 o'clock we reached a point from which we could proceed no further at our present level, and we decided to descend to the river. This was easier said than done, however, and we searched for a long while before we dis-covered a steep gully down which we could climb. In two places the loads had to be lowered by means of a rope. At one of these I had climbed down first, and was standing on a ledge ready to guide the loads down, when someone dis-lodged a rock from above, which hit me on the back of the head. It did not quite knock me out, but I was dizzy and sick for some little while afterwards. The acci-dent was more spectacular than serious, however, as the resulting scalp wound bled with a freedom out of all proportion to the size of the cut. This elicited much tender sympathy from the Dotials, particularly from their old "Captain", and for the remainder of the day they worked with redoubled energy.

A few hundred feet above the river we got into bad bramble, through which a way had to be cut, and at 4.30 p.m. we reached the water's edge at a point about half a mile below the Trisuli Nala. We recognised it as the place at which Longstaff had crossed the river on his way to make his famous ascent of Trisul, twenty-seven years before. We decided to camp here for the night.

When we had distributed the rations and had drunk a cup of tea, Tilman and I went off to make a reconnaissance, and to try to decide on tomorrow's route before nightfall.

I had hoped to reach the junction of the Rhamani and Rishi Rivers on the following day, but we had made very poor progress that day, and the difficulties ahead appeared considerable. A number of large boulders in the river bed offered us an easy place for bridging the river. Dr. Longstaff's party had reached the Rhamani junction by crossing the river at this point; but they had been a lightly equipped party, and even so had found considerable difficulties beyond the Trisuli Nala. We had no idea whether a route along the northern bank was practicable. However, after a careful consideration of the matter, it was decided upon as being at least the more direct one. I was in a hurry, because each day that we spent in getting to our proposed base camp meant at least three days less time for the job above as, so long as the Dotials were with us, we were consuming our food supply at the rate of 32 lbs. per day.

By now the loads were appreciably lighter for, besides the food which was being consumed, we had left a dump of flour at Durashi for the use of the Dotials on their return, and here another dump was left.

We got away at about 6.30 on the morning of May 28th. After a few hundred yards we struck very bad going, but later in the morning we began to make quite satisfactory progress, though held up from time to time by small land-slips, or by fearful tangles of thorn-scrub and bramble. At midday we reached a big scar in the hillside, beyond which we could make no further progress along the river bank. We climbed up for a thousand feet or so and got on to a terrace which took us to a bend in the valley half a mile further on.

The mountain side we were on now steepened up enormously, and it looked very much as if we had reached a dead end. The porters were some way behind so, leaving his load, Tilman went off to prospect round the corner while I waited to rally the men. Now for the first time the Dotials showed signs of despondency. They said they had had enough and they wanted to leave their loads here and go back, and anyhow, they added, they would not face any more difficult or dangerous bits.

It was nearly an hour before Tilman reappeared. He reported that he had got right into a side valley which must have been the Rhamani, and that from the point he had reached it would have been a comparatively simple matter to descend to the stream but that, in getting there, he had had to traverse a tiny sloping ledge without any hand-holds to keep him in balance above a sheer precipice of several hundred feet. He did not think it fair to ask heavily laden men to go across.

We went on for a bit until we arrived at the edge of a deep gully which descended steeply to the Rishi. While Tilman and I examined the possibility of getting on to a higher line of traverse, Kusang and Angtharkay went down the gully to see if the shore of the river would help us. By now the sky had become very dark and a fierce gusty wind was blowing up the valley. It was evident that we were in for a fairly considerable storm. The Dotials huddled together, their teeth chattering.

When the two Sherpas returned with the news that they had only been able to get a hundred yards or so along the shore, we nevertheless gave the word for a general descent to the river, for it was obvious that, apart from everything else, the storm would prevent any intricate climbing on the precipitous ground in front of us. On reaching the river we set to work cutting down trees for the construction of a bridge, while the Dotials made fires on the shore and squatted round them. The actual bridging was not a difficult task with so many hands to assist, as the river was now quite low. By 5.30 p.m. the whole party was safely across.

With a good deal of persuasion we induced the Dotials to come on a little further, telling them that if they did reach the Rhamani junction that night, we would discharge them on the following morning. We told them too that it would take another two hours (though we had not ourselves the haziest notion of how long we should need). A strip of pine forest lay along the southern shore at this point, and as this was free from undergrowth and offered such excellent going, we had actually reached our goal by 6.15. A few minutes later the storm broke, and in a whirl of falling snow we pitched the tents and struggled with a reluctant fire, while the Dotials made themselves snug in a little cave beyond. We did not bother much about food that evening, as darkness had fallen before we had stowed our kit away, and the whirling snow made a mockery of all our efforts to get a fire going.

CHAPTER EIGHT

WHEN preparations for the night were complete, Pasang and I retired to the shelter of a small overhanging rock, while the others took to the tents. Until late into the night the two of us sat huddled over a fire which, after many unsuccessful attempts, we had managed to light in our shelter. Pasang had been suffering from "tummy trouble" for some time, and the heavy work of the last few days had made him feel very weak. It continued to snow heavily throughout the night, and about 1 o'clock I was woken up by Tilman, who had come up to join us, his tent having collapsed under the weight of the snow. He managed to fit some of himself under the shelter of our overhang.

The snow stopped falling in the early hours of the morning and the dawn broke on a cloudless sky. The Dotials paid us an early visit, and we gave them their well-earned pay. They said they did not like leaving us up here alone, but after a touching farewell ceremony, they took their departure. And sorry I was to see them go. They had served us well and faithfully, carrying huge loads over country where a slip would have had serious consequences. Nor should I easily forget their pleasant humour and their courtesy.

The morning was spent in moving our stuff over to the overhang which had been occupied by the Dotials, sorting things out, taking stock of food, and many other little jobs. We found that we had thirty-five days food left.

This section of the Rishi Nala is a fine example of a box-canyon, that is to say, a canyon whose sides rise perpendicularly from the water's edge. The walls of this gorge maintained a tremendous steepness and culminated in peaks of 20,000 feet. Our present altitude was 11,800 feet, and our camp was situated on a small strip of shore on the southern side of the river. The cliffs overhung the shore for about 80 feet above our heads, and afforded fine protection from the rain. In addition, the valley was running nearly east-west, and so our camp enjoyed more sun than would be supposed from the depth of the valley. One drawback to an otherwise ideal site was the lack of clean water. The Rishi was thick with a whitish glacier mud and, though there were several side-streams near by, we could not reach any of them. As we were having our evening meal one night, Angtharkay remarked that now at any rate we had milk with our tea – the milk of the great Nanda Devi!

Our camp was about two hundred yards above the point where Rhamani stream comes into the Rishi Ganga from the north. At the junction itself a huge rock had fallen across the Rishi stream, forming a natural bridge. The crossing was not easy though, and involved some delicate work, especially when crossing with loads. However, it gave us access to the northern side in our search for a route up the gorge, and later was more than useful in our retreat down the valley.

On the afternoon following our arrival, Tilman and I crossed the river to make a reconnaissance on the northern side of the gorge. A hundred feet or so above the rock-bridge we came upon Dr. Longstaff's old camp site – a level grassy platform by an overhanging rock. We climbed up the steep slopes behind it until we could command a good view of the cliffs above our base camp. It was soon evident that it would be impossible to make our way up the gorge at a low level, and that we would have to climb at least 1,200 feet before we could start traversing. We could not see how far this line would get us, but it seemed to be our only chance to get along the southern side of the valley, and it was on that side that Dr. Longstaff had told us to concentrate all our energies.

I found myself to be very nervous and shaky on the steep grass slopes and slabs on which we had to climb. This was due to the fact that I was not yet used to the immense scale of the gorge and its surroundings. Tilman suffered from the same complaint. We also had great difficulty in judging the size and angle of minor features. This made route-finding from a distance very difficult indeed, and we were continually finding ourselves in error. However, the eye gradually adjusted itself, and soon we began to move with more confidence.

That night I could hardly control my impatience to get up on to the cliffs above and start our search for a route through the upper gorge. For a long time I lay awake weighing up in my mind our chances of success. The morrow would show us much, for our reconnaissance that evening had proved to us that there, at the beginning, was but one line of possibility. Should this fail, we should be check-mated at the very outset.

Whatever may have been my enthusiasm or impatience to be up and doing on the night before, the hour for getting up always finds me with no other ambition in the world than to be permitted to lie where I am and sleep, sleep, sleep. Not so Tilman. I have never met anyone with such a complete disregard for the sublime comforts of the early morning bed. However monstrously early we might decide, the night before, to get up, he was about at least half an hour before the time. He was generally very good about it, and used to sit placidly smoking his pipe over the fire, with no more than a few mild suggestions that it might be a good idea to think about starting. Nevertheless, I always boiled (so far as my sleepy state allowed) with indignation, and thought of many crushing arguments (never uttered) why I should be allowed to sleep. Unfortunately it was easier to be a passive obstacle than an active force, and I generally got the better of the silent dispute. But on the morning of May 30th, Tilman's efforts resulted in our leaving camp at 5.20 a.m., that is to say, only twenty minutes late.

Mounting in a series of wide zig-zags, we followed the route we had worked out on the previous afternoon from the opposite side of the valley. After two hours climbing we reached the crest of a little spur which we had taken to be the start of a possible line of traverse, and beyond which we had not been able to see. The spur commanded a fine view of the upper gorge. The immediate prospect looked anything but hopeful, while some two miles further up we saw a huge dark buttress, which appeared to descend in an unbroken sweep from great heights above to the water's edge, and looked to be utterly impassable. This buttress came to be called "Pisgah", for we felt that if we could climb it we would have access to the "Promised Land" beyond.

Directly in front of us was a gully, and beyond the gully was a little terrace running steeply downwards across the face of the precipice we were on. This looked so unpromising that we decided to try it only as a last resort. We climbed the gully for a couple of hundred feet, but were soon brought up short by a line of overhanging rock, and were forced to retreat to the terrace. This led us further than we had expected and we had progressed along the face for some two hundred yards before it petered out below a great scar in the side of the valley caused by a recent landslip. There was no alternative but to climb up to the top of the scar and hope for the best. The rock was "slabby" and very rotten, and we had some unpleasant moments before we surmounted the difficulty. When we reached the top of the crag it seemed as if it would be impossible to get any further, but a search revealed a tiny flaw which enabled us to get round the next corner on to a further sloping terrace.

Our luck held throughout the morning. Above and below us the cliffs were impregnable, and had our present line of traverse failed, I think we should have had to admit defeat; but by a remarkable freak of chance the slender chain of ledges continued unbroken. The complete lack of any alternative, too, enabled us to make good progress, and our eagerness grew as we rapidly approached the gaunt cliffs of "Pisgah". Over and over again the terrace we were on would peter out in some deep cleft, and further advance would seem impossible, but on each occasion there would be a kindly fault in the rock which would enable us to climb over to the continuation of the terrace beyond. Some of the sections were very "thin", and we began to wonder if the route would be possible with loads.

All the terraces were dipping towards the east, and when we reached a point about a quarter of a mile from "Pisgah", we were only 300 feet above the river. Then came the most sensational, though not the most difficult, section of the route. In rounding a spur the terrace or ledge narrowed to a foot in width and actually overhung the river. The passage along it was exhilarating, and it was difficult to believe that a kindly providence had not placed it there to wind up that long chain of improbabilities.

On the opposite side of the river was a strip of shore which ran along the water's edge, until a bend in the river screened it from view. It was possible that if we could get across to it, it might take us past the buttress. We decided to attempt to ford the river and see. It was now 1 o'clock. We should have turned back, but I was desperately keen to "prove" the route we were on, as, if we could do that, further time need not be wasted in prospecting. We took off our lower garments and waded out into the swiftly flowing stream. The water did not reach much above our thighs, but the current was so strong that it was only with the greatest difficulty that we could retain our balance. Also the water was icy cold, and our legs soon lost all sensation. We got across; the passage was painful and unpleasant, but we considered that with due precautions it was safe enough.

The strip of shore did not lead us far and we had to make five more crossings before we were clear of the buttress, and could make our way along the southern side of the valley once more. But it was now getting late, and we had to hurry back. The river of course had to be crossed six times on the way back, making twelve crossings in all, and by the time we reached the gully at the end of the traverse, we had had enough of aquatic sports to last us for some time.

The route we had discovered was far from satisfactory. Many sections of the traverse would be extremely difficult to negotiate with loads; and a route which relied for its practicability on the state of the river was obviously bad. But in the absence of an alternative it would have to serve. Any alternative to the traverse on this side of the river was out of the question, as from what we had seen of the vast precipices of the northern side our chances over there would be remote indeed. Only freak rock formations had made the traverse possible. As for the river, I have already mentioned my reasons for believing that we need not expect a great increase in the volume of water. Also we fancied that, by exercising our ingenuity, some of the crossings could be bridged.

Therefore, after the matter had been discussed at some length, it was decided that we should start at once, relaying the loads along the route discovered that day.

Food was the factor on which all our plans depended. We now had a supply sufficient to last us for thirty-four days. The minimum we could afford to leave at our base for the retreat down the Rishi Nala was enough for three days. That left us thirty-one days for the work ahead of us. A total of 550 lbs. of food and kit had to be shifted.

There were still a good many odd jobs to be done on the morning of May 31st, and we did not get started on our first relay until 11.30. We left Pasang behind for another day's rest, as he had not yet recovered from his "tummy trouble", and we took with us a considerable quantity of light rope and iron pegs with which to construct handrails across the more difficult sections of the traverse, one of which lay just above our base. Here and there we managed to improve upon our previous route, but in the main we were obliged to stick closely to it. At first the work of carrying heavy loads over such difficult ground was exhausting, but gradually we acquired a new rhythm of movement, and the body adjusted itself to the strain imposed upon it. On these occasions my shoulders always gave me most trouble and it generally takes some time for the muscles to get set. The Sherpas support the weight of their loads by means of head bands instead of shoulder straps. This method is much the less tiring of the two, but needs considerable practice. I have tried to use a head band, but cannot manage it over difficult ground.

We decided to make our first camp above the base on the little spur from which we had got our first view of the upper part of the Rishi. It was agreed too to move all our stuff up to the first stage, before going on to the second, and so on. Thus everything was staked on our being able to get through by this route.

The next day, with Pasang to help, we started early, and by making two journeys we got everything on to the spur, where we built up a platform and pitched camp. There was a good supply of juniper fuel with which to make a fire, and we set about the preparation of that ever important item, the cup of tea. It was then discovered that the tea had somehow been left behind with the food dump at the base! I was in favour of leaving it there, but the others would not hear of that, so we drew lots to decide who should make the third journey of the day. Tilman lost and started down at once. However, I think he had the best of the bargain for, as there was still plenty of daylight left, Angtharkay, Kusang and I went off to fix ropes over the big scar at the end of the first traverse. This proved to be an exceedingly tricky job, and was complicated by the advent of a short sharp snow-storm. We returned to camp as night was falling, to find Tilman already returned, and a welcome brew of tea awaiting us.

Seven o'clock the next morning saw us descending into the gully beyond the spur, carrying between us 230 lbs. of gear. All our concentration was needed for the job, for a slip was not to be thought of. (I have often found that so long as the work does not involve complicated movements, carrying a load improves one's climbing technique. Far greater precision is needed, and one naturally abandons all superfluous movements of the body, which often more than counterbalances the weight of the load. This is one reason why a man who is used to carrying loads uphill, when deprived of his load, very often cannot climb as fast or as far as a man who is not used to carrying loads; his movements become jerky, and he finds it very difficult to adjust his rhythm to the altered conditions. Indeed, it is easier to learn to carry a load than to learn how not to carry one. The fact is very evident with the Sherpas, potentially some of the finest mountaineers in the world, but suffering from a tremendous handicap of not being able to adjust the rhythm of their movements as the weight of their loads, or altered conditions of snow, require.)

The scar caused us a lot of trouble. We could not climb the steep crumbling rocks carrying our loads. Three of us had to climb to a stance halfway up, throw a rope down and haul up each load in turn, while those below did their best to prevent it sticking half way, by means of another rope from below. This performance was then repeated on the upper section of the crag. Beyond this was a gully, to cross which the Sherpas removed their boots, so as to be more sure of their footing on the treacherous grass-covered rock.

Climbing out of the gully on the further side, we halted for a moment's rest on a small ridge beyond. While we were there, one of the loads overbalanced and crashed down into the gully some two hundred feet below us. It split open, but most fortunately got hung up on a ledge, which saved it from total destruction at the bottom of the gorge, 1,500 feet below. When we reached the battered sack, we found that some twenty pounds of lentils and rice had been lost, together with some candles. The loss of the food was most annoying, as it represented some two days of our valuable time. But the mishap might easily have been very much more serious, and it taught us to exercise greater care when handling our loads in such unusually steep country.

It was useless trying to hurry along the traverse. Each section had to be tackled with the utmost caution. It was slow work, but very far from tedious, as the job required all our attention. As we gradually became used to the gigantic depth of the ravine above which we were making our way, the early feeling of nervousness changed to one of exhilaration, a glorious feeling almost of being part of this giant creation of Nature. Towards the end of the traverse, the links became very fragile. One spot in particular caused us such trouble that it produced a fairly forceful protest from Angtharkay, and caused Kusang to pause momentarily in his monotonous flow of song. But above and below us the cliffs were smooth and sheer, and the passage could not be avoided. This section came to be known as the "Mauvais Pas", and was certainly the most hair-raising bit of the traverse. The last bit went comparatively easily, and by the middle of the afternoon we reached the river at the point where we had made our first crossing three days before. After stowing the loads under a rock, we hurriedly retreated along the traverse, and reached our camp before dark.

The dawn of June 3rd gave warning of bad weather, and it was in some anxiety that we packed up the remainder of our baggage and hastily got under way. The route was now becoming familiar, and difficulties which had cost us much time and labour before were now being tackled with the confidence and ease of familiarity. We made good time on the slabs of the scar, and the gullies which followed had lost much of their sting. But fast as we went we were still too slow for the weather. By 10 o'clock the lower valley was filled with cloud and by 11 o'clock snow was falling gently in large woolly flakes. This spurred us on to yet greater energy, as the thought of the Mauvais Pas under a covering of snow was not a pleasant one and, if we failed to get across it today, there was no knowing how long we should be held up; for it looked as if the snow had come to stay for some time.

The weight of our loads was forgotten as we raced along the little ledges of the traverse at a frantic speed. By 12 o'clock snow was falling heavily and, when we reached the Mauvais Pas, all the ledges and crannies were hidden under a thick white canopy. We removed our boots in order to be sure of our foot-holds, and proceeded with the utmost deliberation, clearing the snow from the ledges as we went. It was not easy to find places on which to anchor the rope and, though we moved one at a time, a slip would have had very serious consequences. About half way across a narrow slanting cleft had to be negotiated in order to get on to a lower ledge. This was the worst section, as one's load was apt to catch and throw one off one's balance, and my heart was in my mouth as I watched each member of the party negotiate it. The Sherpas worked with a wonderful steadiness and composure, only giving vent to their pent-up feelings when they reached the comparative security of the terrace beyond. Here we halted a moment to rub our feet and put on our boots. A wind started to blow down the valley, driving the snow into our faces as we made our way slowly across the face of the precipice, and Angtharkay suggested that we should stop where we were until the storm had blown over. A more unpleasant idea would have been difficult to conceive, though I must admit conditions had made progress not a little dangerous. By going slowly, however, and taking every precaution, we eventually reached the end of the traverse without a mis-hap.

Cold and wet, we huddled under the lee of the cliff rising from the little strip of shore by the water's edge. A few sodden pieces of wood lay about the beach, having been deposited there when the river was in flood. With the aid of a couple of candles and a good deal of patience we got some sort of a fire started, and "smoked ourselves" until, towards evening, the snow slackened.

On the opposite side of the river there was a wider strip of shore, on which grew a small clump of stunted birches. There was also a fair-sized cave. It was obviously the ideal base from which to tackle the final section of the upper gorge, and the sooner we got there and made ourselves snug, the better, so as soon as the snowstorm had abated we collected all the loads at the water's edge, and prepared for the crossing.

There were ten loads to be carried across. The river appeared to be slightly swollen but, as the snow had been melting as it fell, this was only to be expected. We did not anticipate that the difficulties would be much greater than they had been before.

Fastening an end of the rope to my waist and shouldering a load, I paddled up the edge of the stream, probing with my ice-axe and searching for the best place to begin the crossing. Then I started to wade slowly out into the raging waters. I soon realised that, although the river appeared only slightly higher than it had been before, it confronted us with an obstacle twice as formidable. The force of the current was terrific. As I moved a foot forward, it would be whirled sideways, and it was only by shuffling along that I could make any headway. My legs were slashed by stones swept down by the force of the river, but soon the numbing cold robbed my lower limbs of all sensation. The whirling motion of the water made me giddy, and I was hard put to it to keep my balance. In mid-stream the water was nearly up to my waist; had it been an inch higher it must have carried me away, but by a desperate effort I kept my feet. I tried to turn round, but found that the current was impossible to face, so I had to go on, and at length emerged with bleeding legs upon the opposite beach.

Tilman was a short way behind me. Being shorter, he was having an even tougher struggle. Pasang and Angtharkay were already well in the water, holding on to each other, and on to the rope which was now stretched across the river. My wits must have been numbed by the cold, for I missed the brief opportunity I had of preventing them from coming any further. Too late I realised what they were in for. Pasang was carrying a load of satu, Angtharkay had a load of clothes and bedding, which came down to his buttocks. He was very slight of build and easily the shortest of the five. When he got out towards the middle of the stream, the water was well above his waist, and it was obvious that he was prevented from being swept away only by hanging on to the rope and Pasang's firm hand, which clutched him by the arm. Soon, however, his load became water-logged, and started to drag him down. How he managed to keep his feet will always remain a mystery to me for, in spite of the help afforded him by the rope, his difficulties must have been vastly greater than my own, and I knew that I had had just as much as I could cope with. But then these Sherpas have standards of their own. As they were approaching the northern bank, however, Angtharkay actually did lose his balance and, as he went in up to his neck, I thought he was lost. But he retained his hold on the rope, and Pasang, clutching frantically at his arm, dragged him ashore. They were both rather badly shaken, but immediately set about the task of pitching camp and lighting a fire.

Tilman and I each made two more journeys across with the remaining loads (we left one bag of satu on the southern shore), and on his third trip Tilman came over with Kusang, who had been patiently holding the other end of the rope for us. This time he missed his footing and was submerged, fortunately in the shallow water near the shore. Dusk was falling as, painfully, we lugged the loads across the beach.

It was a cheerless party which sat huddled round the weakly smouldering logs under the shelter of the cave, silent save for the continuous chatter of teeth. I felt very humble indeed for having been fool enough to tackle the river in such haste. It was obvious now that a route which involved several such crossings was out of the question, and except for the fact that we had a decent camp site, we would have been much better off on the southern shore of the stream. However, one must pay for experience, and we were later to find that much was needed in dealing with these fierce glacier streams.

Tilman's pipe had been washed away out of his pocket down the river. He is a confirmed pipe-smoker, and I think that the prospect of a month without one was gloomy, to say the least. Fortunately for him, I had been travelling in Southern Tibet the previous year with Laurence Wager, who had insisted on my smoking a pipe in the evening to keep me from talking. Since then I had continued the habit, and now Tilman was able to get a smoke at the expense of an increased flow of argumentative conversation!

No rain or snow was falling next morning, but it was a dull and cheerless dawn. After an early breakfast, we walked along the little strip of shore to examine the possibility of bridging the river. A little downstream, at the point where the river entered the box-canyon, which stretched almost unbroken for the two miles separating us from our base camp, we found a place where huge boulders in the bed of the stream formed a natural foundation for a bridge. A clump of twisted birches, however, offered us poor material, and it was midday before we had spanned the river with a fragile and rickety structure. Considerable dexterity was necessary to cross the bridge, but it served our purpose so long as it was not washed away.

We now commanded both sides of the river, and it was decided that Tilman and Angtharkay should explore the possibilities of the southern side, while Pasang and I tried to get through on the northern side. I confess that when we started out on our respective jobs, I thought that if anyone got through, it would be Pasang and I; for to get past "Pisgah" on the southern side appeared to be a hopeless task.

Edging along the base of the cliffs at the water's edge, we reached another strip of sandy shore a hundred yards further upstream. From here a steeply sloping corridor led back across the face of the precipice. All the strata we had encountered in the Rishi Nala sloped from west to east in this manner, and we hoped that by following this corridor we might be able to climb on to a terrace which would at least carry us past that formidable buttress on the southern side. But the corridor became more and more difficult to follow, and finally ended in a little platform 500 feet above the river, completely isolated save for the way by which we had come. Further advance in any direction was impossible. We sat down disconsolately, and scanned the cliffs of the southern side of the gorge. High above us, like ants on a gigantic wall, we saw the other two climbing slowly upwards. Presently they started traversing horizontally, and we saw that they were making for the one point in the great buttress where, we had agreed before, lay the only slender chance of success. They reached it and disappeared from view. When after a short while they reappeared, and started up a vile-looking gully, my heart sank. It appeared that the last chance on the southern side had failed, and now it was up to Pasang and me to find a way by hook or by crook.

We descended to the river again and with great difficulty managed to make another two hundred yards upstream, before an overhanging cliff brought us to a dead stop. We tried wading, but the river was even higher than it had been on the previous evening, and we could make no headway. Then we began to search every inch of the three hundred yards we had come from our camp, in the hope of at least being able to climb out of the gloomy canyon we were in. We tried places which were obviously quite ridiculous; just as one searches under the teapot or in the coal-scuttle for a lost fountain pen when one has exhausted every likely place, and I had a similar feeling of hopelessness. But after some desperate rock-climbing, we were forced to admit defeat, and returned to camp, satisfied that at least there was no route along the northern side of the gorge.

It was a cold grey afternoon, and towards evening rain began to fall gently. The gorge wore a grim and desolate aspect, which increased my dejection as I sat in the cave, waiting for the others to return and wondering what our next move would be. If we were forced to retreat from here, we would have to abandon our attempt to penetrate into the Nanda Devi Basin, as there was no other line of possibility. As the evening wore on, we began to scan the crags of the opposite side anxiously for any sign of the others. Their delay in returning gave me some hope that they might after all have found a way; but towards dark I began to fear that an accident had occurred, for they must have realised our failure, and desperation is apt to make people run unjustifiable risks. Then all at once we spotted them, descending through the mist at a seemingly reckless speed. As they approached the river I went over to the bridge to await them. Angtharkay was in front and, as he came nearer, I could see that he was in a state of great excitement; as he balanced his way precariously over the water, above the roar of the torrent I caught the words: "Bahut achcha, sahib, bahut achcha."

When Tilman arrived, I heard from him the glad news that they had found, 1,500 feet above the river, a break in that last formidable buttress, guarding the mystic shrine of the "Blessed Goddess". From where they had stood they could see that the way was clear into the Nanda Devi Basin. The last frail link in that extraordinary chain of rock-faults, which had made it possible to make our way along the grim precipices of the gorge, had been discovered; and this meant at least a certain measure of success to our undertaking.

As I lay in the mouth of the cave after our evening meal, watching the spectral shadows hover in the ghostly clefts of the opposite wall of the gorge, and listening to the mighty boom of the torrent echoing to a great height above our heads, my feeling of despondency was changed to one of deep content.

CHAPTER NINE

THE task next morning of getting the loads back across the river over the bridge was one which required delicate handling. It was easy enough to balance across, unencumbered by any weight, but to do so with a heavy load strapped to one's back was a very different proposition. The bridge sagged unpleasantly in the middle, and, as it took the weight of the body, water swept over it. A rope stretched across the river served as an unreliable handrail. Curiously enough Kusang, normally very sure of foot and steady of head, could not face it. It was as much as he could do to get across without a load, so the rest of us each had to make several of these perilous trips. It was a painfully cold job too in the bitter morning air. But all went well, and by 9 o'clock we were across, bag and baggage, fervently hoping that this was to be our last encounter with the river.

Shouldering five of the loads, we climbed slowly up the mountain side. We encountered several difficult sections, but managed to negotiate each successfully. Twelve hundred feet above the river, we climbed on to a sloping ledge, which led us across the face of "Pisgah" buttress to the foot of the gully up which Passang and I had watched the other two making their way the previous day. Though there were one or two awkward bits, the gully was easier than it had appeared from below, and after climbing some eight hundred feet up it, we were able to escape by way of a narrow chimney, which landed us on the crest of the great ridge which had come so near to destroying our hopes. From here we could see right into the Nanda Devi Basin, though heavy rain clouds obscured all but the mighty ramparts at the base of the great peak.

A short way beyond we came upon two small caves. There was also a plentiful supply of juniper and a small spring; altogether an ideal site for a camp. So we stowed our loads away out of reach of the rain, which was now starting to fall, and romped down the 2,000 feet to the river at a break-neck speed. The second journey up the slopes carrying the remainder of the loads was a slow and tedious business; but when at length we reached the ridge once more, we were rewarded by the pleasant knowledge that for the time being we had finished with the grim austerity of that fearful gorge, and that ahead of us was a new and wonderful world to explore.

Growing in the vicinity of our new camp was a great quantity of wild rhubarb. We had found it lower down the valley, but there it had been scarce. That night we consumed a quantity which now makes me sick to remember!

Towards sunset the rain cleared off and, as we sat round our juniper fire, we witnessed a heavenly unveiling of the great peaks of the basin. First appeared the majestic head of Nanda Devi herself, frowning down upon us from an incredible height, utterly detached from the earth. One by one the white giants of the un-named ranges to the north followed suit; until at last it seemed as if the entire mountain realm stood before us bathed in the splendour of the dying sun, paying homage to the majesty of their peerless queen.

It was after 8 o'clock when we got away next morning. We cached 20 lbs. of food in the cave, together with the remainder of the rope and iron stakes we had brought for the roping up of the difficult sections of the gorge. This left us with 380 lbs. of baggage to be transported through into the basin. It was obvious from what we had seen that we could not hope to make even a rough exploration of the whole thing in the time available before our food ran out. We therefore decided to concentrate on the northern half of the basin, and to return in August, when we hoped that the main force of the monsoon would have spent itself, to explore the southern section. The distance we would be able to cover depended on the difficulty of the ground, and my previous experience of Himalayan glaciers had made me not over optimistic.

The going now became distinctly easier, and by noon we got on to the gentle grassy slopes above the junction of the two streams which came down from the main glaciers of the northern and southern sections of the basin to form the Rishi Ganga River. Half a mile below the junction, we could see a stretch of sand flats where the river broadened out, and, becoming comparatively sluggish, appeared to offer a good fording place. To cross here would save us several hours of toil, which would be necessary if we were to cross the two streams above the junction. But we sadly under-estimated the difficulties, for although we succeeded in getting across, the struggle was almost as severe as it had been in the gorge a few days before and, as there was no possibility of bridging the river at this point, a better way had to be found.

We pitched camp in a little nala formed by a stream coming down from the glaciers of the westerly rim of the basin; then, leaving Kusang to prepare our evening meal, we started out to visit the junction, and to find a better way of getting across into the northern section.

We were now actually in the inner sanctuary of the Nanda Devi Basin, and at each step I experienced that subtle thrill which anyone of imagination must feel when treading hitherto unexplored country. Each corner held some thrilling secret to be revealed for the trouble of looking. My most blissful dream as a child was to be in some such valley, free to wander where I liked, and discover for myself some hitherto unrevealed glory of Nature. Now the reality was no less wonderful than that half-forgotten dream; and of how many childish fancies can that be said, in this age of disillusionment?

Immediately above the junction of the two streams was a curious little plateau, rather resembling a giant tennis-court, which commanded a fine view up each of the rivers. About a mile and a half up the left-hand valley (facing up), we could see the snout of a great glacier. This later came to be known by us as the Main Glacier, and was formed by the ice of all the larger glaciers of the northern section. But although we had a clear view for nearly three miles up the southern stream, we could see no sign of a glacier, though the character of the stream told us that one must exist. This southern stream too contained only half as much water as the other; a clear indication that we must expect a vaster and more complicated glacier system in the section we were about to visit.

It had been decided that on the following day, while Tilman and I were at work with the plane-table, the others would go back to the previous camp for the rest of the stuff. After some discussion the Sherpas assured us that they would be able to find a way back above the junction and, as it was getting late, we decided that it was not necessary to go further that evening. On the plateau we found a quantity of wild onions, which greatly pleased the Sherpas. Beyond the junction, peacefully grazing on the gentle grassy slopes, was a small herd of bharal. We estimated the height of the junction to be about 13,100 feet.

The Sherpas were away shortly after dawn on the following morning, while Tilman and I left camp a little later on our first reconnaissance into the unknown basin. Following a ridge which came down from some of the westerly peaks, we reached at an altitude of about 15,500 feet the crest of a little shoulder, from which we obtained a good view over the lower part of the Main Glacier. I was very surprised at the type of country which lay before us. On the true left bank of the glacier the giant cliffs of Nanda Devi rose sheer and forbidding in true Himalayan style; but, bounding the glacier on the right-hand side, beyond a well-defined lateral moraine, an expanse of undulating grass-land stretched for miles, in lovely contrast with the desolation of the moraine-covered glacier. If the shepherds of the Dhaoli and Niti valleys could only get their flocks through the grim gorges of the Rishi Ganga, they would find here almost unlimited grazing. Now this pasturage is a sanctuary where thousands of wild animals live unmolested. Long may it remain so!

It was a great relief to see that when making our way up the valley we would not be confined to travel on the glacier itself; for conveying loads about on the lower reaches of a Himalayan glacier is a task which demands much time and infinite patience. The ice is generally completely covered with a thick deposit of gravel and boulders. The whole surface is rent and broken into a sea of cliffs and fissures, ridges and hollows. It is almost impossible to work out a good line beforehand, and the traveller has to worry his way through a perfect maze of obstacles. From the point we had reached we could see that by the side of the glacier there stretched gently undulating grass-land, which would provide us with excellent going for the first few miles at least.

Though the views we got were of great interest, we did not have much success with the plane-table, as there was a lot of cloud about, and we could not fix our position with any degree of certainty. Eventually, we were driven down by a shower of sleet and rain. We got back to camp at 7 o'clock, and were surprised to find that the Sherpas had not returned. When darkness fell, and there was still no sign of them, we became seriously alarmed. We were contemplating going out to search for them when from a distance we caught the sound of their voices, and presently they appeared, without loads and obviously tired. We learnt from them that they had had great difficulty in finding an alternative route above the junction of the stream, and that, being overtaken by night, had dumped their loads on the far side of the northern stream.

The next morning (June 8th), there was a great feeling of slackness, and though we got away by 7.20 a.m., we walked without much energy, stopping frequently. The ground, however, was easy and in a few hours we reached the snout of the Main Glacier.

In the afternoon, while the Sherpas went off to fetch the loads they had left on the previous day, Tilman and I climbed over the snout of the glacier, and mounted up the lower buttresses of the main peak of Nanda Devi. We climbed for some hours over rough broken rocks, and emerged at length on the crest of a sharp spur, which commanded a grand view down the Rishi Nala. We saw to its best advantage the majestic sweep of the northern cliffs of the gorge, which culminated in a formidable barrier of mountains forming the western rim of the basin. We worked for an hour with the plane-table, before a mass of evil-looking clouds blowing up from the black depths of the gorge blotted out the view, and we were driven down again, this time by a storm of hail.

Sitting round a blazing fire of juniper that night, Tilman reminded me that in the course of that afternoon we had been the first human beings to have set foot on the main peak of Nanda Devi, a point we had both neglected to observe before!

We cached a further small dump of food at the snout of the Main Glacier, when we left early next morning. We then mounted to a little moraine ledge at the side of the glacier, and soon reached the gentle grassy slopes we had seen two days before. The going could not have been pleasanter: soft springing turf with the grass still short, having only lately got rid of its burden of winter snow. And, owing to our ease of movement, we were able to give our whole attention to the enjoyment of this wonderful new world we were in. Every few hundred yards, some new feature would reveal itself – here a side valley to look up, and to speculate as to where it would lead, there some graceful ice-clad summit appearing from behind a buttress, and looking, in the newness of its form, lovelier than any of its neighbours; there again, a herd of wild mountain sheep gazing indignantly at these intruders who had violated the sanctity of their seclusion. In spite of the heavy load I was carrying, I frequently had difficulty in refraining from running in my eagerness to see round the next corner, or to get a better view of some fresh and slender spire which had just made its appearance.

Towards midday we reached the edge of a big glacier, coming in from the west. After crossing this, we came upon a beautiful lake, shut in on three sides by great mounds of moraine deposit, and on the fourth by dark, frowning cliffs. On the placid waters were reflected the icy crests of the great peaks. We had intended going further that day, but we could not resist the prospect of a camp in such surroundings.

We had previously agreed that not a moment of our time in the basin should be wasted if we could possibly help it. It was all too short as it was, and we were determined to get through as much as we could while our food lasted. Accordingly, as soon as camp had been pitched, we set off to reconnoitre the lateral glacier we had just crossed. The sky was dull and overcast, and presently snow started falling heavily. We climbed on to a ridge which bounded the glacier on the right, and followed it until we were some 2,000 feet above the lake. At 4 o'clock the snow stopped falling, and we erected the plane-table, and waited in a bitterly cold wind for the evening clearing of the mists. At half-past five our patience was rewarded. A rift appeared to the west, and framed in it was a dome of rock and ice, which could belong to only one mountain –

Changabang. There was no mistaking it. Often had I gazed at that wonderful photograph taken by Dr. Longstaff from the Bagini Pass on the opposite side: and here before us was an almost exact replica of that splendid face which Dr. Longstaff describes as "the most superbly beautiful mountain I have ever seen: its north-west face, a sheer precipice of over 5,000 feet, being composed of such pale granite that it is at first taken for snow lying on the cliffs at an impossibly steep angle." As is generally the case with such views, the mountain summit appeared as something detached from the earth, floating in the upper air at a fantastic height above our heads; and moving along swiftly in a direction opposite to that of the drifting mist.

Presently Changabang's sister-peak, Kalanka, made her appearance, and we saw that the glacier at our feet originated in a vast coombe formed by the ridge of the two peaks. Tilman suggested the name "Changalanka" for the glacier, and appeared disappointed when I expressed doubt as to whether that name would be accepted by the authorities!

Soon other summits appeared, each tinted with the fires of the dying sun, and vying with one another to tax the credibility of their puny audience. But Nature is a perfect stage-manager, and when the majesty of the vision was at its height, the curtain of cloud fell about us once more, so, with numbed fingers we packed up the plane-table, and scrambled down to camp in the gathering dusk.

From above the lake we had a view right up the main valley, along the northern base of Nanda Devi. A series of subsidiary valleys coming in from the north-eastern rim offered us a means of exploring that section, and we decided to devote the next week to that task.

The red sunset of that evening was a sure indication of better weather, and we awoke at dawn the next morning (June 10th) to a chorus of birds heralding a gloriously fine day. We ate a hasty breakfast in the frosty air and were away before the sun had reached us, carrying light loads, and having enough food with us to keep Tilman and myself in the necessities of life for three or four days. It was our intention to push as far as we could up one of the eastern valleys, and camp there while the Sherpas came down to relay the rest of the stuff up to a more suitable base. Making our way round the eastern shore of the lake we climbed over the wall of moraine deposit, and were soon worrying our way through the intricacies of a big ice-stream coming in from the north. This came to be known later as the Great North Glacier. At its junction with the Main North Glacier we found an easy route across, and within two hours of leaving camp we found ourselves in a pleasant meadow on the far side of the Great Glacier.

From here the travelling was extremely easy. A wide corridor of flat grass-land ran outside a very well-defined lateral moraine on the right bank of the Main Glacier, and we were able to stride along at a quick walk, until we were abreast of the entrance to the valley we were making for. Then we turned left and plodded up nearly 2,000 feet of slaty shingle, which had been left when the side glaciers shrank to their present dimensions.

By 2 o'clock we had got fairly into the valley and decided to camp at an altitude of about 17,500 feet. The Sherpas built a small stone wall to protect us from the wind, and left us with a promise to return in three days' time.

Later that afternoon Tilman and I went off in opposite directions to make a preliminary reconnaissance of the valley we were in, in order to be able to come to a decision as to our course of action. I took the plane-table with me. Climbing up the scree and snow-covered slope above the camp, I came, at an altitude of about 18,000 feet, to the crest of a ridge. As I did so, I saw a solitary bharal, some twenty-five yards away. He was a noble specimen, and stood so still that he might have been a stuffed beast in the Natural History Museum. We stood regarding one another for some minutes before his curiosity was satisfied, and then he stalked leisurely away and disappeared round the corner of a cliff. Most unfortunately I had left my camera in camp (as was usually the case when I happened upon something which would make a good photograph!) It was difficult to understand what brings these animals to such altitudes. Three thousand feet below was perfect grazing, and neither man nor beast to molest them. Their lives must be wonderfully care-free and one would expect them to be content to grow fat and lazy down below; instead of which they seemed to spend most of their time climbing about precipices of astonishing steepness, risking their necks on crevasse-covered glaciers, and going as far away as possible from food and comfort. Surely then they too have the capacity to appreciate the savage beauty of high mountain places, and to revel in the rhythm of practised movement over difficult ground.

I returned to camp at 5.30 to find Tilman was just back. We compared notes, and formulated a plan for the employment of our time in the valley. We decided first to attempt to reach a col at its head, which we concluded must lie on the eastern rim of the basin. From it we hoped to get a view out of the basin towards the peaks of the Nepal-Tibet border. After that we proposed to attempt to find a high level route into the next valley-system.

We consumed a dish of pemmican soup and, as the sun disappeared behind the distant ranges, we crept into our sleeping-bags, to watch the world give itself over to frozen night. We had with us our tiny bivouac tent, but we had by now got firmly into the habit of sleeping out, using the tent canvas as a blanket. This was due mainly to the discomfort of squashing ourselves into the minute space it afforded, though personally I dislike all tents and use them as little as necessity permits.

The ledge on which we were lying being high above the floor of the main valley on the north side, it commanded a superb view of the colossal northern face of the twin peaks of Nanda Devi. The two peaks were joined by a horizontal rock ridge, some two miles in length. From this ridge, the precipice fell in one unbroken sweep to the glacier which lay at its foot, 9,000 feet below the summit. The rock wall thus formed is perhaps without an equal anywhere in the world. We had recovered by now from the shock which we had experienced on coming for the first time face to face with this sight, but, as I lay there and watched the rays of the setting sun bespangle the mountain with a score of rapidly changing shades, the whole scale of height and depth appeared enhanced beyond belief.

We passed a restless night due, I suppose, to the fact that it was our first visit to that particular altitude that season. We were both wide awake at 2 a.m., though we did not want to be off much before daylight. The little streamlets about us were hard-frozen, and we spent some time melting sufficient ice for what we knew would be our last drink for many thirsty hours of toil to come. We left our bivouac just after 3.30 a.m., about a quarter of an hour before the first glimmer of dawn, and in sleepy moroseness climbed over the boulder-strewn slope to the edge of the dry ice of the glacier. Mounting on to this, we soon settled down to that gentle rhythm which alone makes early morning climbing at high altitudes bearable. For an hour and a half we plodded along in a dreamy silence, only roused every now and then when some large crevasse necessitated an altering of the course. The dry ice gave place to frozen snow, and presently one of us suggested that perhaps it was about time we put on the rope. It was then quite light and, looking back, we saw that Nanda Devi was already bathed in the warmth and splendour of the morning sun, and with this sight a modicum of enthusiasm stirred our lethargy.

The work now became intricate, and several crevasses gave us food for serious thought before we were able to cross them. At about 6.40 we were standing at the foot of a steep slope some four hundred feet below the col. Working on a short rope we started up it, and found it to be composed of a vixenish layer of hard frozen snow, covering pure ice. While the snow remained frozen it was safe enough to kick shallow steps up the incline, but directly the sun came over the col the snow would melt and form an exceedingly dangerous avalanche trap. By first cutting through the snow, and then making large steps in the ice, the slope could probably be negotiated later in the day, but it would be a prolonged and hazardous business, as the gradient was continuously steep and afforded no safeguards whatever. Moreover, the task of cutting such a staircase under the present conditions would take nearly all day. However, from the point he had reached in the course of his reconnaissance on the previous day, Tilman had seen that by climbing one of the peaks adjacent to the col, we would find an alternative route down to the lower part of the glacier we were on; and we decided, after some discussion, that we were justified in continuing the climb by relying on the snow crust alone.

This crust became thinner and thinner as we mounted, and at last we were forced into a longish bout of step-cutting in order to reach some ice-covered rocks just below the col. These too required some careful handling, before we drew ourselves up on to the knife-like crest of the ridge which formed at this point part of the eastern rim of the basin. We sat on a ledge protected from the cold wind and beat our numbed extremities back to a painful life. It was 9 o'clock. With the aid of our barometer we estimated our height at 20,300 feet.

The day was gloriously fine. The view to the east was bewildering. I had never expected to see such an extraordinary array of peaks, and we could make but a poor effort at sorting out the tangled topography. Except for Nanda Kot to the south, there was no particularly dominating feature, but as far as the eye could see there stretched a sea of glistening spires and domes, ridges and icy plateaux, in dazzling profusion and complexity, while in the distance we could discern some mighty giants, evidently belonging to the ranges of western Nepal.

At our feet, far below, we looked down into a wide valley whose glacier flowed away from us into another and much larger one, which we identified as the Milam Glacier.

We were anxious to find a way of escape from the basin in this direction, but even had there been a practicable route down to the Milam Glacier from this point, it would have been an impossible task to get our loads up the ice slopes we had just climbed.

Tilman was feeling the effects of altitude a good deal, and was suffering from the usual sickness and weakness. However, by now our retreat was cut off, and we had to go through with the traverse of a 21,000 foot peak to our north. We sat on the ledge near the col for half an hour, during which time we occupied ourselves by studying the view, forcing bits of biscuit down somewhat unwilling throats, and thawing our chilled limbs. Then we rose to tackle the eight or nine hundred feet of rock and ice which separated us from the summit of the peak. The climbing was not difficult until we got on to a sharp ice ridge which led to the summit. A cold wind was blowing, and it was a tricky job to retain one's balance in the small steps which it was necessary to cut in the crest of the ridge. This was a type of climbing which I disliked, as one had to trust to one's feet alone, and the slightest slip would be impossible to check. But it was exhilarating to see the Milam Glacier System beneath one heel and the Nanda Devi Basin beneath the other; and it is not often that these Himalayan ice ridges are even possible to climb along.

The wind was too cold and the ridge too narrow for us to stop even for a minute on the summit, and we passed straight over and continued climbing down along the ridge on the other side. Soon we were brought up by a vertical cleft in it, and we were forced to cut steps for some distance down the Milam side before we could get round this.

There now followed a very long bout of down-hill step-cutting along a ridge which never allowed any relaxation while we were on it. I felt a mighty relief when after some hours we reached a steep snow gully leading down to the tracks of the morning, and found the snow to be in a safe condition. The snow on the glacier itself was soft and we broke through several times into small crevasses. Nevertheless, we made a very rapid descent and were back in camp by the middle of the afternoon.

As I have said, Tilman had suffered severely from mountain sickness throughout the day, but I was feeling remarkably fit, considering it was the first bit of serious mountaineering that we had been engaged upon at any altitude that year. Presently I felt a considerable pain in the groin, at the top of the right leg. I thought I must have strained the leg slightly in one of the crevasses we had encountered on our descent, but I have since connected it with a mysterious fever which attacked me a few minutes later. It began with a violent attack of shivering, which caused me to pile on all my spare clothing and roll myself up in my double sleeping-bag, despite the scorching afternoon sun. My memory of the next twenty-four hours was distorted by delirium. I had a curious impression that I was lying there in the open for several days, during the whole of which time I was either trying to escape from a fierce tropical sun or from a dead Arctic cold, while the ever-changing face of Nanda Devi writhed itself into hideous grimaces. The fever lasted for about thirty-six hours and then left me as suddenly as it had come. When the Sherpas came on the morning of the 13th, I was able to hobble slowly down with them to a base which they had by now established above the junction of the Great North Glacier with the main ice-stream, and well stocked with juniper fuel collected from the area below the lake.

Having regained my senses, I was extremely annoyed at having lost two days of our valuable time in the basin. Tilman, however, had put in some good work in the meantime, and rejoined us at what came to be known as "Glacier Junction Camp", on the evening of the 13th.

The next morning we started out again, this time with provisions for only one night, for a bivouac in another of the valleys coming down from the peaks of the eastern rim. I still felt very weak, but as I was carrying no load, I managed to follow the others without delaying them too much. This new valley we found to be divided into two sections, and we decided to devote a day to the exploration of the right-hand one, if possible climbing once more on to the eastern rim, where we hoped to be in a position to make a close examination of a complicated knot of peaks to the north which had aroused our curiosity a few days before. We were still hoping too to discover a means of escape which we could use when the time came as an alternative to a retreat down the Rishi Gorge. In this we had small hope of success, however, as a strong party consisting of Mr. Ruttledge, Dr. Somervell and General Wilson, had made an abortive attempt some years previously to find a route into the basin from the Milam Glacier.

As we brewed our evening pemmican, we observed signs which promised an early change in the weather. The evening was warm and still, and our barometer was behaving in an extraordinary manner. However, we "dossed down" in the usual way, using our ridiculous little tent merely as a covering.*

I had slept for about an hour when I was awakened by soft wet snow falling on my face. The tent, an intricate tangle of sodden guy ropes, flaps and ridges, offered very poor covering, as the snow melted and lay in pools of water in the folds of the canvas, and from time to time these would empty themselves playfully down our necks. This prevented us both from sleeping until about one o'clock, when it started to freeze, and though the snow continued to fall our rest was no longer disturbed.

We awoke at 6 o'clock to a dreary morning. The snow had stopped falling, however, and we started up the glacier. Here we encountered the vile snow conditions which were to prevail throughout the summer, and this was to prove to be one of the most serious obstacles with which we had to contend. But the climbing was not difficult, and at 12.30 p.m. we reached another point on the eastern "rim", at an altitude of just about 20,000 feet. A cold wind was blowing sleet into our faces as we peered down from the crest of the narrow ridge. We caught a further glimpse of the valley which contained the Milam Glacier, but

---

*Since then I have come to the conclusion that for the purpose of these light bivouac camps a thin waterproof sheet would be lighter and more satisfactory than one of these small tents people have been at such pains to design of recent years. Tents with accommodation for two people and weighing 15 lbs. or more can be made to stand up against almost any conditions of weather, but I do not think a cloth has yet been discovered which, if made into a tent of much less than 8 lbs., will stand up against weather such as one must be prepared for when doing a series of bivouacs at great altitudes. Such a tent will generally collapse under a heavy weight of snow; it will be torn to shreds if exposed to a really bad blizzard, and will leak even in light rain. Under a single waterproof sheet one is at least as comfortable; it is no trouble either to pitch or to pack up, while in fine weather one need not suffer from the unbearable stuffiness of the midget tent.

beyond that all was obscured in mist. Two thousand feet of steep snow-covered rocks lay at our feet. It might have been possible to climb down, though with loads the risk of snow avalanches would have been too great. From where we stood we were able to get some slight idea of the topography of that part of the watershed, though ten minutes after we had arrived all our surroundings were blotted out and visibility was restricted to a few yards.

The descent to our bivouac took only two hours. The Sherpas were waiting for us, and, packing up the loads, we ran on down to the junction camp as fast as we could.

The present weather was obviously better suited to travel than to the mapping of intricate side valleys, and we decided that on the following day we should push as far as possible up the Great North Valley, so as to be in a position, when the weather cleared, to explore its head. Accordingly, soon after dawn we started in a northerly direction, carrying with us enough food and fuel for six days.

The morning was reasonably fine and it was not until about 10 o'clock that the more distant views became obscured. Travel in the Great North Valley we found to be very different from the easy progress we had made over the gently undulating slopes which bounded the Main Glacier, steep precipices continually forcing us on to the shattered moraine-covered surface of the ice.

We had been going for an hour or so, when Tilman, who had been lagging behind somewhat, complained that his right leg was hurting him. I suggested that he should share some of his load between the rest of us, but this he declined to do. We sat down to argue the point for a moment, when all of a sudden he began shivering, and I realised that he was starting an attack of fever similar to the one to which I had succumbed five days before. I suggested, therefore, that we should remain where we were. But Tilman would not hear of this, saying that if we did not get to a point from which I could make a useful reconnaissance on the following day, yet another twenty-four hours would be wasted. So we divided his load among the rest of us, and carried on, though how he was able to stick at it throughout a long and weary day I cannot imagine, for the work of making one's way over a badly broken moraine-covered glacier is as tiresome and exasperating a job as I know.

As I have mentioned before, it is impossible to work out a line of march over such country beforehand, and the only thing to do is to go straight ahead, and tackle the difficulties as they present themselves. A long ascent of a steep slope of boulders, poised precariously on the hard black ice, and ready at the slightest disturbance to roll down and crush one's foot; a slender ice-ridge, leading across two yawning chasms, one on either side, from which came the dull thunder of a sub-glacial stream; an ice-cliff, down which steps had to be laboriously chipped; these followed one another in monotonous succession, and led perhaps to an impasse, demanding a long, tiresome détour, perhaps to a further tangle of cliffs, ridges and towers. Here was a lake whose dark-blue waters proclaimed it to be of great depth, infinitely placid, save when some little avalanche of ice and rock, crashing down from above, whipped it to frenzy; further on, a raging torrent, rushing madly in no particular direction, barred the way. Our day's work yielded us but some three miles of progress, and we camped in a perfect wilderness of moraine débris. On arrival, Tilman collapsed into a sleeping-bag, and lay for the next thirty-six hours on a rough bed of boulders, waiting patiently for the fever to pass.

The following morning was beautifully clear, and I roused myself out of a half-frozen sleeping-bag in time to resect the position of the camp on the plane-table before the clouds came up and obscured the view. In this brief spell of clear weather I was able to get a general idea of the topography of the valley we were in, and in the gathering shadows of a snowstorm Pasang and I set off to reconnoitre the upper part of the glacier. Working our way diagonally across the ice-stream, we reached a point where the moraine débris from the left bank of the glacier met that from the right bank. The contrast between these two species of rock was very striking. That from the Kalanka side was almost white, while that from the peaks of the eastern "rim" was a dark blue-grey. At this junction we found a wide trough running up the middle of the glacier, providing an avenue of easy going. It closely resembled those glacial troughs which provide such an easy approach up the East Rongbuk Glacier on Everest.

By now it was snowing steadily, and the trough provided our only means of steering a direct course up the glacier. We made rapid progress however, and soon reached the end of the moraine-covered part. Here the trough petered out in a level stretch of ice, which provided going even more unpleasant than that which we had encountered lower down. Slush, knee-deep, covered its surface, which was scored into a maze of channels cut by twenty or more swiftly flowing glacier streams, and it was not until the middle of the afternoon that we reached an extensive lake which lay at the foot of a sheer precipice of ice-worn rock, and seen through the haze of falling snow, bore an uncanny appearance. On either side of the precipice was a confusion of ice-cliffs, which indicated two ice-falls. One, I judged, must come from an extensive ice-plateau to the north, from which the Great North Glacier derived the bulk of its strength. About the origin of the other ice-fall I could form no idea.

After a short rest on the shore of the lake, we worked round to the edge of the "plateau" ice-fall, worked out a route, and ascended some seven hundred feet above the lake. Then, as the weather showed no sign of improvement, we returned to the lake, and plodded down to camp, where we found Tilman still very weak, but better, and determined on making a move on the following morning. We discussed matters, and decided to push a camp as high as possible by the side of the ice-fall which Pasang and I had visited that day.

Snow fell gently throughout a most uncomfortable night, and despite the dreariness of the morning I was glad enough to get going. Our loads were light, as we were carrying only enough food for three men for three days, and we had with us merely the larger of the two tents. The plan was for Tilman, Pasang and myself to occupy the high camp, while Angtharkay and Kusang went down again to the one we had just left. Three is a safer number than two when travelling on extensive snow-covered glaciers as, if one man falls into a crevasse, it is extremely difficult for a single companion to pull him out.

Just before reaching the trough, we passed a curious phenomenon. We were walking along the brink of an ice-cliff about 100 feet high, and below, flowing directly towards the face of the cliff, was a large stream which, when it reached the cliff, entered by way of a tunnel in the ice. A few yards to the left it reappeared, flowing exactly in the opposite direction, until it disappeared once more into another ice channel.

The weather cleared somewhat while we were going up the glacier and, when we reached the lake, we were greeted by a gleam of sunshine which transformed the cheerless waters of yesterday into a pool of radiant loveliness in which danced the images of a thousand sparkling ice pinnacles. We saw, too, up the valley containing the second ice-fall, whose presence had puzzled me on the previous day. It was a narrow gorge-like affair, which bent round to the west and came, we concluded, from the northern foot of Kalanka. Thus its glacier came to be known as the Kalanka Glacier, and Tilman was forced to abandon his "Changalanka" jest and agree to the name "Changabang" for the glacier coming in below Junction Camp.

We sat for a while on the shore of the lake, to bask in the sun and to revel in that brief moment of beauty. Then we turned our attention to some precipitous slopes at the side of the "plateau" ice-fall. Here we became involved in some difficult climbing, which was made no easier by the snow, which soon started falling again, accompanied this time by a blustering wind.

At about 3 o'clock, at an altitude of some 18,500 feet, we started searching for a place on which to camp. The ground was continuously steep, and in the end we were forced to construct a platform on which to pitch our tent. Leaving us to complete the task, Angtharkay and Kusang went off down, climbing at top speed in order to be able to reach the lower camp before darkness cut off their retreat. They had instructions to return in three days' time.

An entry in my diary that evening reads: " . . . The wind dropped and the weather cleared, and gave us a slight idea of our surroundings. The ridge we are on seems to be covered with ice, and probably leads up to peak 113 (on our plane-table sheet). We are closer to the glacier than we thought, and above the worst bit of the ice-fall. The glacier seems to be split into two sections and the bit nearest us leads up to an extensive plateau, which does not look very far away. I suppose that is the thing to explore first; but the snow is now falling heavily again and I don't know what will happen. We have two and possibly three days' food with us. I hope we will be able to do some good in that time. We are having a spell of vile weather. I don't know if it is the monsoon or not. It does not look like it somehow. We all got very cold this afternoon, but are quite comfortable now – about 6.10 p.m. A miserable outlook, and we will soon have to be fighting our way back down the Rishi with scanty provisions.

The presence of three bodies kept the tent warm and in spite of the cramped position we all slept well, and I did not wake until Tilman struck a match at 2 a.m. to look at his watch. I cursed him roundly and went to sleep again, until he woke me again at 3.45. I know of no proceeding more dismal than the preparations for an early morning start from the chaos of an over-crowded tent. One man struggles manfully with a stove in order to provide the party with a drink of melted ice, while the others do their best to knock it over in their efforts to find some missing sock, glove or puttee. Tempers are at boiling point, and the whole business of mountain exploration seems utterly futile and ridiculous. Food in any form is repulsive, and the water, when at last it has been obtained from the ice-blocks, tastes strongly of last night's pemmican, and nearly makes one sick. This, of course, is someone else's fault for not having taken the trouble to wash the pot out the night before! Oh! for a really heavy snowstorm which would give one an indisputable excuse to get back to the only place in the world one really wants to be in – in the warmth of the recently abandoned sleeping-bag. It is stupid to start now anyway – why not wait until we see what the weather really is going to do! But at length all is ready; freezing fingers struggle for some minutes to close the complicated fastenings of the tent, and the party proceeds in silent churlishness until the sun swamps all gloom in the wonder of his early dawn.

On this particular morning, we were threading our way through a maze of ice-corridors whose walls were white, cold, dead, until all in a moment their deathly pallor was changed to a faint rose flush, faint but radiant with life and warmth.

We emerged from the badly crevassed area, and chipped our way up a steep snow slope, at the top of which we found ourselves on the ice-plateau at an altitude of over 20,000 feet. Two great ice-peaks rose in front of us. These numbered 110 and 113 on our plane-table sheet. Between them was a saddle, separated from us by a very gentle slope. We decided to make for the saddle, and from it to attempt the ascent of peak 110, which appeared very easy from where we were standing. I confess that I was vaguely hoping to find an exit from the basin by way of this saddle, though, looking back, that hope seems to have shown poor mountaineering judgment. Peak 113, seen from the plateau, was a wonderfully symmetrical pyramid of the purest ice, standing fully 1,500 feet above the saddle.

The saddle was deceptively far away and, though the snow was still fairly frozen, it took some hours of hard going to reach it. The crest of the saddle we found to be 20,500 feet. Below us to the north and west was one of the most terrific drops I have ever looked down, and it was some seconds before I could adjust the focus of my eyes to see that one could not merely step down on to the moraine-covered Bagini Glacier, 4,500 feet below. It looked as though, if a stone were dropped, it would touch nothing until it struck that glacier, up which Dr. Longstaff's party had made their way twenty-seven years before. Beyond, standing out above a belt of dark cloud, was a wonderful panorama of the Garhwal Mountains. Close at hand on the extreme left rose the slender spire of Dunagiri, whose delicate structure of ice-ridges has presented such formidable barriers to her votaries. Beyond, in the distance, the graceful head of Nilkanta stood in superb contrast to the massive shoulders of the Badrinath group, some of whose secrets we were to be privileged to reveal. Then came my first Himalayan acquaintance, Kamet, ruling despotically over his colony of peaks of the Tibetan borderland; then the untrodden glaciers of Hathi Parbat; and lastly to the north a wondrous mass of mountains of all shapes and sizes, still unnamed and unmeasured.

The wind was too cold to stand for long admiring the view, and we started up the slopes of peak 110. The snow was soft and powdery, and it was exhausting work making a trail. Tilman had not yet recovered from his fever, which was not surprising, considering that he had only risen from his bed of sickness on the previous morning. He seated himself in a shallow crevasse, which was sheltered from the wind and exposed to the warm sun, and told us to carry on and see what we could do with the peak. Pasang and I laboured on for an hour, through snow into which we sank up to our hips. In that time we made some 300 feet of height, and I decided that we would stand no chance of getting to the top, and regretfully abandoned the attempt. From where we had got to, however, there seemed to be no technical difficulties between us and the summit. It was evident too that the good weather would not survive many hours.

When we regained the plateau, we found the snow in a vile condition. As we got lower down, we were out of the wind, and the heat and glare were intense, and the labour of flogging a trail was a hearbreaking one. But we were in no particular hurry, and every now and then we sat down to gaze at the glorious view over the Nanda Devi Basin which our position commanded. The valleys were filled with great banks of woolly storm clouds, and the peaks of the eastern rim and the twin peaks themselves showed up in splendid isolation, which helped us to get a general idea of their relative size and position.

Once, while we were preparing to glissade down a very steep slope of about thirty feet into a crevasse, Pasang started off before we were ready, and, misjudging the length of the rope, both Tilman and I were pulled head first after him. The landing was soft and the fall was not long enough to have any serious consequences, but the incident was an annoying one, as it was a bad mountaineering error caused by pure carelessness. The badly crevassed section of the glacier required delicate handling, as the complicated system of snow bridges, which had been hard-frozen and secure in the morning, were now very unsafe, and we were constantly breaking through and hearing that ominous tinkling sound of icicles falling into the frozen depths of the crevasses below us. We reached our camp without further mishap, just as the usual afternoon snowstorm made its appearance, and spent the remainder of the day brewing and consuming vast quantities of tea and strenuously debating the subject of our next move.

CHAPTER TEN

WE had been keen to climb peak 110 primarily in order to be able to get a comprehensive view of the complicated topography to the north. Our reverse had merely stimulated that desire. Probably a more useful alternative for the morrow would be to continue the exploration of the ice-plateau in that direction. By doing this, if the weather were reasonably fine, we would be bound to see much of interest, whereas if we failed on the peak again, it would be a day of our most valuable time in this unknown country wasted. However, from what I had seen, the peak looked easy and eventually its blandishments won the day.

Pasang had had about enough on the previous day, and at 4 a.m. on the 20th Tilman and I left camp, heading once more for the ice-plateau. We suffered all the usual early morning torments, but were more than adequately compensated by the splendour of the dawn over the Nanda Devi Basin. Having our tracks of the previous day to follow, we climbed at a great pace, and reached our highest point of the previous day while our mountain world was still frozen; but beyond this we were faced with quite unexpected difficulties. A slope of dangerous snow, through which steps had to be cut into the ice below, led us, after some hours of hard work, into a long snow-filled corridor, running across the face of the mountain between high walls of ice. The snow had been swept into the corridor from the ice-slopes above, and was deep and soft. We sank in up to our waists as we beat our way along. We could not see where the corridor was leading us, but it was soon obvious that if we did not escape from it soon, we would have neither time nor energy to go any further. After half an hour or so, I saw a narrow vertical crack or "chimney" in the wall nearest the mountain. I started up it and, by putting my feet against one wall of the "chimney", and my back against the other (a method familiar to all rock climbers) I could make slow progress. But we were now at an altitude of nearly 22,000 feet, and I had not got many feet up the "chimney" before I was gasping like a fish out of water. Also the ice, of course, did not offer much friction to either boot or back, and the tendency to slip was very great. The air in the cleft was deathly cold, and in spite of my exertions my extremities soon lost all sensation. It was not long before I was bitterly regretting my folly in having tackled so severe a climb at such an altitude. The top of the cleft resisted my efforts so sternly that when, eventually, I emerged on to the steep ice-slope above, I sat there faint and sick for several minutes before I could summon up sufficient self-control to take in the rope as Tilman climbed up the "chimney". If it had been cold for me it was far worse for poor Tilman, who had had to wait below while I was wrestling with the "chimney".

When, after ten minutes' rest, we started up the ice-slope, we were both very shaky. The slope was steep and covered with three inches of slush, which made the job of chipping steps a difficult one. Higher up conditions became worse, and we soon realised that our struggle with the ice-chimney had left us too weak for the labour of hacking a safe pathway up ice of such a texture. Also the work called for absolute steadiness, as a slip on the part of either of us would have been impossible to check, and must have resulted in disaster, and we were both too tired to be able to guarantee safe movement. Again we had to admit defeat and turn back. Of course, if we had had time to spend on the job, we would have been able to make a bivouac in one of the crevasses nearby, and so eventually to hack our way up those relentless slopes. But we had come here primarily to explore the Nanda Devi Basin, and we could not afford the two days which would be necessary for a serious attack on peak 110.

The descent to the plateau called for unremitting care, and I was mightily relieved when we got clear of those vicious ice-slopes.

Our second reverse on this peak was another clear demonstration of the tendency to under-estimate mountaineering difficulties in the Himalaya.

After a close observation of the mountain, we had expected to have no serious difficulty in climbing it, and yet we had twice failed to do so. Our camp was only 18,500 feet high, and 4,500 feet is a lot to have to do in a day at that altitude, but this was not the reason for our defeat. In time, when these mountains become more familiar, a great many of their difficulties will be looked upon with less respect; but one wonders if mountaineering technique will ever reach so high a standard as to allow men to climb the more formidable giants of this vast range.

When we reached the camp we found all three Sherpas waiting for us. After slaking a raging glacier thirst, we packed up the tents and sleeping-bags, and hurried on down.

When we reached Great North Glacier, we found that the streams were enormously swollen. There had been a terrific increase in the rate of melting of the surface ice. I imagined that this was a sure sign that the monsoon was at hand, and we became seriously worried about the state of the rivers below.

After an undisturbed night in the open, I awoke at sunrise on June 21st to the song of many birds, which, strangely enough, seemed to be just as numerous far up in these barren moraine-filled valleys as amongst the pastures lower down. At 6.30 on this brilliant morning, while the Sherpas packed up the camp preparatory to going down, Tilman and I started up the glacier once more. We had a busy and interesting morning working with our plane-table at various points about the glacier, and in the afternoon, when the storm clouds had once more re-asserted themselves over the country, we ran at a great speed down the Great North Glacier to Junction Camp. When we reached the main valley, we found that a wonderful change had taken place in the short week we had been away. To a great height the mountain sides were a brilliant green with young grass. Our camp, lovely before, was now set in a garden of wild flowers, whose gay colouring framed the pools and new-born streams, contrasting deliciously with the harsh ruggedness of the higher glacier regions from which we had just come.

That evening we took stock of our food, and found that we had sufficient for only three more days. The weather was very unsettled, and it was evident that the monsoon was at hand. This was surprising, as we had not expected it until after the first week in July. Tilman was suffering from a severe pain in his foot, for which he could not account. There was still much minor exploratory work to be done in the northern section of the basin; this we could not hope to complete.

On the 22nd we took a light camp into yet another side valley leading towards the eastern "rim", and Tilman and I spent that night at an altitude of 18,100 feet, while the Sherpas returned to Junction Camp. We slept as usual in the open, and that evening, after a sharp hail-storm, we experienced again that vision of divine beauty which is, I suppose, the chief object of the strange pilgrimages which men make to the less accessible regions of the earth. It does not come to one at any particular place or time, and may elude the hunter over hundreds of miles of arctic waste or on countless mountain summits, to be found only on rare occasions, when the mind is unexpectedly attuned to the realisation of a delicate perfection of form and colour.

Before us, rising out of a misty shadow-lake of deepest purple, stood the twin summits of Nanda Devi, exquisitely proportioned and twice girdled by strands of white nimbus. This was backed by a liquid indigo, changing to mauve as it approached the south-west, where the icy pyramid of Trisul stood in ghostly attendance. Then, after passing through every degree of shade and texture, the colour died, leaving the moon to shed her silver light over a scene of ravishing loveliness, and to revive within me childish fancies, too easily forgotten in the materialism of maturer years.

We had intended to attempt, on the following day, the ascent of an attractive peak of some 21,500 feet, above our camp. Tilman's foot, however, appeared to be getting worse, and it was deemed wise that he should rest it in preparation for the heavy work which our retreat down the Rishi Nala would involve. Without his early-morning energy to assist me I found it more difficult than ever to summon up the strength of mind necessary to extricate sleepy limbs from the warmth of my sleeping-bag; particularly as the morning was dull and cheerless. Vanished were all the lofty enthusiasms of the previous evening, eclipsed by the hateful obligation of having to expose swollen lips and sore hands to the damp cold. Leaving the bivouac at 7.20 a.m. I crossed Glacier No. 5 on dry ice and climbed up the ridge which divides that valley from the Great North Valley, reaching a height of some 20,000 feet. Although the sky was overcast, the clouds stood well above the peaks and from my perch I obtained the most comprehensive view I had yet seen of the northern section of the basin, and spent an interesting and instructive hour filling in minor detail on the plane-table sheet. Towards 1 o'clock a bitter wind started blowing from the east, and snow fell. I made an unpleasant but quick descent to the Great North Glacier and reached Junction Camp at 4.30 p.m. to find Tilman and the Sherpas already arrived with our high camp kit. Tilman's foot was now badly swollen, and had caused him intense pain on the descent. It was now apparent that the trouble was a carbuncle on the upper surface of the foot.

On June 24th, while the others moved the camp across the Great North Glacier to the side of the lake, I had a long walk up the side of the Main Glacier, principally with the object of sketching the features on the northern face of Nanda Devi. The going was easy and pleasant along the level grass-land beside the glacier. It rained steadily most of the day and although my attention was constantly occupied by flowers, lakes, and herds of bharal, I was able to see very little of topographical interest and returned down the valley earlier than I had intended, reaching camp at 4.20 p.m.

I had hoped that by cutting our rations down slightly we might have time to explore the head of the Changabang Glacier, but it was now evident that the monsoon had broken and that we could not hope for more clear weather. Also we were far from sure how long the return journey would take us and one of the party was lame. We decided, therefore, to begin our retreat at once. And lucky it was that we had no great temptation to stay on in the basin, for our food dumps proved inadequate as it was!

A heavy mist hung over its grey waters as we said good-bye to the lake which had greeted us more than a fortnight before with so much sparkling life. We started very early and had reached the snout of the Main Glacier by midday, to find our fears regarding the state of the rivers only too well founded. The one issuing from the Main Glacier was now a raging torrent, despite the fact that the ground over which it was flowing for the first half mile of its course was relatively flat, and to ford it seemed at first to be a hopeless proposition. Moreover, the alternative of crossing the glacier above its snout and getting to the opposite side of the river in that way was out of the question, owing to a formidable line of overhanging cliffs thereabouts. For a moment our position looked serious, and I began to visualise the unpleasant consequences of having our retreat cut off. We waded out in several places, only to find each time that we could not stand up to the force of the current. After repeated attempts we were standing disconsolately at the water's edge when Pasang suggested a line which appeared to me to be at least as bad as the rest. However, he seized me by the hand, and I was led into the water's edge with a sinking heart. We immersed our lower halves in the seething turmoil, and advanced slowly. One of us moved forward a few inches supported by the other, then he would stand firm while the other moved, and so on. The rushing water made me giddy, and I knew that the least mistake would put us in a false position, from which there would be no hope of recovery. When the water touched my waist I knew that I had reached my limit, and any increase of pressure must sweep me off my feet. Pasang was splendid; never did he relax his concentration on himself or me for a fraction of a second. At length, after what seemed an age, the depth of the water began to lessen, and we bounded out on the other side, Pasang, who had done much more than his share of the "supporting", letting out wild cries of joy.

With the help of a rope stretched across the river, the others got over without mishap, though Angtharkay had an extremely bad time of it and required much support from the other two. Our relief at getting across without mishap was shared by the Sherpas, who danced with delight. But there was no time to waste in celebration, and we started down at full speed towards the junction of the northern and southern streams. To reach it we had to cross a spur coming down from Nanda Devi, and here we became involved in some difficult rock-climbing. However, at 3 o'clock we reached the southern stream just above the junction. After a short search, we were fortunate enough to find a place where the river, running over a stretch of mud flats, was very sluggish and, though the water was deep, we managed to get across without further unpleasant adventures. We found a nest, hereabouts, with three grey-blue eggs belonging, we supposed, to snow-pigeons. These birds were very common in the basin.

We climbed diagonally up the steep slope beyond the river, heading in a south-westerly direction until, about a thousand feet above the junction, we came upon a little grassy shelf with a spring of clear water. Here we settled down for the night, deliciously conscious that a heavy day's work had taken us clear of two serious difficulties, and that we were now well on our way to the Rishi Nala. But as we sat round our blazing fire of juniper wood in the gathering dusk, watching the heavy rain-clouds float lazily over the rolling moors of the basin, my content was marred by a feeling of sadness at having to leave so soon this country, which had provided us with a deep and lasting happiness, and whose beautiful secrets it had been our privilege to explore.

June 26th was a terrific day. During an early breakfast we caught a last fleeting glimpse of Nanda Devi's mighty head through a rift in the heavy monsoon clouds which hung over us. Then we started off towards the west, moving across the steep grassy slopes at a breathless pace which never slackened throughout the morning, and by midday we reached the little cave in which we had camped on June 5th. The Sherpas were as anxious as we were for speed, and I think that the mind of each of us was on the "flesh pots" of the Dhaoli Valley. But this was not the only reason, for the supplies of food left in the dumps were meagre and did not allow for any hitch which might easily occur on the return journey, on account of the early breaking of the monsoon.

Most of us were feeling fairly fit, but Tilman was rendered very lame by the carbuncle on his foot. He insisted, however, in carrying his share of the loads, and never breathed a word of complaint, though the furious pace over such difficult country must have caused him very considerable pain. We halted at our old camp for about twenty minutes, in order to eat a cup-full of satu mixed with cold water. The scramble from there down the very steep slope of 2,000 feet to the river took us two hours on account of the awkwardness of the loads. The river was many feet higher than when we had made its acquaintance before, and of course our little bridge had been swept away. On we went through the afternoon, and darkness found us encamped in a little clump of silver birch beyond the dreaded "Mauvais Pas".

I passed the night in a tiny recess between two boulders, and throughout the first half of it a thunderstorm raged above the gorge. The boulders provided inadequate shelter from the heavy rain which accompanied the storm, and I got very wet. The scene, however, was one not easily to be forgotten. Lightning flashes played continuously upon the grim precipices about me, while the fleecy rain clouds, entwining themselves about ridge and gully, accentuated their already stupendous size. Echoes of the thunder and hissing of rain provided fitting accompaniment.

The next morning, in thick mist and steadily falling rain, we continued our way along the delicate traverses which constituted the only practicable route across the gaunt precipices forming the southern wall of the canyon. The long tedious task of discovering the way and relaying our loads along it had made us familiar with almost every yard of the route, so that in spite of the bad visibility we were now experiencing, we made no mistakes. We were assisted too by the cairns which we had built at various points, and at 1 o'clock that afternoon we reached our base camp on the shore of the river we had left nearly a month ago. We had all been looking forward to a good square meal, but on arrival we found that by some mistake we had left only half the quantity of food which we had intended leaving, and that we now had sufficient only for three more days. This allowed for no contingencies, and there was no time to lose.

Below our base camp we had a choice of several routes. Dr. Longstaff had made his way to this point along the southern slopes of the valley, but he had encountered considerable difficulties, and with our loads and in such weather we would certainly take two and possibly three days to reach the place where he had bridged the Rishi Ganga. The route by which we had come with the Dotials was out of the question, owing to the impossibility of crossing the river in its present state where we had crossed it before. The only alternative then was to cross by the natural bridge to which I have referred before, ascend the Rhamani Nala until we found a place where we could cross it, and try to get on to the high line of traverse which Dr. Longstaff's party had taken after they had crossed the

Bagini Pass in 1907. So shortly after 4 o'clock that afternoon Pasang and I set off to investigate the possibility of this alternative.

We crossed the river by the natural bridge, which Pasang had not seen before. He was delighted, and seemed to think that it solved our last remaining problem. In gently falling rain we climbed up a difficult cliff to Longstaff's old camp site, some two hundred feet above the Rishi. From here we edged our way along a narrow shelf which gave us access to the Rhamani stream, but at a point where the river, issuing from a deep-cut ravine, descended in a series of waterfalls, and offered no hope of a crossing. We retraced our steps, and in some anxiety scrambled up along the steep rhododendron-covered slopes above the ravine, whose smooth unbroken walls overhung the river. We were forced to climb some fifteen hundred feet up before we found another break in these walls, and were able to get down to the river again. This time, however, we found ourselves at a fairly level stretch between two waterfalls, and decided after some discussion that the crossing could be attempted at this point. It was now getting late, and we had to get back quickly if we were to avoid being benighted, but I would have given much to have been able to continue our investigation of that remarkable gorge.

At the base camp we deposited our plane-table, some lengths of rope, candles, "Tommy's cookers" and a few items of clothing, to be picked up when we returned in August for the exploration of the southern section of the basin. This lightened our loads somewhat, and on the following morning we were back at the crossing place by 10 o'clock. We got over without much difficulty, and climbed a further five hundred feet up on the other side. This brought us on to a prominent ridge, from which we had a clear view down the Rishi Nala. Fortunately visibility remained good until 3 o'clock, by which time we had covered about a mile and a half on a fairly horizontal line. Then mist enveloped us, and for the next two hours, in pouring rain, we floundered helplessly about the intricate hillside until we came upon a spacious cave, where we decided to spend the night. There was a quantity of juniper growing nearby, and we were soon drying our sodden gear by a blazing fire.

The weather was still bad when we awoke next morning, and we did not get started until 8 o'clock. Groping our way through heavy mist, we got on to exceedingly difficult ground, and by 11 o'clock we had covered only a quarter of a mile. However, soon after this the weather cleared, and we found ourselves close to the terrace from which we had descended to the river nearly five weeks before. On reaching this we were on familiar ground once more and made such excellent progress that by the middle of the afternoon we were running down the pine-clad slopes to Dibrughita – "the horizontal oasis in a vertical desert". The alp was more beautiful than ever – a vast meadow of lush grass interwoven with forget-me-nots, deep red potentillas, large blue gentians, and flowers of a dozen other varieties, while the stately army of tall dark pines stood in a wide circle as if guarding this little shrine from the demons of the Rishi Gorge.

Our troubles were now over, and as we lay on the damp ground in the gently falling rain before an immense log fire, we basked in contentment undisturbed by sordid considerations of time, distance, and food.

A long slog up the steep slopes of the "curtain" ridge the next day (June

30th), took us to Durashi, where we found that the shepherds from Lata village had been installed for about ten days. These were the first human beings, besides ourselves, that we had seen since discharging the Dotials on May 29th, and our arrival startled them considerably. However, we managed to persuade them that we were not the mythical devils of the upper gorge, and they supplied us with quantities of goat's milk, which I thought at the time was the finest drink I had ever had. It must have strengthened us considerably too, for on the following morning, we made astonishingly quick time up to the Durashi Pass. I had been hoping that some snow would still remain in the gullies, as this would have enabled us to glissade some of the way down to Tolma, but except for a few patches here and there it had practically all gone. We decided to descend diagonally to the Lata village, instead of going down to Surai Tota. We had not much idea of the way, but before we had gone far we struck a sheep track which led us through an intricate network of cliffs in the forest, and soon blossomed out into a sizable path, down which we ran recklessly. Kusang lagged behind to gather considerable quantities of wild strawberries. He gave me all he had picked, and when I asked the reason for his generosity, he said that he had damaged his knee and that eating strawberries would make it worse! I failed to see the connection, but did not argue the point too strongly. We reached Lata village just before 4 o'clock, and immediately set about trying to persuade the inhabitants to sell us some food. We were bitterly disappointed, for the net result of our scrounging was a few unripe apricots and a cup-full of flour. There were no chickens, and therefore no eggs. There were cows, but no milk, and the last year had been a bad one for grain and, with the next harvest still so far off, the villagers could not afford to part with their flour. It was evident that the land of plenty was not yet reached, and we tightened our belts with a grim resolve to reach Joshimath the next day.

That evening we paid a social visit to the village, which we found in a great state of excitement on account of the arrival of an itinerant trader. His wares consisted of a miscellaneous assortment of buttons, matches, jews' harps, soap, etcetera, for which the villagers were eagerly exchanging the grain which had been refused us earlier in the day, though we had offered money some five times the value of the ridiculous trinkets supplied by the pedlar. We could not find out how he disposed of the grain, but it must have been a slow and precarious method of livelihood.

Early next morning, a large section of the village turned out to see us depart and acocmpanied us for some distance in order to see that we got on to the right path. It was a tedious march and we all felt very lethargic, the cause being, no doubt, our enforced underfeeding for the past few days. In the pouring rain we sped down the Dhaoli Valley practically without a stop. Each of us, I suppose, was thinking of hot tea and lots of food; but to a passer-by (if there had been such a phenomenon) we must surely have resembled the demons of the Rishi to whom we had been likened by the shepherds at Durashi. Early in the evening we entered Joshimath, exactly six weeks after leaving it.

1　Eric Shipton (left) and H.W. Tilman setting off on their 1934 Himalaya Expedition from Tilman's family home in Wallesey. Others in the view are Adeline Moir (Tilman's sister), her daughter Pam, the chauffeur and Mrs Tilman (in the limousine).

2　Members of the 1934 expedition: Angtharkay, Pasang Bhutia (Bhotia) and Kusang with Shipton and Tilman sitting behind.

3 (above) The upper Rishi Gorge. The path takes the left-hand slopes. *Photo: John Porter*

4 (left) Lowering loads down a difficult section in the lower Rishi Gorge.

5 (below) A view across the Sanctuary to peaks on the eastern rim – Deo Damla, Bamchu and Sakram (with prominent ice ridge). *Photo: Hamish Brown*

6   The northern aspect of Nanda Devi. The final part of the North Ridge route, first climbed in 1976
     by an American expedition is etched by the sun just below the summit. *Photo: Hamish Brown*

7   Shipton's celebrated photograph of the precipitous North Face of
     Nanda Devi East seen from high on the Uttari Rishi Glacier.

8   Satopanth Col and Chaukhamba seen from the Satopanth Glacier on the occasion of the second crossing of the col in 1998.
Photo: John Shipton

9   (right) The icefall on the south-western flank of Satonpanth Col, the descent of which (in misty conditions) caused such anxiety in 1934. At a crucial stage the couloir on the right was gained and this allowed a rapid but risky descent. This view is from an easier descent route discovered in 1998.
Photo: John Harvey

10   The Gandharpongi Gad or 'Bamboo Valley' which proved so arduous in 1934.
In a renewed attempt to locate the illusive Kedernath/Badrinath pilgrim route, the 1998 traversing party
avoided the valley's dense lower reaches by climbing the northern slopes (photo taken during this
ascent) to reach the adjoining Mandani valley. *Photo: Ben Lovett*

11 After a hard day's descent in the 'Bamboo Valley', Kusang, Angtharkay and Pasang prepare a meal of mushrooms and bamboo shoots.

12 The peaks ringing the northern perimeter of the Sanctuary – the tooth-like Changabang, Kalanka and the summits of the Hardeol/Tirsuli group, including Pt. 6957 attempted twice by Tilman and Shipton in 1934.

13 14 On the lower section of the South Ridge of Nanda Devi, pictures taken during the first attempt on the route in 1934.

Part 3

The First Crossing of the Watershed
(Badrinath – Gaumukh)

CHAPTER ELEVEN

WE had over-estimated the joys of Joshimath. After three or four days of idleness and over-eating we were quite ready for a move to the north, where we fondly hoped we might be beyond the reach of the monsoon. We were bound for the Kedarnath-Badrinath group of mountains which are of great topographical interest since in them lie the sources of three of the main affluents of the Ganges, the rivers Bhagirathi, Mandakini, and Alaknanda, and close to these sources are the well-known temples of Gangotri, Kedarnath and Badrinath.

Our object in wishing to visit these was to cross the range which forms the watershed between the Alaknanda and the Bhagirathi, and so to link up the two chief sources of the Ganges. The range was but twenty miles north of Joshimath and it seemed very likely that there we should escape the influence of the monsoon and enjoy fine weather. (This theory was sound enough – in theory; but like most it did not work out in practice and we found that we were in the same predicament as if we had gone to see the English Lakes in the hope of avoiding a wet summer in the south.)

We knew that in 1912 Mr. C. F. Meade and his two Swiss guides had gone from Badrinath up the Bhagat Kharak Glacier, climbed the ridge at its head, and looked down on the Gangotri Glacier. They did not descend on the other side, but they thought the pass was practicable, and it was our intention to find and cross this pass and thereby not only cross the range, but also explore the unknown head of the Gangotri Glacier.

But there is more than geographical interest in this district. It is believed to be the home of the gods of Hindu mythology, and every feature of the landscape is sanctified by some legend and is traditionally memorable.

It seemed that from earliest Vedic records (Hindu writings), the geography of the mountainous regions sheltering the Ganges sources was well-known. In those distant times when men still worshipped the elements, a region which saw the birth of great rivers and greater storms was naturally regarded with awe; and so, when the worship of the elements was supplanted by the worship of gods, it began to be revered as their home.

The learned and the pious were drawn there for meditation and adoration, and hill and valley, peak and waterfall, came to be associated with particular gods and embellished by stories of their lives. Indeed, in the Hindu legend of the creation, Brahma, Siva and Vishnu assumed the form of mountains. When Brahma desired to create the earth he began by assuming the visible form of Vishnu, the whole universe being covered with water on which floated that god, resting on a bed supported by a serpent. From his navel sprang a lotus from which issued Brahma; from his ears issued two Daityas (or, when transferred to an earthly sphere, Dasyus, the aboriginal black race as opposed to the fair Aryan), who attacked Brahma; and Vishnu and Brahma fought with them for five thousand years until Vishnu finally killed them and from their marrows made the world.

Vishnu then assumed the form of a tortoise and raised the earth out of the water and asked Brahma to create all that the world was of earth, sky, and heaven; divided the earth into nine parts and created wind and sound and time; past, present, and future; work and desire, and anger; from the last-named Siva was created as making the third of the great trinity, Brahma the creator, Vishnu the preserver, and Siva the destroyer.

The story then goes on that during the terrestrial reign of one Prithu, all plants perished by reason of his tyranny, which so angered him that he determined to destroy the earth. The earth sought pardon, and begged the king to remove the mountains which prevented the spread of vegetation. Prithu uprooted the mountains and heaped them on top of each other, but then from the earth proceeded to milk all plants and vegetables. Other gods and demons followed his example and milked the earth of all its virtues, who then fled to Brahma to complain of this everlasting milking. Brahma took her to Vishnu, who made the following promise: "Soon the head of Brahma will fall upon thee" (at Brahm Kapal a great rock in the river at Badrinath); "Siva will come to sit upon the mountains of Tankara" (at Jageswar in Kumaon); "Bhagirath Raja shall bring down Ganga" (Ganges) "to thee. Then I myself will come in my dwarf incarnation and all the world will know that Vishnu has descended on thee. Then thy pains shall be removed and the mountains cease to afflict thee with their load, for I shall be Himalaya; Siva will be Kailas" (a mountain in Tibet north of Kumaon); "Brahma will be Vindhyachal and thus the load of the mountains shall be removed."

But the earth asked "Why do you come in the form of mountains and not in your own form?" and Vishnu answered: "The pleasure that exists in mountains is greater than that of animate beings, for they feel no heat, nor cold, nor pain, nor anger, nor fear, nor pleasure. We three gods as mountains will reside in the earth for the benefit of mankind." (An answer which mountaineers would do well to learn in order to baffle the all-to-frequent inquiry of why they climb mountains, for it leaves the questioner no wiser than before, yet it has an authority sufficiently impressive to silence him!)

Thus Himachal, the Snow Mountains, were invested with sanctity, but the holy of holies is Mount Kailas, in Tibet, and the sources of the Ganges and the mountains which surround it, and here are the ancient temples of Badrinath, Kedarnath, and Gangotri. They are all reached by roads having a common origin at Hardwar, another holy city which marks the place where the Ganges debouches from the hills on to the plains. The three temples are within a circle of twenty miles radius, but between each rises a twenty-thousand-feet ridge of snow and ice, and to pass from one to the other pilgrims must retrace their steps for more than one hundred miles, so to outflank this great barrier.

Kedarnath was particularly associated with the worship of Siva, whose adventures there are definitely not of the kind associated with the life of that grim and terrifying god, the very apotheosis of lust and cruelty. The legend is that the god took refuge here when pursued by the Pandavas (a tribe of the Dasyus whom we have already met) by assuming the form of a buffalo and diving into the ground for safety. Unluckily he left his hinder parts exposed on the surface, and there is still a mountain here which is supposed to resemble in shape the hindquarters of a buffalo and is now an object of adoration.

These high-spirited Pandavas were effectually subdued later, and when told that their power had left them and that they should begin to think on heaven, it was to the Himalaya they retired. The account of their departure is most moving, a pathetic touch being that of the dog who, I suppose, had taken a too prominent part in the buffalo hunt. We read that, "Yudishthira, their ruler, then took off his earrings and necklace, and all the jewels from his fingers and arms, and all his royal raiment; and he and his brethren, and their [sic] wife Draupadi, clothed themselves after the manner of devotees in vestments made of the bark of trees. And the five brethren threw the fire of their domestic sacrifices and cookery into the Ganges and went forth from the city following each other. First walked Yudishthira, then Bhima, then Ayuna, then Nakula, then Sahdeva, then Draupadi, and then a dog. And they went through the country of Banga towards the rising sun; and after passing through many lands they reached the Himalaya Mountain, and there they died one after the other and were transported to the heaven of Indra."

Close to Kedarnath on the north, but reached by a different road, is Gangotri. There is a celebrated temple here and close by is Gaumukh, the Cow's Mouth, which should have proved an even greater attraction, but from what we saw and what I have heard since, is visited by only a few. This is the snout of the Gangotri Glacier, fifteen very rough miles above the Temple, and the sacred source – or rather the most sacred, for there are others – of Mother Ganges. Apparently when the world was young and man was in a state of innocence the Ganges rose at Benares, so that it was an easy matter for believers to visit it. As the earth increased in years and wickedness, the source retreated successively to Hardwar, Barahat, and now to Gaumukh, whither the long and arduous pilgrimage may atone in some measure for the sins of a more vicious age.

In the temple at Gangotri are two images representing the Ganges and the Bhagirathi, and below in the river bed are three basins where the pilgrims bathe. One of these is dedicated to Brahma, one to Vishnu, and one to Siva, and the water of these basins will not only cleanse away all past sins, but ensure eternal happiness in the world to come. It is almost as efficacious if taken away – and returning pilgrims may then hope to get back some of their expenses! The water is drawn under the inspection of a Brahman and by him sealed for a small consideration, and when carried down to the plains it realises a high price. The mighty Ganges is here only about fifty feet across and at Gaumukh perhaps half of that, but in the summer when the snows are melting the current is very fierce.

Such are the interesting legends attached to the Kedarnath-Badrinath country and, the flesh-pots of Joshimath having so quickly palled, we were glad to begin drawing up food lists and to engage the necessary coolies. Unfortunately our eight deserters from Surai Tota had so blackened our characters that we had great difficulty in finding anyone else, but at last we collected six coolies, and two days' march along what is called the "Pilgrim Road" brought us to Badrinath on July 11th. At a village on our way up we stopped to sample some exciting-looking sweetmeats and were led to believe that all the inhabitants were positively clamouring for work as coolies. Now our six were only coming – and that reluctantly – as far as Badrinath with us and we wanted eight to come on to the Bhagat Kharak Glacier, so we promised to give eight villagers the work and received in return an ardent promise that we could rely on them presenting themselves next day in Badrinath at dawn.

This was excellent, and on the 12th we were up at 5 o'clock and had all the loads in readiness, but when 8 o'clock came and there was still no sign of any porter, we began sending out into the highways and byways of Badrinath for recruits. By 9 o'clock we had five men and we then moved over to the bazaar, where we sat, with what small patience we could muster, beside the three extra loads until men could be found for them. Every man in the bazaar joined in the search – which meant that no spare man could be found, but two hours later our complement was somehow made up and we gave the word to start. By then, of course, the first five had drifted off to see their friends or to buy food, but we were assured they would follow. So in ones, two and threes did we straggle out of Badrinath – a distressing sight to an orderly-minded man.

But our fellow-marchers were as happy-go-lucky as ourselves. They had started from Hardwar, a journey of some thirty days from Badrinath and were for the most part townsmen or peasants from the plains; the former in "dandies", or walking before a plodding coolie carrying their baggage: the latter walking – without the coolie. For the majority baggage was not a serious hindrance as a brass bowl for food and a pilgrim's staff was generally enough. One additional thing was carried by all, whatever their station in life. This was an umbrella. Indeed, the almost universal use of this very European article was most striking, and I must admit that the umbrella was a highly incongruous adjunct when borne aloft by a hardy shepherd of the hills, clad in a long, blanket-like coat of homespun fastened across his chest by a metal skewer and chain for want of a button; but seemingly he was sensible enough to prefer dryness to a picturesque appearance.

The pilgrims were of both sexes, and we inclined to believe there were more women than men. Many of the former, could they afford it, were carried in a basket or a "dandy". The basket was high, narrow and cylindrical, not much bigger than a dirty-linen basket, and was hitched to the coolie's back, he carrying a T-shaped staff to support its weight when at rest. The passenger sat facing the rear with only his head showing, and the many we passed appeared to be asleep, with handkerchiefs over their faces to keep off the flies. The "dandy" was rather like a sedan chair without any sides and was carried by four coolies, thus making it a very expensive mode of transport. Slung at each end from a pole which rests on the bearers' shoulders, it was so arranged that they might walk in echelon, and not side by side. The passenger is literally and metaphorically "in the hands" of his carriers, as the following story shows.

Tradition relates that the ruling family of Kumaon, at that time the Katyuris, had their origin here. There is a story about the last Katyuri Rajah which illustrates the steep contours of this country more vividly than can any descriptive writing. Rajah Dham, the last of his line, ruled so tyrannically that he went in fear of his life. In such circumstances the usual safeguard is to wear an extra steel waistcoat or to change the cook, but in this case the Rajah took the precaution of having iron rings fastened to the shoulders of his dandy-bearers. The poles passed through these rings, and so it was impossible for the bearers to drop their royal burden over a cliff without themselves accompanying it. But no one is secure against desperate men, and when oppression grew intolerable, four men were found ready to sacrifice themselves for the sake of their country, who flung themselves off the road, with the Rajah, to their deaths.

The profane like to recount a more recent tradition which also shows how the country lends itself to the arranging of "accidents", but puts the dandy-bearers in a less pleasing light. The pilgrim season is short: it starts in May and none leave Hardwar after the end of August, and so like other seasonal workers the dandy-men try to make the most of it. It is the custom to contract for transport and pay in advance, but if the dandy-men went the whole way, they could at the best make only two full journeys. They therefore hit on the happy plan of tipping their passenger over any convenient cliff into the river, many marches short of Badrinath, and hastening back for a fresh load. They argued that the arrangement satisfied both parties, the pilgrim bathed in the sacred waters as he had desired, and the coolies could earn twice as much in the season. The practice died out with the coming of the British raj, who probably regarded it as a too free interpretation of the contract.

The pilgrims, so we have been told, found the fruition of all earthly desire in a visit to their sacred places, the shrine of Vishnu at Badrinath, the Panch-Sila, the Five Rocks and their respective pools which encircle the throne of Vishnu, and what is called "The Holy Circle of Badrinath", which includes a tract of country from the shrine of Kanwa to the peak of Nanda Devi, on the summit of which is supposed to be a lake, the abode of Vishnu himself. Their day's stage was usually about nine miles and at each halt they found accommodation in long, low sheds open in front to the road and surrounded on the remaining three sides by stone walls supporting a grass roof. The floor was of beaten earth which received daily a fresh wash of mud or clay and along the roadside were a dozen or more little circular fireplaces, also of clay, spaced at four-feet intervals. There were also shops, at which the pilgrims might buy their food and fuel, the purchase of which entitled them to a free night's lodging. Some of these rest-houses were provided with big thatched-reed sleeping mats, but there was no other furniture. Certainly everything looked very clean (owing probably to the frequent washing with yellow clay) but, fortunately perhaps, we were never called upon to put this supposed cleanliness to the test.

The Government, having made the "Pilgrim Road", a well-engineered bridle-track seven to ten feet wide and maintained by the P.W.D. of India, were rightly concerned about the health of the pilgrims, for an outbreak of cholera at any of the rest-houses would be most serious. The greatest difficulty was sanitation, and therefore inspectors were employed along the route to see that at least the most rudimentary regulations were carried out. At most of the villages, too, pipe-lines had been laid down to bring drinking-water from high up the hillsides, where the chances of contamination were less. Even despite these precautions dysentery and, in the lower valleys, malaria took toll of the pilgrims, many of whom, weakened by unaccustomed effort and the cold, were in no condition to resist an attack. We were told that at Badrinath alone that year there had been thirty deaths – but as probably there had been some thirty thousand pilgrims this did not strike us as being an alarming proportion. Besides, more than a few of them were most likely caused by weakness and starvation, since many of the poorer classes start out with little or no money and are soon reduced to begging their way – no easy task in such a sparsely populated district. Doubtless such a method answered well enough for the professional beggar (for whom India is renowned). He had only to pass through a bazaar and thrust his bowl under the noses of unfortunate shopkeepers to have a handful of rice or ata put into it. In this walk of life a disgusting appearance is a positive asset, and I have never once seen the most repulsive-looking individual turned away empty-handed. At Badrinath itself the Temple authorities dispense every day quantities of free food: at mid-day a great bowl of cooked rice is carted into the main street and anyone who asks may be filled.

We were much puzzled by the complete apathy which most of them betrayed. Here was no "Happy Band of Pilgrims", but a procession of woebegone miseries that reminded us of refugees, driven from their homes by an invader. None seemed to derive any pleasure from the performance of a duty which to them meant the principal thing in life, or from the glorious scenery through which this duty led them. One and all went along with downcast head, bestowing no glance upon the grandeur of the hills and deigning but a sour look at passers-by. Possibly, of course, this latter was reserved for ourselves – the outcasts and unbelievers defiling holy ground. (After all, a European on the road to Mecca during the pilgrim season would be lucky to receive nothing more harmful than angry looks.)

But these Hindus were not so fanatical in such matters as the Mohammedans, and on several occasions we found them pleased to show us their temples, so we came to the conclusion that a possible cause of their indifference lay in their awe and fear of mountains. To nearly all of them rocks, hills, snow and ice, were things outside their previous experience and, as we told ourselves, we had not to go so very far back to find similar emotions in our own forefathers. Whether their faces showed these we cannot tell, but what they felt they have very clearly expressed, as, for example, in the writing of Defoe in his *Tours*: "Here we entered Westmorland, a country eminent for being the wildest, most barren, and frightful of any that I have passed over in England, or even Wales itself. . . . Nor were these Hills high and formidable only, but they had a kind of an unhospitable terror in them. . . . But 'tis of no advantage to represent Horror as the character of a Country, in the middle of all the frightful Appearances to the right and left." And a writer of yet later date describing an ascent of homely Saddleback seems to be even more moved, though he does omit the capitals: ". . . views so tremendous and appalling that few persons have sufficient resolution to experience the emotions which those awful scenes inspire."

In addition we had to remember that every rock or pool was supposedly the abode of some god, so that a fearful and downcast air on the part of the supplicant were understandable. In very truth, these pilgrims might exclaim with Kim: "Surely the gods live here. This is no place for men!"

CHAPTER TWELVE

INTERESTED though we were in the behaviour of the pilgrims, the country ahead was yet more interesting, and soon we left the last pilgrims behind, for only a few go much beyond Badrinath.

Three miles from Badrinath we passed through the village of Mana, the last inhabited village on the road to the Mana Pass into Tibet. Its site was picturesque, overlooking the mouth of a terrific gorge and backed by a bleak hillside studded with prodigious boulders, some of which had rolled down, thus completely spanning the ravine. Here the low huts, roofed with rough flat stones, appeared to grow like some fungus out of the landscape, and here the Alaknanda Valley bent abruptly to the west and three miles up gave birth to a river at the adjoining snouts of the Bhagat Kharak and the Satopanth glaciers. But contrary to expectations our pilgrims did not visit this source: instead, they resorted to a place called Bhasudhara, about a mile short of the glaciers. Here, in truth, was the spot where "the slender thread of the Lotus flower falls from the foot of Vishnu", a spot far more fitted to witness the birth of the sacred Ganges than the desolate, moraine-covered ice of the Bhagat Kharak. Almost as soon as one rounded the bend at Mana the eye was drawn, without conscious volition, to a narrow white ribbon of water outlined against a wall of reddish rock at whose feet was a grassy alp. Here the water, cascading from some hidden glacier, dissolved at the bottom into a fine mist with which the wind sported, and so sprinkled a rude shrine and the pilgrims who bowed before it.

This part of the Alaknanda above Mana was a favourite resort for those who wished to commune alone and to practise austerities. We came upon several living the lives of hermits in caves and under sheltering boulders – an existence pleasant enough during the summer months, away from the flies and smells of

Badrinath, and sustained by the milk of the goats which were herded here in great numbers. (In winter, no doubt, these folk descended to a kindlier climate as did the entire population of Badrinath, since from November to May their temple is shut.)

But a far more interesting ascetic than the hermits of the Bhasudhara was a Professor Ram Serikh Singh, known to all in the district as "the Master". We had met him first in Badrinath, whither he came every year, not to stay in the town but to withdraw, with a single attendant, to a tent pitched on a green alp in the shadow of the beautiful Nilkanta. There, in the midst of scenery grand and inspiring, he passed his time in reading and meditation. Deeply learned in Hindu religion and in philosophy, and also in the traditions of these mountain regions, his learning had not been gained from books alone since he was a lover of mountain-travel and had journeyed extensively, even to Mount Kailas in Tibet, which lay some hundred miles to the north-east and was of the greatest sanctity to both Hindu and Tibetan. We spent many delightful hours with "the Master" in his wild and secluded valley, and the memory of them is among the fondest of our travels. His genial countenance and robust figure had at once a resemblance to Mr. Pickwick and to Friar Tuck. Sitting talking in his tent, or poring over a map with his spectacles athwart his nose, his likeness to the former predominated; outside on hillside or road, sturdy of frame, his thick gown girdled at the waist, a mighty staff in his hand, he recalled a favourite picture of Robin Hood's trusted companion. That there is no portrait of "the Master" in these pages is what we call "our fault". He, however, out of the depths of his philosophy, refers to it as Providential (in the strictest meaning of that word). Before setting out to visit him at his camp we constantly reminded each other about a camera, hoping that he would permit us to photograph him – and in the end, both of us inevitably forgot it! When we told him of this omission of commission he displayed great satisfaction, laughingly told us that never had he had his photograph taken, and saw, in this last narrow escape, the directing hand of some Higher Power determined to protect his immunity.

But it is high time we left "the Master" and the "Pilgrim Road" and concentrated upon our reconnaissance of the Kedarnath-Badrinath group!

Our stay in the village of Mana was lengthened by our inability to collect our still scattered followers. But having at last mustered them all, we crossed the grim gorge of the Saraswati by a natural rock bridge and followed the Alaknanda Valley westwards. The valley was pleasantly open and was the grazing ground for all the Mana herds and flocks, and the abode of many anchorites engaged in meditation and the practice of austerities. Had there been juniper wood as well as grass we would have liked it better, for we had no wish to vie with the anchorites in mortifying the flesh. When we camped that night one mile short of the Bhagat Kharak Glacier all hands had to range far and wide to collect enough pitiful little twigs to boil a kettle. Just across the river, tantalisingly close, was a little birch spinney but it might as well have been fifty miles away.

Before reaching the glacier we had to ford a side stream of which we had been warned at Mana and advised to go up it for a mile before attempting to cross. After the Rishi it looked fairly harmless, as indeed it was if taken in the right place, and we scorned to be driven by it two miles out of our way. While we were looking for an easy place the Sherpas tried a line of their own, and Pasang got into serious difficulties. He lost his footing and went right under, but luckily for him his load came free (we again noticed the merit of head-straps), and he was pulled ashore, bruised and badly shaken and minus his ice-axe. The load, containing his own and my kit and bedding, went bobbing downstream, on the way to Calcutta and the sea, and in trying to stop it, Tilman's ice-axe fell a victim to the hungry river. The load grounded lower down on some shallows but the axes were never recovered, and from now on the Sherpas had to use sticks which later proved a serious handicap.

The moraine on the north side of the glacier made a fair path, and two days later we camped at 16,000 feet near the head of the glacier and sent the local coolies back. The glacier was about seven miles long and as soon as we rounded a bend in it half way up we could see there was no pass at the head; there were, however, four subsidiary glaciers flowing in from a south-westerly direction so our hopes were by no means extinguished. The first of these, close to the head of the main glacier was disposed of before camp was pitched, for I went round the corner to look for a better camp site and saw, with disgust, a most forbidding cirque of cliffs at the head.

From the camp we climbed a small peak (19,000 feet), from where we saw enough to rule out a second possible pass, and we also obtained a good view of the northern bounding wall of the Bhagat Kharak, which was to prove useful to us later. We then made a traverse of our peak and came down a new way, in the course of which Tilman made the discovery that glissading on steep ice was too rapid, even in these fast-moving times, and we reverted to slow but safe step-cutting.

Our camp on the ice was not very home-like so we moved it across to a grassy flat on the north side where conditions were pleasant, and where we were well placed for a fresh move, the necessity for which was now looming ahead of us. A walk up the third glacier confirmed our fears, and after much heart-searching we decided the fourth was best left alone. We had caught a glimpse of the col at the head of this on the way up and it seemed to offer some hope, but the approach to the glacier was up a steep and difficult ice-fall which, moreover, was raked by avalanches from the tremendous north face of Kunaling, the giant of this range, some 23,400 feet. The roar of an intermittent bombardment of this glacier from the slopes of Kunaling was ever in our ears.

(Since returning to England we have learnt that it was up here that Mr. Meade went, but he got on to the glacier by some route which avoided the ice-fall and the avalanche-swept area.)

Defeated in the Bhagat Kharak we fell back on a fresh plan. In 1931 the Kamet expedition had gone up the Arwa, a valley system north of the Bhagat Kharak, and in one of its branches had found a pass which obviously led to the Gangotri side of the range, although it was not completely crossed. We therefore decided to cross first to the Arwa and, if our food allowed, to attempt to find a way over the great Gangotri Glacier.

So on July 18th we started relaying loads (including a quantity of juniper wood) to the top of the 20,000 feet ridge beween us and the Arwa. The direction we wanted to take was due north but the only place by which the ridge could be crossed lay well to the east of north, and we were reluctantly driven farther from the watershed. In four days we established a camp on the ridge, where we stayed two days while Tilman and I climbed a peak of about 21,500 feet. It was an interesting ridge climb, but the pleasure we expected, and in fact received, from it was secondary to getting the hang of the geography of the Arwa glaciers on to which we were about to descend. In this object we were disappointed, for the weather which earlier was so good that we flattered ourselves we had outrun the monsoon, now broke up, and snow, rain, and mist were our daily portion.

But our two-day halt here enabled us to eat some of the weight out of our loads and when we started the descent we were just able to carry everything in one shift – everything except our juniper which we abandoned regretfully. The descent was not as exhilarating as descents should be; indeed, soft snow and heavy loads made it purgatorial. We towed the loads behind us like sledges, lowered them in front of us, or sent them rolling down under their own steam; any method rather than carrying them which only sank us deeper and deeper in the snow. At last, after passing at great speed under some hanging glaciers, where the Sherpas called loudly and effectively upon their gods, we reached dry glacier; the first of the Arwa branches which we called "A".

The sun had come out and now blazed down on us as if bent on making up for past deficiencies, and we spread ourselves and the loads out to dry. The Sherpas stretched themselves like lizards on rocks, bottom upwards, for they were over partial to sitting glissades and suffered accordingly. We had dropped over three thousand five hundred feet from the pass and the barometer now registered only 16,200 feet, though it was surprising it could register anything at all after the treatment the load in which it travelled had received. Pasang and Tilman had a little joke of their own about that barometer. When he saw us consulting it so earnestly he often asked Tilman what its name was, and upon being told "Shaitán" (Satan) he seemed to appreciate the name and thereafter took an affectionate interest in "Shaitán's" welfare.

The glacier on which we were camped was three-quarters of a mile wide and the watershed was now two miles west of us, but there was no crossing it here and we had to go still further north. On the opposite side of our glacier two subsidiary glaciers flowed down from the north, and of these we chose the westernmost for our route to the next branch of the Arwa.

The col at the head of this was about 18,000 feet and the approach to it not difficult. We left a small dump of food at our camp on "A" glacier, went up to the col and crossed it, and in the afternoon camped on the "névé" of what we called "B" glacier at 17,000 feet. From here we could see where our pass lay, still two miles north and two thousand feet higher, and the condition of the snow had up till now been so bad that we began to despair of reaching it. Soon after making camp it began to rain and as we had omitted to pitch the tents door to door and there was only the one "Primus", the party of five assembled in one tent to advise and assist in the cooking, thereby raising a very satisfactory "fug".

The rain turned to snow in the night and the morning was overcast, but by

8.30 we were ploughing slowly to the north with the watershed now close on our left hand. Had there been any drying power in the sickly sun which leered at us out of a big halo, sure presage of foul weather, Tilman would have made a passionate appeal for a later start. It was his privilege to carry the tents and he preferred them dry, the extra weight being a consideration but not nearly so objectionable as the water which seeped through on to his back.

That virtue is its own reward we were beginning to learn, for in the matter of early starts we found there was no other. At whatever hour in the day we were afoot the snow crust would never bear our weight, and we sank to our knees or waists as much at dawn as at midday. To-day we encountered an exceptionally bad patch in which we wallowed to the point of exhaustion, but as we neared the col conditions improved and by midday we gained the top (19,500 feet).* A desultory snowstorm prevented us seeing much but it was very noticeable how, as we came north, the hills assumed a more Tibetan aspect; the rock being reddish and loose, the slopes more gentle, and the tops flatter.

Below us a steep, loose gully led down for three hundred feet to a small glacier. The bottom of the gully was iced, and below the *bergschrund* gaped hospitably. We descended one at a time in order to avoid the danger of loose stones. On the icy bit Pasang parted company with his load which headed straight for the abyss, but fortunately jumped it and was fielded by myself on the far side. Long-suffering "Shaitán" had had yet another narrow escape!

The glacier we were now on was badly crevassed and to Tilman, who was in front, it seemed to fulfil somebody's definition of a sieve, "a lot of holes held together by wire". He duly fell into one but his load got wedged and held him up very comfortably. Pasang, the next man, was unaware of this and before Tilman could explain matters had nearly pulled him in two with the rope, thinking, not unnaturally, that he was dangling over space. For the next fortnight every deep breath fetched a groan from poor Tilman's battered ribs, the burden of their groaning being "Save me from my friends".

Above a deep ice-fall we forsook the glacier for a scree slope and were soon at the bottom on another much bigger glacier, fortunately "dry", and flowing due west. We camped on some rocks in the middle of this and now the snow which had fallen fitfully all day, stopped for a moment. There, looking down the glacier, we saw in the distance the wall of another valley crossing it at right angles, unmistakably the Gangotri. This was a cheering sight – moreover we now had water at hand instead of snow to melt, and one of us, gifted with a strong imagination, conceived the happy idea of mixing raisins in the dough for our "chupatties" – and so in great content to bed.

Again it snowed all night and was still at it in the morning, so we stayed in bed singing doleful songs which presently had the desired effect, for the snow stopped. Dumping two days' food here we started down the glacier, doing the first mile on "dry" ice very quickly. Then we got into a jumble of moraine and spent the next two hours clambering in and out of great hollows. Finally we won clear and got on to a smooth lateral moraine on the right bank, and soon the

*The cols and glaciers of the Arwa are mapped in detail on p.280 of *Kamet Conquered*. Although *Abode of Snow* states that they used Birnie's Col, this is probably incorrect – an easier pass to the north providing the route. (Editor)

sight of a few flowers gladdened our ice-weary eyes. We made five miles that day in spite of a long, luxurious halt at midday, when the sun came out and we basked and dried our sodden loads. The colours in this valley were most striking, for besides the vivid patches of green provided by the grass there were bold splashes of red, blue, and white rock. As yet we had found no juniper but we promised ourselves a fire next day.

We camped that night in a pleasant alp only two miles from the Gangotri ice-stream, but our friendly moraine had petered out and the going promised to be rough. For once we woke to a fine morning (July 27th) and looking out of the open tent-flap we saw a sight which fairly made us spring from our bags. West across the Gangotri floated, high up, a silvery spire, graceful as that of Salisbury, and sparkling in the early sun.[1] It seemed poised in mid-air, for the base on which it rested was momentarily hidden and revealed by the mists writhing upwards from the valley.

By 10 o'clock we reached the junction of our unknown "X" glacier[2] and the Gangotri, and we halted on a friendly alp to discuss our next move, watched by an inquisitive herd of bharal from the cliffs behind. We had imagined that the glacier which we had come down would join the Gangotri five miles above the snout, and we were now, at a guess, ten miles from the head. We much wanted to visit both, the head because no one had seen it, and the snout because many had. We felt that to come to the Gangotri Glacier and not see Gaumukh, the Cow's Mouth, the birthplace of Mother Ganges, would be like going to Cairo without seeing the Pyramids; at least one of us felt this but the other was not so sure, and an interesting debate began as to whether sightseers and trippers (which we were in danger of becoming) were to be emulated or despised. Before the question was put, the debate being still in progress, the clearing mist revealed a river not three miles away, a sight which altered things considerably for it meant we could go down to Gaumukh and back in the day. We camped where we were and unashamedly set forth as trippers.

We made our pilgrimage to Gaumukh from the wrong direction, and if the merit acquired is proportionate to the energy expended, ours must have been great. There was no lateral moraine on our side and we toiled by devious ways through chaotic hills and valleys of ice strewn with gigantic boulders, the short two and a half miles taking us a long two hours. On the way we passed the mouth of a valley lying parallel to the glacier we had descended, but there was no indication of it on our map and this omission gave us a feeling of quite unmerited superiority to map-makers in general and the author of this map in particular. We ought to have blessed him for giving us something to correct, whereas we made lofty and scornful remarks about slipshod work; but in less exalted moments we did appreciate at their true worth the labour and skill which had gone to the making of a map that was never meant for mountaineers.

Drab though the scene was, like the tongue of any glacier, it was impossible to be unmoved at sight of the turbid flood rushing from a black ice cave under the towering wall of ice which marked the end of the Gangotri Glacier, and to reflect that here, where it was a bare thirty feet wide, the Ganges began a journey of fifteen hundred miles to the Bay of Bengal into which it poured

[1]Probably Shivling   [2]The Chaturangi Glacier (Editor)

through many mouths, one alone full twenty miles wide. When one further reflected that from sea to source it was regarded with veneration by more than two hundred million human beings who, in life, believe that to bathe in it is to be cleansed from sin, and at death ask no more but that their ashes may be cast upon its waters, one had a combination of stupendous spiritual and physical marvels which could hardly be equalled elsewhere in the world.

Not wishing to acquire a double dose of merit, we returned by an easier way on the south side of the glacier where, beyond a high moraine, were grassy flats brilliant with flowers and watered by meandering streams. Opposite to our camp we recrossed the mile-wide glacier and the Sherpas welcomed us with a cheerful juniper fire and a dish of wild rhubarb, not quite equal in flavour to that of the Rishi Ganga, but rare and refreshing for all that.

We had left dumps of food on the way for the return journey but we still had two days' food in hand, and the question was what we should now do. Our tripper instincts being satisfied, the explorer instinct was asserting itself. We wanted to traverse the whole length of the Gangotri Glacier, but with only two days at our disposal we could not get far. As we were discussing alternatives inspiration came to us, borne perhaps on the wings of the wild rhubarb, and such was the attractiveness of this fresh plan that we decided to return to Badrinath forthwith to put it into execution.

On July 28th we started back up "X" glacier and two days later camped at the foot of the small glacier leading to the pass; the weather was clearer than when we came down and we could now sketch in the many lateral branches. Mindful of the loose stones in the gully we made an early start on the 29th and went up to the pass as fast as we could in order to tackle the gully while it was yet frozen up. Tilman, as last man, was in the best position for feeling the results of and criticising careless movements on the part of the others, but thanks to our early start, and the Sherpas' Agag-like tread, we reached the top without shifting a stone. On the other side snow conditions were now better and we pushed on past our old camp and straight down "B" glacier, for instead of crossing the second pass back to "A" glacier and our food dump, we had decided to go round by the Arwa Valley and camp at the foot of "A" glacier, retrieving our food next day.

By the time we were clear of "B" glacier and heading down the valley the weather became very thick and we had some difficulty in locating the snout of "A". At last we came to a stream issuing from a glacier, and assuming it was "A" we camped. Next morning Angtharkay and Pasang started early up the glacier, which we devoutly hoped might be the right one, though any doubts we had we kept to ourselves. They found the dump, but did not get back till afternoon, by which time it was raining, so we declared our half-holiday a whole one.

We now held all streams, of whatever size, in the greatest respect and to avoid having anything to do with the one by which we were camped, we went up to the glacier and crossed on the ice. In these uncongenial surroundings we were surprised to meet a large flock of goats going up the valley, and it is to be assumed the shepherds knew where they were going for as yet we had not seen a blade of grass, and even a Tibetan goat would jib at a stone and water diet.

The nearer we approached to home the worse became the weather, as it had in the Rishi, and a searching wind blew up the valley, bringing with it a cold rain. We huddled in the lee of a boulder to brew the last of our tea and then, pushing on, we got on to the track which came down from the Mana Pass. Here we met a Tibetan and two women living in a tent which was remarkable for its superior ventilation, and with them the Sherpas had a long chat. In appearances there was not much to choose between our party and the Tibetan; of both it was true to say that they were without visible means of support. But it seemed that they were the less destitute and they presented the Sherpas with a handful of twigs. I was struck by the kindliness of this gesture, for it was no more than that, the twigs hardly sufficing for tinder, let alone a fire. In this, however, I was under a misapprehension, because when I mentioned it to the Sherpas I was told that the gift was tea!

We carried on till 5 o'clock, getting wetter and colder, hopefully expecting to find some juniper wood, but at last we resigned ourselves to the bleak prospect of one more fireless night which a brew of the Tibetan's firewood did something to ameliorate.

Next day, August 2nd, we crossed the upper end of the same remarkable Saraswati gorge whose lower end we had crossed on the way out. It ran for half a mile to the mouth of the Alaknanda Valley like a gigantic slit, and was but a few yards across at the top, while the river roared through, heard but not seen, two or three hundred feet beneath. The track crossed it here, as below, by a natural rock bridge and passing through the village of Mana we were presently in Badrinath and busy with letters and preparations for our next venture.

Part 4

The Second Crossing of the Watershed
(Badrinath – Kedarnath)

CHAPTER THIRTEEN

TWO days' rest enabled us to explore Badrinath and its surroundings more fully. On our first view of the town itself we had been greatly disappointed as, upon breasting the last steep rise from Joshimath, our minds filled with the severe grandeur of the country through which we had passed, we looked down on a hideous huddle of tin huts and were grieved by the thoughtlessness of man in introducing such ugliness to the mountains. The roll on the drum, which welcomed all incoming pilgrims and had its length and loudness nicely adjusted to the stranger's probable generosity, was an added irritation and the temple itself did nothing to modify our first impressions. It was of no great height and so hemmed in by houses that little could be seen until close up to it, while even the façade, upon which there was some really fine carving, had a ramshackle appearance.

But on our second visit, when we viewed the temple from the far side of the river, we realised better the extraordinary atmosphere of the place and the lure that had drawn men to it throughout the ages. For at Badrinath, Krishna, probably the best beloved of all Hindu gods and one of nine incarnations of Vishnu (a tenth is expected in the future) was supposed to have "practiced austerities", as the saying goes. Since "he stood here for one hundred years on one foot, with arms aloft, subsisting on air, with his outer garments thrown off and his body emaciated and with veins swollen," and since but one of his exploits was to lift a huge mountain on one finger to shelter some milkmaids from the wrath of Indra, the god of the skies and rain, we felt that "austerities" was an understatement to say the least.

On the bank opposite the temple was a bathing pool fed by a hot spring, with steps leading down from it to the leaping, icy waters of the Alaknanda, where a ring-bolt was sunk in the rock so that the pilgrim might cling to it while undergoing his ceremonial bath. By this baptism and by worship by Badrinath a man might obtain whatever he desired and all sins of former births were cleansed if the deity was supplicated through the priest. A legend proving the efficacy of this relates how one Janami Jaya slew eighteen Brahmans (whether rivals for or guardians of the lady we are not told), in order to possess a beautiful girl whom he met out hunting. Even for this enormity a visit to Badrinath was sufficient atonement! When one remembers that the Rawal or priest here, and at Kedarnath and other important centres, is usually a Brahman from southern India of the Vaishnava sect, and that he is assisted by a secretary or clerk who is also from these parts, the above story seems all the more remarkable.

The origin of this custom of a Brahman priest seemed very remote, but apparently, at one time the ancient religion was supplanted by Buddhism until there arose the reformer, one Sankara, a native of Mysore. The century in which he lived is doubtful but is thought to be about the eighth A.D., and he was particularly active in Nepal and Kumaon, where he drove out the Buddhists and unbelievers and restored the ancient faith. He displaced the Buddhist priests of Badrinath and Kedarnath and in their places introduced priests from the Dhakin and Mysore. Everywhere through his followers he preached the efficacy of pilgrimage to the holy shrines, and there is no doubt that the consequent – and lasting – influx of orthodox pilgrims prevented Kumaon from a second relapse into Buddhism.

Brahmans, the priestly caste, are thus seen to be very powerful, but in many proverbial sayings the lower castes have published their defects. The most glaring seems to be an eye for the main chance, as hinted at in the saying: "Brahmans and vultures spy out corpses"; while in another instance we see a case of diamond cut diamond or two of a trade when we are told: "The Brahman blessed the barber and the barber showed his glass."

But these legends, if believed in and acted upon wholesale, might lead to results which would tax the forgiving powers of even the Badrinath deities, and to offset this there is another little story which inculcates more desirable conduct. A wealthy trader who had ten sons was told to go to Badrinath with his family and his property, there to give all his possessions to the Brahmans and to make his home, thus securing his admission to Paradise. But while living there his wife (who seemingly had her own views as to property) lost a valuable ivory ring, and the sages then told her that as penance for this duplicity in holding back a valuable article, the family must once more do the round of the "tirthas" or places of pilgrimage. When this had been accomplished and they were back in Badrinath, the elephant whose tusk had provided the ivory for the ring suddenly appeared and conveyed the whole family at once to the paradise of Vishnu.

Of men brought up on such traditional tales, none who believed could resist the promises of desires fulfilled and past misdeeds forgotten, and at some period in their lives the majority of Hindus visit one or more of the holy shrines. Judging by the swarms of pilgrims met with on the road and in the town most of them had chosen Badrinath.

Among the many legends of these parts believed to have been founded on fact is a story that, many hundred years ago, there was no high priest of the

Kedarnath Temple, and that the high priest of Badrinath used to hold services in the temples of both places on the same day. The shortest known route between the two temples was well over one hundred miles, and over a high mountain pass at that. Tradition has it that a quick way across the watershed was known to the priests of those days. But although the natives believe that the two places are only two and a half miles apart, in actual fact, the distance is some twenty-four miles as the crow flies.

Our observations from the Bhagat Kharak had suggested to us that if a pass could be found from the head of the Satopanth, it would lead us into the Kedarnath Valley system. If this proved to be the case, we should stand very little chance of getting down on the other side, owing to the immense depth of the valley there. However, a view from the crest of the watershed would solve for us many interesting problems.

We had intended to return to the Rishi Ganga about August 10th, and August had already come round. But by now we were thoroughly absorbed in the manifold problems of this range, and to have come away without investigating the head of the Satopanth Glacier would have left our task only half finished.

We did not have the same difficulty as before in collecting men to accompany us, but on the morning of our departure, the porters, despite an early appearance, had neglected to have any food before they left their homes three miles away. Consequently we had to fume for a full hour while they made good this oversight – an unpropitious start!

A dense mantle of cloud still hung over the peaks, as we began to plod up the valley towards Mana and, remembering our little *contretemps* with the Bhasudhara River of a few weeks earlier, we kept this time to the southern bank of the Alaknanda. This provided us with only a narrow walking space under great perspiring, mossy cliffs, down whose black sides streamed a thousand tiny waterfalls, but luckily there was quite a presentable sheep track which allowed our attention to wander from the main business of getting along to the enjoyment of impressive scenery about us, and, a mile or so further on, the valley widened out and provided a stretch of moderately flat grass-land.

Suddenly, with a shout of joy, the Sherpas dumped down their loads and set to work collecting some small, light-blue berries which grew in great quantities amongst the grass. They brought us handfuls of these with great enthusiasm, saying that the berries were considered a delicacy in Sola Kombu, where they came from. On tasting them we found that they had a flavour remarkably like that of tooth-paste, and were certainly pleasanter to look upon than to eat.

At 3 o'clock we came to a small isolated wood of birch and rhododendron about half a mile below the snout of the glacier. We had seen this from the opposite side and had looked forward with relish to the luxury of a blazing camp-fire. But by now it had started to rain again and the locals were still a long way behind. Before we could get the tents pitched we were wet through. There was no dry wood at hand and it was an hour or so before we had sufficient fire to brew some tea, and that only by dint of continuous blowing on the part of

Kusang. The rain having cheated us out of a blissful lounge before blazing embers we retired to our leaky tents with an unpleasant foreboding of what was in store for us higher up.

Awakening to the song of birds and the exhilarating freshness of a perfect morning, our spirits rose and eclipsed the gloom of the night before. Our meal of satu and tea completed, we were content to sit and dry ourselves and our tents in the slanting rays of the morning sun.

It was with an effort that we packed up and started up the boulder-strewn valley. We found that the locals had spent the night in a nearby cave in company with some shepherds, who when we passed their shelter appeared to have not the least intention of stirring themselves for some time to come. What a delightfully carefree life they must lead, requiring nothing but the bare necessities of life, living always up in this wonderland of Nature, with little to worry about and nothing to hurry about; knowing nothing of the filth and squalor of our modern civilisation!

Shortly after leaving camp we came to the corner of the Satopanth Valley and turning half left we made our way along the grass slopes at the sides of the glacial moraine. The slackness of the morning remained with us and we made frequent halts to gaze up at the huge ice-clad precipices about us.

Soon we came in sight of the head of the glacier, still many miles away, and were able to get an uninterrupted view of the gap we hoped to cross. From now on little else interested us and we talked of nothing but the "col". Was it practicable even from this side? Where would it lead us? Back on to the great Gangotri Glacier? Or over the range to Kedarnath? We argued that point over and over again. I felt most convinced that if we succeeded in reaching its crest we would see a great snow-field descending gently before us, turning northwards and forming eventually the Gangotri ice-stream which we had reached a few weeks before. Tilman on the other hand held the other view, that the main Gangotri-Kedarnath watershed was to the north of us and that if we succeeded in crossing the gap we would find ourselves amongst the Kedarnath valleys. The discussion waxed heated in spite of Tilman's common-sense suggestion that we should wait and see.

As was the case on the Bhagat Kharak Glacier our chief concern now was how far we could go up the glacier before our supply of firewood ended. We could not expect the locals to spend a night above the limit of fire-wood, though we could transport sufficient for one night. So we had to aim at pitching our camp as near as possible at the upper limits of the dwarf juniper. As the valley ascended at a very gentle angle this line was by no means easy to gauge.

The going was easy and we made rapid progress, walking on the crest of a kindly lateral moraine which ran for miles down the southern end of the Satopanth Glacier.

Late in the day we came upon a lateral glacier flowing into the main ice-stream from the south. This glacier was fed almost entirely by ice-avalanches falling from the ice-cliffs of Nilkanta, and in the angle formed by the junction we found an alp whose attractions as a camp site were irresistible. So we spread ourselves out in the sun and basked until the chill of evening sent us to our sleeping-bags. Mine that night was squeezed in between two rocks, a position which was more suitable for contemplation of the infinite than for sleep.

The Mana shepherds occasionally brought their sheep far up these moraine-covered glaciers, and we came across a great many piles of stones hung with prayer flags as in Tibet. These prayer flags were simply bits of rag on which were written prayers. Each flap was supposed to emit one repetition of the prayer written thereon, and consequently on a windy day the hanger of a flag could get through many thousands of prayers in the course of a few hours.

(A similar, and, I should judge, a more effective praying-machine is the prayer-wheel which is commonly used in Tibet. This consists of a drum wrapped round with paper on which are written countless thousands of prayers. Each revolution of the drum emits one repetition of all the prayers written on it. The large prayer-wheels are worked by water power and must get through sufficient praying in one week to insure for each member of the village a high place in the hereafter.)

The going now became very rough as we had to cross a succession of side glaciers, each bringing down on its surface a perfect wilderness of boulders. This meant the usual wearisome performance. Toiling up a long slope of large stones balanced precariously on the ice, balancing along an edge above a yawning crevasse, jumping from a boulder or slithering down some icy slope beyond.

At about 2 o'clock on August 7th we reached a point at which the moraine-covered surface of the main glacier gave place to bare ice only half a mile or so from the cliffs which enclosed the Satopanth Glacier. Across the valley we recognized our old friend Kunaling*, from this side presenting a very much more formidable appearance.

We decided that this was the best point from which to launch our attack on the gap, and dismissing the Mana men, we pitched our tents just before a strong wind descended on us from across the ice.

Shortly after an ominous dawn on the following morning we shouldered our heavy loads and tramped slowly across the ice in the direction of the col.

It appeared to us that there was not much choice of route. A steep ice-fall descending direct from the col seemed to be the only way. The line of rock cliffs which bounded it on the left appeared far too steep in its lower section to offer much chance even of getting a footing on them from the glacier. The ice-fall did not look too difficult, though it was certainly very broken in its upper section. So it was towards the ice-fall that we turned.

Over the level stretch of ice we made quick time, but when the angle steepened up our heavy loads made themselves felt and the straps bit cruelly into our shoulders. It was a sultry, windless morning and we were oppressed by an intense lassitude. The ice was bare of snow and steps had to be chipped, though the angle was quite moderate. Our pace became painfully slow.

Soon the ice became broken and complicated, and we came to a section where climbing with a load on one's back was impossible. The leader had to cut steps up the rickety piece of ice and haul the loads after him. The section was only some thirty feet high, but it cost us a good hour to negotiate, and from here the climbing needed the utmost care and called for much step cutting.

*The peak referred to is probably Chaukhamba – the highest in the Gangotri area. (Editor)

However, it had the advantage of taking our minds off our sore shoulders and aching thighs.

We climbed steadily for some hours, making long detours to avoid crevasses and ice-cliffs and we were within a thousand feet of the crest of the gap when we were brought up by a yawning chasm whose bottom was lost to view, hundreds of feet down the icy depths below us. Dumping our loads, we hunted this way and that, but could find no place which offered the slightest chance of crossing this formidable obstacle.

This was a bitter disappointment. After all that weary toil we had but one thousand feet to go to learn the solution of the riddle which had been occupying our minds for so long.

We descended for a few hundred feet when it occurred to us that we might be able to find a way off the ice on to the upper part of the rock cliffs to the south. Dumping our loads once more, we worked our way over towards the edge of the ice-fall. Reaching it we saw that just below us was a point at which we could get on to the rocks immediately above the steep section below. We could not see how far the rocks would take us, but it was worth trying, and with fresh hope we returned to our loads and pitched camp in the midst of the tangled mass of the ice-fall.

By now it was snowing heavily, and our small tents soon resembled chips off the great ice-blocks which surrounded them. Night fell to the accompaniment of an almost continuous roar of ice-avalanches from the great cliffs of Kunaling above us, and into the early hours of the morning the thunder of falling ice continued. Though our position was quite safe, being well protected by the crevasses and ice-cliffs about us, several times during the night I was brought to a sitting position, trembling, as some particularly large avalanche fell close at hand.

Snow fell gently all the while, and was still falling when we awoke to a grey and unpromising dawn. In consequence of this we made a later start than we had intended. The tents were wet and the loads were heavier in consequence.

Through the mist we could see only a small section of the face of rock above us. Several of the gullies showed signs of recent stone falls and the rock was damp and slippery. When we reached it, however, we found that the angle was easier than it had appeared from below and we mounted at quite satisfactory speed, hurrying here and there when we were obliged to cross one or other of the stone-swept gullies.

Higher up the mist became really thick and we had to grope our way up the rock face – through the still gently-falling snow as if blind-fold.

On the previous day Tilman had fallen and injured another of his ribs, and climbing under such a heavy load as he was obliged to carry caused him considerable pain.

The route-finding now became complicated and we had to trust mainly to a sense of direction. Ridge, gully and rock-facet followed one another in monotonous series, until after a step round an awkward corner we found ourselves at the base of a blunt ice-ridge which we had seen from below.

Chipping small steps in the ice we mounted to the crest of the ridge. From here we caught a glimpse below us of the ice-fall in which we had camped. We followed the crest along until it landed us on what appeared to be a great ice-plateau. The mist was still thick about us and we could only guess at the direction to be followed. We plodded on for half an hour and then halted and pitched the tents.

Our height was 18,400 feet and we calculated that we must be just about on the crest of the col.

Snow was still falling lightly and a southerly wind was blowing. All five of us crowded into one of the tents and sat huddled up waiting for the Primus stove to melt some ice and heat the water sufficiently to make tea. But the Primus had sprung a leak somewhere and had to be pumped up continuously. We waited for two hours before the water was sufficiently warm to absorb any colour from the tea-leaves, and we began to realise that if we were to have a prolonged sojourn on the glaciers we would not have enough fuel for anything but the simple production of water.

That night we were content with a cup of tepid pemmican soup before we turned into our sleeping-bags. At dusk it started to freeze very hard and we became more hopeful about the weather.

Our cheerless camp had done nothing to damp our excitement at having reached the col, and we could hardly curb our impatience for the view which would tell us where the col was leading us.

I still held to the theory that we were at the mysterious head of the Gangotri Glacier. The level stretch of ice over which we had come seemed to indicate the head of a long, gently-flowing glacier. Shortly after dark there was a momentary clearing of the mists above us and we caught the sight of the great buttresses of Kunaling to north of us and those of another, unnamed peak to the south. But in front, a great sea of cloud still withheld from us the secret of our whereabouts.

I spent much of the long, cold night praying fervently for a fine morning, which the frost gave me good reason to expect.

I was disappointed, however, and when I looked out of the tent door at dawn it was into the same "pea-soup" as on the night before.

After a cup of warm satu, Tilman and I left the camp and started off in a south-westerly direction to reconnoitre.

The surface of snow we were on soon began to fall away in front of us in an ever steepening curve. Shortly after leaving camp we were jumping over and threading our way through a network of small crevasses, and we had not gone far before we were brought up short by a vertical drop of about one hundred and fifty feet. Beyond this a great tangle of ice-cliffs showed us that we were on the brink of an ice-fall.

It was useless to attempt to find a way through it with a visibility of only fifty yards, and we sat down on the edge of the cliff and waited. The outlook was pretty hopeless as the glacier was narrow at this point and the ice-cliffs seemed to stretch the whole width.

We had been waiting for half an hour when all of a sudden the fog rolled away from below us, and we found ourselves looking down into the immense depths of a cloud-filled valley at our feet. The glacier we were on descended in a steep ice-fall for about a thousand feet, then flattened out into a fairly level stretch of ice before it heeled over for its final colossal plunge into the gloom of the gorge six thousand feet below us.

This was obviously not the Gangotri ice-stream, which at its snout, some twenty miles from here, is 13,000 feet high. Tilman had been right and we were looking down into the Kedarnath Valley system, from the "pass" said to have been known to the ancient high priest of Badrinath.

Our little problem was solved, but the grim aspect of the ice-falls below us offered little hope for our succeeding in our project of finding a direct route between the two temples.

After some search we were able to trace a route through the first ice-fall. We hurried back to the camp, reaching it just as Angtharkay and Kusang were starting out to look for us, fearing that we might have come to grief in a crevasse.

Packing up the tents we shouldered our loads once more and made our way down towards the ice-fall. By now the clouds had enveloped us again and we had a difficult job to find the route we had traced through the maze of ice-cliffs and crevasses of which the ice-fall was made up.

In and out of great ice-corridors, past towers and turrets of all shapes and sizes, we worried our way; balancing across slender ice-bridges, which spanned gaping crevasses whose icy depths seemed illimitable; toiling up some bulge which obstructed our path and clinging our way down the slippery banks of its further side.

At length we found ourselves on the flat stretch of ice we had seen from above. Going to its further edge we halted for a few moments to gaze down upon the head of the second and very formidable ice-fall. It was appallingly steep, and for a long time we could not see any way of attacking it which offered the slightest hope of success.

Immediately in front was a sheer drop of some hundreds of feet to the head of the ice-fall itself.

After a careful examination it occurred to us that it might be possible to descend the ice-fall for some distance on its right-hand side, and then force a way off on to the cliffs which bounded it in that direction. Beyond this we could not see, but these cliffs appeared to fall away vertically to the valley still some five thousand feet below.

We worked over to the right and descended for some time before we were brought up by an impassable crevasse. Search as we would we could not find a way of descending a yard further or of reaching the rocks to our right; so very slowly we toiled our weary way back to the level section where we sat for some minutes sucking lumps of ice in vain attempt to assuage a burning thirst.

By this time the weather had cleared somewhat and as we made our way over to the left-hand side of the glacier we saw that by traversing along an ice ledge under some evil-looking seracs we might get down five hundred feet below the level section. Beyond this the glacier disappeared from view on account of the steepness of the angle.

We started to traverse below the seracs and the Sherpas as usual burst into their monotonous praying chant, evidently beseeching the demons of the ice world not to throw things at us.

Hurrying across the débris of a recent fall, we found ourselves at the brink of the glacier's final downward plunge. So steep was it indeed that we thought that we must be standing on the upper part of a hanging glacier.

We dumped our loads on the ice and set off down on what seemed to be an utterly futile errand. But it was the last chance, and we thought we might as well finally prove the thing to be impossible so as to be able, later, to find comfort in that fact. Also the Sherpas, for some reason, were almost frantically keen to get down, and would not admit that the thing could not be done. Whether this attitude of theirs was an outcome of their extreme loyalty to us, or whether they were taking a personal interest in the exploration I cannot say. But in any case it was typical of the fine spirit of these men that, from the time we had left the Satopanth Glacier, they seemed willing to go almost to any lengths to get over that pass. Their loyalty to the expedition did not cause them merely to carry out our instructions; they understood our aims and did everything in their power to see that we realised them.

With these allies we hope, one day, to reach the summit of Mount Everest; without them we would have little hope of doing so.

I have often found that towards the end of a long, tiring day's mountaineering one gets a sudden rejuvenation, particularly when faced with a problem of unusual severity . It was certainly the case this evening and we set about that ice-fall as if our lives depended upon our getting down.

The work was intricate and needed delicate handling as a slip would have had serious consequences. The further we advanced the steeper became the ice until further downward progress on the glacier itself became an impossiblity.

We worked our way over to the left until we came to the left-hand edge of the ice-fall. Standing on a small promontory we looked down a sheer drop of some two hundred feet into a steep gully which separated the ice-fall from the rock cliffs bounding it on that side. We saw that if we could reach the floor of the gully we might be able to work our way down between the ice and the rock. But the two-hundred foot drop at our feet appeared quite impossible. Tilman and I sat down feeling that we had reached the end of our tether.

But Pasang and Angtharkay refused to admit defeat and asked to be allowed to try the wall below us. We consented; and they roped up on a short rope and gave us an exhibition of calm, surefooted climbing whose equal it has rarely been my fortune to witness.

After some twenty minutes they were back with us admitting that the face below was too much even for them. But Angtharkay's blood was up and no sooner had he recovered his breath than he started traversing to the left and soon disappeared from view behind an ugly ice bulge.

Minutes passed as we waited with bated breath. Then, crash! a great chunk of ice hurtled down and smashed itself into a thousand pieces on the floor of the gully, sending up along the cliffs a rolling echo. I think my heart missed several beats before a shout from Angtharkay assured us that all was well. Presently his head appeared from behind the ice bulge, and we saw that his face wore a broad grin.

He informed us that he had found a ledge from which it might be possible to lower our loads and ourselves.

With this hope we raced up our steps back to the loads. It was beginning to get dark and we had yet to find a suitable camp site and get ourselves fixed for the night. To have attempted to get down into the gully that night would have been too much to expect of them. Also, lower down, the gully was overhung by some ice-cliffs and it would be dangerous to pass under these at any other time than the morning.

I spent most of the night tossing about our uncomfortable perch, though it was not so much the discomfort of my bed as excitement which kept me awake.

CHAPTER FOURTEEN

WE had decided not to bother about food or drink in the morning, and as soon as it was light we were packing up the tents and getting ready to start. It was a fine morning and for the first time we were able to get a view down into the valley we were making for, the upper part of which was now only two thousand feet below us.

A level stretch of glacier some three miles long ended in what looked like a pleasantly wooded valley. About a mile below the glacier there seemed to be a bit of a "cut-off", and below that dark vegetation stretched away as far as the eye could see. This we took to be pine forest, while far beneath we could see patches of light green interspersed amongst the forest.

Two days marching at the most, we thought, would take us through this pleasant looking country to some habitation. Also it seemed reasonable to suppose that we would strike a forest path or game track and be able to cover, if necessary, some twelves miles a day. We knew that it could be no very great distance from the snout of the glacier to the great Kedarnath pilgrim route.

Working along Angtharkay's ledge, clinging close to the cold clammy walls of glacier ice, we reached the little platform from which we were to lower ourselves and our kit. It was an unpleasant place, enclosed on all sides by walls of sickly green ice, and it required but the slightest slip to send one crashing into the depths below, while the most careful handling was needed to save the loads from a similar fate.

Pasang was lowered down into the gully and he stood there ready to receive the baggage. It was painful work. The rope, wet from contact with the snow on the previous day, was now frozen stiff and cut cruelly into our numb fingers.

It took us two hours of hard work before we were safely assembled on the floor of the gully, and it was with feelings of some relief that we turned our backs upon the scene of our labours.

Now the climbing became more straight-forward and for the first time since leaving the Satopanth Glacier we were able to dispense with the rope. Hurrying over the section threatened from above by the ice-cliffs we were soon able to break out of the gully to the left where the angle of the cliffs eased off about a thousand feet above the level stretch of glacier in the valley. This we managed to reach by means of an intricate zig-zag course down the intervening slopes.

After a few moments "breather" we raced down the glacier at top speed, leaping the crevasses in our stride. We were full of pleasant anticipation of a camp in some grassy meadow below the glacier. We were doomed to disappointment. For on leaving the glacier we found ourselves immersed in a tangle of sappy, green vegetation about eight feet high through which we had to hack our way. So thick was it, that we could not see where we were going and all we could do was to stumble on blindly.

We cleared a small space and sat down for a meal, after which we flogged our way on in the hope of finding a better camping place before nightfall. By now it had started raining and the contact with the sodden undergrowth soaked us to the skin. In addition to this the floor of the valley was made up of large boulders which were completely screened by the undergrowth, and at every few steps one stumbled into some pot-hole between the rocks. Brambles soon made their appearance and added to our difficulties.

Late in the evening, after some two hours of this work, we reached the edge of the great cut-off which we had seen from above. This proved to be a sheer drop of some one thousand two hundred feet in the floor of the valley. There was no time to look for a way down the gaunt crags and we had to make shift for the night. After an hour's work we had cleared a muddy space underneath a boulder and collected some sodden stumps of juniper with which to make a fire.

Squatting huddled up under the boulder which afforded scant protection from the rain, vainly trying to dry our sodden garments before the smouldering logs, we discussed our position. Our supply of food was beginning to run low and we had no idea how far we would have to go before we reached the first habitation where we could obtain more supplies with which to carry on. If the going had been good, there would have been little doubt that we could force our way through, however pressed we were for food. But our experience since leaving the glacier had given us an unpleasant taste of what we must expect lower down. The precipice below us might prove to be impassable or cost us much of our valuable time; and with time went food.

Again: what of the side-streams which we must meet further down the valley? By now we had considerable respect for this form of obstacle, which we knew could not only hold us up but completely block our way.

The only alternative was to struggle back up the ice-fall and over the pass back to Badrinath. The matter had to be decided here and now, for as it was, we would have to go all out to get back over the pass before our food and fuel ran out altogether.

The prospect of retracing our steps and committing ourselves once more to the icy slopes we had just left, did not appeal to us in the least. Moreover, the weather showed no signs of improvement and we might quite well be held up by a fall of new snow on the pass.

Starvation high up on the glacier, besides being more unpleasant, would be very much harder to fight against than it would be in a forest, where at least we would be able to make a fire. On the other hand, in going down we were taking a step into the unknown. The difficulties of the forest might easily take us some weeks to overcome, though, of course, we might strike some sort of a path tomorrow, or the next day. It was a difficult problem on which to make a decision, and we sat discussing it long into the night before retiring to our damp sleeping-bags.

On visualising the position over again I think undoubtedly the wisest plan would have been to go back up the ice, and several times during the week which followed, we sincerely wished we had done so. I am afraid that the fact that we wanted to make the complete crossing of this most intriguing range weighed too heavily on us all, and the downward course was decided upon.

The rain had stopped by the morning and we optimistically delayed our departure in order to get some of the water out of the tents and sleeping-bags. That this was a mere waste of time we were soon to realise. However, it gave us time to look around and decide on the best course of action for attacking our immediate problem, the descent of the thousand foot cut-off.

It was an impressive affair. The river, here of quite sizable dimensions, disappeared underground for a short distance above the bank of the precipice and issued forth in a great waterspout to crash down into the depths below. Owing to this we were able to get from one side of the valley to the other without difficulty and could choose either side down which to make our descent.

A short examination of the left-hand side of the valley convinced us that there was no practicable route to be found there, and so, striking camp, we committed ourselves to a search on the right-hand side. Here we fought our way for a quarter of a mile up and along the side of the valley and then began to descend. Clinging on to handfuls of matted undergrowth we clambered down, cursing our loads the while for their insistence on slipping sideways and often nearly dragging us down with them.

Soon we came to a vertical cliff whose rocky sides were too steep to hold any scrub, but whose cracks and crevices were filled with damp earth and moss. Balancing ourselves precariously above this we lowered Angtharkay, the lightest member of the party, on a rope, until he was able to get a footing on a grassy ledge below. Our loads followed in a similar manner. Then, tying two lengths of rope together and doubling them over a convenient juniper root, we slid down to join Angtharkay on his perch below.

Fortunately the side of the valley on which we were was made up of a series of terraces, which were not too widely separated from each other, and by repeating the process described above we eventually reached the densely forested floor of the valley.

Under the spread of the giant forest trees the undergrowth was not so thick and, walking for once in a normal attitude, we made fairly good progress until we reached the upper limit of bamboo. There, at least, was help against the exhaustion of our meagre food supply, and at 1 o'clock we called a halt and set about gathering a goodly quantity of the small soft cylinders which form the edible portion of the bamboo shoots. This, and the fact that lately we had not been battling through bramble scrub, put us in better spirits, and we almost forgot to call down curses on the rain which had by now started to fall again.

The bamboo was certainly our ally and was later to prove our salvation, but it was not an unmitigated blessing. Really dense bamboo provides an obstacle second only to thickly matted bramble, and when the valley narrowed and we were forced up on to its steep sides, the bamboo jungle reduced us once more to our weary hack, hacking of a way.

The almost impenetrable density of the jungle down by the river forced us to climb up the steep sides of the valley until we were about fifteen hundred feet above the stream. There we found ourselves in a zone of tall straight plants about nine feet high. The plants were crowned with a spray of most beautiful blue flowers, in shape rather like snapdragons. The growth was as dense as that of a good stand of corn, and, viewed from above, the general effect closely resembled a forest of English bluebells.

Through these lovely blue flowers we waded for three hours, each taking it in turns to go ahead and flog a path with our ice-axes.

Constantly throughout the day we came across fresh spoor which provided ample evidence that large numbers of bears inhabited the forest we were in. These animals, though not wantonly vindictive, possess very poor senses of sight and hearing and should one stumble upon them by accident they are liable to attack through sheer fright. The Sherpas were very alarmed at seeing the tracks of these beasts, and kept up a continuous shouting to give warning of our approach. They were very anxious too that the party should keep well together.

At about 5 o'clock the ground in front of us began to fall away steeply and, from the change in the tone of the river's roaring, we realised that we were approaching a sizeable side stream, coming down from the peaks of the Satopanth range. Pressing on through the forest we soon arrived at the edge of a ravine from whose unseen depths the thunder of a mighty torrent reached our ears. Looking up to the right we could see the turbulent white river booming its way down towards the gorge.

Here was a problem the seriousness of which we were not slow to recognise, for, if we could find no way of crossing the stream in front of us, we would be in a sorry plight, as now it was too late to think of a return across the pass by which we had come.

Going to the edge we examined the cliffs below us and saw at once that a direct descent into the ravine was out of the question. Moreover, even if we could get across thereabouts, it would be impossible to scale the sheer walls which formed the opposite side of the gorge.

Two alternatives were open to us. Either we could go down to the junction of this torrent with the main river, or we could follow the stream towards its source in the hope of being able to cross it higher up.

We could see that, above the junction, the stream issued from the confines of the ravine and ran for some twenty yards between moderately sloping banks before emptying itself into the main waterway. But here the stream was very broad and there appeared to be but small chance of bridging it at this point. On close scrutiny of the cliffs above the ravine, however, it seemed to us that there was one point where the opposing walls of rock met high above the level of the water.

At first I was sceptical about this and declared it to be an optical illusion produced by a bend in the river; for, although we had seen many such natural bridges during our travels in this amazing country, such formations are rare.

But after studying it for some minutes, I agreed with others that it was indeed a
natural bridge.

To reach it, however, would involve a climb of some two thousand feet, over
difficult ground, and we decided to pitch camp as soon as we found any water.
This was not an easy matter and we had climbed a long way up towards the
"bridge" before we came to a small trickling spring shortly before dark. We
were lucky in finding a nice level space on which to camp, and, after pitching the
tents and collecting a vast quantity of firewood, we settled down to an evening
which for sheer enjoyment would take a lot of beating, despite the fact that five
yards from the camp was a bear's lair. Luckily its recent occupant kept well
clear of the vicinity during our occupation of the camp.

Growing close at hand we found small clumps of forest fungus, which the
Sherpas declared to be edible. We collected a large quantity, but each piece was
subjected to a searching scrutiny by Angtharkay, and, for some obscure reason,
more than seventy-five per cent were rejected. However, in solidity they made
up for what they lacked in taste, and, together with the bamboo shoots, the
remainder provided us with a square meal. And this was more than welcome,
for on unpacking our sacks we found that what remained of our satu was
soaking wet and was rapidly going bad; this in spite of the fact that it had been
carefully packed in canvas bags.

Indeed, by now almost all our kit was water-logged an we resigned ourselves
to living in a state of perpetual wetness.

By now the rain had slackened, and after Kusang had blown the sodden logs
for an hour or so we sat before a blazing fire. But though it blazed and needed
no further encouragement, Kusang continued to blow late into the night.
Tilman conjured up a pleasant picture when he remarked that should Kusang
happen upon a house on fire, while others were fighting the flames, he would be
unable to resist the tempation of blowing on them!

Lying on a soft, sodden bed of leaves we basked in the glow of the fire. Warm
now and, for once, not hungry, we allowed our tobacco smoke to drug us into
forgetfulness of the worry which had seemed so acute throughout the long day.

It is astonishing how quickly warmth and a well-satisfied belly will change
one's outlook. We were too happy to question whether the bamboo and
mushrooms would remain with us all the way along, or whether kindly nature
had provided natural bridges over all the side streams which would cross our
path. Considering that we had had the "cut-off" to negotiate that morning our
estimated distance of a mile and a half did not seem bad. Later we came to look
upon a mile and a half as good progresss for a day's labour! Meantime we lay
peacefully in a half-doze, watching the firelight flickering on the great gnarled
branches above us and making weird play with their shadows.

It was raining more heavily than usual when we shouldered our loads next
morning and toiled on and up through the forest. Soon we came to dense
bramble and began once more the tedious job of fighting our way through it.
Our water-logged kit made our loads doubly heavy, weighing us down and
causing us to overbalance as we bent and twisted to rid ourselves of the clinging
thorns. Soon a dense mist descended upon us and we had to grope along the
ever-steepening side of the nala with only a hazy notion of where we were

going. Every now and then a steep-sided gully would bar the way and we would have to scramble up some hundreds of feet before we could find a place at which we could cross it.

After some hours of this, the mist cleared and we saw that we were near to the place where we thought we had seen the natural bridge spanning the gorge. Immediately we realised that we had been mistaken, and that the supposed "bridge" had indeed been an optical illusion!

Leaving our loads where we halted, we clambered on through the still heavily falling rain towards the stream. The rocks were steep and very slippery and we had to exercise extreme caution, for a slip would have deposited any one of us in the turbulent waters of the torrent some hundreds of feet below.

At length we reached a point from which we could command an uninterrupted view of the stream for some considerable distance above and below us. Below us the cliffs dropped sheer to the water's edge, while above, the river, descending in a series of waterfalls, did not permit the faintest hope either of fording or of bridging the stream.

We held a hurried consultation. Either we could go down to the junction in the small hope of bridging the torrent down there or we could work on upstream on the chance of finding better things above the point to which we could see. The Sherpas were very much against going down to the junction. On the other hand, to have gone up even to the spot to which we could see would have involved the best part of a day's climbing, and then what chance would we have had of finding a place to cross up there? Fording was out of the question and higher up we would find no trees with which to build a bridge. Much as I respected the judgment of the Sherpas, which in country of this sort had usually proved sounder than my own, at that moment I just could not face, on such a slender chance, the toil which the upward course would involve.

It was decided, therefore, that we should return to last night's camp site, leave our loads there, go down to the junction to examine the possibilities of bridging the stream, and return to the old camp for the night. This latter prospect was the one bright patch in a gloomy outlook.

We returned to our loads and made our way slowly back down the bramble-covered slopes, reaching our old camp at about 3.30. While Kusang blew upon the seemingly dead embers of the morning's fire we stood shivering in our soaking garments and reviewed our position. This certainly appeared unpleasant enough, for, if we failed to get across at the junction, two more days at least would be wasted before we could hope to find a way across on the higher route, and probably more, if indeed we could manage it at all. The work involved in getting along was heavy, and without food it would be well-nigh impossible.

At 4 o'clock, after swallowing some tepid tea, we raced off down towards the junction, leaving Kusang to build the fire and prepare a meal of the few bits of fungus which still grew near the camp. We were some eight hundred feet above the junction of the two rivers, but sliding down on the sodden carpet of leaves which formed the floor of the forest we reached it in a few minutes. That is to say we reached a point about a hundred feet above it, for the only way we could get down to the stream itself was by way of a steep gully. From a rock above we surveyed the stream as it issued from the mouth of the ravine. The water was obviously much above its normal level, and carried with it great quantities of mud. In the short stretch between the mouth of the ravine and the actual junction there was only one point which offered the slighest possibility of our constructing a bridge. There two rocks stood up well above the surging water, one close to either bank. If we could balance a tree trunk on these two rocks so that it lay across the stream, we could lay other trees diagonally across it and so make a sufficiently sound structure to enable us to cross. But from above, the rocks appeared much too far apart for us to be able to do this.

We climbed down the gully to the water's edge and, measuring the distance across roughly by means of a rope, we came to the conclusion that the thing must be attempted, then reascending the gully we selected some suitable pines which most luckily happened to be growing in small numbers hereabouts.

As it was growing dark we climbed the steep slope back to camp at a pace set by Pasang which left us with aching lungs and thudding hearts. And so we camped in exactly the same position as on the previous night, but with so much less food, considerably less confidence in our ability to cross the stream and with our sleeping-bags wetter than ever. As we ate our vegetarian meal, therefore, we lacked much of the content that had been with us twenty-four hours earlier.

The dawn of August 14th saw us sliding once more down the leafy slopes, albeit with more caution than previously by reason of our heavy packs. Dumping our loads at the water's edge, and noting thankfully that the stream was no more swollen than on the previous evening, we clambered back up the gully and set to work on the trees which we had marked the night before.

Pasang gave us a fine display with his kukri and after a few minutes the first tree crashed to the ground. Stripping it of its branches we dragged it to the edge and, heaving it to an upright position, tipped it into the gully, down which it crashed its way to the water's edge. Angtharkay and I then descended the gully to make the necessary preparations while the others worked above.

In a surprisingly short time three more trees had arrived at the edge of the stream and Tilman and the other Sherpas began to climb down the gully. Angtharkay and I were engaged in building a rock platform at the water's edge, when all at once there was a crash and looking up I saw a huge boulder hurtling down. The others seemed to be well to the side of the gully and I resumed my work thinking how lucky it was that they had not been lower down where the route lay in the actual floor of the gully.

A few moments later, chancing to look up, I saw Pasang leaning against one of the walls of the gully some way above me. His face was very pale and he was trembling. I scrambled up to him and found that the boulder had hit him a glancing blow on the left arm and left foot. It had even torn the lacing from his boot.

Helping him down to the foot of the gully I examined the damaged members. The arm, though temporarily useless to him seemed only to be badly bruised. His foot was very badly swollen and he could not move his toes. It looked as if one of the small bones on the top of the foot had been broken.

It was a nasty blow to us all, though I could not help being devoutly thankful for his lucky escape, for had he been a foot or two further on the boulder would have hit his head and would have crushed it like an egg; for the rock weighed a good two hundred-weight.

After treating Pasang's wounds as best we might we set to work once more on our task of bridging the stream. We tied the end of a climbing rope round the top of the longest tree trunk, and placing its butt on the rock platform we had built, we heaved it up to a vertical position. Then taking careful aim we let it fall out across the stream. The top of the log hit the rock on the other side and bounded off into the stream to be swept off by the current. Hanging on to the rope for all we were worth we played it into the side.

Having strengthened the structure of the rock platform, we repeated the process with a similar result, but at the third essay the tip of the log remained balance precariously on the slimy edge of the rock opposite us. We then placed another shorter pole diagonally across the first. This scarcely reached the rocks on the other side.

On this flimsy structure Tilman, with a rope fastened to his waist, started to balance across the raging torrent. We stood watching him with bated breath as, inch by inch, he crept along the swaying poles. It was obvious that he *must* not either slip or upset the balance of the poles, while the further he went the more difficult was his task owing to the thinning of the tree trunks towards the top and the consequently greater sag of the poles. But at length, with what looked like a cross between a leap and a fall, he landed on the other side. We sent up a cheer which was drowned by the roar of the river.

After Tilman had performed this feat the rest was easy, and with all four poles laid across and lashed together with strips of bark, and a rope stretched across as a hand rail we had a bridge over which we could transport the loads without further difficulty. It was now about 10.30 a.m. and we halted for about half an hour on the further side of the river, partly to give Pasang more time to recover from his shock and partly to distribute his load between us. Of course Kusang and Angtharkay insisted upon adding the lion's share of Pasang's load to their own, which made their packs of water-sodden gear quite enormous.

We followed the bank of the main stream down for a few hundred yards and were then forced by cliffs to climb high up into the forest. Here the going was very bad indeed. The side of the valley was exceedingly steep and we had to hang on to the undergrowth above to prevent ourselves sliding down into the undergrowth below while we hacked our way through. At times it took us as much as an hour to cover twenty-five yards.

At first I went ahead with the kukri in order to cut a passage through. It was gruelling work and my shoulders, already burdened by my load, began to ache fiercely. We soon found that except in a few places we could get along faster without the cutting.

The rain was coming down in torrents, but (while on the march) except for making our loads heavier, it could no longer increase our discomfort.

At about 3 o'clock a small side stream, which had cut deeply into the side of the valley, caused us some trouble and by 4.30 p.m., being by a small spring of water, we decided that we had had enough and began to prepare for the night. This was no easy job. There was no place level enough to pitch a tent on, and we had to dig with an ice-axe into the slope for a long time before we could construct a suitable platform. In the pouring rain it was out of the question to make a fire in the open. Here again the woodcraft of the Sherpas was equal to the occasion. Cutting great quantities of bamboo they set to work to construct a shelter under which to make a fire.

These various jobs kept us busy and warm until dusk. Meanwhile poor Pasang sat huddled under the lee of a tree-stump, shivering with cold – the picture of misery. And small wonder, for his struggle with the undergrowth on that steep slope must have been cruel, and now he was incapable of lending a useful hand.

At length, the shelter finished, we huddled under its scant protection. With numbed fingers (we were still at an altitude of 9,500 feet) we struck match after match. (It was fortunate that we had got a good supply of these stored away in sheep-skin gloves!) In this manner we had got rid of two boxes and had started on the third before we succeeded in lighting a piece of rag steeped in paraffin. Once this was accomplished we soon had a fire going. We found that dead bamboo, however wet it may be, catches fire very easily and makes most excellent kindling. Indeed, without it, in such rain as we were experiencing it would have been impossible to light a fire at all. Thus the bamboo plant was providing us with house, fire and food; and without it our lot would have been a sorry one indeed.

Stripping ourselves of our sodden garments we lay naked before the fire while boiling a large pot full of shoot. With a modicum of "ghee" added after the water had been drained off, these were served and eaten as one would eat asparagus. Indeed Tilman's imaginative palate detected some slight resemblance to that delicacy. Unfortunately we had found no more fungus, and our meal failed sadly to satisfy our all too robust appetites.

It had been the busiest day of a hectic week, and I fell asleep without much difficulty only to be roused by Tilman in what seemed a few moments to find it daylight once more.

CHAPTER FIFTEEN

SO tired were we that the morning was already well advanced before we woke. Hurriedly packing our loads, we left our lonely little shelter to engage once more in fierce strife with the tangled vegetation. While amongst big trees the undergrowth was fairly sparse, but where the trees were small of spread or few and far between, there did the brambles grow in profusion, their large thorns clinging and tearing at our clothes, hands and faces as we kicked, flogged and pushed our way through them.

Here and there the valley was broken and rocky. Such a place could provide a formidable obstacle, for, fighting one's way along, one would be brought up suddenly at the edge of a cliff and a long weary ascent would have to be made before a way was found round it. Further on maybe, one would fall into one of many booby-traps in the form of a deep pit filled with bramble and thus disguised better than any man-made game trap. Down one would crash for ten or fifteen feet with load on top.

But it was the gullies which we came to dread most, for here, on account of some old land slip, or the rocky bed of an ancient stream, there were no trees to keep the lesser vegetation in check, and the brambles ran riot.

There was very little variety. At first, struggling to the crest of a ridge full of hope of better things "round the corner", we felt disappointed when we saw before us yet "another —— gully!" Later we got resigned to it and accepted what came without comment.

Five hundred feet up we went and then five hundred feet down; now to avoid some impassable cut-off, now in the hope of better going above or below as the case might be. Generally speaking we kept between fifteen hundred and two thousand feet above the river.

At 1 o'clock we made a brief halt and at 3 o'clock we came to the edge of a steep lateral valley. Through the falling rain we could see two moderate-sized streams coming down the valley in a series of waterfalls, and uniting just before they flowed into the main river far below. Separating the two streams was a high ridge.

Scrambing down a steep slope we reached the first stream and, crossing it without much difficulty, we climbed the ridge beyond. For some while we could see no way of crossing the second stream. The water was coming down with tremendous force and the bank beyond rose in an unbroken line of slimy cliff.

Following the ridge along, however, we soon came to a place where a large tree trunk spanned the torrent. In order to reach this we had to prop a small pine up against it, and clamber up this improvised ladder until we could swing ourselves on to the broad back of the giant – no easy task with our loads.

The further side of the valley provided a steep climb at the top of which, for the first time in some days, we found ourselves on a stretch of level ground. Moreover, owing to the gigantic spread of the branches overhead there was little or no undergrowth. It was now 5.30 p.m. and the temptation to spend the night in this delectable spot was too great. The only snag was the lack of a stream. This difficulty was overcome by spreading the tents on the ground and it was not long before we had sufficient water for our modest culinary needs. During the whole of our sojourn in the forest the torrential rain hardly ever slackened.

The net result of our day's labours in actual distance we reckoned to be one mile. Our altitude was now about 10,000 feet. We had two reasons for keeping so high: one, the fact that the valley was steeper and more broken nearer the river, or so it had seemed from our distant views; two, our fear of getting out of the bamboo zone. (On most tropical mountain ranges there is a narrow belt of altitude where bamboo grows in the forest.) If the bamboo were to fail us our plight would be serious indeed.

An entry in my brief diary for this day is fairly representative of the tone of the rest and runs: ". . . Pasang is no better. The job is becoming very tedious;

always wet, not enough food, and can't see where the —— we are going. . . ."

Pasang was bearing his lot with great courage. He was hard put to keep up with us, even though he was carrying no load, and the frequent stumbles into pot-holes must have caused him agony.

The procedure on this evening was the same as before and we had a difficult task to get our various jobs done before nightfall. There was water to collect, firewood to gather and cut and the shelter to build before we could light a fire, strip off our clinging garments and huddle round its in-sufficient heat.

The level stretch on which we camped enabled us to make good progress next morning for a bare two hundred yards, before we plunged once more into a gully where the going was worse than any we had struck so far. For two hours we made hardly any progress at all, and when we had succeeded in forcing our way across that gully we found ourselves in another almost as bad as the first. At 1 o'clock we halted for a quarter of an hour on the crest of a ridge. Looking back we caught a glimpse through the rain-mist of the ridge where we had camped the night before – about one-third of a mile away. Late in the afternoon we came to a cliff of open rock up which we had to climb in order to continue our traverse along the side of the valley. In two places the climbing was too difficult to be done with loads and these had to be left behind to be hauled up after us.

The weather cleared slightly and from the top of the crag we got our first real view down the valley. A mile away we saw two large patches of grass-land, a strangely welcome sight. We saw too that we were about to descend into a side valley from the bottom of which the boom of a river reached our ears.

We had dropped a good thousand feet before we reached the water, and at about 5.30 p.m. we started looking for a camp site. Presently we espied a large overhanging rock which would provide us with shelter and an ideal place to camp. We were some ten yards from it when a large black bear emerged from the darkness of the cave. Angtharkay, who was in front, dropped his load and made as if to run for it. But the bear was in an even greater hurry and ambled off into the forest without a sound. However, we had to alter our ideas of a camp site for the Sherpas refused to remain in the vicinity of the cave.

That evening we found that the bears were our rivals, not only in the selection of suitable camp sites, but for that all important commodity, the bamboo shoot. Wherever we went we found that the bears had been there before us and ravished the supplies. We had to search far and wide before we could collect enough even for a frugal meal.

Nevertheless, it was in a more cheerful frame of mind that we sat before the blazing furnace which Pasang had made. This, I think, was wholly due to the fact that for once we were not being rained upon and could hang our things before the fire to dry. For it had been a long hard day and we had no reason to be pleased with our progress. We decided that if we did not strike something soon we would have to leave our loads behind and push on without them.

The next morning the stream provided us with no small problem until we found another friendly tree trunk spanning it. The going now became decidedly

better and we made such excellent headway that by midday we had reached the
first of the two patches of open grass-land. The grass was thick and tall, but, oh!
what a relief to emerge for a while from the oppression of the forest. Rain had
fallen early as usual, but now it stopped for a space and we actually saw an
anæmic sun appear. Perched upon a rock we basked awhile in the feeble rays.

Our respite was short-lived and being forced down again into the forest we
found ourselves once more immersed in bramble, the rain falling more heavily
than ever.

At 3.30 p.m. we came to a cave which bore the signs of previous human
habitation, and hunting about, the Sherpas declared that they had found a
track. This latter proved to be a mere figment of the imagination however,
though the evidence in the cave certainly made things seem more hopeful.

We continued on our way until 5.45 p.m. and arriving at a small stream
decided to halt for the night. By now the bamboo was very scarce and, search as
we could, we could find no more than a few pieces for our supper. Darkness fell
before we were prepared for it and we passed an uncomfortable night in a small
cave high up in the face of a small crag.

The next morning was a most unpleasant one. The going was just as bad as it
had ever been and I began to experience that nasty feeling of faintness caused
by hunger and heavy work together. So it went on, hour after hour, in and out
of those pitiless gullies, flogging every inch of the way.

At 1 o'clock, suddenly, dramatically and without warning, came relief from
our worries.

We had found our tedious way across a gully, resembling in appearance
many of its fellows, and clambering up a steep slope had breasted the ridge
beyond. The point marked a slight bend in the main valley. In front of us
stretched an open grassy hillside. A mile down the valley on the opposite side
we saw two fields of standing crops. Leading from these down to the water's
edge was a path, ample evidence that the village from which the fields were
worked was on our side of the valley.

At first we could not believe our eyes, then with one accord we gave
expression to our feelings of joy and relief with a prolonged and lusty cheer.

Two hundred yards beyond the fields a large river joined the one which we
had followed for the last week. This we knew to be the Madmaheswa in whose
valley was the remote Hindu temple of that name.

Even Pasang's foot seemed to have recovered somewhat as we sped joyously
along the steep grass slopes. For two hours we kept up a breathless pace when,
mounting a spur beyond, we saw far below us a tiny hamlet consisting of some
four oblong buildings. When we first spied it we felt like castaways who had at
last sighted land. The Sherpas were if anything more relieved than we were, for
it was only in the last day or two that the unpleasant possibilities of our position
had begun to dawn on them. It was a suitable moment for an oration on our
part, but all Tilman could say, mindful evidently of late descents into some
Lakeland dale, was "We shall be down in time for tea"; while I merely
stuttered: "Thank heaven for that!" We hurried on rejoicing, the Sherpas
yelling with delight when we met a herd of cows, and so frightening the man in
charge of them that he took to his heels.

There were but three houses in the village and, when we arrived, only two old women out of whom we could get nothing but a cucumber. It was still raining hard so we billeted ourselves in a barn which some goats kindly vacated for us, and waited on events. Presently a greybeard appeared with some apricots which went the way of the cucumber, and when we had got it into his head that we wanted some real food, he brought along some flour. He was not slow to realise how sore was our need, for only after prolonged haggling did we get four pounds of it in exchange for an empty bottle and one rupee; the bottle representing the actual price, and the rupee a souvenir of the occasion, for it would be of no use to him.

We slept well that night, unmindful of bugs and fleas, but we paid dearly for it as many days elapsed before the last flea evacuated our sleeping-bags.

It was pleasant to be once more on a track, but as we got down the valley villages became more numerous and tracks led in all directions. We kept getting off our road and none of the villagers seemed anxious to put us right. At 5 o'clock we were still three long miles from the place we were making for and, as usual, were drenched to the skin, so at the next village we parked ourselves in the one dry spot under a balcony, and started a fire.

Our reception here was frigid, and the woman of the house flatly refused us the use of an empty room which opened off where we were sitting, and added insult to injury by ostentatiously locking the door. The Sherpas got annoyed at this lack of hospitality, and Pasang had to be restrained from coming to blows with some of the villagers who had gathered to hear the old lady's apparently vivid description of our manners and appearance. But after peace had been restored the owner of a nearby house took pity on us, and offered us the use of his balcony where we had a comfortable night.

As no one was robbed during the night the atmosphere next morning was more friendly, and we opened negotiations for two men to accompany us as porters for we were tired of losing our way, and still more tired of carrying heavy loads. Their indecision would have been amusing had it not been so annoying, for we were impatient to start. After a long wrangle over rates of pay and finally seeming agreement, the men would calmly announce they were not coming, and the whole business started over again. Patience was at last rewarded, and two of the more enterprising recklessly consented to cast in their lot with us for at least one day.

By the time we reached Kalimath, the place we had hoped to reach the day before, it was raining harder than ever and even the inhabitants were heard to complain of the weather. We had now got to something more than a village; there was a temple and, at that moment of more interest to us, a shop. Sheepskins were spread for us and tea made, and hoping for a few luxuries we held an informal stock-taking. First we got hold of some almonds which were good, and then we found some jaggary (lumps of raw sugar), excellent if one was not averse to eating one's obligatory peck of dirt at one sitting. We had been without sugar for a week so we bought two pounds of it, and Tilman, who suffered from a sweet tooth, seized the biggest lump. After only a couple of bites he rose hastily, and showing all the symptoms of violent nausea rushed outside – he had eaten a piece of soap! After this we were more careful but it was difficult to distinguish the soap from the sugar without biting it.

Late that afternoon we got on to the "Pilgrim Road" leading to Kedarnath and were greatly tempted to turn in that direction, but we had already spent too long on this journey and, turning our backs on it regretfully, we headed south. A long day ended at Okhimath where there was a hospital, a bazaar, and an important temple. As usual now, food was uppermost in our minds and we made straight for the bazaar to get the taste of soap out of our mouths. While sitting there the doctor and the clerk of the temple (a Madrassi) came along and took us over to it. Here we were given tea, a room and beds were prepared for us, and the clerk lent us some of his clothes, as of course all our kit was still wringing wet. Meanwhile he and the doctor plied us with questions about our journey, the news of which had apparently gone before us, and were eager to hear about this legendary pass to Badrinath, the crossing of which had invested our party with some merit, the temple authorities treating us as honoured guests, and the doctor doing what he could for Pasang's foot which was still giving him considerable pain.

The temple buildings were arranged round a courtyard in which stood the shrine, and our room opened off this yard. It served the purpose of the village green and was full of gossiping men and playing children, who with one accord adjourned to our room to have a look, filling it to overflowing. It was several hours before they left us to ourselves.

Our quarters were all that could be wished, but the temple precincts were a bit noisy at night what with praying and ringing of bells, and the dawn of another day was heralded (we thought prematurely) by rolling of drums. When it came to making a start our local men refused to go any further and we had to send out for volunteers. The first to answer the call blenched visibly at the sight of the heavy load which Angtharkay had thoughtfully got ready for him, and incontinently fled. At last we persuaded a sturdy, cheerful little man with an alarmingly large goitre to come with us, and our kind host saw us several miles on our way.

As we were toiling up the long ascent to the village which was our next stage, we had a very pleasant meeting with an old native officer who was going up to Kedarnath with his family. He and Tilman exchanged reminiscences about the War and Neuve Chapelle (the mud and wet had left more impression on him than the bullets), and his fine, open manner and obvious pleasure at our success were very charming. The village was grandly situated only a few hundred feet below a ten thousand foot pass, but the bad weather we were still experiencing deprived us of a view back to the Kedarnath peaks which we much wanted to see.

Five miles of descent through forests of oak and sycamore brought us to a small village where we joined a group of returning dandy-bearers who were sitting round the hut of the village milkman and baker. We got this worthy to boil us up a great bowl of flour, milk, and sugar, and the result was a fine, filling batter pudding. Fortunately the road was still downhill and with this weighty cargo on board we were hard put to check our momentum.

That evening a very violent storm made the thought of our tent so unalluring that we prepared to risk a pilgrim doss-house. Just as we were settling down, one having authority came along and opened for us the Dharmsala, a sort of village meeting-hall. He was an ex-havildar of the Garhwal Rifles with eight years war service, who besides making us comfortable insisted on bringing us presents of milk, ghee, rice, and pickled mangoes.

Our cash resources now began to worry us considerably. A whip round amongst the five of us produced exactly seven rupees and we still had to buy food for the four remaining days to Joshimath, so it was clear we should have to eschew luxuries. We might have raised the wind by becoming strolling players, for Kusang could juggle with three stones and Tilman and I had a varied repertoire of hymns, but on the whole we thought it would be more dignified to try what our credit would do at Chamoli, the first important place we came to on the "Pilgrim Road". Arrived there we went to the postmaster, who having communicated on the "buzzer" with his colleague at Joshimath, readily advanced us some money.

Chamoli is under four thousand feet above the sea and the heat is almost tropical; after dinner that night we sat outside the bungalow in long chairs talking with the Tahsildar, a local magistrate. He was very interested in Yog and pronounced the theory that Christ, many years of whose life are unaccounted for, had spent part of this time in India studying Yog.

At our next stopping place, Pipalkoti, there was a little stone-paved square in the centre of the village, and round this the bazaar was ranged. While waiting for our men we sat here with one of the shopkeepers discussing tea and politics. The all-important question for him was not Dominion Status but whether Pipalkoti should have its post office back or not, and he showed a touching faith in our power and influence as Englishmen to right all wrongs. Apparently through some delinquency on the part of the postmaster, the village had been deprived of its post office, which was now placed in a much smaller village three miles away. Our public-spirited friend had been battling manfully to restore the lost prestige of his village, as a file of letters a foot thick well showed; and though we could afford him only sympathy he was determined to spill his last drop of ink in the cause.

On the last march to Josimath we had an interesting encounter with the young Prince of Nepal who was returning from a pilgrimage to Badrinath. He was a boy of about ten, spoke very good English, and was travelling on foot. Unfortunately our Sherpas were a long way behind so that we missed seeing what took place at the meeting of a Prince and his subjects.

And so on August 26th, once more to Joshimath to get ready for our final campaign.

Part 5

The Second Nanda Devi Venture

CHAPTER SIXTEEN

ON August 27th we began hurried preparations for our second Nanda Devi venture. We had, by good fortune and the experience of those who had gone before us, met with far more success than we had deserved in the first penetration of the basin which I have already described. But, greatly interested as we were in the Badrinath Kedarnath topography, the major task of exploring the Nanda Devi Basin was yet unfinished.

Now that the monsoon had abated somewhat there was no time to waste and Angtharkay was despatched with instructions to recruit fifteen men from the Mana Valley and to return with them as soon as possible. Meanwhile we were busy working out our ration lists, collecting food, packing up and planning our last little campaign.

Pasang's foot was by no means healed, and I expressed some doubt as to whether we would be able to take him with us. But the mere suggestion that he should be left behind hurt him so desperately that I had not the heart to insist and weakly agreed that, as it was two weeks since the accident and he was no longer feeling pain, he could come along.

The rest of the party, although there was much work to be done, were glad enough of the respite from marching, and a newly arrived batch of letters and papers provided Tilman and myself with a certain amount of recreation, although through these we learnt for the first time and with profound sadness of the terrible disaster which had overtaken the German expedition to Nanga Parbat early in July, when four Europeans had perished together with six of our gallant Sherpa comrades from the 1933 Everest expedition. We thought it wiser to keep this news from our three men, and it was an unpleasant ordeal when, some six weeks later, we broke it to them, for nowhere can be found a more warm-hearted friendship than amongst these great little men of the Himalaya.

Late on the night of August 29th Angtharkay arrived with as tough a squad of men as we could have wished for, amongst whom I recognised several whose aquaintance I had made on the Kamet expedition in 1931. He brought too kind messages of congratulation from His Holiness the Rawal and other of our friends in Badrinath. We were particularly gratified to receive a message from "Master" Ram Serikh Singh who, on hearing of Angtharkay's arrival had rushed down from his camp in the lovely valley below Nikanta to hear our news. Later I had the pleasure of receiving a long and charming letter from him in the course of which he says: " . . . When you and Tilman Sahib started from Badrinath to explore the Badri-Kedar snowy ranges the rains began to fall, and they were not only heavy but record rains. I have never experienced such heavy and continuous rain for the several years of my residence in this part of the Himalaya. I was expecting you to return without success. When nothing was heard of you I expected that both you and your porters must have perished in the snow. They were anxious days for me. But when I received your letter in my camp from Joshimath with the news of your unique success I hurried down to Badrinath to send a message of my heartfelt congratulations to you and Tilman Sahib . . ."

We managed to get away just before noon the following day. The weather was bad and we experienced heavy rain as we marched once more up the Dhaoli Valley. After our recent experiences we were anxious about our food supply getting wet. As usual it consisted mainly of flour in the form either of ata or satu. At Tapoban, where we spent that night, we came across a thermal spring. Near its source the water was so hot that one could hardly bear to immerse one's hand. The Sherpas have very great faith in the benefits to be derived from these springs and even Pasang was persuaded, contrary to his Tibetan custom, to have a bath.

Our next day's march took us to Lata, where we billeted in an ancient barn, innocent of roof. We hoped that we would now be able to obtain some food from the inhabitants so as not to have to broach our new stores until we were well on our way; however, as usual, nothing very substantial was forthcoming. Two cucumbers and some potatoes were brought to us by an old woman. When we asked her how much she wanted for them she burst into tears and replied that as her child had recently died she would rather that we did not pay her. We failed to see the connection, but could not induce her to take any money. However, a gift of matches so delighted her that she seemed to forget her late bereavement. An old man actually brought three eggs for which he demanded eight annas (9d.) each. We told him that we could not possibly pay such a ridiculous price, but when he started to go away with the eggs I panicked and gave him the money without further discussion. At that moment an egg seemed an almost priceless luxury.

We were told that at Tolma rice was obtainable, and Kusang volunteered to start very early next morning and go with one of the Mana men to purchase the rice and catch up the rest of us in the evening by taking a short cut from Tolma. We agreed to buy the rice on condition that there were no complaints later about the weight of the loads.

The weather was fine during the morning and we had a most pleasant march along a well-defined path amongst the tall sombre pines of the forest through which we had raced exactly two months before. Now we were not spurred on by the pangs of hunger and we were going uphill instead of down; so we had time to linger in the shady glades of the lovely, open forest. It was a long pull up however as Lata was under 7,500 feet and the little alp of Lata Kharak which we were making for was nearly 13,000 feet.

We pitched camp at the upper limits of the forest just in time to bundle the loads of food inside the tents as a heavy rain storm burst upon us. But it did not last long, and after it had cleared away we collected great masses of rhododendron firewood, and were soon sitting round blazing fires, I for my part lost in wonder at the sight of the ranges across the valley, flooded in that unbelievable blue light which occasionally follows a heavy evening shower in the hills. From far down in the forest there came a faint shout which was at once answered by the full strength of the party, after which the job of guiding the wanderers was taken in turn and shrill whistles broke the silence of the forest at intervals of a minute or so. Kusang and his companion eventually turned up long after dark and after what must have been a very hard day. They had secured a maund (80 lbs.) of rice, the arrival of which was greeted with great jubilation.

The rain came on again and continued to fall throughout the night, with the result that we had some difficulty in getting the men started next morning and did not leave before 9 o'clock. By then the rain had stopped but a damp mist enveloped the mountain side and a cold wind beat in our faces. This seemed to have a good effect on the coolies, who displayed a remarkable turn of speed. We managed to hit off the sheep-track which led us once again over the scene of the exhausting labours of our first visit in May. It was interesting to pick out old landmarks – here a ridge to reach which had cost us half a day of weary flogging; there a gully into which we had floundered up to our armpits. Now we were swinging along a well-defined path at the rate of miles an hour. We passed a short way above our old bivouac place, and pointed out to the Bhotias the little platform on which we had passed the night; how different it looked from that little island of rock which we remembered so well!

When still in thick mist we reached the Durashi Pass, the Sherpas, led by Kusang, insisted on building an enormous cairn for old times sake. On this they deposited various tattered garments which had hitherto clung miraculously to their bodies. Pasang sacrificed his hat in order to create a huge joke by placing it on top of the edifice and leaving it there. I think he would have abandoned his boots if he had thought that it would make a better jest!

The Bhotias were mightily impressed by the sheep-track which ran from here across the face of the cliffs to Durashi, as indeed anyone must be who sees it for the first time. We found some juniper growing in some of the steep gullies, and remembering the scarcity of firewood at Durashi we gathered great quantities so that the party resembled a small army of itinerant bushes. When we reached the alp, we found that a new lot of shepherds had taken the place of those we had met before. With their tall, strong frames, flowing hair and handsome, weather-beaten features, their appearance harmonised wonderfully with the prodigious splendour of their surroundings. They told us that the weather was becoming too cold for their flocks and that they were starting their retreat to the Dhaoli Valley on the following day. This retreat must have meant a long anxious job for them, as most of the new-born lambs were still too small to walk far, and there were hundreds of these little creatures to be carried over the difficult ground which led to the Durashi Pass. Indeed, it was difficult to imagine how they hoped to achieve the passage without a considerable loss. Their dogs were beautiful animals and had wonderful control over the sheep.

The morning of September 3rd was gloriously fine and the view from the "Curtain" ridge appeared to make a deep impression on the Bhotias, who demanded a detailed explanation of the topography. They were very thrilled to see a distant view of their own mountains, the Badrinath and Kamet ranges, and started a heated debate amongst themselves as to the identity of certain features. But it was the sight of the graceful curves of their Blessed Goddess, Nanda Devi, as she stood framed between the dark walls of the upper gorge which most excited their admiration. Several of them asked to be allowed to remain with us until we had finished our travels. What an extraordinarily nice lot they were! Always cheerful, they kept up a constant stream of good-humoured back-chat amongst themselves. They had not, of course, to undergo the hardships which the Dotials had suffered on our first journey, but before very long I came to have considerable respect for them as cragsmen, while their every-ready wit and carefree laughter will remain as one of my pleasantest memories. They and the Sherpas came to be the very best of friends and I think there was a measure of genuine regret when the time came for the Bhotias to leave us. In camp in the forest beyond Dibrughita that evening they treated us to a concert of part songs which reminded me very much of those of the Welsh singers. After this one of their number produced a book which was apparently written in Nepali from which he read laboriously to the Sherpas.

During the next few days, as we traversed once more high up on the flanks of the Rishi Nala, we were able to appreciate the tremendous advantage of possessing local knowledge when travelling over difficult country. Across places which had previously cost us hours of anxious toil we were now able to lead our party safely in half the time. We found, however, a great many landslips had occurred in our absence, and that portions of the country were quite considerably altered. The rains must have been terrific. Small, steep-sided nalas, normally dry, and with very little collecting capacity, showed signs of having had as much as seven feet of water coming down them. We soon realised that the delay which had been caused by our experiences on the Satopanth Pass had been a blessing in disguise, for the Rishi Nala would have been no place to be in during such weather as we experienced in the forests of the Kedarnath valleys.

In order to preserve our rapidly disintegrating climbing boots, we wore rubber-soled shoes on this journey. They slipped about horribly on the damp grass and earth-covered rocks and made the traversing along narrow ledges a most unpleasant business. On one occasion Tilman did slip and for a moment I thought he was lost as he swayed on the brink of a dreadful drop.

From Dibrughita we followed the high level route by which we had returned in June. On September 5th we crossed the Rhamani, one thousand five hundred feet above its junction with the Rishi. The stream was still in spate and we experienced some difficulty in getting across. Most of the Bhotias were very frightened of being swept away and left the task of getting the loads across mainly to two young "tigers" each of whom made some half a dozen crossings. One old man flatly refused to wade into the stream and was eventually carried across. Later it transpired that he was the "egg wallah" who had achieved a certain amount of fame on the Kamet expedition in 1931, by being washed away in a river in the Alaknanda Valley, only I had not recognised him. That evening we reached our old base camp at the entrance of the upper gorge. At one period during the monsoon everything had been flooded, though as we had walled in the belongings which we had left we found that they were still intact. There were several things which we did not require, but we soon came to wish that we had pitched them into the river as the Bhotias spent most of the night noisily dividing the spoil.

As we knew every inch of the route through the upper part of the gorge we decided to take ten of the Bhotias on with us, while the rest returned. Huge segments of the cliffs had broken away and it was very lucky for us that none of the vital sections of the route had been touched. One landslip might well have rendered the gorge impassable, though it is possible that it might have the reverse effect. The men climbed splendidly and on the evening of September 8th we pitched camp some miles up the main valley of the southern section of the basin. The Bhotias were astonished at the country. Such enormous areas of splendid pasturage and no one was able to get their flocks through to graze it! Pasang said he would like to bring a few yaks through into the basin and live there in peace for the rest of his life!

Our camp was situated near the junction of the two main glaciers of the southern section, and promised to serve as a useful base for our work. Besides the exploration of the country to the south of Nanda Devi we meant to reconnoitre the southern ridges of the mountain to see if we could find a practicable route to the summit. But our chief ambition was to force our way out of the basin either to the south or to the east, for besides not wishing to return by the way we had come, Dr. Longstaff's words, "I can think of no more interesting or arduous task for a party composed of mountaineers than to follow up the great glaciers under the southern face of Nanda Devi and to cross the ridge on which I camped in 1905 into the Milam Valley," had fired our imaginations.

Our activities in the southern section were governed largely by this ambition. We had two possible alternatives. One was the col reached by Dr. Longstaff from the Lwanl Glacier on the Milam side, the other was the depression on the southern "rim" by which Mr. Ruttledge and his guide Emile Rey had tried to gain access to the basin in 1932. Both these ways were likely to prove extremely difficult, but we were inclined to favour the former proposition as Longstaff had proved the practicability of the further side of the Lwanl Col by climbing it from that direction, whereas from what we had heard of Ruttledge's col it seemed very doubtful whether a reasonably safe route could be found down the southern face even if we succeeded in reaching its crest from the north.

It was mainly then with the object of obtaining a clear view of the unknown side of the Lwanl Col that on September 9th Tilman, Angtharkay and I, after bidding farewell to the Bhotias, left camp heading in an easterly direction. We crossed the stream to the northern side of the valley by means of a snow bridge formed by a huge avalanche cone which had fallen from the cliffs of Nanda Devi. Presently, as we made our way along a moraine ledge under these cliffs, we were alarmed by the ominous whirr of falling stones accompanied by some shrill whistles, and, looking up, we saw a number of bharal high up among the crags above us. Never have I seen a more extraordinary display of rock climbing. The cliffs on which these animals were scrambling about looked from where we were to be utterly unclimbable; and yet here were four-legged creatures, young and old, running about on them as if they were horizontal instead of being almost vertical. Later we found out that owing to the inward dip of the rock strata the cliffs of this side of the mountain are not so difficult as they appear. Nevertheless, although I had often watched chamois in the Alps, I never before believed that these animals could move about on rock faces of such appalling steepness. I do not imagine that such agile climbers would be so careless as to knock stones down by accident and I strongly suspected that they were bombarding us purposely and probably enjoying a good laugh at our obvious alarm as the stones shattered themselves unpleasantly close to us.

Soon we got on to the big glacier flowing from the west under the southern face of Nanda Devi, and crossed it diagonally to its left bank, where we found a well-defined lateral moraine along which we could make good progress. We had gone for some miles before we rounded a corner and came in sight of the head of the glacier. There was a lot of cloud obscuring the peaks, but after we had waited for half an hour or so we got a brief and distant view of the col. What we saw made us somewhat uneasy. From the col itself a steep ice or snow gully descended for about two thousand feet to the head of the glacier. If the gully consisted of good snow throughout its length it would not be difficult to climb it even if it were steep. But from where we stood it appeared to us to be composed of ice, particularly in its upper part. If this proved to be the case the task of cutting steps all the way up it, at the same time carrying loads of 50 lbs. and being responsible for the safety of the Sherpas, who would be carrying at least 70 lbs., was one which neither of us was very keen to face; for on steep hard ice it is almost impossible to check a bad slip, while there is nothing easier than to make one. Moreover, several deep ruts in the gully and piles of débris below indicated that the route was swept by stone falls, while the rocks on either side of the gully did not appear to offer a satisfactory alternative. Our view, however, was too fleeting and too distant to be at all satisfactory or conclusive, but we saw enough to make us decide to examine the possibilities of the Sunderdhunga Col, as Ruttledge has named the depression on the southern "rim", before making a serious attempt to force a route up the grim precipices of the south-eastern wall.

Across the glacier from where we stood the great southern ridge of the main peak swept up into the drifting clouds at an appalling angle. I could not repress a shudder as I looked at its great glistening flanks and reflected that it had been our intention to look for a route up it. The lower section was hidden from view;

but higher up the icy cliffs mounted without a break to support the majestic head of the virgin goddess, near ten thousand feet above us. I do not remember even remarking upon the apparent inaccessibility of the ridge, and I began to hope that we had proved the mountain to be unclimbable.

We returned to camp in the evening by way of the left bank of the glacier. The Bhotias had taken their departure and Pasang and Kusang, having performed their numerous duties about the camp, were busily engaged as usual with their intricate coiffure. As they wore their hair long it was in constant need of attention, and long continued practice had taught them much which would make many a Paris hairdresser sit up and take notice. Sometimes a long and richly ornamental pigtail was allowed to hang down the back; sometimes it was wound round and round the head; on other occasions the hair was bunched coquettishly behind the ears. A parting, when such was worn, was ruled with the most scrupulous accuracy. This evening I watched, fascinated, while Kusang (he did not know I was looking) ran a short stump of pencil up his nose and over his forehead to make sure that his parting ran exactly down the middle of his head. He repeated the process over and over again before he was satisfied, squinting the while so grotesquely that I began to wonder if his smiling eyes would ever be the same again.

CHAPTER SEVENTEEN

ON the morning of September 10th we were greeted by a warm sun. As it was the first we had experienced for nearly two months we were tempted to bask in its kindly rays for some time before embarking upon the more serious work of the day. We decided to go up the great glacier which we had seen coming in from the south, at the head of which we suspected the Sunderdhunga Col must lie. We intended to camp near the head of the glacier, push a camp on to the crest of the col if that were possible and spend some days examining the ice-cliffs on the southern side in the hope of being able to find a way down. If we were successful we could return to continue our work in the basin for as long as our food lasted, in the comfortable knowledge that an escape over the rampart was possible. If we failed we would have to make an attempt on the great ice-gully leading up to Longstaff's col. We started, carrying heavy loads, and were content to take things gently. By the time we got into a position which would command a view of the glacier the clouds had come up from the south and we could get no idea of the type of country for which we were making. The going was good on the dry ice of the glacier and we made steady progress, passing one or two remarkably fine specimens of "glacier tables". These somewhat surprising phenomena are caused by a large slab of rock falling on to the surface of the glacier and protecting the section of ice on which it has fallen from the rays of the sun, so that as the rest of the glacier melts the slab is left perched upon a pedestal of ice which it has protected. In the case of smaller rocks the process is reversed, the stone becoming heated by the sun and sinking into the ice instead of being left perched above it.

Soon after midday a bitter wind blew up from the south and sweeping across the glacier drove hail and sleet into our faces. This caused us to put on a spurt and before we camped we were a great deal further up the glacier than we had expected to go that day. With difficulty we erected the tents and got the Primus going. The wind dropped towards sunset, and chancing to look out of the tent I saw that the clouds had retreated down the valley leaving the peaks to the south clear. We saw that we were near the head of a very wide glacier-filled valley from which gentle ice-slopes rose to a broad saddle which we knew must be the Sunderdhunga Col. To its right was a massive ice-peak. This we concluded must be the triangulated peak, 22,360 feet, which is such a conspicuous landmark when seen from the south, and which is known by the Survey of India as East Trisul*. The delicious purity of the summit snows, tinged as they were by delicate rays of the setting sun, filled me with desire for a closer acquaintance with the peak. Moreover, unlike most of the peaks in the vicinity, there was an obviously practicable route to the summit, and the prospect of a view from such an elevated point in this wonderland was irresistible. Arguments against the present plan were not difficult to find. The col was easily accessible from this side and in order to find out whether a descent on the south was practicable or not, one would have to go down several thousand feet of very difficult ice, and once one had done that, one would probably be disinclined to climb back again. So it was decided to cut out the reconnaissance, and make a full-dress attempt when our work in the basin had been completed.

We passed a very cold night and in consequence did not emerge from our tents until the sun was well up. Carrying one tent, bedding for three and food and fuel enough for three days, we started in the direction of the ice-peak. The weather remained fine all day, and as hour after hour we threaded our way laboriously through a badly-crevassed area which stretched for a long way up the mountain side, the heat and the glare from the newly-fallen snow was almost unbearable. We aimed at getting our camp up to 20,000 feet. Tilman had been feeling very unfit all day, and in the afternoon when we were at an altitude of about 19,000 he decided not to go any further, and suggested, most unselfishly, that Kusang should stay up at the camp in his place and attempt the peak with Angtharkay and myself, while he went down with Pasang. I, too, was not feeling in very good form, and was suffering from a bad attack of that mysterious complaint loosely known as "glacier lassitude", so that I was glad when 500 feet higher up we came upon an excellent camping site in a crevasse.

With three of us crammed into a two-man tent, we settled down to a most uncomfortable night. Lack of space did not permit independent movement and when one man wished to turn over the others had to turn too, in order that each should fit spoon-wise into the curves of the other. The Sherpas thought this a tremendous joke and as far as I could make out simply laughed themselves to sleep. I suppose I must lack much of that priceless gift – a sense of humour, for I could see in the situation very little to laugh at, with the consequence that I lay long into the night hiding my head and trying to decide which of my companions snored the loudest.

I roused them at 4 a.m. and after a great deal of struggling we contrived to melt ourselves a drink and wrap our shivering bodies in all the clothing which we could extract from the tangled mess inside the tent. Boots then had to be thawed out and forced after a frightful struggle on to feet which had apparently swollen overnight. Soon after 5 o'clock we issued reluctantly out into the bitter morning air.

It is curious how the Sherpas, when they have no loads to carry, seem to lose all power of controlled, rhythmic movement which is such a vital necessity in mountaineering and particularly at considerable altitudes. Their steps become jerky and impulsive, they rush along for a few minutes and then sit down, with the result that they soon become exhausted. All that their life of mountain wandering has taught them about the best methods of walking uphill seems to be lost and they are like raw novices who are amongst the mountains for the first time in their lives.

Today this was very evident and before we had been climbing an hour the party was feeling very sorry for itself. Higher up, too, the snow conditions became bad and the work of kicking steps extremely laborious. We began to feel as we had felt at a considerably higher altitude on Everest the year before. We started off by going for an hour without a halt, then the hour was shortened to half an hour, half an hour to twenty minutes, twenty minutes to a quarter of an hour, and at length we would subside gasping into the soft bed of snow after only ten minutes' struggle. But the morning was fine and as we lay there, we gazed out over a scene of ever-increasing grandeur until even the gigantic southern face of Nanda Devi became dwarfed by the mere extent of the panorama.

I can never hope to see a finer mountain view: the Badrinath peaks, Kamet, the Kosa group, Dunagiri and the great peaks of the northern part of the Nanda Devi Basin – all mountains amongst which we had been travelling for the past four months, served merely as a foil to set off the stupendous ranges lying beyond Milam and across the borders of western Nepal. What a field of exploration lay there – the heritage of some future generation.

Only one frame of mind is possible when working one's way up bad snow at high altitudes. One must shut out from one's mind all but the immediate task of making the next step. To start fretting about the slowness of one's progress or about the time it is going to take to reach the goal would render the whole business unbearable. On a larger scale, this frame of mind, the firm concentration on immediate necessities, made possible those terrible months of sledging through the blizzards of the Antarctic.

As we approached the summit the wind, which had been unpleasant in the early morning, now became very strong indeed and it was the fear of frost-bite which spurred what little energy we had left. My hope of seeing something of the southern side of the watershed was disappointed, for when we reached the summit ridge we looked down into a boiling cauldron of cloud a few feet below us. This was rising rapidly and soon enveloped us. However, we did get one brief glimpse down to the little Simm Saga range which lay at our feet; and also into the head of the Sunderdhunga Valley which we were so hoping to reach. What we saw went a long way to quenching that hope for there seemed to be very little break in the 10,000 feet of precipice which lay between us and the grassy floor of the valley below. I had refrained from taking any photographs on the way up in order to preserve the exposures for the summit. But before my numbed fingers would open and set the camera we were wrapped in a dense cloak of cloud, and we passed the remainder of our stay on the top clapping our hands and banging our feet about in an attempt to restore rapidly diminishing circulation. Then we bustled off the summit and embarked upon a descent which proved to be almost as trying as the ascent. On reaching the camp we packed up the tent and sleeping-bags, and in spite of the loads we had now to carry, we shot down over the lower ice-slopes at a tremendous speed, paying little respect to the crevasses which had caused us so much trouble on the previous day. Tilman greeted us with apparently unlimited tea. He had put in a useful day's work with the plane-table and had succeeded in fixing several important points about the glacier.

On the following day we went down to our base and, leaving a dump of flour there just sufficient to enable us to beat a retreat down the Rishi Ganga in the event of our failing to escape from the basin to the east or south, we carried the remainder of our stuff to a pleasant little alp a couple of miles up the left bank of the main glacier. By now we had been able to make a fairly lengthy examination of the southern aspect of Nanda Devi. We had seen a curious diagonal spur running down in a south-easterly direction from about half-way up the main south ridge. This appeared to be accessible in its lower section and it seemed to us that we might be able to work our way for some distance along it. We decided to attempt to do this in order to get a comprehensive view of the southern section of the basin, though it did not even occur to me that we might also find a practicable route to the summit.

The morning of September 14th was brilliantly fine, and we started early carrying with us the usual light camp and enough food for Tilman (who was now recovered) and myself for two or three days. We crossed the main glacier and made our way again along the valley which lay at the foot of the great black buttresses of the southern ridge, fixing our position on the plane-table as we went and taking shots to distant landmarks. We camped that night by a pool of crystal clear water, on a lawn of close-cropped grass over which snowy eidelweiss grew in profusion.

It was an hour after dawn the following morning before we got away. It seemed as if the last remnants of the monsoon had departed. The glacier was silent, bound under the iron grip of frost; and we joyously sped over its desolate stony surface. Forty minutes of hard going took us to the foot of the black precipices which girdle the base of the great southern ridge. Here we found that the rock was well broken but firm and that the strata sloped in our favour which made the climbing a great deal easier than we had anticipated. Within an hour of leaving the glacier we had reached the crest of the diagonal spur which we had seen from a distance. This was as far as we expected to get and we sat down contentedly in the warm sunlight and gazed lazily at our unique surroundings.

We saw that the spur we were on, coming down from the main southern ridge of Nanda Devi, formed a gigantic glacier cirque. In front of us across a deep valley rose a stupendous ice-wall which formed the southern face of the twin peaks. We were too close and, for all our 18,500 feet, far too low to get anything but a very fore-shortened view of the face and it was a long while before the colossal scale began to impress itself upon my imagination. The ice-wall was fringed on top by a band of rock forming the actual summits of the twin peaks and the two mile ridge connecting them. By now the sun had been shining on this band for some hours and had already started to dislodge masses of rock, which set up an almost continuous moan as they hurtled through the air towards us, yet so great was the distance of the peaks above us that throughout the day we did not detect a single of these avalanches which must have involved several hundreds of tons of rock. The whole effect was very uncanny.

As it was such a brilliantly fine day and as yet quite early we decided that we would investigate the possibilities of climbing further up the spur. A virtual tower rising straight out of the ridge blocked a way along the crest, but we soon found that we could traverse along under the tower on its eastern side and climb diagonally towards a gap in the ridge beyond. This we reached in a couple of hours without much difficulty, and were surprised to find that here again the inward sloping strata made progress comparatively easy. By now we were about nineteen thousand feet high and beginning to get really excited. We had already overcome the apparently inaccessible lower part of the ridge and were still going strong. Was it possible that we had discovered the one key to the innermost defences of this amazing mountain? Of course, we would not be in a position to make an attempt on the summit but to have discovered the way was sufficient to work us into quite a frenzy of excitement. Up and up we went without finding any place which gave us more than a moment's hesitation. Our pace was slow by reason of the fact that the rocks were still under a deep covering of monsoon snow, but our progress was steady enough. The higher we got the more fully could we appreciate the immensity of the glacier cirque on the rim of which we were climbing.

We climbed on until about 2.30 p.m. when we halted and decided that we had come far enough. We estimated our height at close on twenty-one thousand feet. The ridge was certainly showing signs of becoming more difficult but for the next few hundred feet there did not appear to be any insuperable obstacle and we came to the definite conclusion that if a well-equipped party were to spend a couple of weeks over the job that there was a good chance that the ridge could be followed to the summit. It would be no easy task and the party would have to be supremely fit and competent. Prolonged siege tactics (which are so much the fashion in the Himalayas nowadays) would be too dangerous to be justifiable, since this method would involve too many men in the upper camps, and if it were overtaken by bad weather high up such a party would be in a very serious plight. In high mountains, mobility is the keynote of efficiency and safety, and it is for this reason that I find it hard to believe that a large, heavily organised expedition will ever achieve success on Everest.

We were now sufficiently high to get a true idea of the immensity of our surroundings, and even though I had been living for months amid perpendicularity on a huge scale I suffered from a feeling of panic which resembled the delirium of a fevered mind.

Our slow rate of descent was evidence that we had climbed too fast earlier in the day and night was falling as we made our way back across the glacier after yet another unforgettable day.

The morning of September 16th was spent mainly in plane-tabling, on the slopes above the camp, and in making further examination of "Longstaff's Col". This more detailed study confirmed our first impressions that an ascent of the couloir with heavy loads would be too difficult and dangerous a job. We could not, however, tell for certain as so much depended upon whether the gully was composed of snow or ice. By now we had become really worked up about our chances of being able to force an exit over one of these gaps. In doing so, we would make a complete crossing of the range, thus linking up with the explorations of those who had attacked the rampart from the south and east; we would see for ourselves those valleys, which though not unexplored, we knew to be of surpassing loveliness; and the last phase of our quest would be through country new to us. If we were to fail we would be forced to retreat once more down the Rishi Nala, and from Joshimath to journey back by the way we had come, thus missing a rare and glorious climax to our little season of perfect happiness.

When we returned to camp early in the afternoon we found that the Sherpas had come up and were busily engaged in their hobby of building cairns. Packing up, we ran off down the glacier, reaching our little green alp before sundown, here to spend one more night lying in the open, dozing in the light of the half moon and waking to watch the rosy light of dawn steal gently down the east-turned face of the "Blessed Goddess".

The week which followed has left with me a richer and more varied stock of impressions than any other I can recall. We started up the glacier to the south that morning, staggering under the weight of very heavy loads. I was feeling lazy and lagged behind the others, sitting down often to gaze at each new aspect of the peaks around me. Once I found myself by a deep pool in the ice of the glacier, and stayed as if hypnotised by the reflections on the placid blue surface of the water. It was irresistible. I threw off my clothes, plunged in and swam for some seconds under water along the glistening walls of ice. The day ended in camp far up the glacier, under the icy cirque standing at its head.

A frigid night was followed by an even colder dawn and we were hurried along in spite of our cruel loads by the bitter morning breeze. The snow was iron-hard, and as the slope steepened the already burdened shoulders of the leader would ache painfully as he chipped steps, while those behind were frozen with inaction. The arrival of the sun changed all this and we were soon stamping a way, and sinking up to our knees at every step, while a fierce glare scorched our faces unbearably. Several large crevasses caused us some trouble, but we worked at full pressure and at 11.15 a.m. we reached the crest of the "col". We found that this consisted of an extensive snow plateau which sloped gently towards the south, so that we were obliged to descend some five hundred feet before we could get any view of the southern precipices on which all our thoughts were concentrated. From the edge of the plateau we could look down into the cloud-filled Sunderdhunga Valley up which, as I mentioned earlier, Hugh Ruttledge and his guide, Emile Rey, had come in 1932 to attempt to gain access into the Nanda Devi Basin. In order to save the reader the trouble of referring back to that incident it may not be out of place to requote here, Mr. Ruttledge's description published in *The Times* of August 22nd, 1932, of the obstacle which now faced us:

"In a mood of hopeful anticipation our party, on May 25th, trudged up the narrow glacier which leads from Sunderdhunga itself to the base of the wall, of which the greater part has been invisible from a distance. The Sherpas cheered derisively as a little avalanche had an ineffective shot at us from the cliffs above; and raced round the last corner. One step round it, and we were brought up all standing by a sight which almost took our remaining breath away. Six thousand feet of the steepest rock and ice. 'Nom de nom,' said Emile, while Nima exclaimed that this looked as bad as the north-west face of Kangchenjunga in 1930. However, we had come a long way to see this, so we advanced across the stony slopes to a point from which we hoped, by detailed examination, to reduce terrific appearance to milder reality. But the first impressions were accurate. Near the top of the wall, for about a mile and a half, runs a terrace of ice some two hundred feet thick; in fact, the lower edge of a hanging glacier. Under the pull of gravity large masses constantly break off from this terrace and thunder down to the valley below, polishing in their fall the successive bands of limestone precipice of which the face is composed. Even supposing the precipice to be climbable, an intelligent mountaineer may be acquitted on a charge of lack of enterprise if he declines to spend at least three days and two nights under fire from this artillery. An alternative is the choice of three knife-edge arêtes, excessively steep, sometimes overhanging in their middle and lower sections, on which even the eye of faith, assisted by binoculars, fails to see a single platform large enough to accommodate the most modest of climbing tents."

We dumped our loads in the snow and set about our task immediately. Remembering Ruttledge's description we decided that our best chance of success was to get on to one of the three rock arêtes or ridges, for though they were referred to as being "excessively steep", at least their crests would be safe from the bombardment of ice-avalanches. The clouds had now come up from below and our view was very restricted. After working over to the left for some distance, however, we came to the edge of a tremendously steep gully from which came an incessant rattle of stone falls. Beyond we could make out a dark mass which we concluded was the first of the rock arêtes. After hunting about for some time we found that in order to reach the arête we would be forced to run the gauntlet of the rock falls in the gully. As these were coming down at very short intervals the chances of our getting across without some member of the party being killed was very small, and the risk was quite unjustifiable. So that was that.

The ice-fall below us plunged out of sight. We returned to our loads and worked over to the right. In about twenty minutes we were brought up short and found that we were standing on the edge of the ice-terrace overhanging six thousand feet of polished limestone. It was a wonderful sight. Every now and then enormous masses of ice would break away from the cliffs we were standing on and crash with a fearful roar into the cloudy depths below. After satisfying ourselves that there was not the slightest hope in this direction we waited for some while to watch this unusual scene. It is not often that one gets a chance of watching a display of ice-avalanches from so close, and rarer still to see them breaking away from the very cliffs on which one is standing.

We returned disconsolately to our loads for a meal at 2.30 p.m. A cup of tea and satu put new heart into the party and we set off to tackle the last line of possibility. This was the ice-fall which lay immediately below us and which separated the ice-terrace from the rock arêtes. A few feet of twisted and riven ice was all that we could see: beyond this the ice-fall plunged out of sight into the whirling mists which filled the depths below. It was useless to attempt to work out a line of attack from above and all we could do was to go straight at it and worry our way down by the tedious processes of trial and error. We had plenty of food with us, however, and we could afford to take our time. As long as we kept fairly well out of the line of bombardment from the ice-cliffs of the terrace and avoided a slip we could carry on for several days if necessary.

Soon we found ourselves on ice more torn and complicated and more frighteningly steep even than that which we had tackled six weeks before on the southern side of our Satopanth Pass. It was exceedingly strenuous work trying line after line without success, but as the evening wore on our energy seemed to increase, probably from a growing feeling of desperation. A series of slender ice-ledges suspended over space by some conjuring trick of Nature would lead us downwards to the brink of an impassable chasm. Then a wearisome retreat back by the way we had come to try a new and perhaps equally futile chance. The further we went the more involved became the precipitous maze we were in, until my head began to whirl and I began to think we should neither find our way on or back. By dark, however, we had managed to get some hundreds of feet down and we crept into our sleeping-bags in a slightly more hopeful frame of mind.

The night was an extremely cold one and we decided not to start before the sun was up on the following morning as our clothes had become sodden in the soft snow of the previous day and an early start would almost certainly have resulted in frost-bite. This decision gave us a moment of leisure in which to watch a sunrise whose beauty far surpassed any I had seen before. In the right and left foreground were the icy walls, steep-sided and grim, enclosing the head of the Maiktoli Valley; in front beyond the brink of the ice-ledge on which we were camped, and immensely far below was a lake of vivid colour at the bottom of which we could see the Sunderdhunga River coiling like a silver water snake, flowing away into the placid cloud-sea which stretched without a break over the plains of India.

The day was one of heavy toil, over-packed with thrills. Hour after hour we puzzled and hacked our way down; sometimes lowering our loads and ourselves on the rope down an ice-cliff, at others chipping laboriously across the steep face of a tower or along a knife-edged crest, always in constant dread of finding ourselves completely cut off. The bitter cold of the early morning changed towards midday to a fierce heat and glare which robbed us of much of our strength and energy. Our heavy loads hindered every movement and threatened to throw us off our balance. But we were all absorbed in our task, and worked on through the day without pause.

Evening found us working on dry ice three thousand feet down. Beside us to our right was a prominent rock ridge, which, though lying immediately below the higher line of hanging glaciers, offered us a heaven-sent alternative if only we could reach it. We cut steps to the edge of the glacier and from there we looked down a sixty-foot ice-cliff into a steep slabby gully. The gully was evidently a path for ice-avalanches, but it was narrow and once in it we could run across in a couple of minutes. By chipping away the ice in a large circle we soon fashioned a bollard. Round this we fastened a rope, down which we slid, recovering the rope from the ice-bollard without difficulty. A short race across the gully with hearts in our mouths took us to a little ledge under the overhanging walls of the ridge, which offered a convenient and well-protected site for a camp. No sooner had we got the tents pitched than there came a fearful roar from above and for fully a minute a cascade of huge ice-blocks crashed down the gully, sending up a spray of ice-dust, while a number of ice-splinters landed harmlessly on the tents.

The day, begun with the sight of a dawn fair beyond description and crowded with so much vivid life, closed with us stretched luxuriously on our ledge, perched high up amongst the precipitous glaciers of one of the grandest of mountain cirques. Lightning flickered somewhere to the east; the distant thunder was almost indistinguishable from the growl of the avalanches. Mists floating stealthily in and out of the corries about us, forming and dissolving as if at will. Far to the south the placid sea of monsoon cloud still stretched over the plains, and the silvery light of a full moon lent to the scene an appearance of infinite depth.

Three thousand feet of precipice still remained to be descended and this took us nearly the whole of the following day. Frequently we had to rope down the more difficult sections. On one of these occasions one of the sacks came open; most of the contents fell out, bounced once and hummed out of sight. In the afternoon we were enveloped in mist and had considerable difficulty in groping our way downwards; but Antharkay distinguished himself by a really brilliant piece of route-finding and in the evening we reached a collection of rude stone shelters, used by shepherds, and known as Maiktoli. The shepherds had departed some weeks before.

The high mountains were now showing signs of approaching winter, a sharp reminder that our season of freedom and perfect happiness was at an end. But the marches which followed have left their quota of memories. A struggle to find an exit from the grim gorge in the upper Sunderdhunga Valley into which we had blundered in a heavy mist; our last encounter with a swollen mountain river; an enormous feast on wild raspberries and Himalayan blackberries lower down the valley; the generous hospitality of the first villagers we met, and the sweetness of their honey; the sparkling sunlit mornings, as one lay, sleepily watching the smoke of a distant wood fire mounting straight up into the clear air; a dawn on the distant ice-clad giants, whose presence we had just left.

Return to civilisation was hard, but, in the sanctuary of the Blessed Goddess we had found the lasting peace which is the reward of those who seek to know high mountain places.

THE ASCENT OF
NANDA DEVI

by H.W. TILMAN

First published by Cambridge University Press, 1937

Contents

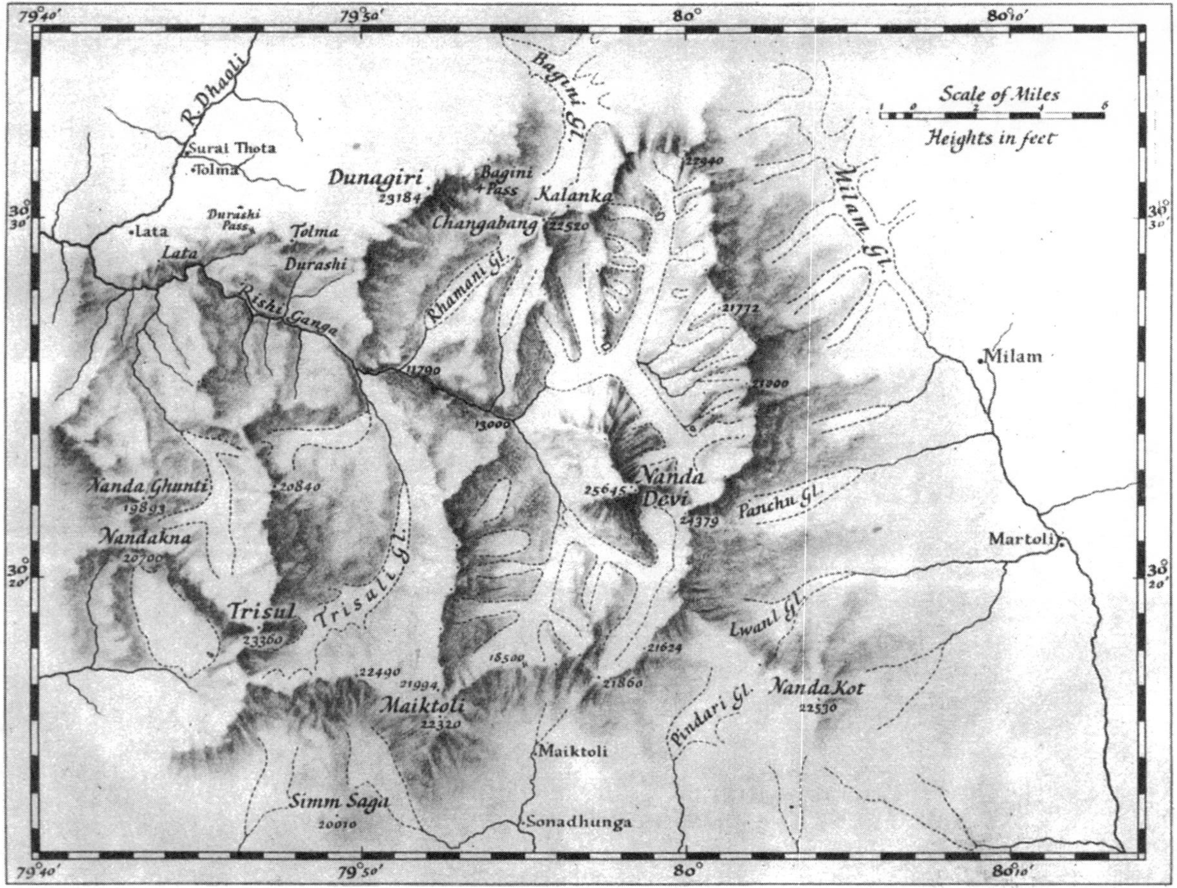

By courtesy of the Royal Geographical Society

CHAPTER ONE

Mythological and Geographical

I⊤ is questionable whether the story of a successful attempt on a new peak will be as acceptable as a story of failure; at any rate to lovers of mountains or to those who know one end of an ice-axe from the other. These will perhaps be more inclined to echo the words of David's lament and cry, 'Tell it not in Gath, publish it not in the streets of Askelon.'

If an account of the climbing of Everest is ever written, I take leave to doubt whether it will be as widely read as have been the stories of successive failures. For, say what one may, when the summit is reached some of the mystery and grandeur surrounding a peak hitherto untrodden by man is lost; and a book recounting the fall of one of the giants will be bought—or by mountaineers more likely borrowed—with misgiving and read with loathing. But so complex is our make-up that the pleasure which success brings far outweighs any remorseful pangs, and friends, even mountaineering friends, congratulate the triumphant party sincerely instead of damning them heartily. And, as if that was not enough, pressure of various kinds results in the members of the expedition putting on record their experiences so that all profit by them, and the invincibility of yet another great mountain is thereby imperilled. Perhaps when the millennium dawns, of the writing of books there *will* be an end, at least of mountaineering books; if there are then any unconquered peaks remaining, come what may, successive generations will think them still unconquered to the end of time.

Stories of unsuccessful climbs are in a different category. The splendour of the mountain is undimmed or even enhanced, and the writer can be trusted to see to it that the honour of man is, at the lowest, not diminished. But having now hinted at the motives impelling the writing of this account it is time to cut the cackle and come to the 'osses; for it would puzzle a conjuror to explain satisfactorily a habit (not confined to mountaineers) of believing one thing and doing another.

Before leaving for the Himalaya in May, I was asked by an otherwise intelligent man whether it would be summer or winter out there when we arrived. This is mentioned in no critical spirit, but only to show that what one man assumes to be common knowledge may be known only to very few. A banker, for instance, popularly supposed to be without a soul, may know nothing and care less about mountains, but be deeply interested in music or literature; and, conversely, mountaineers may not know the most elementary principles of banking or, possibly, grammar.

To some the Himalayas may be only a name vaguely associated perhaps with a mountain called Everest: to geologists they provide a vast field for the starting and running of new hares; to other learned men, glaciologists, ethnologists, or geographers, the Himalaya are a fruitful source of debate in which there is no common ground, not even the pronunciation of the name; while to the mountaineer they furnish fresh evidence, if such were needed, of the wise dispensation of a bountiful Providence. For, lo, when the Alps are becoming too crowded, not only with human beings but with huts, the Himalaya offer themselves to the more fanatical devotee—a range of fifteen hundred miles long, containing many hundreds of peaks, nearly all unclimbed, and all of them so much higher than the Alps that a new factor of altitude has to be added to the usual sum of difficulties to be overcome; and withal to be approached through country of great loveliness, inhabited by peoples who are always interesting and sometimes charming. Here seemingly is a whole new world to conquer, but it is a world which man with his usual perversity, flying in the face of Providence, has reduced to comparatively small dimensions: for what with political boundaries, restrictions, and jealousies, the accessible area is less than one-third of the whole. And though European travellers and climbers may grouse about this state of affairs, Europeans are, I suppose, largely to blame. For with the present state of the outside world before their eyes the rulers of Tibet, Nepal, and Bhutan can scarcely be blamed, and might well be praised, for wishing their own people to have as little as possible to do with ourselves.

Sikkim, Kashmir, and Garhwal remain open to travellers, though the first two are not without their restrictions; restrictions which we were to experience. Garhwal is a small district almost in the centre of the Himalayan chain and lying about two hundred miles north-east of Delhi. It is divided into British Garhwal and the native state of Tehri Garhwal, but here we need trouble ourselves only with the first, which did not come under British control until after the Nepalese War of 1815. Originally the country was in the hands of a number of petty chieftains, each with his own fortress or castle; the word 'garh' itself means a castle. In the early years of the nineteenth century it was overrun by the Ghurkas, who, not content with this acquisition, extended their ravages down to the plains and thus came into collision with the ruling Power and brought about the Nepalese War. In the early stages of the war we reaped our usual crop of defeats and disasters, but in the end (and up to the present this also has been usual) we muddled through and drove the Ghurkas back within their present boundaries; and, as a slight reward for the trouble to which we had been put, we annexed the greater part of Garhwal for ourselves. It is roughly rectangular, about a hundred miles from north to south and fifty from east to west, and diagonally across the northern half runs the Himalayan chain. In this short section of the range there are two peaks

over 25,000 ft., including Nanda Devi (25,645 ft.), the highest peak in the
Empire, and over a hundred lesser peaks all over 20,000 ft. To the east lies
Nepal, on the west is the native state of Tehri Garhwal, and north is Tibet.
The Tibetan border runs on the north side of the highest axis of elevation, the
northern slopes of the range merging into the high Tibetan plateau, and south
of the range are the foothills running down to the plains of British India. It is
noteworthy that the watershed lies near the Tibetan border on the north side
of the line of highest elevation, which would naturally be expected to form the
watershed. The rivers have either cut back through the range or the country
has been elevated since the existence of the rivers.

There are three main rivers flowing roughly south, cutting through the
range at right angles, and between these river valleys are the chains
containing the highest summits, forming, as it were, spurs thrown out from
the main range. From east to west the rivers are the Gori, the Dhauli, and the
Alaknanda. The last two flow into the Ganges, the Alaknanda constituting
one of its main sources, and at the head of all three valleys are high passes
leading into Tibet. Between the Gori and the Dhauli lies the range containing
Nanda Devi, and at its southern extremity this range bends round to the west
towards Trisul (23,360 ft.), and culminates in Nandakna (20,700 ft.), and
Nanda Ghunti (19,983 ft.). Some ten miles north of this abrupt westerly bend
another spur of approximately equal length branches off, its western
extremity marked by Dunagiri (23,184 ft.). Between these two short parallel
spurs is a yet shorter one composing Nanda Devi itself, so that we have here a
sort of reversed letter 'E', the short middle stroke representing Nanda Devi,
the longer top stroke the Dunagiri, and the bottom stroke the Trisul massif.
But that is not all; subsidiary spurs branch off from Trisul and Dunagiri and
converge upon the middle stroke, thus almost encircling Nanda Devi with a
ring of mountains.

The space between the foot of Nanda Devi and its ring-fence of giant
peaks, in extent some two hundred and fifty square miles, contains many
lesser peaks and ridges, an extensive glacier system, rock, scree, and,
surprisingly enough, grass slopes of wide extent. The whole is known as the
Nanda Devi Basin or, more felicitously, the Sanctuary, a name first bestowed
on it by Mr Ruttledge of Everest fame, who in the following passage
graphically describes the unique situation of the mountain:

> 'Nanda Devi imposes on her votaries an admission test as yet beyond their skill
> and endurance. Surrounded by a barrier ring, 70 m. long, on which stand twelve
> measured peaks over 21,000 ft., and which nowhere descends lower than 18,000 ft.,
> except in the West, where the Rishi Ganga river, rising at the foot of Nanda Devi,
> and the sole drainage of 250 sq.m. of ice and snow, has carved for itself what must
> be one of the most terrific gorges in the world. Two ridges converging on the river
> form as it were the curtain to an inner sanctuary within which the great mountain
> soars up to 25,645 ft. So tremendous is the aspect of the gorge that Hindu
> mythology described it as the last earthly home of the Seven Rishis—here if
> anywhere their meditations would be undisturbed.'

The Rishis mentioned here were seven wise men, Hindu sages, and they are
now said to be represented by the seven stars of the Great Bear.

The superstitions, myths, and traditions relating to mountains, are most of them interesting and some beautiful. The mountains of Garhwal are particularly rich in such stories, because Garhwal is the birthplace of the Hindu religion, the traditional home of most of the gods of the Hindu Pantheon, and the terrestrial scene of their exploits. Every mountain and river, almost every rock and pool, is associated in legend with the life of some god.

Of the population of Garhwal, the orthodox among the immigrant Brahmans and Rajputs worship the five great gods, Vishnu, Siva, Devi, the Sun, and Ganesh, the elephant-headed god of wisdom. The bulk of the people, Khasiyas, a race of a caste lower than the Brahmans or the Rajputs, but yet generally allowed to be also immigrants from an Aryan source, adore principally the mountain god Siva; while the Doms, less than a fifth in number of the rest and believed to be the aborigines of the country, propitiate the local gods and demons who were in existence long before the coming of the Brahmans and Hinduism. But all, even the hillman such as the Bhotia, who has little respect for things sacred, finds a common subject for reverence in the majesty and aloofness of the snowy ranges. At any sudden revelation of one of these giants, the home of one of the deities, coolie and priest alike will fold their hands and with bowed head utter a word of prayer.

Nor is worship at the high places of Himachal, 'the abode of snow' sacred to the Hindu gods, confined only to the nearer inhabitants. From all parts of India pilgrims make their way annually to this Hindu 'Palestine' to 'acquire merit' by enduring the privations of the road, and, by worshipping at the shrines, to receive forgiveness for past sins and assurance of future happiness.

At Kedarnath Siva, or Mahadeo, the god of everything destructive and terrible, is the object of adoration; at Badrinath the temple is dedicated to the benignant Vishnu, and a third famous shrine is found at Gangotri. All three lie amongst the great group of mountains which separate the valleys of the Bhagirathi and Alaknanda, rivers which unite lower down to form the Ganges.

At Kedarnath the tradition is that the god in the form of a buffalo took refuge from his pursuers the Pandavas (a tribe of the Dasyus who represent the original black race as opposed to the fair Aryans). For further safety he dived into the ground but left his hinder parts exposed, and a mountain there, in shape something like the less dangerous end of a buffalo, is still an object of adoration. The remaining parts of the god are worshipped at four other places along the Himalayan chain; the arms at Tungnath, the face at Rudrnath, the belly at Madmaheswar, and the head at Kalapeswar. Together these five places form the 'Panch-Kedar', and to visit them in succession is a great ambition of the Hindu devotee, but one, I imagine, which is not often accomplished. I have in mind particularly Madmaheswar, which lies up a valley that few plainsmen would care to penetrate.

Bigoted followers of Siva or Vishnu visit only the temple dedicated to their respective god, but the great number of pilgrims make the round of as many of the sacred places as possible. Badrinath probably receives the most, and derives from its fifty thousand annual visitors a far greater revenue than that of Kedarnath. Badrinath also has its five sacred places, the 'Panch-Badri', comprised within the Holy Circle of Badrinath, which extends from the shrine of Kanwa to the summit of Nanda Devi, on which there is a lake, the abode of Vishnu himself. The Bhagirathi, which is a lesser stream than the Alaknanda, has a greater reputation for sanctity, but it does not attract as many pilgrims as do the sources of the Alaknanda, particularly the fall of Bhasudara. The temple of Gangotri is ten miles below the place where the Bhangirathi issues from the snout of the Gangotri glacier, a very holy spot called Gaumukh or the 'Cow's Mouth'. It is here that, according to Hindu mythology, the heaven-born goddess first descended upon earth. Water from the river at Gangotri, sealed in flasks by the priests, is taken to the plains as being of great value.

Of the exact meaning of Nanda Devi, or rather of 'Nanda', it is not easy to get any precise information. According to one interpretation it means the 'Blessed' or 'Revered' Goddess, but if there is anything in a story I was told it means the goddess Nanda. Nanda was the daughter of a Kumaon king (Kumaon is a division of which Garhwal is part, and was formerly a separate native state) whose hand was demanded in marriage by a Rohilla prince. He was refused, and war followed, a battle taking place near Ranikhet. Nanda's kingly father was defeated and the future goddess fled and, after many vicissitudes, took refuge on the top of Nanda Devi. There are two other mountains in the vicinity in which the name 'Nanda' occurs. Nanda Ghunti to the west has already been mentioned and this, I was told, means 'The halting-place of Nanda'; it is only 19,893 ft. high and was probably used as a stepping stone to Nanda Devi itself. To the east is Nanda Kot (22,500 ft.), which means 'The stronghold of Nanda', and south is Trisul, 'The Trident', a defiance to any rapacious Rohillas.

Amongst the local natives this belief that the mountains are the abode of gods and demons is less strong than it used to be. In 1830 Mr Traill, the first Commissioner, accompanied by local coolies, crossed a pass between Nanda Kot and Nanda Devi. The story goes that he suffered severely from snow-blindness, which the coolies attributed to the wrath of the goddess, and they affirmed that he only recovered after making an offering at the temple of Nanda Devi at Almora. The story may not be strictly accurate, but only a pedant would have it otherwise.

In 1855 the same route was taken by Adolph Schlagintweit, and of this crossing Mr A. L. Mumm in *Five months in the Himalaya* related the following. A promise of additional pay and a rich offering to Nanda Devi had to be promised before any coolies could be persuaded to start. On top of the Pass, 'Schlagintweit commenced taking observations but was disagreeably interrupted by three of the hardiest men being seized with epileptic fits . . . A cry rose up that Nanda Devi had entered into them and Adolph, fearful lest the seizure might spread further, took aside two Brahmans whom he had with him, and after pointing out that he had given Nanda Devi all that they had demanded, and that this unpleasant scene was only the result of their own folly in calling on the goddess at every difficult place on the way up, ordered them to put a stop to it at once. This they achieved, partly by prayers, and partly by putting snow on the head of the sufferers, the latter remedy being, in Adolph's opinion, the more effective of the two.'

A later traveller, W. W. Graham, in 1883 had trouble with the local natives when he attempted to approach Nanda Devi by the gorge of the Rishi. His men all deserted, ostensibly on the grounds that the gorge was infested with devils. But in 1934 when Mr Shipton and the writer penetrated the gorge our Dotial and Bhotia coolies evinced no superstitious fears, though they, of course, are not really local men. Some men from the Dhauli valley whom we employed did desert, but I think the devils they feared were more tangible—the devils of discomfort and hard work. In 1936 we took a few coolies from a village at the very mouth of the Rishi Ganga and for them superstition either did not exist or was overcome, and this was the more remarkable because they came up the Rishi and joined us at the foot of the mountain, unaccompanied by any European.

On the other hand, shortly after our return, a local correspondent of a well-known Indian newspaper published a report to the following effect. In 1936 the monsoon rainfall was exceptionally heavy in the United Provinces and Garhwal, and on August 29th, after a severe storm, the Pindar river, which is fed by the glaciers of Nanda Kot and Trisul, rose many feet and wrought considerable havoc in the village of Tharali; a village, by the way, through which we had passed on the way to the mountain some weeks before. Forty lives were lost, several houses destroyed, and many cattle drowned. It was on the same day, August 29th, that we climbed the mountain and thus provoked the anger of the goddess, who immediately avenged, blindly but terribly, the violation of her sanctuary.

CHAPTER TWO

Historical

THE reader who blenches at the chapter heading will be pleased to hear that it is not necessary to recall the history of previous attempts on the mountain because there have not been any. For fifty years the problem which engaged the attention of many experienced mountaineers was not how to climb the mountain but how to reach it. But as the approach to the mountain was not the least serious of the problems which we had to face, perhaps it will not be out of place to outline briefly the story of these attempts, although they have already been recounted very thoroughly in Mr Shipton's *Nanda Devi*.

The truism that we climb on the shoulders of our predecessors is sometimes forgotten, and it is difficult to exaggerate the importance of the part which earlier failures play in the final success. The Himalayan peaks over, say, 23,000 ft. which have been climbed at the first attempt can be numbered on the fingers of one hand, and even if the present climb be cited to the contrary, the answer is that we had the inestimable advantage of knowing where to make our efforts and how to get there—knowledge gained for us by our forerunners. And apart from previous experience on the actual mountain there is the vast fund of accumulated knowledge of high climbing in general to draw upon; for though experiences may be 'the name men give to their mistakes' it does not lessen their value to those who are willing to learn.

The earliest expedition was that of W. W. Graham in 1883, who was accompanied by two Swiss guides and who hoped to reach the mountain by way of the Rishi gorge. This river, as has already been said, drains the whole of the Nanda Devi Basin. It has two sources at the snouts of the two glaciers encircling the north-east and south-west sides of the mountain, and the streams from these glaciers unite at the foot of the west ridge. From this point the river, by now a formidable torrent, flows west through a gorge or series of gorges until after a distance of about eight miles it joins the Dhauli river near the village of Rini. Graham's party started to follow the river up from near its junction with the Dhauli, but were stopped almost at once by the difficulty of the terrain; nor to this day has anyone succeeded in passing the lower portals of the gorge.

Repulsed here Graham and his two guides, Boss and Kaufmann, moved round to the north and, after an unsuccessful attempt on Dunagiri, learnt from shepherds that there was a way into the Rishi *nala* over the northern containing wall which avoided the insuperable difficulties of the lower four miles. 'On the evening of the second day', Graham wrote, 'we reached a lovely little table-land called Dunassau (Durashi). The last day's route had been extremely wild running along the southern face of the ridge, sometimes with a sheer drop to the river below—some 7000 to 8000 feet. Such wild rocks and broken gullies I had never met before.' Here most of their coolies deserted, but they pushed on: 'Occasionally we had to hang on to a tuft of grass or a bunch of Alpine roses, and I do not exaggerate when I say that for half the day's work hand-hold was as necessary as foot-hold.' Several days of this sort of work brought them to a place where they were finally stopped by the smooth cliffs of the north side and inability to cross the river to the more accommodating south bank. The desertion of their remaining coolies put an end to their hopes and they abandoned their loads and struggled back as best they could.

In 1905 Dr Longstaff, a name for ever associated with mountain exploration in Garhwal, attacked the problem from the opposite side. In that year he and two Italian guides, the Brocherel brothers, were in the Gori valley to the east of the Nanda Devi massif with designs on East Nanda Devi (24,300 ft.). This mountain is the highest of the encircling peaks and from it extends that short ridge, the middle stroke of the reversed letter 'E', which links it with Nanda Devi itself. Starting from Milam in the Gori valley Longstaff's party got on to the rim of the Basin at the foot of the south-east shoulder of the lesser Nanda Devi, at a height of 19,100 ft. They were thus the first ever to look down into the mysterious sanctuary; but the descent looked formidable, nor was it their objective. It had been a close thing, but the Sanctuary remained inviolate.

In 1907 Dr Longstaff returned to the attack with a strong party which included General Bruce, Mr Mumm, and three Alpine guides. Their first attempt was by what Dr Longstaff called the 'back door', the route which Graham had learned of from the shepherds. Half-way up the gorge from Rini on the north side of the river, and a couple of thousand feet above it, there are two hanging valleys. Here is valuable grazing to which, in the summer, are brought the sheep and goats from many neighbouring villages, some enterprising but unknown shepherd of a bygone age having found a remarkable route to these alps, or Kharaks, as they are called locally. The route involves the crossing of a 14,000 ft. pass which in late spring is still snow-covered, and a rather hair-raising, or since sheep form the bulk of the travellers, wool-raising, traverse across a mile of cliffs. The pass, however, was found to be still blocked by snow, so the party moved round to the north and east of Dunagiri and proceeded up the Bagini glacier in an attempt to cross the northern wall of the Basin, the top stroke of our reversed 'E'. There was a pass at the head of this glacier which according to the map then in use should have led into the Basin, but this region of ice and snow had of course not been included in the survey, and though the map did credit to the maker's imagination it was apt to mislead. The map of Garhwal in use up to 1936 was made from a survey in 1868 which was, rightly, only carried up to the snow-line, and above this, not so rightly, it was largely filled in by guess-work. There is nothing but praise and thankfulness for the accuracy of the surveyed portion, but for the unsurveyed part we should all prefer to have a map which, like the crew of the *Snark*, we can all understand, 'a perfect and absolute blank'.

In 1934 we had the same experience as Dr Longstaff's party in other parts of Garhwal. From an explorer's point of view it may seen inconsistent and ungracious to gird at inadequate maps, for it is the explorer's job to fill them in. But this is only a plea for blanks instead of fancy; blanks, of which there are, alas, but few remaining, thanks to the energy of the Indian Survey. At the present moment a new survey of Garhwal is in hand, and this year (1936) we had the advantage of a provisional new issue of the old map incorporating the results of much private and official work done in Garhwal in recent years. Is it not time to start a Society for the Suppression of Abolition of Maps and Guide Books, not necessarily confined to the Himalaya? With the accumulation of exact knowledge comes the desire to put it to use, and we shall presently have a Five-Year Plan for the Himalaya and learn that the Sanctuary is one of those eligible sites 'ripe for development'. To show that this is not completely idle fancy I might mention that 'Pilgrimage by Air' is, if not an actual fact, at least an advertised one. The following appeared in *The Times* dated from Delhi this year: 'An aerodrome among the Himalayas, 10,500 ft. above sea-level, is being constructed by the Air Transport Company here to cope with the pilgrim traffic to the Badrinath shrine, sacred to the Hindus. The present terminus (long may it remain so) of the air route to the shrine is situated at Gauchar, about 70 miles from Hardwar. The return journey between Hardwar (*sic*) and Gauchar takes about eight weeks by road, and could be done in twelve hours by rail.' The words in parenthesis are the author's. For Hardwar, in the last sentence, I suggest read Badrinath; we have been told the distance is seventy miles, and four weeks for the single journey is a little slow even for a pilgrim travelling on his hands and knees or measuring his length on the ground at every step, as some of them do.

To return to our exploring party on top of the Bagini pass; they found, after crossing the pass and descending another glacier, that they had got into the Rishi gorge at the point reached by Graham and were still separated by three miles of cliff from the Inner Sanctuary. Shortage of food compelled them to hurry with all speed down the Rishi instead of attempting to force this upper passage, and they finally emerged by the 'back door', which was now clear of snow. After a rest they came up the Rishi once more and Dr Longstaff with two of the guides (the Brocherel brothers) climbed Trisul, going from a camp at 17,500 ft. to the top in one day—an amazing *tour de force* which is not likely to be repeated.

Trisul was climbed on June 12th, and the 14th saw Dr Longstaff and two Gurkhas trying to force a way up the south bank of the Rishi. Foiled here, they crossed to the north side by a natural rock bridge and camped near the entrance of the Rhamani torrent down which they had come on the previous journey recounted above. The height was 11,700 ft., and the next day they climbed to 13,500 ft. up the cliffs of the north bank, but found this side even less encouraging than the other. In view of the difficulties and at the instance of other plans still to be carried out, no further attempt was made to penetrate the grim defile and Dr Longstaff rejoined his party in the lower Rishi.

In 1932 Mr Ruttledge, who as Deputy Commissioner of the Almora district had had opportunities for studying the problem of Nanda Devi and the Basin both from distant Almora and from journeys to the east and north, thought that he had discovered a breach in the outer rampart. About half-way round the southern rim from Trisul to East Nanda Devi the surrounding wall falls to its lowest elevation, about 18,000 ft. or slightly less. From a distance this depression seemed a likely place for a crossing of the wall, but rising as it did from a deep and steep valley very little of the approach to it could be seen. Accompanied by Emil Rey, an Italian guide, and six Sherpa porters, Mr Ruttledge went up the Maiktoli valley to get a closer look, but from beneath so forbidding was the aspect of the proposed pass that not even a closer inspection was required.

'We were brought up all-standing by a sight which almost took our remaining breath away. Six thousand feet of the steepest rock and ice . . . Near the top of the wall, for about a mile and a half, runs a terrace of ice some 200 feet thick. Under the pull of gravity large masses constantly break off from this terrace and thunder down to the valley below, polishing in their fall the successive bands of limestone of which the face is composed. Even supposing the precipice to be climbable, an intelligent mountaineer may be acquitted on a charge of lack of enterprise if he declines to spend at least three days and two nights under fire from this artillery. As alternative, there is a choice of three knife-edge arêtes, each one excessively steep, sometimes overhanging in the middle and lower sections, on which even the eye of faith, assisted by powerful binoculars, fails to see one single platform large enough to accommodate the most modest of expedition tents.

'The jury's verdict was unanimous; and so vanished the last hope of a straightforward approach to Nanda Devi; and the goddess keeps her secret.'

Prior to this Mr Ruttledge had made two previous attempts. One in 1926 accompanied by Dr Howard Somervell and Major-General R. C. Wilson, when an approach by the Timphu glacier to the north-east was tried but found to be even more hopeless than that by the south or west. And again in 1927 with Dr Longstaff, when the lowest point of the wall, 17,000 ft., at the head of the Nandakini valley to the south-west was reached. Further progress was barred by bad weather, but this approach would but have led into the lower Rishi Ganga and not into the Basin.

In 1934 Mr Shipton and the writer with three Sherpa porters went to Garhwal, having as our main objective the entrance and mapping of the Basin. As with a man making a second marriage, hope triumphed over experience, and by Dr Longstaff's advice we directed our attention to the Rishi gorge. The gorge was passed and a month was spent exploring and mapping the Promised Land of the Basin, and in the autumn a second journey was made to complete the work. On this second occasion a way out was found over the low depression in the southern wall but, of course, in the reverse direction to that which Mr Ruttledge had intended, and in consequence a much simpler affair.

In the course of the six weeks spent in the Basin we had ample opportunity to study the mountain from every side. As a result of this study, having exhausted all other possibilities, we concluded rather unhopefully that a lodgement could be effected on the south ridge, but it seemed unlikely that the ridge would 'go'.

We took a camp up the south-east glacier to within striking distance and, fully expecting that a closer acquaintance would only strengthen our first impressions, we devoted a day to the ridge. We reached a height of about 20,000 ft. and found it easier than we expected, which only goes to show the value of an oft-quoted piece of mountaineering advice by Dr Longstaff, that 'you must go and rub your nose in a place before being certain that it won't "go"'. It was a perfect autumn day and we sat for some time on our airy perch, following in imagination a route up the ever-steepening southern ridge, and fascinated by the grand sweep of the horse-shoe cirque at the head of the glacier, a 3000 ft. glacis of glittering ice. Despite our height and the clear day we were not well placed for judging the difficulties of the ridge above our heads. We were looking at it *en face*, we were too close, and the whole was very much foreshortened, but with due allowance for this our opinion was summed up by Mr Shipton in *Nanda Devi* as follows: 'The ridge was certainly showing signs of becoming more difficult but for the next few hundred feet there did not appear to be any insuperable obstacles, and we came to the definite conclusion that if a well-equipped party were to spend a couple of weeks over the job there was a good chance that the ridge could be followed to the summit. It would be no easy task and the party would have to be supremely fit and competent.'

Two things may be noted in this brief summary: first, that Sherpa porters made their first appearance in Garhwal in 1927 with Mr Ruttledge, for it was not until after the earlier Everest expeditions that the possibilities of these men were realised. The first travellers in Garhwal, like Traill and Graham, had only the local natives as porters, and these could only be relied upon below the snow-line, and not always then. Later their place was taken by European guides, an infinitely stronger substitute but a monstrously expensive one. Secondly, that the parties become successively smaller, ending with two Europeans and three Sherpas, for with a problem such as the approach to Nanda Devi the advantage lies obviously with the smaller party. I might add that in the last case smallness was dictated almost as much by motives of economy as of mobility.

When attempting a high mountain the party may have to be larger, but how much larger, if any, is a debatable point, and we still have what for convenience may be called 'Big-endians' and 'Little-endians' with us in the mountaineering world. A great deal must depend on the peak to be tackled, but there is no question which is the best for purposes of mountain exploration as opposed to an attack on single peak. It may be thought that the expedition to be described, comprising eight Europeans, was a successful reversion to type, but apart from the number of climbers (actually seven) there was nothing big about it and in the course of the narrative it will appear that there is every justification for classifying it as small.

CHAPTER THREE

Preliminaries

WHEN an expedition is on foot a certain amount of preliminary work, proportionate to the size, has to be done. For some the whole of the winter may be all too short for this, while, on the other hand, I think the preparations for our two-man show in 1934 could, if necessary, have been completed in one day. However, for those concerned with the organisation of something which intends calling itself an 'expedition', the winter is a busy time, and since it is the custom to be very reticent about plans, the organisers meet and go about their business with the air of conspirators. One reason for this is that it is annoying, or ought to be, to read in the Press of what an expedition is going to do before it has even started; nor is it any consolation to know that the information bears as much relation to fact as an official communiqué did during the War.

The notion of a British-American expedition to the Himalaya was first mooted in America, and plans were very far advanced before any climbers on this side were approached. The objective was Kangchenjunga, the third highest peak in the world, and preparations were on a correspondingly large scale. It was not until February 1936 that W. F. Loomis came to England to collect four climbers, more equipment, and, most important of all, to apply to the Indian Government for permission to go. This was cutting it rather fine, for no one, least of all a Government, likes to be bounced into making quick decisions, and if they are so bounced the decision is usually unfavourable. Fortunately we were warned that such might be the case and we selected Nanda Devi as a second string for our bow. Here, as has been explained, there were no political complications, and moreover, for this objective, we had the goodwill of all who had had anything to do with the mountain.

Meanwhile, Loomis, having drawn up two equipment lists, one of rather staggering dimensions for Kangchenjunga and a more modest one for Nanda Devi, returned to the States, leaving me to collect our Nanda Devi requirements and to await the result of our application before ordering the rest.

The British party was now complete and comprised, in addition to the writer, T. Graham Brown, F.R.S., an eminent physiologist, who has climbed in the Alps for many years and who was one of the party which in 1934 climbed Mt Foraker (17,300 ft.), a difficult peak in Alaska, for the first time; N. E. Odell, a geologist, who in 1924 climbed twice to Camp VI (27,000 ft.) on Everest, and who, in addition to the Alps, has climbed in Spitsbergen, Labrador, and the Rockies. And lastly Peter Lloyd, another experienced Alpine climber with many fine guideless ascents to his credit, and a brilliant rock climber.

How many of the original American members would go was still uncertain and much depended on what our objective was to be. It was decided that the party should assemble in India at the end of June, as this was the earliest by which most of them could arrive. This was of course unusually late, for at that time the monsoon would already be active, but according to the experience of two German expeditions this would be no disadvantage for Kangchenjunga. July and August were said to be the most favourable months; the reason given being that prior to the monsoon particularly severe winds were the rule. For Nanda Devi the advantages of climbing during the monsoon were not very obvious, indeed anyone who had seen the mountain and knew the conditions in the gorge would consider that our chance of success was in consequence materially diminished.

It was important that one of us should go out to India in advance to collect porters and arrange transport, so I decided to leave in March, hoping that before then we should know whether we were going to Sikkim or Garhwal, seven or eight hundred miles apart. But it was not to be, and when I sailed at the end of the month, accompanied by only part of the food and equipment, the oracle at the India Office had not yet spoken. For my part I sailed in the hope and expectation that we would be permitted to try Kangchenjunga, mainly because for me it would be new ground. But correspondence with the others gave me the impression that they were prepared for a refusal with a most Christian-like resignation; in fact, I suspected they might even welcome it. To them both mountains were new, but there was more freshness and originality about Garhwal and Nanda Devi. Kangchenjunga is seen by everyone who goes to Darjeeling, various parties have prowled around it, and it has received three full-dress assaults, and possibly to their minds it was getting a bit moth-eaten. And moreover, though both mountains gave us an equal chance of putting up a good show, there was vast inequality in the chance of getting to the top; Kangchenjunga is probably as formidable as Everest.

We tied up at Calcutta on a Monday, and a blacker day, in both senses, I have seldom experienced. The first letter to be opened informed me, with regret, that the British-American Himalayan Expedition would not be permitted to enter Sikkim to attempt Kangchenjunga; like most oracular pronouncements no reasons were given. It seemed a pity to have to accept this fiat without some protest, but there was nothing to be done except write a 'forlorn hope' of a letter asking for reconsideration and the reply to that was merely an official 'raspberry'.

I now went round to see the Customs, for the Indian Government very generously allow expeditonary equipment to come in free of duty. We had already written asking to be accorded this privilege, but unfortunately no instructions had yet been received from Simla, so nothing could be disembarked. Feeling a bit subdued, I thought it was time to enlist some local aid and began hunting up the few people I knew in Calcutta. All were either in England or Darjeeling and, feeling more like a pariah every minute, I slunk away to a hotel. On the way I noticed one or two people staring rather hard and, looking down, I discovered a dark blue sea of ink the size of a plate on an otherwise spotless white coat. At the hotel I handed it over to a boy telling him to get busy with milk, lemon juice, india-rubber, and any other ink-remover he knew. An hour later it was brought back, but not by the same boy, and one soon understood why, for the last state was worse than the first, the inky sea being now suffused over half the coat, and though the deep rich blue had paled to a watery grey the effect was still too bizarre for me to carry off.

My suitcase had now arrived, and in it another exciting discovery awaited me in the shape of the havoc wrought by an uncorked bottle of ink. Few things had escaped unmarked, and for the next few days I must have looked a bit mottled because in a temperature of 100 degrees colour is apt to run. But soon a wire from Simla allowed me to land and store the equipment and to escape from the Turkish bath of Calcutta in April to the freshness of Darjeeling.

The question was what to do, for now there was no preparatory work to be done in Sikkim, and the others would not arrive in India for nearly two months. There was the possibility of making a journey into the Basin to form a dump, but I had only a small amount of the food with me and, further, there was always the chance that bad weather might prevent the main body getting through and necessitate a change of plans—we should look uncommonly foolish if all our food was inside the Basin and we outside unable to reach it. Nor was it weather alone that might bring about this contingency; the first burst of the monsoon might break the slender thread of the route through the gorge by rock-falls or by washing off from the underlying slabs the thin covering of earth and grass upon which one depends mainly for holds. The most useful way of spending the time seemed to be to go into Sikkim with a few Sherpa porters to test their abilities, and then to take them up with me to Garhwal at the end of June.

For a stay of more than a fortnight in Sikkim a pass has to be obtained from Gangtok, the capital, and, being in a hurry, I was unwise enough to wire for this without explaining my intentions. The name must have aroused suspicion, for the reply was a request for full particulars of my intended journey; evidently I was regarded, figuratively, as the thin end of a British-American wedge. Telegrams were abandoned in favour of the typewriter and various other people were written to for assistance in this crisis. As a friend remarked, if the pen is mightier than the sword, the typewriter is mightier than the ice-axe. All Himalayan expeditions should carry one, even if it means leaving their ice-axes behind.

After a week's delay I started with four Sherpas, obtained only with difficulty. Even in England it had been clear that good porters would be hard to come by, and this was found to be true enough. The Everest expedition had of course skimmed the cream, a French expedition had taken thirty Sherpas to the Karakoram, and there was a small British party in Sikkim with another twenty. In consequence it was difficult to scrape together even four, and two of these were complete novices. On the eve of a long-delayed start a cable was received saying that Loomis would arrive in Bombay on May 21st, and asking if a journey into the Basin would be done before the monsoon began. A reply was sent advising him to wait and come out with the others, and then we made a double march from Darjeeling which put me well beyond the reach of any more cables.

After an all too brief but peaceful fortnight on the glaciers south of Kangchenjunga, I began worrying about what was happening and decided to return to Darjeeling, where we arrived on the 21st. Sure enough there was a letter to say that they had not been able to get in touch with Loomis to stop him and that he would be in Bombay on the 21st. Something had to be done, and now, contrary to previous notions, I thought it might as well be done in Garhwal. If we went straight there and moved fast we might be able to take some loads into the Basin and get back in time to organise the main party as well. By doing this we should have fewer loads to take in after the monsoon had started, and the party would therefore be less cumbersome; during this Sikkim trip the weather had been such as to remind me forcibly how unpleasant conditions might be in the monsoon, so that the fewer coolies we then had with us the better. I forgot how many wires I sent to Bombay, for I did not know where Loomis was and feared he might have already started for Sikkim. The American Consul, all the Travel Agencies, and the Shipping Line, seemed a wide enough net, and next day I had the satisfaction of knowing that I had caught him.

We arranged by wire to meet in Ranikhet on May 28th.

Some arrangement hád now to be made about the Sherpas. Of the four, I had already decided that only one was worth a place on a serious show; this was Pasang Kikuli, who was quite outstanding. He had been to Everest in 1933 and carried to Camp V, where he got slightly frost-bitten hands, but having been treated with oxygen suffered no ill-effects. He had also been twice to Kangchenjunga and was on Nanga Parbat in 1934, where he was one of the five porters to get down alive from the highest camp, six porters and three Europeans dying on the mountain. It was strange that he should have been overlooked by the Everest and other parties, but their loss was our gain, and he turned out to be a treasure. When the time came for me to leave Darjeeling no more porters had come in, so I took two of the original four, one of course Pasang Kikuli, and left instructions for four more to be sent up later when there might be some more likely candidates available. Pasang's companion was one Pasang Phuta. A good average porter but with no outstanding qualities except a disarming grin. The Americans called him a bit 'dumb', and anyone who knew Pasang Phuta would not need to be told that this is a briefer way of saying that he was not highly endowed mentally.

CHAPTER FOUR

A Telegram to the Temple

RANIKHET, whither we were now bound, is a hill station in the United Provinces. From Kathgodam, thirty-six hours' journey by train from Calcutta, it is reached by a good road of fifty miles. Numerous buses ply on this fifty-mile stretch of road and competition is so fierce that the fare is only three shillings, luggage included, and perhaps an extra sixpence for the doubtful privilege of sitting next to the driver.

Ranikhet is 6000ft. above sea level, and the relief on reaching it and breathing the pine-scented air, after a journey by rail through the sweltering plains, has to be felt to be believed. On many days of the year this feeling of having left hell and arrived somewhere near heaven is intensified by the sight of a hundred and more miles of snow peaks: distant, it is true, but near enough to stagger by their height and fascinate by their purity. At this time of year though, before the monsoon, they are seldom seen to advantage, owing to the dust haze which drifts up from the plains.

Apart from the view there are no distractions for the casual visitor to Ranikhet, and this was as well, because we had no time to waste. We had to get up the Rishi gorge, into the Basin if possible, and I had decided that we must be back by June 25th, in order that we could have things well in hand before the others arrived. Normally, it would take eighteen days to get there, not allowing for any delay *en route*, and in this case delay was almost inevitable. The food and equipment which I had brought out was still on the way up from Calcutta by goods train and none of the American consignments had yet arrived, so that the only loads we could take were coolie food, which could be bought locally; that is rice, atta (wheat flour), and satu, for feeding the local coolies on the way in and the Sherpas while on the mountain. Satu is the same thing as the Tibetan tsumpa—barley, or wheat, which has been parched and then ground into meal. It has one great advantage in that it needs little or no cooking; you can put it in tea and make it into a thick paste, or moisten it very slightly with water and mould it into a cake; it can even be eaten dry, but that is not a method I can honestly recommend. It also makes an excellent porridge, and, if there is a little milk to help it down, tastes more like food than some of the shavings and sawdust sold as cereals. This food could be bought at Joshimath, nine marches from Ranikhet, so there was no need to take any coolies until Joshimath was reached. These men I proposed getting from Mana, a little village in the extreme north-west of Garhwal near the Tibet border. It was only twenty-one miles from Joshimath, and men from there had been up the Rishi with Shipton and me in 1934, and their stoutness and rock-climbing ability were beyond all question.

If delay was to be avoided these arrangements had to be made before we left Ranikhet, because it would take time to collect 900 lb. of food and to get the men down from Mana to Joshimath. Fortunately this could be done. There is a telegraph line to Joshimath, and a wire and a money order to a man in the bazaar there set on foot the collecting of the food. There remained the problem of the porters. Mana is twenty-one miles from Joshimath, and to go up there, find the men, and return would take a good three days. But the problem was solved in a rather unlikely way by invoking the aid of the priesthood.

The telegraph line does not stop at Joshimath but follows the Pilgrim Road up to Badrinath, which is only three miles short of Mana. Of Badrinath, the Mecca for fifty thousand Hindu pilgrims, something has already been said. It consists of a temple, a number of pilgrim rest-houses, and shops, situated in an open valley on the right bank of the Alaknanda river, only twenty-five miles below the Mana Pass into Tibet. The fall of Bhasadura, one of the sacred sources, where 'the Ganges falls like the thread of a Lotus flower', is not far away, and there are bathing pools in the river, and thermal springs, which are all efficacious in cleansing believers of past offences.

The temple, however, is the centre around which the life of Badrinath revolves during the short pilgrim season between May and October. Badrinath is 10,280 ft. above the sea, and during the winter snow lies everywhere, the temple is closed, and the officials, shopkeepers and others migrate to a less inhospitable clime. The temple is close to the river. It has a very modern appearance, but the foundation dates from the eighth century and the first building is said to have been erected by Sankara Acharya, the great Hindu reformer. This building and several subsequent ones are believed to have been destroyed by avalanches but, considering its situation, this is difficult to understand unless great changes have taken place in the formation of the surrounding country. The idol in the main temple is of black stone, stands about three feet high and is clothed with rich brocade, and wears a tiara of gold in which is a large diamond. The dresses and ornaments are reputed to be worth at least ten thousand rupees. The idol is served daily with two meals, and after a decent interval has elapsed the food is distributed amongst the pilgrims, many of whom are too poor to feed themselves. Offerings are of course made by the pilgrims in cash, kind, or ornaments, according to their means; strict accounts are kept by the treasurers, and the business affairs of the temple are in the hands of a secretary. Other members of the temporal council for the affairs of the Badrinath temple are the Bhotias of Mana, so that this village is intimately connected with its larger neighbour.

At the height of the pilgrim season the scene in the one narrow street of Badrinath brings back memories of *Kim*. Wealthy babus in 'jhampans', or dandies, carried by four sweating coolies, the more economically minded in long cylindrical baskets carried by only one; old men and women of all classes arriving on foot travel-stained and weary, clutching their pilgrim's staff; all welcomed by a roll of drums nicely proportioned in length and loudness to the probable state of the pilgrim's purse; naked fakirs smeared with ashes, long-haired saddhus, blind and deformed beggars thrusting their wooden bowls under the nose of every shopkeeper in the bazaar, getting here a little flour or a handful of rice, there some spices or salt, and nowhere a refusal; all these jostle each other in the narrow stone-flagged street between the open-fronted shops where yak-tails and Manchester cottons, musk and cheap photographs lie huddled together; and over all, aloof, watchful, stand the snows of Himachal where the gods live.

To find amongst all this a Post and Telegraph Office savours of banality if not impropriety, but to us it proved invaluable. In 1934 Shipton and I had twice visited Badrinath and made the acquaintance of the Rawal or Priest of the temple (to give him his full title, His Holiness the Rawal Pandit Basudeva Numbudri), a high-caste Brahman from Southern India. This custom of appointing a Brahman from the south as the Rawal of a temple in the northernmost confines of India dates back to about A.D. 800, when the great Hindu reformer, Sankara Acharya, drove out encroaching Bhuddism from Garhwal and took measures, of which this was one, to maintain the purity of the restored religion. It was this same Sankara who preached the efficacy of the pilgrimage to the holy places of the Himalaya. I was now reminded of this friend in need and felt confident that a wire to him, asking for a dozen Mana men to be sent to Joshimath on June 6th, would be all that was needed.

One more day was spent in Ranikhet having a big tarpaulin made up, buying a few necessities, and arranging for a bus. In the course of the day a reply came from Joshimath assuring us that the food would be ready. None of our equipment had yet arrived, a fact which made it the more easy to travel as light as we intended. My sleeping bag, which had an inner and outer lining, would do for both of us, the tarpaulin would cover the food, the two Sherpas, and ourselves, while extra clothing was not wanted as we would not be going above 14,000 ft.

So on May 30th, two days after arriving, we started out, the party consisting of two Sherpas, a 10 lb. Cheddar cheese, and ourselves. The cheese was one out of a case of six which I had luckily brought up from Calcutta in my own compartment to spare them the prolonged suffering of a ten-day journey by goods train in the hot weather.

From Ranikhet you can get a flying start in a bus, and this dropped us fifty miles away at a place called Garul, where the road ended, by half-past ten in the morning. The height of this place is only 3000 ft., and Gwaldam, where we stopped for the night, is over 3000 ft. higher and ten miles away. It was fairly cool, thanks to a dust cloud which hid the sun, but otherwise this march can be a trying one. At Gwaldam a bungalow welcomes the traveller. That and a few unhappy looking tea bushes are the only remaining evidence of a once flourishing tea estate. It rained hard in the night, but next day we were permitted to remain dry until two o'clock, when it began again with some violence. A fair interval persuaded us to push on from the village where we were sheltering to the next stream, and there we got our tarpaulin rigged just before another deluge began. It was open at both ends, and when the four of us were lying cheek by jowl there was a foot or two to spare at each end—on fine nights the outer berth was very desirable. Rain in Garhwal may be heavy, but usually it seems to be unaccompanied by wind and the tarpaulin kept us dry very effectively.

When reading accounts of travel in Garhwal the peculiar nature of the country should be borne in mind. The whole country is an intricate tangle of valleys and ridges with their attendant ravines and spurs, which, even in the foothills, are all on a scale undreamt of in this country. The stages of a march may seem short, but involving, as most of them do, a rise of 3000 ft. or more and an equally great descent, they are quite long enough. It is possible to be in a valley not more than 3000 ft. above the sea, the home of a vegetation which is almost tropical, and at the same time to be within fifteen miles of snow-clad peaks 20,000 ft. high.

The following story seems to me to provide as apt an illustration of the country now as it did then. 'In the reign of Akbar, that prince demanded of the Raja of Srinagar (the ancient capital of Garhwal) an account of the revenues of his raj and a chart of his country. The Raja being then at court, repaired to the presence the following day and in obedience to the commands of the king presented a true statement of his finances and a chart of his country by introducing a lean camel and saying: "This is a faithful picture of the territory I possess—up and down and very poor." The king smiled at the ingenuity of the thought and told him that from the revenues of a country produced with so much labour and in amount so small, he had nothing to demand.' It was over the humps and hollows of the camel's back that we had now to pass.

There are three possible routes from Ranikhet to Joshimath and we took the most easterly, which is the one generally used and one which has been frequently described. It is supposedly the shortest, but that is doubtful, for it certainly involves more climbing than the other two. There are three big valleys between Garul and Joshimath, all running from east to west directly across the route; the valley of the Pindar river which comes from the south of Nanda Kot, the Nandakini from the slopes of Trisul, and the Bireh Ganga from Nanda Ghunti; and naturally the farther east and the nearer the mountains these are crossed, the higher are the intervening ridges.

The most westerly route is the Pilgrim Road, which avoids crossing any of these valleys by following the main valley of the Alaknanda. It is usually shunned by expeditions, at any rate on the outward journey, on account of the risk of picking up dysentery, cholera, or malaria; curiously enough these diseases seem to lose their terrors when the expedition is on the way home. It is provided with bungalows at every stage and a variety of food can be bought, which perhaps explains the curious fact noted above; whereas on the route we took there is only one bungalow and no food. We had brought from Ranikhet for our own use rice, lentils, and flour, sufficient to last until Joshimath, but the Sherpas, expecting to be able to buy at every village, had brought very little. For most of the way all they could get was barley flour, and it became quite pathetic to hear them asking, hopefully but vainly, at every house they passed for wheat flour.

Eggs and milk were our desideratum, but this was a much fonder hope than that entertained by the Sherpas for their atta. The absence of eggs is understandable because to Hindus hens are unclean and are seldom kept, for in some ways the Garhwali is a very orthodox Hindu. Sometimes one comes across ex-soldiers who have served the British Raj in the Garhwal Rifles who have so far lost caste that they are sufficiently abandoned to keep hens. The rarity with which milk could be got is less easily explained. Every village possessed livestock in abundance, cows, water buffalo, goats; and one could not help thinking that it was the will to help which was lacking, not the ability.

This wet night in a forest glade was a dismal one owing to a new brand of midges, new at least to me. An ordinary midge observes regular hours and knocks off as soon as darkness sets in, but here they carried on business all night long without intermission—if you left your head out you were driven frantic, and suffocated if you put it inside the sleeping bag.

Next day we crossed a pass on the ridge between the Pindar and Nandakini valleys at about 10,000 ft. and dropped down through oak and rhododendron forest and grassy alps to Kanol. It was just too late in the year to see the rhododendrons in flower, which are at their best early in May; they are found between 8000 and 10,000 ft., and this route is particularly rich in this gorgeous kind of forest—gorgeous when in flower, but at other seasons drab and grey. It rained again all the afternoon, and an inside that was far from well added to my gloom; but apart from that we had good reason to be pleased because we were already a day ahead of time. It required a desperate effort next day to retain this lead, for the usual bridge over the Nandakini had gone, and a long detour, five miles up stream and five down again, had to be made. Then we got into trouble crossing a smaller river, where the bridge consisted of the usual two pine logs and flat stones in between. Those with experience are careful to stick to the logs, but Loomis trusted to the stones, which naturally slipped through and in he went, losing both topee and ice-axe. Pasang Kikuli recaptured the topee after an exciting race down stream, and we wasted half an hour at the pool below the bridge while Loomis stripped, tied on the climbing rope, and searched the bottom for the axe. The loss of this axe led to the loss of another, nor was the topee destined to live much longer.

We finally made the appointed stage late that evening, wet, weary, and cold, the result of a very violent hailstorm which we had encountered. In my infirm state I was glad to find shelter in a sort of rest-house; it had a mud floor and no furniture, but a roof and an excellent fireplace made up for these deficiencies.

The next obstacle was the Bireh Ganga, across which we were relieved to find there was still a bridge albeit with little to spare between it and the surging water. I began to wonder how we would fare six weeks later when the river would certainly be very much higher. Our camp that night was amongst some large erratic boulders near the village of Kaliaghat, and a convenient rock overhang preserved our fire from what was now the inevitable afternoon rain. It seemed that the monsoon had already broken, but we talked ourselves into believing that this was merely the 'chota Barsat', the little rains, which are supposed to precede the monsoon proper.

The last and highest ridge was yet to be crossed, that between the Bireh Ganga and the Alaknanda valley in which lies Joshimath itself. The way over this ridge is by the well-known Kuari Pass, 12,400 ft., which is usually crossed on the second day's march from Kaliaghat. We, however, put on steam and reached Dekwani, the camping place at the foot of the Pass, by midday, and went up and over in the afternoon.

Dekwani is a grazing ground just above the tree-line and 1000 ft. below the Pass, and that day there must have been at least a thousand sheep and goats present. It lies on a route which is much used by sheep and goat transport into Tibet. This route follows the Dhauli valley down from the Niti Pass (16,600 ft.) and, leaving the valley short of Joshimath, crosses the Kuari Pass and so reaches the southern valleys of Garhwal. It is a route favourable to such a form of transport because it is high and cool, there is plenty of grass, and few villages. Grain is the usual commodity carried going up to Tibet and salt and borax on the return. A sheep can carry about 20 lb. and a big goat 30 lb., so that a flock of one hundred, which is a small one, can shift a ton or more. The saddle bags are made of coarse wool or hemp strengthened with leather, and are carefully balanced on the back and secured by what corresponds to a breastplate and a crupper; there is no girth. When halted the saddle bags are stacked into a high wall which affords some shelter to the drovers.

We halted at Dekwani to have some food and pass the time of day with the sheep drovers. They were inclined to be surly and took time to thaw out; in fact when the Sherpas borrowed their fire to boil some water they spat ostentatiously and muttered imprecations. A little tobacco soon mollified them, for these Bhotias are inveterate smokers, smoking stuff which looks for all the world like plum pudding, and smoking charcoal rather than nothing at all.

From Dekwani we were on top of the Pass in fifty minutes, but of the glorious view which often rewards the early morning traveller there was no sign. Lowering clouds and mist veiled the horizon in all directions and when, an hour later, we camped below the tree-line these burst in furious squalls of wind and rain. In the evening when the rain stopped we were able to appreciate the best camping ground we had yet had. A smooth flat carpet of grass to lie on, a sparkling brook at our feet, unlimited firewood for the gathering, and at our backs the shelter of a mighty cedar. As if that was not enough, the clouds lifted, and for a moment, before darkness fell, the great bulk of Hathi Parbat, the 'Elephant Mountain', loomed up across the valley, and far to the northwest the shapely white cone of Nilkanta seemed to stand alone in a darkening sky.

Next day we reached Joshimath, a day in advance of the time appointed for the Mana men. Of these there was no sign—and the telegraph line to Badrinath was broken.

CHAPTER FIVE

The Rishi Gorge and Back Again

JOSHIMATH is a village of some importance on the Pilgrim Road to Badrinath and two marches short of that place. It is 6000 ft. above sea level and 1500 ft. above the confluence of the Alaknanda and Dhauli rivers. At the junction is the temple, so often seen at the place where two rivers meet, built on a tongue of rock between the two. This is known as the 'prayag', and the shrine and the few huts are called Vishnuprayag. There are five such 'prayags' at the five sacred confluences of the Alaknanda. The river here, and for a few miles up, is called the Vishnuganga. A flight of stone steps leads down to the water, which is cold, swift, and deep, and in it the pilgrims bathe ceremonially, hanging to chains and ringbolts to avoid being carried away. Even with this precaution several lives are said to be lost every year. The long zigzag path from Vishnuprayag to Joshimath is cut into steps faced with stones.

The temple, or rather collection of temples, is built round a courtyard and is of great antiquity. Some of them are in a state of dilapidation owing, it is said, to an earthquake, but the temples of Vishnu, Ganesh, the Sun, Navadevi, and Narsinha are in fair preservation.

The idol of Vishnu is of black stone, well carved, and about seven feet high. That of Narsinha is reputed to have an arm which diminishes daily, and when it falls off the road to Badrinath will be closed by a landslip and a new temple will be erected at Tapoban, seven miles up the Dhauli valley from Joshimath. The legend giving rise to this forecast is that Vishnu, in his man-lion incarnation of Narsinha, visited the palace of an early Raja of this region and asked the wife of the absent prince for food. Having partaken he lay down on the bed of the Raja, who found him there on his return from the chase and struck him on the arm with his sword. Instead of blood, milk flowed from the wound, and the startled Raja, sensing that he must have struck a god, asked that his crime might be punished. The deity disclosed himself, and having

ordained that the Raja must leave the pleasant vale of Joshimath, added:
'Remember that this wound which thou hast given me shall also be seen on
the image in thy temple, and when that image shall fall to pieces and the hand
shall no more remain, thy house shall fall to ruin and thy dynasty shall
disappear from amongst the princes of the world.'

In one of the Hindu writings is the following:

> The road to Badri never will be closed
> The while at Joshimath Vishnu doth remain;
> But straightway when the god shall cease to dwell,
> The path to Badri will be shut to men.

There is a dâk bungalow at Joshimath for the use of travellers and the
Rawal of Badrinath has a large house here in which he resides during the
winter months. The streets are paved with stone flags and the houses are
neatly built with squared stone and roofed with shingles or heavy slates; they
are usually of two storeys. The ground floor being devoted to a store or shop
while the family live above. Traders, cultivators, and temple officials make up
the population of about five hundred.

There are two bazaars, where all native foods can be bought; the Sherpas at
last got all the atta they wanted and we were able to replenish our stock of
sugar, rice, and lentils, and make ourselves sick on the local sweetmeats,
which are very good indeed. There were far too many flies about for the
fastidious, but, in Garhwal, if you eat only what the flies have not touched
then you go hungry. The flies are no doubt worse in Joshimath and along the
Pilgrim Road generally, but it would not be right to ascribe this wholly to the
pilgrims and their small regard for sanitary rules. All the villages of Garhwal,
even up to 7000 and 8000 ft., are plagued with flies, but as a good part of the
Pilgrim Road lies in a comparatively low and hot valley they are naturally
more numerous in villages on the Road. Chamoli, for example, twenty-five
miles below Joshimath, is only 3000 ft. above the sea.

Malaria, dysentery, and cholera, though not exactly rife, are nevertheless
prevalent along this Road in the summer. A great deal has been done by the
Government to combat this by piping down a clean water supply to the
villages, enforcing sanitary rules, and placing a Medical Officer in charge of
the Road. Cholera was active in Joshimath and neighbouring villages when
we returned there a fortnight later and the Medical Officer, who was then in
Joshimath, told us how difficult it was to control, particularly in the outlying
and more inaccessible villages to which it sometimes spreads. Bodies are left
unburied by the banks of streams which carry infection to lower villages, and
the terrified inhabitants migrate, panic-stricken, to other places, taking the
infection with them. Corpses are left to rot in the houses and the sick lie
untended.

The pilgrim season was in full swing and Joshimath was alive with devotees
of all ages and all classes, men and women, rich and poor. To an outsider their
demeanour gave the impression that this pilgrimage was more of a disagreeable
duty than a pleasure, that the toil and hardships of the road were supported
with resignation rather than accepted joyfully as a means of grace—incidents

on the road to heaven. But this downcast air may rightly be attributed to the awe and terror which most must feel in the presence of such strange and prodigious manifestations of the power of the gods. Savage crags, roaring torrents, rock-bound valleys, hillsides scarred and gashed with terrific landslides, and beyond all the stern and implacable snows—all these must be overwhelming to men whose lives have been passed on the smug and fertile plains, by sluggish and placid rivers, with no hill in sight higher than the village dunghill.

Nor is it remarkable that they should attribute the faintness felt in the rarefied air of Badrinath and Kedarnath to the influence of superhuman powers; or believe that the snow wreaths blowing off the Kedarnath peak are the smoke of sacrifice made by one of Siva's favoured followers, or that the snow banner flying on Nanda Devi is from the kitchen of the goddess herself.

The accomplishment of such a journey by such men must be a tremendous fact in their lives, something to remember when all else has faded. To reach the temple alone is a sign of divine favour, for the gods turn back those with whom they are displeased. The daily exercise, the months of frugal living, the hill air, the sacrifice of time and money, all these must play no small part in the moral and physical regeneration of the pilgrims; and if this salutary discipline of mind and body were to be enjoyed there would perhaps be the less merit. For the mountaineer, it is to be feared, though he penetrate to the ultimate *sanctum sanctorum* of the gods, there is, like the award of the Garter, 'no damned merit about it'—his enjoyment is too palpable.

By midday of June 6th the telegraph line to Badrinath was working and an exchange of telegrams brought the good news that the porters would be down next day. Meantime our 900 lb. of food was ready, half here and half at another village, so that all was set for a start on the 8th, and only a day had been lost. In the perverse way the weather sometimes has, both of these days spent sitting idle in Joshimath were gloriously fine.

Fourteen men from Mana arrived in the evening, among whom were three who had accompanied us in 1934, and on the 8th we did a short march to Tapoban, where the balance of the food was collected and three more local porters enlisted. One of these men, hailing from Bompa, a village higher up the Dhauli, was an amusing character. His name was Kalu and he had chits from previous expeditions in which he appeared to have distinguished himself by going high on Trisul. He was a shameless cadger with an ingratiating manner, and a habit of placing both palms of his hands together as if in prayer whenever he spoke to you. As a mountaineer he thought no small beer of himself, particularly if the conversation should turn to Trisul as it always did if he was taking part in it, and then he would slap his chest like a gorilla, and cry out in a loud voice what great feats Kalu had performed and what greater he was about to do. For all that he worked so well on this trip that at the end I placed too much faith in him and was let down.

At Tapoban we had a fortunate meeting with two British officers out on a shooting trip, who invited us to use their camping ground and join their mess, an invitation we were not slow to accept, as I knew from previous experience that on these shooting trips the doctrine of 'living on the country' is not carried to extreme lengths. But for this chance meeting and the existence of a hot spring, Tapoban would have left nothing but evil memories. The flies were unusually fierce, and as soon as they stopped work at dusk the midges began, and at dawn the reverse process took place.

The hot spring I mentioned is up a little side valley a couple of hundred yards from the road. There is a stone tank about ten feet square and three feet deep, into which gushes a stream of water at a temperature of about 90 degrees. The water is clear and sparkling, and has no taste. Close by is a shrine and a hut for its guardian, an emaciated hermit whose hair reached almost to the ground. On this occasion he was absent and we could lie in the bath at ease, increasing the pleasure by running a few yards to a brook where the water was as cold as the bath was hot, and smelt deliciously of wild mint.

A more detailed description of our route may be left for the moment; sufficient to say that after one more vile night of midges in the warm valley we began the climb to the 14,000 ft. pass where flies and midges ceased from troubling. On our way up we met a flock of sheep, and the shepherd was understood to say that one of his sheep had fallen over a cliff and it was ours for the carrying. The Mana men soon found it, skinned it, and went on their way rejoicing; it certainly looked fresh enough, but there was suspiciously little sign of it having suffered a fall. In camp that night when Loomis and I had, after some argument, come to a decision about the respective merits of grilled chops and boiled neck, the inquest was resumed, and we were calmly informed that the sheep had died through eating a poisonous plant. Somehow or other mutton chops ceased to allure and we generously gave our share to the Sherpas. I should hesitate to accuse them of using this stratagem to bring about such a desirable result, but they showed no reluctance to accept fortune's gift and suffered not the slightest ill-effect.

We crossed the pass, now clear of snow, and got down to the Durashi grazing alp. There were no sheep there and we had the place to ourselves, the Mana men finding shelter in some caves, ourselves under the tarpaulin, and the Sherpas in a stone hut used by shepherds. It required a certain lack of imagination to sleep in this hut, because the roof of enormously heavy stones was only supported by some singularly inadequate pieces of wood, one of which was already cracked.

We woke to a wet morning and did not leave till nine o'clock, though this was not much later than usual, for the Mana men are very independent and dislike being hurried. After a leisurely breakfast, the pipe (they had only one) would be passed round several times before they even thought of hinting at a readiness to begin packing up, and unless there was some urgent reason for an early start it was useless to try and hurry them. It was the same on the march; they knew how far they were going and took their own time getting there, sitting down whenever they felt the need for a pipe, which was frequently, and remaining there till all had smoked enough.

The pipe has a ritual of its own: it is a water pipe with a stem about two feet long which is carried by one man; another carries the bowl, a clay affair the size of a jam dish; the bamboo mouthpiece, also two feet long, is carried by a third, the tobacco by a fourth, and the flint and steel by a fifth. If there is any straggling on the march it is some time before the whole is assembled and yet longer before the thing is fairly alight; unless there happens to be a fire handy, when they simply put a burning brand on top of the bowl and leave it there. These dilatory habits are somewhat exasperating, but the men are withal so active and sturdy and reliable that it is impossible to find fault, and if a special effort is required they can and will move quicker than most. Nor is there ever any trouble about making up their loads and deciding who will carry what, a blessing which only those who have travelled with African porters can really appreciate. In their case this unenviable task of apportioning loads usually begins with a free fight and ends with the abandonment of the heaviest load.

Between Durashi and the lower grazing alp of Dibrugheta lies an easy grass pass involving an ascent of 1000 ft. from Durashi and a descent of 3000 ft. to Dibrugheta. The ridge which is crossed by this pass was, by Dr Longstaff, aptly named 'The Curtain'; away from the pass towards the Rishi the ridge rises and the grass slope changes to enormous slabs of smooth, grey rock, which jut right out to the river and completely hide the lower part of the gorge, like the fire curtain on some vast stage.

We sat for some time on the ridge waiting in vain for a view up the gorge to Nanda Devi. Then the Mana men, having had their smoke, took it into their heads to build two enormous cairns and to dedicate them to Loomis and myself, first asking our names, which the scholar amongst them then wrote in Urdu on a stone with a piece of charcoal. This cairn building and stone balancing is the national pastime amongst Tibetans and kindred people such as Sherpas, who are likewise Bhuddists, and these Bhotias who, though nominally Hindus, possibly came from Tibet originally and have maintained a connection with that country ever since. They will run up a noble cairn out of the most unlikely material in a very short time, and crown the whole with stones of diminishing size, skilfully balanced, one on top of the other.

Meanwhile it had started raining again, but the cairns had to be finished off, and in no slovenly manner either, before we were allowed to go on. Rain on the march was to be particularly dreaded at this time, because although the flour and rice were put up in Willesden canvas bags these would not stand a prolonged soaking, and the food was going to be left for six weeks or more before being eaten.

At Dibrugheta we were once more down among birch and pine forest and the Mana men made themselves elaborate huts roofed with birch bark. This invaluable material has many uses. We have all heard of birch-bark canoes, here we were using it for thatching, and it was strongly recommended to me by a former traveller in these parts as a substitute for tobacco, though after trying it I decided that this was a joke in rather bad taste. The Mana men were full of beans this evening, and when they had finished their meal the lads amongst them started throwing lighted brands on the roof of each other's huts, and the whole mob roared with delight when someone's hut was burnt down.

The next camp beyond Dibrugheta is the Cave Camp and here all hands can be accommodated in caves. That is true at least of a party of reasonable size such as ours was then, but it puzzled us to know what we should do when the main body of fifty or more came, because of tent sites there were none. Loomis and I slept that night on a mattress of bags of food to escape the adamantine hardness of the cave floor.

We made the first small food dump here where it was dry, and where it was beyond the reach of those in the villages who might be curious to know what we had done with so much food. It was now the 13th and it was time to think of turning back. But things were going well, the farther we got the food the better, and above all I wanted to have a look at the difficult part of the gorge to see if the route would still 'go'. It was conceivable that since 1934 a fall of rock or the disappearance of some grass or trees from the cliff faces would have made the gorge impassable. One of the charms of the route then discovered was the weakness of some of the links in it and the absence of any alternatives. We therefore decided to go on for another three days, long enough to take us beyond all difficulties and to the threshold of the Promised Land.

Our march that day took us to what had been our base camp in 1934, a pleasant camp under a big rock overhang on the south side of the Rishi Ganga, which can be crossed here by a natural bridge. Before dropping down to the crossing of the Rishi, the glacier-fed torrent of the Rhamani, coming down from the north, had to be crossed. At this time of year it was not a serious obstacle, but for all that it was no place to cross without the support of the third leg which an ice-axe provides. Accordingly as soon as I had crossed, instead of waiting for the rope, I foolishly threw my axe back for Loomis, whose own axe, it will be remembered, had been lost. The bank on that side was steep and high and, instead of landing on top, the axe hit a boulder and bounced back into the river. Loomis made one unavailing grab and then jumped into the river after it, and the net results of two pieces of foolishness was the loss of his topee and my ice-axe.

After carrying an axe for some days one feels lost at first without it, but in the Rishi, where it is better to have both hands available rather than one hand and an axe, it was really more of a hindrance than a help. The loss of the topee might have been serious for anyone with a sensitive skull, but none of us found such things necessary in Garhwal, which is outside the tropics and in about the same latitude as Cairo.

The natural bridge over the Rishi, which is formed by an enormous boulder, caused some delay. All loads had to be lowered down to it and on the boulder itself a rope was necessary because the branches, which in 1934 we had placed there as ladders, had all gone. However, all got safely over and there we were only two days from the Basin, with ten loads of food, and a dry overhang under which to sleep.

From this point the way lies straight up the south wall of the gorge to a height of about 1500 ft. above the river, and from there pursues a horizontal or slightly downwards course—what we call a traverse. The first 400 or 500 ft. out of the river bed are steep and exposed, and the climber is disquietingly dependent on branches of trees and tufts of grass for his safety. No further difficulty is encountered until the beginning of the traverse. From a grass terrace a rock chimney leads up to what we called the 'Slabs', smooth rock sloping upwards at such an angle, that with a load on, it is difficult to stand up with any confidence. These slabs form the floor of a wide gully, which just below here plunges down to the Rishi at a much steeper angle. Above the slabs is a rock wall which can be climbed on the left by men without loads, and these can then be hauled directly up the wall.

We arrived at this place and found the slabs dry, and Loomis and I, who were in rubbers and had only moderate loads, got up without a rope. The Mana men go barefoot and most of them climb like cats, but here only a few of them, and neither of the Sherpas, despised the aid of the rope. Loads were dumped and some of us climbed to the top of the wall and began hauling while the others remained below to tie on. It is a slow job at the best, and I climbed down again to hasten matters, as I wanted to get finished before the rain started; we had a rope 120 ft. long so that both ends could be used—tying a load on one end while the other was being hauled up. To superintend this I was standing on a narrow ledge about twenty feet above the floor of the gully and, thick-headedly enough, almost under the rope. Things then happened quickly. Gazing at an ascending load I was petrified to see a large flake of rock, probably loosened by the rope, sliding down the wall straight for me. Whether it hit me, or whether I stepped back to avoid it, is only of academic interest because the result was the same, and next instant I was falling twenty feet on to the slabs, head first and face to the wall, for I distinctly remember seeing it go past. Hitting the slabs I rolled for a bit and then luckily came to rest before completing the 1400-odd feet into the river.

In a minute or two I was able to sit up and take notice, and having told the load-haulers to get on with it, crawled up the slabs to a more secure place and assessed the damage. A sprained shoulder and thumb, a bruised thigh and a cracked rib, and a lot of skin missing was the sum total. None were serious, and it might have been much worse; in which case, I thought, the last lines of a little verse about the man who tried to hurry the East would not have been inapplicable: 'And the end of the fight is a tombstone white with the name of the late deceased, and this epitaph drear, "A fool lies here who tried to hurry the East."'

It was necessary to get moving before stiffness made this impossible, so with a rope on and some men shoving behind, I was got up to the top of the wall, and when the loads were all up we started for Halfway Camp, which was still a mile distant.

Next day Loomis went on with the men and dumped all the remaining loads at Pisgah Camp within sight of the Sanctuary, and returned the same day to Halfway Camp. I lay in camp and felt sorry for myself, wondering how I was to get back, for the slightest movement was difficult, tomorrow was the 17th, and we were due in Ranikhet on the 25th.

With Pasang Kikuli assisting I started very early next morning, in advance of the others, who caught us up at the 'Slabs'. These were difficult for me because both arms were useless, but the Mana men were very solicitous and skilful and before midday we reached the overhang by the Rishi. After an hour's rest we pushed on over the bridge, which had now been made easier by placing trees there, and Cave Camp was reached the same day.

Another double march followed, Kalu and the Mana headman taking care of me. The 3000 ft. climb up to the 'Curtain' ridge from Dibrugheta was enlivened by a violent hail storm and we were so perished with cold that, on arrival at Durashi, Loomis and I shared the stone hut with the Sherpas, caring little whether the roof fell in or not. Still marching double stages we crossed the pass and got down to flies and the Dhauli valley next day, and on the 20th reached Joshimath, not omitting to wallow for an hour in the hot spring at Tapoban in the hope that it would ease my battered limbs, which, when they realised they were not likely to get any rest, began to respond to this 'healing by faith' treatment.

Here we paid off the Mana men, giving them a liberal tip at which they grumbled loudly for, unlike the Sherpas who do this sort of work more for its own sake than for the money, they are out for all they can get and value their services highly. For all their complaining, they let it be understood that they would be willing to come with us again next month, despite our illiberal notions about baksheesh. Kalu had already engaged himself, and had undertaken the collection of another ten loads of coolie food, assuring me that I could rely on him to have it ready waiting for us, an assurance I was foolish enough to accept.

Now that the Mana men had gone, Loomis and I had no one to carry our loads, and for me it was painful enough to get along at all, without having to carry a load. We combed the bazaar for a coolie, but at ten o'clock gave it up and left in pouring rain and in a very sour mood. It was late evening before we camped amongst the pines not far below our old camp site. On the 22nd we crossed the Kuari, went on through Kaliaghat and down to the Bireh Ganga. The bridge was down but a repair gang were at work on it and, after a short wait, two logs were got into a sufficiently stable position to cross with the aid of a rope. Spray was dashing over the logs and Pasang Phuta was rash enough to try it in rubber shoes, slipped on the wet wood, and hung suspended with his load in the water and his head not far off it. He was soon rescued from this undignified and perilous position and we pushed on and camped in the gathering dark some way above the river.

We seemed to be getting into a defiant sort of mood and evinced a growing determination to reach Ranikhet in five days from Joshimath, cost what effort it might. Next day we crossed the ridge, got down to the Ramni bungalow at midday and, encouraged by hearing that the bridge on the direct route was repaired, crossed the Nandakini and trudged the 2000 ft. up to Kanol, camping at six o'clock in a field.

I was rapidly recovering under this treatment, but Loomis was not well; yet on the following day we eclipsed all previous efforts and covered what are normally three stages, reaching the Gwaldam bungalow at half-past seven at night. We learnt that the Ranikhet bus left Garul at five in the morning, and we toyed with the idea of leaving Gwaldam again in the small hours to catch it. But in the night there was tremendous rain and it was so jolly sitting once more in a chair with a roof over our heads and a fire at our feet that we consigned this particular bus to the devil and strolled down to Garul like gentlemen late in the forenoon. By paying rather more than the usual fare we persuaded another bus to start and got back to Ranikhet on the evening of the 25th, twenty-eight days after leaving it.

CHAPTER SIX

'Scrapping and Bagging'

THANKS to the goodwill of the Forest Service we had been given the use of the Ranikhet Forest Bungalow, and here we installed ourselves to begin work and to await the arrival of the others. It is a big building of eight rooms, with a wide verandah running round two sides which made an ideal place for the reception of the flood of cases which was about to engulf us. Furthermore, it is one of the most pleasantly situated bungalows in Ranikhet and commands a complete panorama of the snows from the Kedarnath peaks in the west to Nepal in the east.

We were told that the weather had been atrocious ever since we left, the monsoon having set in exceptionally early. Comparing notes it seemed that the weather had been less severe where we were, farther north, and personally I did not consider monsoon conditions really established in the north until we returned to Joshimath on the 20th. However, there was no doubt about it then, for it rained all the way back and, except for a short break, continued to rain throughout our stay in Ranikhet; so much so that the later arrivals never got a glimpse of a mountain until we reached the Kuari Pass. During this brief fine spell Loomis and I, and Arthur Emmons, the second of the American contingent to arrive, had some clear views of the Range. The side of Nanda Devi which can be seen from Ranikhet is that by which our attempt was to be made, and after studying it through glasses and telescope we could only express a pious hope that it was not so bad as it looked.

Emmons, who joined us on the 28th, had done some climbing in Alaska and was one of the party which in 1932 climbed Minya Gonkar (24,900 ft.), a peak in the south-west of China near the Tibet border. While at the highest camp on this mountain Emmons had been severely frost-bitten in both feet, which he was fortunate not to lose altogether. He was still able to climb, in fact he had since been to the Alps; but he was not able to go high because frost-bite is very apt to recur in a limb which has already been attacked. He was to take charge of the base for us and carry out a survey.

Most of the food and equipment had now arrived, and although a considerable quantity of food was purposely left at Delhi, we yet had far more than we could use, due mainly to preparations having been made on a Kangchenjunga scale for a party of twelve. This was not such a happy position as it may sound. Some stoicism was required for the scrapping of so much good food, and even with only three present whose tastes need be considered, it was hard to satisfy everyone. It was all the more important therefore to get this job done before any other members of the party arrived, further to darken counsel by urging the claims of their pet foods.

Without wishing to appear over-righteous I may say that I was indifferent to what we took so long as it was food and not chemicals, and gave value for weight. That this attitude involved no self-sacrifice I might add that in my opinion all tinned foods tasted the same, and that if we had to take a hundred pounds of tinned meat the proportion of ham, tongue, chicken, roast beef, bully beef, or even sardines was of no consequence. And the same might be said of cereals, of which we had a weird and wonderful assortment of every hue and texture, but which in the end all boiled down to porridge. Tinned jams too are more distinguishable by colour than by taste and, when these came up for selection, I put in a mild plea on behalf of honey to the exclusion of all jam, a plea which received more favourable hearing because its advocate had taken no part in the fierce contests which raged over, say, oatmeal versus hominy grits, and corned beef against roast beef. Having fixed the total weight of food required and deducted what I considered the essentials, namely all the pemmican, cheese, biscuit and, if possible, honey, that we had with us, plus sugar at the rate of half a pound a day a man, the remaining weight was then apportioned between meat, cereals, sweet-stuffs, and miscellaneous, and Loomis and Emmons filled the lists in detail, tossing up, presumably, for first pick. The method might not have been approved by a dietician, but the results were satisfactory and nobody groused about the food, at least not until circumstance compelled us to jettison a lot more.

Saving weight was to my mind all-important, and this doctrine found ready backers amongst the others, especially those who had climbed in Alaska or British Columbia, where porters as understood in the Himalaya are non-existent, and everything has to be carried on the climber's back. When porters *are* available, as in this case, it may seem immaterial whether we took forty or fifty, apart from the small extra cost. But the route up the Rishi is difficult for heavily laden porters and a slip might have serious consequences, so that every coolie in excess of the minimum was an added responsibility. It was not like climbing on a mountain with a few Sherpas, when Europeans are roped to the porters and able to look after them. Roping together large numbers is not very practicable nor can you festoon three miles of cliff with fixed ropes, and in most of the places where a slip might occur no safeguards are possible.

When a large amount of tinned food is taken the packing is no small proportion of the total weight. For example, 30 lb. of bully beef packed in 1 lb. tins, or sometimes ½ lb. tins, weighs nearly 40 lb.; it is seldom safe to allow less than one-fifth of the total for packing, and more often it is a fourth. We saved what weight we could by bulking where possible, and things like cereals and dried fruits were put in waterproof bags. In only one instance did our zeal for saving weight outrun discretion, when a certain much advertised drink in powder form was put in bags and promptly coagulated into a stiff, glutinous mass. To some of us it was more palatable in this toffee form than as a drink.

When the remainder of the party arrived, the results and implications of this scrap and bag policy were regarded with mixed feelings. 'Scrapping and bagging' became a stock jest and dark hints were thrown out that the leader of the 'scrap and bag' school should himself be scrapped, or at any rate bagged. It was a job for a Fisher and I am afraid that unlike him none of us were sufficiently 'ruthless, and remorseless'.

The weight suggested for our personal gear, including sleeping bag and boots, was 35 lb. Boots were included among gear to be carried, because for the approach march everyone used the highly unorthodox footwear of rubber shoes, usually without socks too, until beyond Joshimath, and some of the more impious wore them on to the glacier. If the weight was kept down to this poundage per person each Sherpa could carry his own kit of 25 lb. and his Sahib's, and the Sahibs would march unladen, at least as far as Joshimath. In practice this was unsatisfactory, for most people then proceeded to burden themselves with a private rucksack and another 20 lb. or more of personal belongings. Very little of this extra stuff was used, but was dumped at various places from Tapoban onwards and later solemnly carried back again. It is rather a problem deciding what you must take and what you can leave behind, but it is amazingly simplified when you know that you have to carry it all yourself.

The Sherpas' personal effects wanted a lot of overhauling to keep them within the stipulated weight, and in *their* case it was possible to be dictatorial. But, despite the severest scrutiny, when we arrived in the Basin one of them suddenly appeared wearing a wholly unauthorised and very unexpeditionary pair of trousers, another a favourite pair of buttoned boots.

To conclude, this overlong dissertation on weight, I should add that on the day before starting, when most of the others were out or too preoccupied, Charles Houston and I had a glorious hour amongst the 'kitchen' and 'miscellaneous junk' loads, which resulted in the scrapping of most of the innumerable articles included for the time-honoured reason that 'they might come in useful', and the reduction of our eating utensils to a mug and a spoon apiece.

The four additional Sherpas arrived on July 3rd. One of them, Nuri, had been with me in Sikkim, two I had looked at in Darjeeling and turned down on the score of age. These were Da Namgyal and Nima Tsering, who were both on Everest in 1924 but who now seemed, from one cause or another, to be past any really strenuous work, as indeed the event proved. The fourth was Kitar, who had an extraordinary record of expeditionary work to his credit but who did not seem to us a very likeable type of Sherpa. He had been on the Everest expeditions of 1922, 1924, and 1933, Kangchenjunga expeditions of 1929, 1930, 1931, and Nanga Parbat of 1934 when he, Pasang Kikuli, and three others were the only survivors of the eleven high-camp porters.

The remainder of the party, excepting Odell, arrived on July 6th and included Graham Brown, Peter Lloyd, and Charles Houston. The last named was the third American, and had organised the attempt on Mount Foraker in which Graham Brown had taken part. Odell, in the tradition of learned professors, was last, and we were still one American short. This was Adams

Carter, who on this particular date was believed to be in Shanghai, rather a long way from Nanda Devi. Apparently there had been some misunderstanding, and he was under the impression that we were not going to tackle the mountain until after the monsoon. I thought it would be hardly worth his while to come, but in this I reckoned without his resource or the possibilities of air travel. Anyhow, we sent him a cable to the effect that we were starting on the 10th, and that if he could not reach Ranikhet within a fortnight of that date, he might as well stay in Shanghai.

Odell, who was intending to do a lot of geological work, and who as a scientist lent seriousness to our otherwise frivolous proceedings, had gone to Simla and was not to arrive until the 8th. This was a source of worry to me, who had to arrange the transport, for it was credibly reported that he was accompanied by a mountain of luggage, would probably acquire more scientific instruments in Simla, while others of the same genus were said to be converging on Ranikhet from various parts of Europe and America. Meantime we had to tell the coolie agent with whom we were dealing exactly how many coolies we required, for these Dotial porters have to be sent for from some distance and would have to start in advance of us. Making a guess, I mentally devoted two coolies to the service of science, and prayed fervently that the reports were exaggerated and that the instruments on the way would arrive too late; as happily they did.

The Dotial porters do not come from Garhwal but from Doti, a corner of Nepal bordering on the Almora district, which perhaps accounts for some of their toughness. They are a class of professional porters and most of the carrying in Garhwal is done by them: an exception to this is on the Pilgrim Road, where the men who carry the dandies all come from the native state of Tehri Garhwal. They are very strong and the normal load for a Dotial on a good road is 80 lb.

In 1934 Shipton and I employed eleven Dotials to carry from Ranikhet to the entrance of the gorge, and, when eight coolies from the Dhauli villages deserted, these men stood by us, added all but two of the abandoned loads to their own, and carried 80 lb. over the 14,000 ft. pass when it was still deep in snow. Their behaviour then had left me with a very high opinion of their qualities, and though, on that occasion, we did not take them over the most difficult part of the gorge, I was confident of their ability to tackle it.

Yet there was a risk in relying entirely on them, because amongst the large number we proposed taking there were likely to be some who were not equal to difficult climbing, and coming, as they do, from a comparatively low, hot country, the cold and wet conditions we expected to encounter in the gorge might knock all the stuffing out of them. The Mana men, on the other hand, could climb anything and were pretty well impervious to weather, the result of living part of the year at 10,000 ft. and most of it at yet higher altitudes tending their flocks. But on the last trip they had told me that we could not get forty Bhotias because not many would be willing to come on an engagement of only three weeks' duration, being at this season more profitably employed trading with Tibet. I therefore decided to rely mainly on Dotials and to leaven the lump with a few Mana men.

For this purpose thirty-seven Dotials paraded in the bazaar on July 7th and, having been signed on and given an advance of pay, were instructed to meet us at Garul on July 10th. Two of these were of the gallant eleven of 1934, and one, Aujra, appointed himself as headman, but on the understanding that he would carry a load. The aid of my friend the Rawal of Badrinath was again invoked, and I asked him to send ten Mana men to meet us in Joshimath on the 19th.

But for this man Aujra we employed no headman, cooks, or other idlers, but each Sahib had a Sherpa allotted to him as servant. There were seven of us, and only six Sherpas, so Pasang Kikuli was detailed to look after Graham Brown and myself while the others had each a Sherpa. This was not so unselfish as it appears, because Pasang could and did attend to the needs of two better than his fellows could look after one, doing most of the camp work into the bargain. Da Namgyal was chosen for Odell and proved to be the perfect 'gentleman's gentleman'; and this was most fitting because Odell was the only one amongst us capable of doing his man credit and of upholding the white man's prestige. By talking to Da Namgyal very loudly and clearly in English, Odell at once arrived at a complete understanding, and thenceforward he was attended by a perfect valet who, with a little encouragement, would have pressed his master's shorts and polished the nails of his climbing boots.

To Da Namgyal the rest of us were rather low and common, scarcely Sahibs in fact; the Americans, especially at first, were rather impatient of too much attention, and I must say it is a bit corrupting to have your boots put on and your pipe lit for you. However, I noticed that before long they acquiesced not unwillingly in the ways of the country and were as ready as the rest of us to shout 'koi hai' on the slightest pretext.[1]

Nima Tsering, who was large and tough-looking, was given to Loomis who was even larger, so that if necessary he could be repressed. He turned out to be our second best man in spite of his age and the effects, as they told me in Darjeeling, of a life-long belief that 'beer is best'. Fortunately, or unfortunately from some points of view, Garhwal is 'dry', at least I have never, or seldom, come across any beer in the villages, though that might be because the search was not diligent enough. Had it been there I am sure the Sherpas would have found it, but we never had any trouble from them on this account. Nima was as strong as a horse and very ready and active, with a prodigious grin in front and a magnificent pigtail behind. He was the only one of our six to wear a pigtail, and I confess to being prejudiced in favour of Sherpas who do wear one, if only because it may mean that they have not been enervated by long residence in Darjeeling.

Pasang Phuta, who, as I have remarked, was a bit bovine, and Nuri, who was small and frail, were allotted to Lloyd and Houston respectively because they seemed least in need of assistance. Emmons took Kitar because he was not travelling with the main body, but was riding to Joshimath by the Pilgrim Road to save his feet and needed someone reliable with him. Kitar knew the

1 'Koi hai' means 'anyone there?'—the usual way of calling a servant.

ropes, having been to Garhwal some years ago with Mr Ruttledge and again, only a month previously, with an Austrian traveller.

All was now set for a start. On the evening of the 9th two lorries came up to the bungalow and were loaded with our 2500 lb. of stuff to facilitate an early start next morning. To save weight nearly all the loads were packed in gunny bags instead of boxes. These served the purpose well enough and managed to last out the wear and tear of a rough journey; the only disadvantage was that when anything was wanted they had first to be unstitched and then sewn up again: we carried a supply of twine and packing needles. It speaks well for the honesty of our men that although very little was under lock and key nothing was stolen.

A mass of surplus kit and equipment was now carried over to a neighbouring bungalow and stored there against our return. For this and many other kindnesses we were indebted to Mrs Browne, an old resident of Ranikhet, who has travelled extensively in Garhwal and as far as Tibet. Carter's kit and a small tent were left here ready for him should he arrive, and Mrs Browne undertook to take charge of him and see him started on the road to Joshimath. It had rained without pause for the last forty-eight hours and next morning, when we piled ourselves and the Sherpas into the lorries, it looked like continuing for another forty-eight. No one was there to see us off—a few words of chaff passed with Emmons—and so we started with hopes which no rain could quench.

CHAPTER SEVEN

The Foothills

THE fifty miles of road between Ranikhet and Garul are carved for the most part out of abrupt hillsides and are as full of kinks as a wriggling eel. The heavy rain had started many small landslips, and rounding everyone of the innumerable bends I half expected to find the road completely blocked. Nor was it comforting to reflect that only yesterday a lorry from Kathgodam had slipped off the road and gone down the *khud* with fatal results. Such gloomy thoughts must have been roused by a too early and too heavy breakfast, and it was with a feeling of having been delivered from a great peril that I got down at Garul at midday.

Our thirty-seven Dotials were all present and correct, one or two capitalists sheltering under battered umbrellas, for it continued to rain cheerfully. The thirty-seven loads were dumped in the mud and presently these were adjusted to the satisfaction of all, the headman, having successfully palmed off most of his on to the more complacent of his followers, contenting himself with an umbrella and a canvas bucket, perhaps with a view to being prepared for both contingencies—flood or drought. There was some talk of stopping for the night at a dâk bungalow two miles away, the headman arguing with some cogency that it was raining (a fact which might have escaped our notice) and quoting the time-honoured rule that the first day's march should be a short one. To this I replied that if we only marched in fine weather we should not march at all, that they had already marched for two days from Ranikhet so that it was not their first day, and as for ourselves, though it was kind of him to think of us, we would for once make an exception to the rule.

Gwaldam was therefore our destination, ten miles away and a long climb, and it must have been a portentous sight for the Garulians to see this long caravan sliding and slipping out of their muddy village, most of us brandishing an ice-axe in one hand and an umbrella in the other, some draped in green oilskin cycling capes, and one even crowned with a sou'wester. I remembered the march to Gwaldam in 1934 as a decidedly grim affair, for it was a grilling hot day in May, and when we finally crawled into the bungalow we were more dead than alive. Today nobody seemed to feel it much, not even those who had only recently stepped off a ship, and the slowest of the porters was in by half-past six. There is much to be said for travelling in the monsoon.

The Gwaldam bungalow is a poor place, at least for a party of six; its best feature is the magnificent view which of course we were not to see, save only for a patch of snow which, through a break in the clouds, appeared for a moment high up and seemingly belonged to no earthly mountain. Nor were we more favoured with material things; the usual inquiry for eggs and milk met with the usual reply.

The Dotials had been asking questions about the route, and, hearing that the bridge over the Nandakini was again down, had mapped out a new route for us some distance to the west of the more usual way. Accordingly next morning, when we dropped down through a forest of noble 'chir' trees (*Pinus longifolia*) to the Pindar river, instead of crossing it, we turned west and marched down the valley to a place called Tharali. Here the river was crossed by a wire suspension bridge and the camping ground, a green flat on the river bank, was pointed out to us. It was too public and looked too wet to be very inviting, and since the march had been but short we asked if there was nothing better ahead. There is only one answer to such a question, even should there happen to be a stream round the next corner, and we were hastily assured that there was no water for at least ten miles. For once the liars who told us this did us an inestimable service, for, in consequence of believing them and stopping there, we got three dozen eggs on the spot and two dozen more next morning. Blessings on Tharali! And the more pity that it should have been singled out for vengeance by the flooding of the Pindar river. No doubt the more pious Garhwali considered that Tharali was doubly damned and deserved all it got, not only for keeping the unclean hen but, worse still, for selling the product to the defilers of the shrine of the Blessed Goddess.

The camping ground belied its wet appearance, the sun shone for a brief interval, we broached a 10 lb. cheese of perfect maturity, bathed in the icy Pindar, and were the subject of much amiable curiosity on the part of young Tharali.

It rained again at night and in the early morning, but we got away in good time, for it was advisable to inculcate good habits while the expedition was in its infancy. The usual routine was for me to get up about five and rout out the Sherpas, or rather two of them, for the others seldom came to life until much later. Nima was very good and was generally out first to light the fire, with Pasang Kikuli a close second ready to cook the food I gave him. A great beaker of tea all round was the first thing and then, while the porridge was cooking, Pasang and I started making the chapatties. Pasang was an artist at this and what is more he always washed his hands before getting to work. The mathematically perfect circles of thin dough which he cleverly slapped down on to the hot plate were the envy and despair of all who tried their hands at this game of skill. The amateur's effort was of any shape, varying from an ellipse to something resembling the map of England, that is if it ever reached such an advanced stage; more often it was beaten to fragments or slipped out of the hands on to the ground before ever it was ready for the neat backhander which should, but seldom did, spread it flat on the iron plate. The beaker of tea and the noise we made whacking away at chapatties were the signal for the others to 'rise and shine', though precious little 'shining' was done after the first few days.

When our breakfast was off the fire the Sherpas started cooking theirs—at this stage of the journey usually a vast mountain of rice and a mouth-blistering sauce containing 100 per cent chillies to help it down. Some might have preferred the breakfast order reversed, Sherpas first and Sahibs last, but as it was we had a pleasant interval for digestion, smoking a pipe, writing up diaries, or any other odd job before having to pack up and march.

Today we turned north up a pleasant side valley through more pine forest, and then west again, heading for a gap in the ridge. Camp was made on a delightful green terrace set amidst oak trees, three miles beyond the last village and 8000 ft. up. Odell and I were in first, and while waiting for the porters we stripped and walked back down the road to a nearby waterfall for a bathe. Odell was out of luck; he was surprised by a bevy of ancient beldames and was forced to flee in confusion pursued by a volley of Garhwali Billingsgate.

It began to rain as the porters arrived and all our seven tents had to be pitched for their accommodation. We slept three in a tent, the Sherpas five, the Dotials seven, and those who were left over sought shelter in some shepherds' huts close by. One function of a tent is to keep out rain, but we were now beginning to suspect that the makers of our tents were not aware of this. Every seam dripped, and, where the guys joined the fabric, rivers flowed out to collect on the floor into young lakes, which were summarily dealt with by stabbing a hole in the ground-sheet with a knife. These tents were not made in America, but poor Houston, who was responsible for them and who, under the sheltering roof of the forest bungalow, had waxed eloquent over the impeccable behaviour of the same type in Alaska, came in for some merciless chaff. 'Were they equally good in snow?' we asked, 'and was the rain in Alaska very dry?' And an insect common in Garhwal, though hitherto unknown to science, was discovered for Houston's benefit—a flying leech, which we assured him would fly through these precious tents as easily as the drops of rain.

The mention of insects constrains me to add the following. The seven tents were in two sizes, 6 ft. × 7 ft. and 7 ft. × 8 ft., but in appearance all were alike and now, having given them out to the Dotials, I suddenly called to mind a little roadside incident I had witnessed only that morning. Two Dotials were resting by the wayside, one of them subjecting an indescribably dirty shirt to a close scrutiny, while his companion, sitting behind, did a like office for his head. I kept this disturbing memory to myself and there and then went out, armed with an indelible pencil, and marked with a large 'S' the tents used by ourselves and the Sherpas.

While on the subject of tents I may say, to anticipate matters, that on the mountain the tents were severely tested and behaved very well.

Next day's march took us down to the Nandakini river, about ten miles down stream of the old route, at a place called Ghat. It was not a long march; indeed the stages on this route seemed to me much easier than those of the other, and the Pindar-Nandakini watershed was crossed at a height of only 8900 ft. instead of 10,000 ft. From the pass we followed a delightful river, in which we bathed, down to its junction with the Nandakini; bathing was rapidly becoming an obsession and we did it again in the Nandakini, across which Houston swam, greatly to the astonishment of the natives.

At Ghat a dâk bungalow was in the last stages of construction; there were no doors or windows and the debris which always accumulates during building operations lay thick on the floor—but for all that we occupied it, most of us, even Houston, preferring to be dry though dirty. There was nothing interesting to eat here, and though a man went down to the river at dusk with a net the hopes thus aroused were not fulfilled. Mahseer are found in these bigger rivers where the water is not too cold.

At breakfast next morning we were entertained by a party of strolling minstrels, two bold-looking hussies who sang and an insignificant little man playing a drum with his fingers. We gave them a rupee, which was apparently far too much, for they were quite beside themselves with delight and I feared they would follow us up the mountain.

The Nandakini was crossed by a permanent bridge and for four hours the road zigzagged steadily up a steep slope bare of trees. From the top there was an uninterrupted view up the valley, where the river slowly uncoiled itself like a silver snake between the dark olive green of the forested slopes, flecked with sunshine and shadow. We gazed for a long time, waiting vainly for the great white dome of Trisul to reveal itself at the valley head, while a wandering shepherd beguiled the time for us with the music of his pipe.

The road now contoured the hillside, converging gradually towards the old route and finally joining it in the little village of Ramni, where we took up our quarters in the same ramshackle bungalow.

A Garhwal village is, at any rate from a distance, a very delightful and humanising incident in the Himalayan landscape. It is generally built on a spur or half-way up the slope of a hill, so that the cultivation extends both above and below. Regard must of course be had to the water supply, and this should preferably be from two sources, so that the low-caste Doms shall not foul the water of their betters the Biths (Brahmans and Rajputs). The houses are of stone and are two-storeyed and in front is a stone courtyard bounded by a low stone wall. It is here that the threshing, winnowing, and weaving are carried on. Fruit trees are sometimes planted round the courtyard, peach trees in the higher valleys and bananas or plantains in the lower.

The village with its solid stone houses, sometimes having the walls white-washed, surrounded by terraced fields, has a very satisfying appearance—an appearance of comfort, warmth, and prosperity that is many times accentuated for the traveller who first views it after many weeks above the tree-line.

It rained during the night, and in the morning we climbed in dank mist through dripping rhododendron forest to the top of the ridge at nearly 11,000 ft. Between Ramni and Kaliaghat, the usual halting-place, is a delightfully situated grazing alp called Shim Kharak. I had pleasant recollections of camping there in 1934, but hearing a report that the bridge over the Bireh Ganga was down, we decided to push on and camp closer to the river, so that we could learn the truth of this report and if necessary begin building operations.

We camped a mile short of the bridge and 500 ft. above the river, and Aujra, the headman, went on down to look at the bridge. He reported that the bridge, a tree-trunk affair, was still standing, but that the river was almost lapping it. This news made us very uneasy; it was fine at the moment, but if it rained in the night the bridge would probably go.

Sure enough it rained all night and was hard at it next morning when we hurried down to the river expecting the worst. From half-way down we caught sight of the river through the trees, and there was the bridge with the water a clear two feet below it. It seemed doubtful whether Aujra had gone to the bridge yesterday or merely drawn on his imagination, but I was too thankful to press the inquiry, and rather felt it was a job one of us ought to have done. Had the bridge gone we should certainly have been held up for a day or more, for it would have been no easy matter to throw fresh logs across the forty feet of rushing water.

Climbing up the north side of the valley we could see where the river widened out into the Gohna Lake, the result of a great landslip which occurred in 1893, damming up the Bireh Ganga until a lake of many square miles was formed. At first reports from the local headman that a mountain had fallen were ignored, but when the place was visited by Lieut.-Col. Pulford, R.E., Superintending Engineer, it was found that a succession of slips had formed a dam 900 ft. high, 11,000 ft. wide at the base, and 2000 ft. wide at the top. His opinion was that nothing would happen until the water topped the dam and, in spite of other experts holding contrary views, this opinion was adopted and acted upon, and in the event was triumphantly justified.

An engineer was put on to watch the rise of the water and a light telegraph wire erected for the purpose of warning the towns and villages down the Ganges valley. The danger limits of the expected flood were marked out by masonry pillars beyond which the inhabitants were warned to retreat. Suspension bridges were taken down and pilgrim traffic diverted to other routes.

Final calculations predicted that the flood was not to be expected until August 1894, and on August 25th the water began to trickle over the dam and at midnight it collapsed with an appalling crash. The flood lasted until the morning of the 26th, when it was found the lake had fallen 390 ft. Only one life was lost, but much damage was done all down the river, the town of Srinagar being swept away. From the permanent lake which now exists, the water escapes over the sound remains of the huge barrier.

The enormous grey scar on the hillside above gave us but a faint notion of the cataclysmic nature of the event. The steepness of the valleys, the nature of the rock, and the heavy rain combine to make landslips a frequent occurrence and the maintenance of roads a task of Sisyphus.

It was still drizzling when we reached Kaliaghat at midday and camped amongst the giant boulders, the Dotials boldly and, as it chanced, unwisely deciding to use the spare tents instead of walking a mile to the village. After a fine afternoon it began again in earnest that night, and was raining heavier than ever when we got up. Breakfast was cooked under difficulties, or, to be accurate, under an umbrella. When this dismal rite was over, the flood continued unabated and the porters were averse to starting, saying that a river at the foot of the Kauri Pass would be unfordable. They had already abandoned the tents and taken refuge in a derelict cowshed, and since everyone was wet and miserable we made their faint-heartedness an excuse for 'lying at earth', as Mr Jorrocks would express it, when the weather was too bad for hunting. This decision cost us Rs 37, a day's pay for the Dotials, and the words 'milksops' and 'sissies' were freely bandied about in self-accusation, but it is difficult to conceive a process better calculated to promote universal misery than striking water-logged tents and packing up soaking bedding in a deluge of rain.

We lay in our tents all day watching the drips and rivulets, stabbing holes in the floor to keep the lakes at a reasonable level, and blessing our stars that we were the right side of the Bireh Ganga. It was a day for song if ever there was one; on such a day, pent up in a leaking tent, the most mournful hymns have been found to have a very composing effect. But we were singularly deficient in this useful accomplishment and I do not remember a single chorus. Perhaps we were too serious-minded and certainly the ship was heavily freighted with learning. In one tent you could listen to a discussion on geology or, if not a discussion, at any rate a monologue; in another poetry was not only discussed but also written, while in a third medicine would be the theme, for we boasted no less than two doctors in embryo, and one *ci-devant*. It was possible to have a fellow-feeling for Walpole, the Prime Minister, who said that he always encouraged the guests at his table to talk bawdy because that was a subject in which everyone could join.

So many would-be doctors were rather a thorn in the flesh at times, because there was a ban on unboiled water and it was impossible to drink out of a stream unless they were out of sight, and then it was done furtively and with a sense of guilt. Even some apples which we got in Joshimath, straight off a tree, were subjected to the indignity of a potassium permanganate bath; I suppose they deserved it for not moving with the times, and omitting to grow a cellophane wrapper as well as a skin.

Meantime it is still raining, as it was when this digression started, and so it continued for a second night until by dawn it had rained itself out. After crossing another 11,000 ft. ridge above Kaliaghat we dropped again to the stream which had to be forded. The approach to it was down the loose debris of a comparatively recent landslide, flanked on the right by the horribly unstable-looking precipice of yellow rock off which the slip had broken. The road crosses the river below a waterfall issuing from a gorge which is almost a cave, and which Loomis compared to the Bee Rocks of *The Jungle Book*. Normally this ford is only ankle-deep but now it was impracticable, and we had to cross by a fresh place a hundred yards down stream where the bed widened. The previous day even this would have been impassable, as the porters had feared.

On the far side we passed many clumps of bamboo and, partly for old times' sake, and to amuse the others, I got the Sherpas to gather some young shoots, which we had cooked for dinner. On one occasion in 1934 bamboo shoots had been our 'manna'. We enjoyed another gastronomic treat that day when we found wild strawberries almost as large as a cultivated variety.

And talking of gastronomy, we ourselves provided a gastronomic treat for the leeches that were here in considerable numbers. It has always puzzled me what these creatures live on in the normal course of a dull life, and whether blood is a necessity. The banquets provided by human beings must be of rare occurrence in the dense, wet, tropical forests which are their usual habitat. We had met a few in the lower country earlier in the march, but it was curious to find so many here at an altitude of over 9000 ft. Leeches have always been associated in my mind with hot, wet climates, but I suppose no one from the forests of Assam or Burma, where there really are leeches, would admit that we had seen any; half a dozen on one's feet in the course of a march would to them appear negligible. We found our footgear, or rather lack of footgear, namely rubbers and no socks, as satisfactory as any for combating these revolting beasts. One generally noticed them at once on shoe or bare leg and could pull them off before they had a good hold, whereas boots, socks, and puttees will not prevent them from getting at the feet; the leech on them is harder to spot, and, once in, it is not discovered until the boots are removed in camp and found to be full of blood and gorged leeches.

Now began a long, steep grind to the 12,400 ft. Kuari Pass, but today we were bound only for Dekwani, the grazing alp 1000 ft. below the ridge. When we were here in June the air resounded with the bleating of sheep, and white flocks covered the hillside, but now the place was empty of life except for some choughs and a questing hawk. This camping ground is just above the tree-line and in consequence rather bleak; instead of pitching their tents the Dotials retired to the woods to sleep—only the Europeans were hardy enough to endure the rigours of the ". . ." tents.

When we passed this way in 1934 we made a special effort to be on top of the Pass at dawn and virtue was for once rewarded by the unsurpassed panorama of the Garhwal Himalaya, which is seen from here in fair weather. But that was in May, and now in this month of rain and mist not much was to be expected, so we were content to be up there by eight o'clock. There was a lot of cloud to the north but all was not hidden and to the majority of our party, who had not yet seen a Himalayan mountain, the little that remained was a breath-taking revelation. Dunagiri to the north-east claimed pre-eminence of beauty and of stature, and her perfectly proportioned shape shone dazzlingly white in a frame of massive cloud. Across the Dhauli valley the great bulk of Hathi Parbat stood up like an iceberg from a sea of vapour, while to the north, near Badrinath, the country was bathed in sun and the warm glow of a glacier there was for all the world like pink snow.

For long we looked, trying with camera and cinema to capture some record of the changing scene, and then, having added each a stone to the cairn which guards the Pass, we began the long and easy descent. The grass merged into pine forest and 1000 ft. lower, where two tracks diverged, Pasang Kikuli and I turned west for Joshimath while the bandobast[1] went on down to Tapoban.

1 Bandobast—a useful term meaning organising or the organisation itself.

CHAPTER EIGHT

The Rishi Once More

IT was July 19th when we reached Joshimath and inquiries for Emmons in the bazaar elicited the information that, arriving two days ago, he had gone up to Badrinath and was expected back that day. Having collected the mail, we repaired to the dâk bungalow and half an hour later Pasang Kikuli reported that he could see Emmons and Kitar riding up from Vishnuprayag, the temple at the junction of the Dhauli and Alaknanda rivers, 1500 ft. below Joshimath.

A little later he and Kitar arrived and we swopped news. He had thoroughly enjoyed his journey along the Pilgrim Road, particularly the day spent at Badrinath, where he was very kindly received by the Rawal, and shown the Temple, the hot spring, and the steps leading down to the frigid waters of the Alaknanda, where the pilgrims bathe ceremoniously, clinging to a ringbolt.

The next to arrive was a wire from Carter saying that he was leaving Ranikhet that day, so that here were two members of the party who had not allowed the grass to grow, however leisurely may have been the progress of the main body.

Finally, in the evening, ten Mana men arrived with the chest-slapping Kalu. Kalu I had hoped was up the valley at Tapoban collecting food, but here he was with the Mana men and, seemingly, rather the worse for wear. I soon learnt that, if we were relying on him to find coolie food, we might whistle for it; the month that had elapsed since he left us had apparently been spent at Mana or Badrinath, and from his blear-eyed look very ill-spent. I hurried down to the bazaar to see what could be done, but the man I had dealt with previously was away and all that his underling could promise was one load of atta. Here was a pretty kettle of fish, for it might take two or three days to collect the ten loads we wanted and the prospect of further delay was maddening. Returning to the bungalow, I gave the Mana men sufficient rupees and told them to scrape together all the food they could find in the bazaar. The result was beyond expectation, and two hours later they had got together eight loads of atta and two of rice.

Early next morning two Dotials and Phuta came in from Tapoban as arranged, and I spent the morning again in the bazaar buying odds and ends for them and the Bhotias. The Mana men are Bhotias and the name gives some indication of their origin, for Tibet was known as the land of Bhot.

The Garhwal Bhotias number about five hundred, divided between the villages of Mana and Niti. They themselves claim that they are Hindus who crossed the Himalaya into Tibet many generations ago, and after a long sojourn there, during which presumably they intermarried, they returned to their present home. They are not identical with Tibetans, but they are of a Mongolian type, sturdy, thick-set, with olive complexions sometimes tinged on the cheeks with a ruddy glow. The men wear a long blanket coat of homespun reaching to the knees, over trousers of the same material, which are tight at the ankles, baggy above, and tied at the waist like pyjamas. None of them are fanatical about cleanliness.

The village of Mana is 10,500 ft. above the sea and is set on a boulder-strewn slope, where the low stone houses of the village seem as natural as the great erratic blocks which litter the hillside. It overlooks the Alaknanda river at its confluence with the Saraswati and only a few miles below the glacier source of the first-named. The shrine at this river junction is called Keshoprayag and is sacred to Vishnu. Immediately above here the Saraswati flows through a very remarkable cleft, the walls of which almost touch above, the river flowing heard but unseen several hundred feet below. Some cultivation of barley and buckwheat is carried on and there is one tree, of which the Mana people are rightly proud; but sheep, goats, and the Tibetan trade are their main interest.

The trade from Mana is neither so extensive nor so lucrative as that carried on over the eastern passes from the Milam valley in Almora. The Mana Pass is 18,650 ft. and comparatively more difficult than the others, and the trade seems to have fallen off considerably in recent years. Here, as in Milam, the Tibetan Jongpen sends an official to Mana to ascertain whether there is any disease amongst men or cattle before declaring the Pass open for the summer. The official is given a stone (who determines the size I have not learnt) and the Bhotias undertake to forfeit its weight in gold if any disease be introduced into Tibet. A licence to trade has to be paid for in cash or kind, and a commission is exacted on all deals. The chief exports are food-stuffs of all kinds, cloth, sugar, spices, tobacco, and dried fruits; and the imports salt, borax, wool, ponies, dogs, jubus (a cross between a yak and a cow), rugs, Tibetan saddles, tea, butter, gold, yak tails, and horns.

Now that we were about to leave the habitation of men, our porters had to be supplied with a few extras, both luxuries and necessities, and it was interesting to compare the respective wants of our three different breeds.

The Bhotias' needs were hard to satisfy either in variety or quantity. They evidently believed in doing themselves well if someone else footed the bill, and seemed not to have heard anything about pipers and the tunes they played. Eight pounds of tobacco was their first demand, cut down by me to four; then half a dozen different spices were selected and equal quantities red and black lentils. Ghee was the next item, and several shops were visited before a superfine quality was found, and then I had to put in another demurrer as to quantity, for good ghee is more expensive than butter. Several 2 lb. cakes of jaggery wrapped in leaves were next added to the growing pile; it is unrefined sugar like solidified treacle and indistinguishable from their tobacco. Tea and salt were bought after another wrangle over quantities, for they seemed to think they were fitting out for a year.

That met, if it did not satisfy, their wants, and I wondered apprehensively whether the Dotials had the same generous notions about what was requisite for their well-being. Fortunately the headman himself had not come, no doubt only because he realised that something might have to be carried back, and the two men he had sent had not been properly coached. When asked what they wanted, they were quite at a loss, and tea, sugar, salt, and tobacco had to be pressed on them. The Sherpas' needs were similar to the Bhotias', except that they took cigarettes instead of tobacco, and made no attempt to take advantage of having *carte blanche* to get what they wanted.

While this was going on, Loomis and Lloyd arrived, having come in to see the sights of the metropolis, and at one o'clock we all started back together carrying the morning's purchases, ten loads of coolie food, and some apples for ourselves. There is a small orchard at Joshimath and earlier in the year peaches of enormous size can be had.

Before leaving, arrangements were made for Carter's possible coming, and instead of turning Kalu off, as he deserved, I gave him the job of waiting here to take charge of Carter when he arrived and, with the help of another Mana man, to follow us into the Basin. He was very repentant, praying constantly with his hands palm to palm, and seemed pleased at having this responsibility put upon him.

We reached Tapoban at three o'clock and, jealous of the others who had spent the morning wallowing in the hot bath, we three lost no time in visiting it. To our annoyance the hermit was there sitting outside the hut, his long hair reaching to the ground, and his eyes fixed vacantly on the stone tank. It is *infra dig.* to strip in front of natives, but I got rid of him by the simple expedient of holding out a four-anna piece and pointing to the hut. His mind was not as blank as his face, for he at once understood, got up and went into his hut, and I placed the money on the stone thus vacated. When we had done boiling ourselves and dashing from the hot to the cold and back again, he came out of the hut, took up the money, and resumed his contemplation of the infinite.

The camping place at Tapoban is on a grass plateau the size of a tennis court, which has the appearance of having once been part of a fort. Close by are three very old and completely neglected shrines, beautifully built of massive stone put together without any mortar. They are said to date back to A.D. 800. The only inhabited building nearby is a school for the children of the neighbouring villages. After school hours it serves the purpose of an inn, for I remember we slept in it in 1934 and now it sheltered the Mana men. Some slight re-adjustments of loads were made here when most of us found we had brought too much, and some articles of food found to be in excess were also left. From these we made up an assortment of food for Carter's use, and the whole was handed over to the care of the schoolmaster.

It was important that the Dotials and the Mana men should get on well together, but I had always had a lurking fear that this pious hope would not be realised—that in fact it might be far otherwise. The Bhotias did not strike one as being good mixers, although they were friendly enough with the Sherpas, but I think they despised the Dotials and resented the fact that we were employing them instead of Bhotias. I watched them when they first met that evening and, though neither side was effusive, they talked together a little, in a distant manner, like two strange dogs smelling round each other. Once the ice was broken I hoped that good relations would be established, but an incident next morning showed that of this there was little likelihood.

The Mana men were as usual the last to start, and as they were coming up the road to collect their loads they met the Dotials starting off, already laden. Unfortunately one of the Dotials had taken one of the food loads which the Mana men had brought yesterday from Joshimath—a handy compact bag of 60 lb., very comfortable to carry. The Mana men had marked all their loads and promptly claimed this one. The Dotial refused to give it up and both sides gathered round to join in the argument. We were still at the camp, but the row attracted our attention and I hurried down to see what was happening. All loads had been downed and the more hot-tempered on both sides were shouting and grimacing and threatening each other with fists and sticks. The headman, instead of pacifying them, had got his face about an inch off the head Bhotia's, shouting away with the best. A first-class riot seemed imminent. They were so excited that little attention was paid to me, but with the arrival of one or two Sahibs we managed to separate them, and giving the Mana man his load sent them off out of the way. The Dotial who had been the most aggressive in flourishing his stick I paid off and sacked on the spot, 'pour encourager les autres', and in the heat of the moment overpaid him to the extent of Rs 7. Perhaps this was lucky, because without that accidental inducement he might have refused to go home alone and would probably have been backed up by his fellows. He was the strongest of the Dotials and a good man, and I was sorry to lose him.

Later, when I caught up with the Mana men, I gave them a talking to, and declared fiercely that at the least sign of trouble they would all be sacked—a piece of bluff which to have had called would have been exceedingly inconvenient. For the next day or two I lived in constant dread that some triviality would blow up the smouldering fires, and took care not to leave them alone together on the march. There were no rows but there was no cordiality, and the notion previously entertained, that the Mana men would extend a helping hand to a Dotial in difficulties, was obviously false—they were more likely to push him down the *khud*.

Our route that day followed the Dhauli valley, and the aspect of this valley differed widely from those mild and beautiful valleys which we had crossed on the way to Joshimath. Here the scene was grander and sterner, in places almost savage, and no imagination was required to guess that close behind the steep enclosing walls lay the ice, rock, and snow of high mountains. The Dhauli river rises near the Niti Pass and its course down to Tapoban is almost one great gorge, through the bed of which the water roars and rages with incredible violence. It is milky white with glacial deposits.

Four miles above Tapoban, where the road crossed by a stout cantilever bridge from the south to the north side of the river, the Rishi Ganga flows into the Dhauli. We looked with newly awakened interest at the grey rushing waters that were a living witness to the mysterious Basin, and at the gorge above which still kept its secrets.

Beyond this we recrossed to the south bank of the Dhauli by a rather amateurish suspension bridge, the flimsy flooring sagging and swaying a few feet above the boiling water that dizzied the eye to look upon. Frail though it was, it was comforting to feel that two-foot wide flooring underfoot, unlike the home-made bamboo bridges of Sikkim, where one shuffles one foot after the other along two slippery bamboos, clinging affectionately to the handrail the while.

After crossing the bridge we climbed up from the river to the village of Lata, the porters sweating hard and resting frequently under a hot sun, which we noticed was surrounded by a wide halo. Lata is no place to camp at if it can be avoided, but the next water is a long way up the hill, and the need of shelter and food for the coolies make it advisable to stop near a village if there is one. One very remarkable fact about this village was that there were three eggs in it, but even this paled before the yet more remarkable fact that the owner wanted half a rupee (about 9*d*.) for each of them.

Lata was the last link with the outside world, and from now on we and our fifty-three porters were dependent for food and shelter on what we carried. We could not afford to waste any days now, for when the porters are not marching they still eat. They were consuming nearly one hundred pounds of food every day and the number of days we could keep them was dictated by the food we had. Of course the longer their services were available the farther, within limits, we could push our base, and any time wasted meant that we should have to dismiss them before this goal was reached.

Bad weather might hold us up, as it had at Kaliaghat, and it was with gloomy foreboding that we observed the sun halo, but the next day turned out as fine as any we had had. The road climbed almost without break for 5000 ft. to Lata Kharak, which was to be our camping ground. It is a grassy hollow just above the tree-line, which here is over 12,000 ft.; birch trees and rhododendrons are the only trees able to grow at this height, the pine having given up the struggle a little lower down. One variety of pine which grew here, the 'chir' or *Pinus longifolia*, is a most useful tree because, being full of resin, it burns like a torch, and a few slivers of it make excellent kindling. Pasang Kikuli generally carried some, and with it a fire could be started under the worst conditions. Rhododendron makes a good fire too, but it is not easy to start.

The Dotials were on their mettle today and out to show the Mana men what they could do, with the result that they climbed this 5000 ft. in five hours and were in camp by half-past twelve; the Bhotias took it easy, as they usually did, and were not up until two o'clock. A chill wind and mist are the rule at this camp but today it was fine and warm. The Mana men retired to the woods to sleep, despising tents at this moderate altitude even had tents been available, as they were not. The Dotials occupied all there were, probably more with a view to depriving the Mana men of them than from any renewed faith in their weather-resisting powers.

It was wet when we got up at half-past five, but when we started two hours later this had turned to fine mist. The crest of the ridge overlooking the Rishi valley from the north is first gained at a height of about 13,000 ft., and then the path traverses along the north side, ascending gently, until it crosses the ridge by the 14,000 ft. Durashi Pass. From the Pass views of peaks both to north and south should be obtained, but though we sat there an hour to give it a chance, the mist refused to lift. From here a sensational traverse leads across a mile of some of the steepest and most rugged cliffs imaginable. At first glance a man would despair of getting himself across, let alone a flock of sheep, but every summer many hundreds of sheep and goats are taken over it, and back again in the autumn with young lambs at foot. In May, when there is snow and ice about, step-cutting is necessary, but when the snow has gone all is plain sailing and it is merely an airy walk.

At the further end of the traverse is much dead juniper wood, and those who know the scarcity of fuel at Durashi add as much of this as they can carry to their loads. The traverse ends in a long steep gully full of loose stones, and at the bottom of this I waited to see the porters come down, thinking that someone might get hit by a stone. I need not have worried—not even a pebble was dislodged. A steeper but shorter gully was then climbed and there below us lay Durashi, but no tinkle of sheep bells reached our ears, and the place was apparently deserted. The Bhotias accounted for this by saying there was not enough grass, but I think it more likely that the shepherds had been driven out by excessive rain; sheep had certainly been there recently.

We had already reduced the loads appreciably by eating, and now we were able to pay off five Dotials, which made a useful reduction in the number of mouths to be fed. I had expected some trouble in selecting the five victims, but two of them chose themselves by being sick and the other three made no bones about going. The Dotials are much more amenable than the Bhotias; when Loomis and I were here in June I had tried to send some of the Mana men back because there were no longer any loads for them, but it only led to trouble. They presented a united front and said that all would go on or all would go back, so we had to submit to paying and, what was more important, feeding four unnecessary men.

The march between Durdashi and Dibrugheta is short, and again, as in June, we lingered long on the 'Curtain' ridge, expectant of a view, for on a clear day Nanda Devi herself is visible. The mist however was thicker than ever and even the Dibrugheta alp immediately below us was hidden. From the ridge to the alp is a drop of some 3000 ft. down an excessively steep grass slope, and the few who now remained faithful to rubber shoes had some very unhappy moments, which were accentuated when it began raining. At the bottom is a stream, and the way out up the opposite bank lies over steep rock clothed with a thin layer of mud, grass, and other vegetation. Here it went hard with the rubber school and the porters with awkward loads, one of whom had to have his load carried up piecemeal. This was an unlucky Dotial carrying a load, part of which consisted of tent poles, the most troublesome and impracticable tent poles that ever were. Each pole weighed 4 lb. and was in two sections, each four feet long; one section telescoped into the other but at the slightest provocation telescoped out again. If carried horizontally they caught on every projection near the path, and if carried vertically they bruised either the man's head or his backside. The seven poles made up half the load and the other half was something just as unwieldy but rather less necessary, a glacier drill. This is a scientific instrument and not, as one might suspect from its presence in a mountaineering party, some device to facilitate glacier travel. Of its subsequent history all that need be said is that like the immortal Duke of York's men it 'was marched right up the hill, and then marched down again'.

Having disentangled ourselves from these perplexities we emerged on to the small plateau of the Dibrugheta alp, an emerald gem in a sombre setting of dark green pines. The flowers which, earlier in the year, make this meadow a Joseph's coat were past their best, only a few white anemones remaining to set off the rich crimson of the potentillas. Of greater interest than these to the materially minded were the wild shallots which mingled with them.

It was raining too hard when we arrived for a due appreciation of our surroundings. As Dr Johnson said, 'the noblest prospect is improved by a good inn in the foreground', and no time was lost by us in thus augmenting the beauty of the scene. The tents were pitched, the loads stacked on top of a flat rock and covered with a tarpaulin, and at last a fire was started under a sheltering canopy of umbrellas. At dark the rain ceased, fresh logs were piled on, and we sat round enjoying the blaze like so many salamanders. Then the moon rose, outlining for us in a silver silhouette the summit of Niti peak and emphasising the black profile of the 'Curtain' which towered above us, while, across the dark cleft of the Rishi, pinnacle upon pinnacle of rock was etched against an indigo sky.

CHAPTER NINE

To the Foot of the Gorge

THE sheep track which we had so far followed ends at Dibrugheta and from here to the foot of the gorge and through it the going becomes progressively difficult; the first stage from Dibrugheta to the Cave Camp gave the Dotials a taste of what was in store for them higher up. It might be said of them as of the crew of a more famous expedition:

> The danger was past—they had landed at last,
> With their boxes, portmanteaus, and bags:
> Yet at first sight the crew were not pleased with the view,
> Which consisted of chasms and crags.

The march begins in a brutally abrupt manner with a stiff climb of 1000 ft. through grand pine forest. We were off before eight on a fine morning and an hour later had cleared the pines and were sitting on the ridge getting a first sight of our objective, Nanda Devi. The lower part was hidden in cloud, giving an added effect of height. Gazing with wonder at the great wedge of the summit, supported on the south-west by a fearfully steep sort of flying buttress, all who were looking at the mountain for the first time were profoundly impressed. In the immediate foreground ravines and ridges alternated with rock walls and grass slopes to confuse the eye, until in the distance a great grassy shoulder screened the whole of the upper gorge.

The porters went well and by eleven o'clock we reached what Shipton and I had christened 'Rhubarb Gully', a gully with a stream running down it, full of lush vegetation, including a quantity of wild rhubarb. The porters like to eat the tops of this when it has gone to seed, but the stems stewed with sugar are every bit as good as the cultivated variety. We ate them whenever we could.

We continued our march, groping our way through thickets of rhododendron, balancing along narrow ledges of rock, and stepping gingerly over the smooth water-worn slabs of the ravines, until we reached the most critical piece of the day. This was a smooth cliff several hundred feet high, liberally provided with holds in the shape of grass and short furze. Although I had been up and down it five times I never was fond of it, disliked it especially coming down, and dreaded it when wet. Luckily today the rain was holding off and everyone made a special effort to get there before it started. The Mana men in their bare feet simply romped up, and most of the Dotials seemed equally at home, but the little man carrying the tent poles broke down completely. He could not face it, and even after dumping his load he had to be shepherded all the way up, Emmons and I keeping an eye on him from behind while a Dotial in front held his hand. His load was again brought up piecemeal.

There followed a trying half mile over a chaotic scree of enormous blocks, amongst which we dodged and climbed, coming frequently to an impasse. The Cave Camp, reached at three o'clock, consists of one big cave with a very uneven floor and a through-draught which by means of a vent at the back draws the smoke of a fire right through the cave, thoroughly fumigating the occupants. We appropriated this, the Bhotias found another cave, and the Dotials pitched tents in the most unlikely places. There is ample juniper wood here, rhubarb grows luxuriantly, and the cave is dry, so that altogether it is a refuge not to be despised.

In June we had dumped a bag of atta and a bag of rice here and we were relieved to find the atta was only slightly affected by damp. For food on their return journey we now left some atta for the Dotials and some rice for the Bhotias. The Dotials had asked for nothing but atta and this was their sole food, morning and night, in the form of chapatties; nor could they use rice had they wanted it, because they had no cooking pots except the shallow iron bowl in which chapatties are baked.

So far everything had gone well; true, it had rained most days, but this had neither damaged the loads nor depressed the spirits of the porters. But on Sunday, July 26th, the tide of fortune seemed to be on the turn. It rained heavily in the night and in consequence we made a late start, not getting away until nearly nine o'clock. Our destination was the old Base Camp, hereafter called the Bridge Camp, on the south bank of the Rishi, and to get there we had to go over the big grass shoulder and cross the Rhamani torrent which lay beyond. Neither in 1934 nor in June this year had we experienced much trouble in crossing this stream provided it was tackled before afternoon. It is fed by a glacier and like all such streams it increased in volume as the day wore on, reaching its maximum at evening, owing to the melting of the glacier as the warmth increased. With this in front of us then, it was desirable to make an early start, but having failed to do this I tried to keep the porters moving and was not unduly worried about the river.

We reached the top of the grass shoulder at midday, when the mist which had been hanging about all morning turned to rain. This was fortunate in a way because the ridge was a favourite halting-place for the Mana men, who loved to sit there and smoke. On fine days there is a magnificent view of Nanda Devi and the gorge. We were quickly driven off by rain, which increased in intensity as we descended to the Rhamani until it became so blinding that it was difficult to find the crossing-place. It was essential to hit off the right place because the Rhamani flows in a miniature box canyon and in that place only was it possible to climb out on the other side.

When we finally reached the river at one o'clock it was running fast and high and looked very uninviting. Loomis and I waded out, tentatively, hand in hand and tied to a rope. We got about half-way and then turned back, for it was over our thighs, or at any rate mine, and running too fast for the porters to be expected to face it. Various futile expedients were tried, such as pushing big boulders into the water. This was the Sherpas' idea, but I think it was more for the pleasure of seeing a boulder go in than from any thought-out plan. A boulder of anything less than five hundredweight would not stand against the current, but there were plenty of big ones about and the Sherpas managed to roll one of nearly half a ton down the bank into the water and the prodigious splash it made was greeted with happy cries—it was a comfort to know that someone was getting some fun out of our predicament. Operations then ceased, for even they were not capable of standing on this and dropping another of equal weight on the far side of it, and so on until the fifty feet of rushing water were bridged.

We cast up and down the bank, but fifty yards either way was all that could be made before cliffs barred further progress. Meantime we were all very wet and cold and it was at last borne in upon us that we must wait here for better times. The word was given to camp, and soon the already water-logged tents were pitched on the narrow bed of shingle, and the Bhotias, as was their way, had found a snug cave some way above the river. It was more annoying to be stopped because once across the Rhamani it was no great distance to the Bridge Camp.

Within an hour of our arrival the river appeared to rise another foot but after that it began to drop a little. Our camp was quite safe because we were six or seven feet above the water, but it was puzzling to know whether the rise was caused mainly by rain or was merely due to the melting of the glacier. If the rain had brought it about we might be here for a day or two, for there was no sign of it stopping, but we hoped that most of the rise was normal, in which case we should be able to get over early in the morning.

We found an overhang that gave enough protection to keep a fire going, and after a hot meal we felt more cheerful, though the outlook was gloomy enough. Before dark I had a talk with the Dotials and told them I wanted four more to return from here. The headman approved of that and though he confessed to being sick himself he did not ask to be one of the four. This sudden illness was probably diplomatic, but had he been at death's door he could not have looked a greater picture of woe, squatting under a tattered umbrella with his head enveloped in a pink shawl. On that I went to bed, but the noise of the river, which seemed to have a note of malice in it, made sleep difficult. Just as I was dozing off, a head was thrust through the tent door and a torrent of words rose high above the roar of the river. It was one of the Dotials, the most vocal of them, a demagogue with a fearful rush of words to the mouth. By his tone I guessed he had not come to tuck me in and say 'goodnight', but it was some time before I grasped the gist of his tirade—they were all going home.

He had chosen the best time for belling the cat because I was not sufficiently awake to be interested and could only tell him to take his face out of the door and shut both. The news was disturbing but was not taken very seriously, and I thought that tactful handling and a lower river would bring about a change of mind.

It rained all night and was still drizzling at dawn when I went outside to have a look at the river. It was still pretty high, but better than yesterday, and routing out Loomis I got him to hold the rope while I went over. We then hauled the rope taut and made fast at each end, spanning the stream, and I hoped that this little surprise arranged for their benefit, would put fresh heart into the Dotials. Early morning bathing in glacier streams might be enjoyed by the hardy souls who break the ice in the Serpentine, but for my part I made a beeline for the kitchen fire to still my chattering teeth.

Here Nima pointed with glee to a great slab of rock which had peeled off the rock of the overhang in the night, falling flat on the fireplace. Another piece now threatened to do the same, but Nima was blowing away at the fire quite indifferently. A Sherpa blowing up a fire is a rare spectacle. He has only to put his head down, and after a few well-directed and long-drawn blasts, which scatter wood and ashes in all directions, a fire which is seemingly past praying for will burst crackling into life; and for dealing with fires, and all that fires imply, food, drink, and warmth, which in this sort of life seem almost as important as life itself, they possess equally useful adjuncts in hands which can lift up live coals and boiling saucepans, and in eyes and lungs which are impervious to smoke.

The Dotials were now stirring, but when they saw the rope across the river it was not greeted with the joyous and enthusiastic shouts that we expected, and presently my eloquent friend of last night was reaffirming their determination to have nothing to do with the river. I told him the river was lower, there was a rope to hang on to, and that all the loads would be put across for them, and on that he retired to take the sense of the meeting. After breakfast the Bhotias descended from their cave and their resourceful minds soon hit on the right method for roping the loads over, putting our scientific brains to shame. Several of them went across by the fixed rope and took up a position on a rock ten feet above the water; others took up a position high up on a cliff on our side immediately opposite. Two 120 ft. climbing ropes were slung across and soon the loads were being tied on and hauled over as fast as they could be carried up the cliff. The fact that the taking-off place was much higher than the landing-place made the hauling quite light work.

The Dotials helped us in getting the loads up instead of sulking as might have been expected, and from this I argued they were going to change their minds and come with us. No loads fell in, the last went over, and then the remaining Bhotias and Sherpas crossed followed by the Sahibs.

It was beginning to rain again when I turned to make a last fervent appeal to the Dotials before crossing myself. The headman, still under his umbrella and wrapped closer than ever in his pink shawl, looked yet more disconsolate and took no interest in the proceedings. I asked for a few to cross, even if only to carry our loads to the Bridge Camp, but the only response to all entreaties was that they were frightened of the river, and that they wanted to be paid off and dismissed. It was time to play the last card, a card that I fondly hoped would be a trump, and I pointed out that all the money was now on the other side so that they would have to cross anyhow to get their pay—to which the reply was, that I could go across and fetch it back.

For a moment it looked as if they would go home without their pay, but bribing one of them with the gift of my umbrella, I persuaded him to cross with me hand in hand. The rupees were unpacked and, sitting by the river with Pasang holding the umbrella over us, we counted out the money due. The transaction was soon completed, for the envoy was too cold and wet to argue about it, and we were spared the importunites of the whole mob for more baksheesh, and the abuse of the headman at receiving none. The man recrossed and with no more ado the Dotials climbed out of the river bed and disappeared in the driving rain.

We discovered much later, on the way back in fact, that they took it out of the Mana men by eating or taking away all the rice left at the Cave Camp, which was two days' rations for the Mana men, a mean act which might have had serious consequences for anyone less tough and less able to look after themselves than the Bhotias.

It was time to consider our own position. Our porter strength was now sixteen instead of forty-eight, but by increasing the Sahibs' loads to 60 lb. we could reckon on shifting about twenty full loads. We still hoped to reach the Bridge Camp that day, and if everyone piled on a bit extra all the loads might be got there in two journeys. The route followed the precipitous bank of the Rhamani down to its junction with the Rishi, a distance of about half a mile. Just above the junction was the natural bridge across the Rishi formed by a giant boulder, but the short approach to the bridge was a sheer wall and loads had to be lowered down. The rock of the bridge too was smooth and slippery, as was the descent on the far side, but all these places had been made easy, if not very safe, when we were here in June by fixing branches as ladders. The camp was only a couple of hundred yards upstream from the crossing-place.

The Bhotias seemed in good heart, rather pleased, I imagined, at the defection of the Dotials, and carrying very big loads we cautiously began the descent to the Rishi. It was infernally steep and slippery, but we got down to a point close above the bridge without incident, dumped the loads there under a tarpaulin, and went back for the remainder. It seemed to me that if we went right on to the camp with this lot it would, under the prevailing weather conditions, be difficult to make anyone turn out again.

By midday everything was assembled at the dump. The loads had then to be carried down to the roping-up place and Loomis and I went down first to receive them as they were lowered. The first load to come down however was received, not by us, but by the Rishi. Apparently Phuta slipped while approaching the dump, which was about 100 ft. higher up; he managed to stop himself rolling, but his load shot down the slope, just missed the party who were busy tying loads on, flew past Loomis' head, and on into the river. I was still lower down and just caught sight of a two-gallon tin of paraffin and the fragments of an oxygen cylinder spinning through the air before they hit the water. I was not sorry to see the oxygen thus taken off our hands, for clearly the time had come for some more scrapping, but the loss of the paraffin could be ill afforded. [The oxygen apparatus had not been brought to assist climbers, but for use in case of illness or frost-bite.]

After this Phuta, very shaken and frightened, was lowered down and parked out of harm's way near the bridge. Then the loads began to arrive, not unaccompanied by small stones, and soon there were enough assembled for the Mana men to start carrying them across the bridge. It was desperately cold work standing there in the pitiless rain and the first fine enthusiasm of the men was evidently on the wane. Once they had carried a load over and dumped it under a convenient overhang it became increasingly difficult to make them leave the shelter for another journey.

At long last everything was down and all hands turned to carrying across the bridge. Bridge is not quite the word for a place where you first had to climb down a wet slab putting all your weight on a branch of wood—a branch for the apparent security of which no one could see any valid physical reason—then to step across a narrow gap with the river roaring and boiling twenty feet below, traverse across another slab and finally descend to *terra firma* by another branch. But by now the Mana men had had enough and began drifting away to a cave which one of them had discovered on the Rhamani side, and in which he had started a fire. The Sherpas were still good for a bit, and with them we started carrying loads up the south bank of the Rishi to the camp site, which was quite close. It consists of a big overhang which is usually bone-dry but where now there was hardly a dry spot. At four o'clock we called it a day; there were still a number of loads by the bridge, but we had enough for our immediate needs and the call of hot tea and food was too insistent.

The chronic state of wetness of our clothes, sleeping bags, and tents did not make for cheerfulness as we discussed the turn which events had taken. For the moment our star was not in the ascendant, but the situation was by no means bad. By cutting down weight a little, only one relay would be necessary and no load need be more than 60 lb.; nor had I any fear of the Bhotias leaving us in the lurch, for they had worked like Trojans until cold and wet finished them. Indeed in one respect the loss of the Dotials could be borne philosophically, if not cheerfully, in that I felt our responsibilities were considerably lightened, and there was now no doubt of our having sufficient food for the porters. I still think it was the river which upset the Dotials and that in good weather we could have got them up the worst part of the gorge, now immediately ahead of us, though some of them might have needed a lot of assistance.

Against these meagre benefits was the fact that it was going to take us longer to reach the mountain and that there would be less time available for climbing it, and, moreover, that from now onwards we ourselves would have to carry heavy loads—not the best preparation, I thought, for heavy climbing. If we did, it would be 'magnificent but not war', that is we would be exhausting ourselves before ever the mountain was reached. In most Himalayan expeditions the object is to spare the climbers any work at all until on the mountain in order to conserve their strength, and here were we proposing to carry 50 or 60 lb. loads over difficult country for the next ten days or more. The alternative of Sherpas and Mana men, meant that the extra time required would not leave us enough food to finish the job. These preconceived ideas were upset and our policy justified by the event.

For all that, I felt that my misplaced confidence in the Dotials had let the party in for this and would not have been surprised to hear some hard things said. But there was not a word of reproach and the aim of all seemed now, more than ever, to be to spend themselves rather than spare.

CHAPTER TEN

The Gorge

THE day after these memorable events dawned fine, and having discussed the position and decided on a plan, we started sorting out loads and rebagging the food. Food was almost the only item on which much weight could be saved, so it was arranged that only enough for forty days should be taken on from here. Having fixed the amount of each kind, it was easy to fill in the varieties, for by now we knew our likes and dislikes. Even so it was a long job which was only just finished before the rain began again at ten o'clock.

One other way in which weight was saved was the abandonment of two pressure cookers. Their scrapping did cause us some heart-burning, since it was from here onwards that their need would be felt. Cooking at high altitudes becomes difficult owing to the low temperature at which water boils; even at 15,000 ft. this temperature is 85 degrees instead of 100 degrees and of course it decreases as you go higher. Tough things like rice, lentils, beans, or dried vegetables will not cook properly at these temperatures, but the difficulty is got over by using a cooker that cooks by steam under pressure, and in which, I think, even a pair of boots would be made edible. It is a thing like a heavy saucepan with a steam-tight lid, fitted with a safety valve, and a whistle which can be adjusted to go off when the desired pressure is reached. We had two of them, and they were left behind with less reluctance because, so far, we had used hardly any rice or lentils—perhaps Loomis and I had had a surfeit of them on the earlier trip.

By the time this work was finished the Mana men had brought everything up from the bridge, and although they were rather expecting to have the day off we persuaded them to make the trip. The plan was to carry some loads as far as the foot of the 'Slabs' and to return here for the night, and at midday we all moved off in drizzling rain carrying 60 lb. loads. It was about 1500 ft. up to the 'Slabs' and the first few hundred feet immediately above camp were as steep and exposed as any part of the route. Numerous birch trees growing out of the cliff face were of great assistance, and provided the branch did not break or the tree pull out bodily it was impossible to fall.

At the top of this bad stretch was a short rock pitch known to us as the 'Birch Tree Wall', where considerable amusement could be had watching the efforts of the purists to climb it *with* a load on and *without* a pull from above.

The difference of climbing without or with a load is not always realised; when bowed down under a load places, which otherwise would not be given a thought, appear to bristle with difficulties and have to be treated with the utmost respect. The centre of gravity has shifted so much that balance has to be learnt afresh and any slight movement of the load may have very untoward results. The Bhotias carry their loads by shoulder straps as we do, but the Sherpas and the Dotials use a head strap which must be far more unsafe for any delicate climbing. On this trip we had brought light carrying-frames provided with a belly band which did much to obviate the risk of a load shifting. They were very successful but, without careful adjustment and judicious padding, at the end of a long day one's back felt as though it had been flagellated.

For the remaining thousand feet there was little difficulty but much labour, and it was with sighs of relief that we dragged ourselves up to the cairn, built in 1934, which marks the end of the climb. From here we descended slightly to a wide grass ledge lying at the foot of a rock wall, and a short way along this we dumped the loads under a little overhang. Taking a couple of Mana men, a quantity of light line, and some rock pitons, I went on up the shallow rock chimney leading to the top of the wall and the foot of the 'Slabs'. We secured the rope at the top of these by means of the pitons so that it hung down the full length of the 'Slabs', affording invaluable assistance to a laden man. This done, we started back and reached the Bridge Camp in an hour, thoroughly wet, but very pleased with our day's work.

Next morning, the 29th, was again fine, and we took advantage of it to do some much-needed drying before packing up. The 'Slabs' were reached by ten-thirty and the slow business of getting the loads up began. Some were busy carrying up the 'Slabs' from the dump while others attended to hauling them up the wall. Luckily the rocks were dry, everyone worked with a will, and by one o'clock all were got up without incident.

From here it took nearly two hours to cover the mile to Halfway Camp with half the loads; the route is intricate, involving much up and down work, and there are one or two bad places. The height of this camp is about 13,000 ft. and it is sited on a very uneven boulder-strewn ridge on which the making of tent platforms is hard work.

It was almost three o'clock when we reached it, and it would have been pleasant to devote the rest of the day to making ourselves comfortable. The Sherpas and the Mana men were of this opinion and lost no time in getting to work digging out boulders and levelling sites. It seemed a pity to disturb them, but I had to remind them that the remainder of the loads had still to be brought from the 'Slabs'. It took some time to overcome their passive resistance to this suggestion but finally all, less Graham Brown and Emmons, started back for a second load.

When put to it the Mana men can move at tremendous speed over rough country, and on this occasion we were left toiling hopelessly in the rear. Knowing their leisurely way, one could only surmise that they had gone mad, but there was method in this madness because the first on the scene had the pick of the loads. There was not much to choose as far as weight went, but we still had our old friends the tent poles with us, and there were other loads which vied with them in popularity, such as a sack of miscellaneous junk of which the *least* angular part was the needle-pointed tripod legs of a plane table; and there were several sacks of sugar which had got wet and started to sweat, so that the shirt of anyone unlucky enough to carry one became like a treacle paper for catching moths.

Better time was made on this second journey, camp being reached soon after five. Graham Brown and Emmons had delved out a tent platform and it was not long before the Sherpas had us all comfortably housed. I say the Sherpas, because at work such as this they are in a class by themselves. No boulder is too big for them and no trouble too great, and when they set to work on a tent platform they remind me of so many terriers digging away at a rat hole.

We were blessed with another fine morning, so that it seemed as though fortune had relented and was smiling on us again. Whilst we were tackling these two difficult stages of the gorge, one of which was now completed, dry weather was an inestimable boon. Of the two I think that over the upper half of the gorge is the worse. There is no place so awkward that loads have to be taken off and roped up, but there are many which are very exposed, which cannot be made safe, and where a slip would be fatal.

Today we reversed the procedure, taking the camp forward and leaving the rest of the loads to be fetched next day. A gully of smooth water-worn slabs had first to be crossed, where the rubber-footwear school could for once tread with more confidence than those clad in orthodox nailed boots. A gently descending terrace brought us to the crux of this part of the route, a place which in 1934 had earned the name of the 'mauvais pas', and for which, at least on my part, familiarity had bred no contempt. Here the general angle steepens until, when standing, you can touch the slope with your elbow. A narrow grass ledge leads to a projecting nose of rock which has to be rounded and then, with no pause, a short steep chimney leads down to another narrow ledge. This continues for about fifty yards of varying degrees of difficulty until finally a high rock bulge is surmounted and the security of a wide terrace reached. The whole distance is so great that there is no means of securing anyone engaged on this traverse, nor is any encouragement derived from the prospect below, where the steep rock and grass slope continues relentlessly to the river a thousand feet below.

The Mana men crossed unperturbed and did not even bother to wait for us at the other end. I took off my shoes and made the Sherpas take off theirs—an advisable precaution, because the trouble with these sort of places was that as more people went over them so they got worse. Many of the footholds were grass tufts and by the time the last man used them they were reduced to a small sloping rugosity of slippery earth. One or two of the Sherpas were unable to negotiate the rock nose and Pasang enjoyed himself carrying their loads for them; he was always ready with a helping hand for the weaker. We made three journeys over the 'mauvais pas' and on each were lucky enough to have it dry; when wet it is hazardous, and once in 1934 when there was a covering of fresh snow it became a nightmare.

Descending by easy grass terraces the route approached the river and the Pisgah Buttress, the last defence of the gorge, and so called because from it can be seen the Promised Land of the Sanctuary. It is a great buttress of rock which springs sheer from the river and then slants less steeply upwards for 2000 ft. The original route in 1934 dropped almost to the river before turning to ascend the gully and grass spur flanking the buttress; but the Mana men have improved on this, and now, by what we called the 'Mana variation', the old route is joined high up the grass spur so that descent to the river is avoided.

This 'variation' we took and, though in places rather exposed, it saved us a lot of hard work. From where the routes joined we climbed a slope almost bare of grass. Working over to the left, we gained a grass terrace backed by a high wall, up which we climbed by means of a rock staircase. On top were slabs, overlapping like tiles on a roof, but set at a moderate angle, and these took us up to another grass terrace, where we rested before tackling the final problem. This was a vertical rock wall only about ten feet high, and a little overhanging chimney was the solution. With a load on, it was a severe struggle, but there were plenty of willing hands above and below. From here to the ridge of Pisgah was long and steep, and Nuri's condition began to cause us some anxiety. He was going slower and slower and at last gave out altogether, so we relieved him of his load and told him to come on at his own pace.

It was nearing two o'clock as we approached the crest of the ridge, but the sun still shone in a clear sky and as we finished the climb and stepped round a rock boss out on to the ridge, Nanda Devi stood there in all her majesty, the cloud veil for once rent aside. All eyes were drawn to the south ridge on which our hopes centred and we prayed that the face which it hid might be less grim than the profile.

Camp was but a short distance away and we took up our quarters on a ledge in front of the low cave in which Loomis and the Bhotias had dumped the seven bags of food in June. It would not hold a tent and sites for these had to be made, a task that the Sherpas set about in their indefatigable manner, digging out and heaving down phenomenal lumps of rock which in their descent threatened to demolish the Mana men who were camped below.

Some of the food bags that had been left here were found to be damp; we turned them all out, spread the flour and satu in the sun, and rebagged it in dry bags. Only about five pounds from each bag had to be thrown away.

Nuri had to be helped into camp and our united medical talent did their best to diagnose his case without much success.

The days spent at Pisgah camp we shall not easily forget. Apart from the view of Nanda Devi, which is probably more striking from here than from anywhere else, a good part of the northern Basin lies spread out below one like a coloured map. In the middle is the great main glacier which terminates in a hundred feet ice wall from beneath which the Rishi rushes; on the left are smooth grass downs broken only by the white moraine of the Changabang glacier; on the right are the variegated rocks, rust red, yellow, and black, of Nanda Devi's pedestal, while in the far background the kindly grass runs up to warm-coloured scree, the scree merges into glacier, and high over all towers the crenellated snow wall of the Basin.

During the two days spent here we were privileged to see all this not only under a bright sun and blue sky but also by the light of a full moon. Even when we had done admiring the miracle of colour performed at sunset, the distant snow-white wall would be suffused with the delicate pink flush of the afterglow; and then as this faded, snow blending with greying sky as the stage was darkened, the curtain rose gradually on yet a third scene. The grey of the sky changed to steely blue, and the snow wall, at first vaguely outlined, shone out clearly like white marble as the moon sailed up from behind a screen of jet-black rock.

The last day of July dawned fine and after a more leisurely breakfast than usual we started back for Halfway Camp. Nuri, who was a very sick man, and three Sahibs remained behind, as there were only nineteen loads to be fetched. The Mana men again set a furious pace and as we were descending the 'variation' we could see them on the 'mauvais pas'. Going flat out, we did the journey in an hour and they must have beaten us by nearly fifteen minutes. It would be interesting to enter some of those men for the Guides' Race at Grasmere where, I feel sure, they would astonish the natives.

Travelling unladen after a week of heavy packing, one felt as if walking on a different planet, perhaps Mars, where the force of gravity is but half that of the earth. Even so the 'mauvais pas' was treated with respect, and on the return journey, grievously burdened as we were, with much more.

We were back soon after one o'clock, observing on the way the beautiful sky phenomenon of an iridescent cloud. The border of a high patch of cirrus cloud appears coloured like a rainbow, the red and green being particularly clear. Until recently their origin was not known, but it is now believed that these coloured patches are fragments of unusually large and brilliant coronae, a corona consisting of a number of concentric rings, rainbow-coloured, which are sometimes seen round the sun or moon when it is covered by a thin cloud veil. It is caused by refracted light from the ice particles which form high cirrus cloud and differs from a halo in having a much smaller radius and a reverse order of colours, blue near the sun and red farthest away. Coronae can be seen frequently round the moon and no doubt they form often round the sun, but owing to the intensity of the light they can only be observed under favourable conditions. I have seen both iridescent cloud and sun halos several times in the Himalaya but nowhere else.

A sun halo is usually regarded as heralding the approach of bad weather, but the period between the omen and the event is indefinite. It seemed to be hardly ever less than a day, but sometimes there was no change in the weather for several days; indeed it was often difficult to see any connection at all between halos and weather. If a corona round the moon is observed and the diameter contracts, it shows that the water particles are uniting into larger ones which may fall in rain; conversely, an expanding corona indicates increasing dryness. The open side of a halo is believed by some to foretell the quarter from which bad weather may be expected. Like most weather signs, halos and coronae are not infallible.

However, the rain, which had held off for so long at this critical time, and now could no longer hinder us, started again the same afternoon. It was with relief and thankfulness that we saw the last load brought into camp and realised that the gorge was now behind us and the way to the mountain lay open.

CHAPTER ELEVEN

The Sanctuary

IN 1934 the next camp from here was close to the snout of the South glacier, but it seemed improbable we should be able to get as far as that with the first loads because we had to return to Pisgah the same day. However, I had a lingering hope that we might, and accordingly made a fairly early start.

Most of the precious time thus gained was wasted before we had gone fifty yards. Close to camp was a broad band of smooth slabs set at an angle of about 30 degrees, caused by the slipping away of the surface soil and the exposure of the underlying rock. The Mana men waltzed across this with no more ado than crossing a road, indeed it was not unlike crossing a road but, of course, less dangerous, and then they sat down on the far side to see how we, the eminent mountaineers, would fare. It was not a prepossessing place to look at and the first few tentative steps soon convinced us that this time appearances had not deceived us. The wretched loads were of course the trouble, for with those on one had not the confidence to stand up boldly and plank the feet down. Each man took the line that seemed good to him, but all got into difficulties, and then was seen the comic sight of seven Sahibs strung out over the slabs in varying attitudes, all betraying uneasiness, and quite unable to advance. The Mana men, having savoured the spectacle to the full and allowed time for the indignity of our situation to sink in, came laughing across the slabs to our aid and led us gently over by the hand like so many children.

Fighting a way down through a heavy growth of bush, we crossed a stream, contoured the other side of a valley, and rounding a high ridge set our faces towards the south. We were now fairly within the Sanctuary, but there was another hour of very rough going over scree and boulders before we trod the grass downs for which we were all longing. After so many days traversing a country so hopelessly askew as that of the Rishi valley, our ankles had developed a permanent flex, and great was now the relief and joy of getting them straight again, of walking without having to hold on, and without watching the placing of every step.

Keen as we were to reach the old camp near the glacier, it was difficult if not useless to drive the Bhotias. All that could be done was to push on as fast and as far as possible, and hope that, in their own good time, they would follow; but it was exasperating to look expectantly back and see them sitting like so many crows on some distant ridge over a mile back. At last about two o'clock, when still some one and a half miles from the glacier, I felt that they would not follow much longer, and sat down to wait for them.

A cold wind blew up the valley, but there was a sheltered grass hollow close by a stream which would make a delightful camp. There was no juniper wood at hand, but we had passed some half a mile back and I knew there was more in front. When the Mana men came, an effort was made to get them to push on a little, but they assured me there was no water for a long way. Two of them had been here in 1934, and when it came to pitting their memory for a country against mine I was quite prepared to give them best; but later we found that this particular piece of information, which I was not prepared to dispute, was a flat untruth. However, it had been a long march, so we dumped the loads and hurried back, reaching Pisgah about five o'clock. Nuri had been left in camp but appeared no better for the rest, and we wondered how he would manage tomorrow when camp had to be moved. It had been yet another fine day despite the omens of the sky, and again from our vantage point we watched the pageant of setting sun and rising moon, beyond the means of a painter, either in words or colour.

We had carried extra-heavy loads on the first journey, hoping that on the second there would be little left but our personal kit, but when the porters had made up their loads it was so arranged that we had each a tent to shoulder: Nuri was able to travel but of course without a load.

All felt slack, the result of our efforts yesterday. Emmons had gone off at the first streak of light to set up his plane table, but when we joined him at his station half-way to camp he told us he had not been able to fix his position. I was not surprised, because from inside the Basin this is by no means easy. To effect it you have to be in a position to see and recognise three known triangulated peaks, all at the same time; and owing to cloud and mist you may have to wait many hours on some bleak and wind-swept spot before this happy event occurs, and when it does you probably mistake one of the peaks and get a completely false result. Before going out to Garhwal in 1934, we had some instruction in plane-table work in Richmond Park, but somehow conditions in the Basin seemed quite different.

Loomis and I reached camp long ahead of the others and impatiently raided the dump for cheese and biscuits, which were still our daily lunch and of which we never tired. On their arrival no time was lost in getting up the tents, for the same cold wind was blowing and presently a drizzling rain set in. The height of this camp was about 14,000 ft. and now for the first time the Mana men condescended to sleep in the despised tents. I confess to some disappointment at this evident sign of degeneration. In 1934, in much the same spot, they appeared quite happy in the lee of a large boulder. Did they but know what our tents were like, their hardihood in proposing to sleep in them might have been admired, but since they expected to find shelter in them their softness was to be lamented. Were the Mana men becoming 'sissies' like their employers?

This camp site was a delicious change after the cramped asperity of the quarters to which we had now been long accustomed, and it was difficult to say which gave us most pleasure, the space, the flatness, or the absence of rock. Below our little hollow the rounded slope curved gently down to the southern branch of the Rishi and the contrast between the opposite bank and our own was as great as it might well be, and could be adequately summed up in the words 'frowning cliffs' and 'smiling downs'. On our side wide slopes of short, sweet grass extended in all directions; a herd of cattle grazing on some distant rise or a flock of sheep coming over the hill would have caused no surprise, so peaceful was the scene. But across the river, savage, reddish-brown cliffs, seamed with dry gullies, rose sheer from the river, presenting a seemingly unbroken alternation of buttress and gully along four straight miles of river frontage; and beyond these the snow and rock of the western ridge of Nanda Devi loomed vaguely in the swirling mists.

It was now August 2nd, and we still had food to feed the Mana men for another five days. Within that time we had to establish a base camp as high up the mountain as we could. The South glacier consists of two main branches which join almost at the snout, one coming in from the south and the other, with which we are concerned, from the south-east. In 1934 we went up this South-East glacier by the true left bank, that is, the side farthest from the mountain, and some two miles up we had found a very pleasant camp at about 16,000 ft.—a sheltered grass flat tucked away behind the moraine and watered by a spring. From this camp we had crossed the glacier, there half a mile wide, and by means of a scree slope gained a serrated rock ridge which, higher up, curled round and merged into the south ridge of Nanda Devi.

It was on this serrated ridge at a height of about 18,000 ft. that we hoped to find a site for a base camp, but the immediate problem was whether to make for the old camp on the far side of the glacier or to go up the unknown right bank. The grassy flat and the spring were very great attractions, but it was more than doubtful if they could be reached in a day from our present camp, so far below the glacier snout. On the other hand by hugging the mountain on the right bank the way would be shortened, and only one camp would be necessary between Sanctuary Camp, where we now were, and the proposed base camp. We decided to eschew the delights of the 1934 camp and to take our chance on the unknown right bank, time being a more important factor than soft lying and spring water.

We got off at eight on the 3rd, all, including Nuri, carrying loads, most of them 60 lb. We had not gone half a mile before coming to a delightful stream of clear water, flanked by an acre patch of dry juniper wood, the sort of camp one only finds in dreams. I was rather ashamed at not having remembered it myself, but I had no doubt that the Mana men knew of it and could not refrain from asking them how they reconciled this with their statement of two days ago, and whether perhaps the stream and the juniper had both come into existence within the last two years. They had lied, and knew that they had lied, but they were not the least abashed, and laughingly replied that we had gone quite far enough that day and they were not to be blamed, indeed we ought to be grateful to them for furnishing such a good excuse for stopping.

About an hour from camp we came to another of our 1934 camp sites, the one near the snout of the glacier. Cached under a rock were a bag of satu and a spring balance. I opened up the satu and, finding that beneath a hard core the inside was still good, was cautious enough to dry it, rebag it, and add it to our reserve.

Opposite this camp is a tremendous avalanche cone of snow which has slid down one of the gullies of the opposing cliffs and formed a permanent bridge over the Rishi. When it first fell it must have dammed the river, but now this flows underneath it by a passage which it has burrowed out for itself. We crossed by this and climbed up the hard snow of the avalanche for a couple of hundred feet before leaving it for the grass of an old moraine. This took us close under the ciffs at the base of the mountain to a corner where their general direction changed from south to south-east. Here the moraine petered out and we had to commit ourselves to the hummocky, boulder-strewn surface of the South-East glacier. Still hugging the cliffs, we advanced slowly, either on the glacier or in the trough lying between it and the cliffs; on these a wary eye had to be kept, for at one point there was a continuous fall of stones that necessitated a wide detour.

At about midday we halted on top of one of the miniature ice-mountains of the glacier to take stock of our position and to allow the Mana men to catch up, for they were finding it heavy going in bare feet on the rough surface of the glacier, though it was seldom that they had to tread on ice. We eagerly scanned the ground ahead, between the glacier and the base of the mountain, for some suggestion of a camp site, but it was clear that grass flats and springs formed no part of the landscape on this side. Half a mile up was a high bank of talus which looked as though it might conceal something, so, leaving the others, Graham Brown and I pushed on to investigate. When opposite the bank we dumped our loads, got off the glacier, and climbed on to the top of the bank by a stone gully. Following up along the edge we came first to a stream and then to a dry flat of sand and mud lying between moraine and cliffs. It appeared to be clear of stone-falls, so we decided it would do and hastened back to call up the others. Pasang dashed ahead, and before Graham Brown and I had reached the foot of the stone gully he was coming down from the glacier carrying both our loads and his own!

By two o'clock everybody was in and, after a long rest, we started back, satisfied at having found in this wilderness of rock and ice such a comparative oasis, but fearing that it might yet prove too far from where we hoped to put our base camp. While we rested here a herd of bharal, or wild sheep, was seen traversing at a gallop the yellow cliffs nearly 1000 ft. above us and stopping occasionally to utter a sort of shrill whistle. On the grass downs of the Sanctuary there are at least two large herds, but this time we did not come across them. Had we seen any, the sight of so much fresh meat walking about might have made us regret our decision against bringing rifles, but to disturb a peace, which for them has never been broken, would be almost sacrilege, nor were a rifle and ammunition worth their weight for the sake of supplementing an ample diet with an occasional haunch of venison. Shooting for the pot may in some circumstances be necessary, but in the Sanctuary both sentiment and expediency are strongly opposed to it. It has been proposed that the Government of the United Provinces make this a sanctuary in fact as well as in name, and it is to be hoped that the game here will continue to enjoy by law the immunity hitherto conferred on them by reputed inaccessibility.

At this Moraine Camp, as it was subsequently known, there was of course no fuel. The limit of height for the invaluable juniper bush is about 14,000 ft. and the height of this camp was 15,000 ft. It was essential to keep our small stock of paraffin, now reduced to 6 gallons, for use on the mountain, so arrangements had to be made to bring wood up to here and on to the next camp, which we hoped would be our base. I wanted to stock the base camp with fuel for three weeks and use no paraffin at all there.

On August 4th we were able to make a start by bringing up two full loads of wood and the rest of us made what small additions of fuel we could to the loads which had still to be carried from Sanctuary Camp. As soon as we reached the new camp at one o'clock it began to rain heavily and a recess under the cliffs had to be burrowed out in order to light the fire. As far as space and flatness went, it was almost as good as the last camp; with all seven tents pitched, and a neat pile of loads under their tarpaulin, it had a most business-like appearance. In fact some were so attracted by it that there was a suggestion that it should be made our base.

It was I think this proposal—no more than a proposal—that led to a very happy evening and, as we realised later, a very timely one. Loomis apparently, had been carrying, buried in the recess of his kit, a small flask of Apricot Brandy, and, on the grounds that we had now reached what could, might, or ought to be our base camp, he was moved to produce it.

The secret had been well kept and when, supper over, our mugs, contrary to custom, were returned to us clean, we assumed that someone was going to make a brew of cocoa. Judge then of our surprise and pleasure when instead of that flaccid beverage this small bottle of beautiful amber liquid appeared, and was with due reverence uncorked. One's sense of smell gets a bit blunted in the course of an expedition—it has to—but grateful, oh most grateful, was the aroma of that Hungarian nectar which by some subtle alchemy overcame the fetid atmosphere of the tent. The flask was small and our pint mugs, seven in all, were large, but Napoleon brandy itself could not have been sipped with such gusto or lingered over so lovingly.

As the brandy was good so it was potent, and that distant country Alaska, of which we had already heard more than a little, assumed, along with its travellers, new and terrifying aspects. The already long glaciers of that frozen land increased in length, the trees which seemingly burgeon on these glaciers grew branches of ice, the thermometer dropped to depths unrecorded by science, the grizzlies were as large as elephants and many times as dangerous, and the mosquitoes were not a whit behind the grizzlies in size or fierceness, but of course many times more numerous. And amid all these manifold horrors our intrepid travellers climbed mountains, living the while on toasted marshmallows and desiccated eggs, inhabiting tents similar to ours, and packing loads which to think of made our backs ache. To echo and amend Dr Johnson, 'Claret for boys, port for men, but Apricot Brandy for heroes.'

CHAPTER TWELVE

The Base Camp

THE morning following this debauch we sent all the Mana men down the valley for fuel. The Sherpas and ourselves set out with the intention of finding a base camp, carrying 60 lb. and 40 lb. respectively: as the height increased we should find this quite enough, for we hoped to get somewhere near 18,000 ft., which would be higher than most of us had ever been.

We pursued the same tactics as yesterday, keeping where possible in the trough between the glacier and the cliffs, sometimes being forced out on to the glacier. Progress was rather laborious, but in an hour and a half we reached the foot of the scree slope up which Shipton and I had gone in 1934, and this was now the scene of a regrettable incident, nothing less than the loss of one of our scientists. On the way up the glacier Odell, either through excess of zeal or insufficiency of load, had led the field at a rare pace and the field had got rather strung out. By the time we plodders had reached the foot of the scree he was out of sight. I told him that we had to turn up a scree slope but, perhaps in the traditional absence of mind of the professor, or, more likely, because his eyes were glued to the ground after the manner of geologists and prospectors, he had steamed past without noticing it. We sat there for some time wasting valuable breath, which we should presently need, shouting for him, but with no effect.

I forget what load he was carrying. It may have been, and poetic justice demanded that it should have been, the unmentionable glacier drill; but I hardly think it was, because I remember we were flattering ourselves that that would be dumped at Moraine Camp where there was what seemed to be, at least to our ignorant minds, a fair sample of Himalayan glacier within a stone's throw, waiting to be drilled.

Anyhow we wrote Odell off for that day at least and addressed ourselves to the task presented by the steep scree. It was not as loose as scree can be, but it was loose enough to make it very hard work for the man in front, whose feet sank down several inches at every step. We rejoiced to see a stream of water coming down, indicating that we might find water on top of the ridge. We had had some doubt about this and later it was disappointing to see that the source of this stream was a good 500 ft. below the crest.

It took over two hours to climb the 1500 ft. to the top, and, before it was reached, rain, which presently turned to snow, began to fall. We gained the crest at a notch just below the fantastically weathered 'coxcomb' of crumbling yellow rock which gave the ridge its serrated appearance and also its name, for we now preferred the 'Coxcomb', *tout court*, to the former 'Saw-tooth' or 'Serrated' ridge.

Where we stood the ridge runs roughly east and west. On the south side, up which we had come, is the South-East glacier, one branch of which flows round the eastern foot of the ridge from its head beneath the southern slopes of East Nanda Devi, Nanda Devi itself, and the mile of snow ridge connecting the two. These slopes, together with the south ridge of Nanda Devi, make up a tremendous cwm, comparable, though on a lesser scale, to the West Cwm of Everest. From our position on the ridge then it will be understood that we looked down on to the upper névé of the South-East glacier and across it to East Nanda Devi. Had our erratic (I use the word in its strict sense of 'wandering') scientist continued his course up the right bank of the glacier, we would now have seen him on the glacier below us; but this we neither hoped nor expected, and I mention it merely in an attempt to explain the topography.

We now turn west along the crest of the ridge until driven off it by the steep and jagged rocks, below which we traversed on the north side. There was no sign of water, nor did it appear likely that we should find any higher up. The only alternatives for a base camp were on the névé of the glacier 200 or 300 ft. below us or near the source of the stream which we passed on the way up. The former would have been a fairly frigid spot for a base camp and the presence of water was problematical; the advantages were its height and the fact that the whole of our proposed route up the mountain would be in view. On the south side of the ridge the camp would be on shale, which is as preferable to ice for sleeping on as a feather bed is to a 'donkey's breakfast'. Also water was plentiful; but against this was the 500 ft. plug up to the ridge and the fact that the mountain would not be in view at all, though some of us thought this was a point in its favour. Emmons was the only one who preferred the glacier site. As he would have to spend most of his time there his opinion carried weight, but he was overruled, and I hope he was duly grateful.

While this discussion was going on, we were getting colder and wetter, so we dumped the loads under the 'Coxcomb' wall, covered them up, and hurried back. These loads contained nothing that we could not do without at the base, and we could therefore leave them here to be picked up when we returned this way to establish Camp I. Plunging and scree-riding down the southern slope, we reached the bottom in about twenty minutes, where we found a note from Odell saying that he had left his load and gone back to camp.

We followed him there, arriving at half-past three, and were mightily surprised to find Carter. We had calculated that he could not get here for another two days and I am afraid our first reaction was a feeling of relief that the Apricot Brandy had been drunk last night. Kalu was with him, his damaged reputation somewhat mended, and two other coolies, one from Mana and one from Lata—an acquisition of strength which would have been more welcome had we not got to feed them. The Bhotias got back later with big loads of wood.

The morning of the 6th was as unpleasant as it could be, raw, wet, and misty. The Sherpas, less Da Namgyal, and the Sahibs, got away with loads by nine o'clock, but the Bhotias were extremely reluctant to leave their tents. They disliked the glacier travel and made anxious inquiries about the route, but luckily I was able to assure them that it was free from ice or snow. Even so, much patience was required, but at last, an hour later, they made up their loads of fuel and started. Da Namgyal remained in camp because his cough was troubling him. He had suffered from this almost from the start and every night we would hear him coughing in the most distressing way; he must have made sleep difficult for his tent-mates, who were probably relieved when I sent him down.

The Mana men needed coaxing on the way up and I was fearful lest they should jib; indeed on one occasion when I had got too far ahead they were so long in coming that I went back to look for them, fully expecting to find that they had had enough. However, they brightened up when we reached the scree slope and I could point out our destination, nor were they long in reaching it. We were joined here by Odell, who had retrieved yesterday's error and was now carrying two loads. The others passed us on the way down, but by three o'clock the last of us were back at the Moraine Camp, having dumped the loads and the wood on a fairly flat site close to the highest water. Into the remainder of the short afternoon we crowded the writing of letters and the further weeding of our kits, for tomorrow the Base Camp would be occupied and the Mana men dismissed.

A wonderfully fine morning greeted us on this important day. On account of the Mana men there was no time to waste since they had to carry loads to the Base Camp, receive their pay, and then get down to the wood and warmth of Sanctuary Camp because they would be without tents.

More kit was left here, things that we should not need on the mountain and things that never should have been brought. Odell and I had some harsh words over the glacier drill, because in making up the loads for the men this had been left out on the assumption that it would stay here, an erroneous assumption, because we now learnt that what to our uninstructed minds appeared to be a perfectly good bit of glacier was to the scientific mind beneath contempt. The glacier down here was too old, worn, and decrepit to yield the desired results; its temperature at depth—'the be-all and the end-all' of our hopes, the sum of our ambition, that which we had left England to find—this could only be taken where it was young, fresh, and unsullied by a covering of stones. The glacier drill went with us.

We made good time and reached the new camp at half-past eleven and immediately began paying off all the men, except Kalu, who was to stay with us in place of Da Namgyal, whose job was to go back with the Bhotias as far as Joshimath, where he could have a week or ten days' rest. Then having collected six men from Lata village he was to return up the gorge, bringing our mail and two loads of coolie food, and to arrive at the Base Camp by September 1st.

Kalu was overjoyed at being promoted to the ranks of the Sherpas, though I take leave to doubt whether the joy was mutual. He indulged in a little of his

customary chest-thumping but retained sufficient presence of mind to claim
D'a Namgyal's high-altitude clothing and boots, which Da Namgyal was very
loth to surrender. That important point settled in his favour, Kalu then made
the round of the Sahibs, praying diligently, and cadging tobacco. He was the
most inveterate smoker I have ever met and would smoke charcoal, paper, or
old rags if there was nothing else. Now that the Mana men were leaving he
was without a pipe, but he got over that in a very ingenious manner. He made
a long sloping hole in the earth like the adit of a miniature mine, and then
sank a vertical shaft to cut this at the lower end. The shaft was filled with
tobacco, or in Kalu's case anything inflammable, and the smoker's mouth was
applied to the mouth of the adit. It gives, I imagine, a very cool smoke, and
does away with the tiresome necessity of carrying a pipe about, and to this day
I regret that I did not get Kalu to try the same method during his very brief
residence on snow.

The paying off of the Mana men took place under circumstances very
different to the last pay-day, even if only because it was a fine hot day instead
of a pouring wet one. These men had done all, and more, than was expected
of them. We could be liberal ungrudgingly, and we parted, at any rate on our
side, with feelings of esteem and almost affection. They are the most likeable
of men and in character not unlike the Sherpas; given the opportunity, they
might in time become as useful on a mountain as the Sherpas, but if that was
ever the case I should hate to have the paying of them. For once they now
appeared satisfied with what we gave them, true they asked for more, but only
as a matter of form, and the demand was not pressed very hard. Many and
profound were their salaams, and then they ran down the scree, laughing and
shouting like schoolboys on a holiday. To them we owed a lot.

It was a great satisfaction to be here. We felt that at last after nearly a
month, or in some cases two months, of preparatory drudgery the stage was
set and the supernumeraries dismissed; or like a builder who, having finished
the prosaic task of digging the foundations, was about to begin the more
exciting job of erecting the walls. To be rid of all coolies and to have no one
but the Sherpas and ourselves to look after gave a new feeling of confidence,
for, capable though the Bhotias are of taking care of themselves, they can yet
be a source of worry. It is one of the drawbacks of Himalayan climbing that
coolies should be necessary, but I think that anyone who has travelled with
the better type of Sherpa would like to have them along with him whether
necessary or not, just for the fun of their companionship.

We had good reason to be pleased with the result of all this preliminary
work. We were not more than a week behind schedule, we had a comfortable
Base Camp stocked with a month's food and three weeks' wood fuel, and
everybody except two of the Sherpas was in good health and spirits. None of
us had had any sickness on the way up, apart from a few septic sores. Loomis
was the worst sufferer in this respect, but his were now practically healed,
thanks to Houston's assiduous attention.

There were too many unknown factors for us to gauge with any accuracy
our chances of getting to the top, but at this stage we were decidedly hopeful.
The view of the south ridge from Pisgah had rather dashed us, but a closer,

though fleeting, look from the 'Coxcomb' ridge *en face*, even with due allowance for foreshortening, had been encouraging. But if the first appearance had proved to be false, common sense might have told us that the other need not be true. That this was so we were presently to learn.

CHAPTER THIRTEEN

A First Footing

I HAVE always admired those people who before ever reaching a mountain, perhaps even before seeing it, will draw up a sort of itinerary of the journey from base camp to summit—a complicated affair of dates, camps, loads, and men, showing at any given moment precisely where *A* is expected to be, what *B* will be doing, what *C* has had for breakfast, and what *D* has got in his load. It always reminds me of the battle plans an omniscient staff used to arrange for us in France, where the artillery barrage and the infantry went forward, hand in hand as it were, regardless of the fact that while there was nothing whatever to impede the progress of the barrage, there were several unknown quantities, such as mud, wire, and Germans, to hamper the movements of the infantry.

Parallels drawn from warfare are apt, and difficult to avoid, but they assort very ill with the spirit of mountain climbing; yet any programme that includes a human factor is liable to go amiss, and in our case almost every factor was unknown. Moses himself, who was no mean organiser, could hardly cope with a problem of movement which included such imponderables as the route, the state of the snow, the rate of climbing, the weather, the porters, and the powers of acclimatisation of a party only two of which had been over 17,300 ft. before.

In the final stages of a climb, when the unknowns have been greatly reduced, a time-table is essential, but we made no attempt to elaborate any such miracle of organisation and foresight at this early hour. We might have succeeded in keeping in step for one day, but, as will appear, the second and third days would have played the devil with it.

The first thing to do was to find a Camp I and take up everything we should need on the mountain, including food for twenty-five days, leaving at the Base Camp a week's extra food and twenty days' food for Emmons, who was stopping there. We had the advantage of knowing that there were no difficulties up to 19,000 ft., so we were able to start without waiting to reconnoitre. We completed our loads from the dump on the ridge and continued traversing below the 'Coxcomb', the Sherpas carrying 60 lb. and ourselves 40 lb., which we found was as much as we could well manage at this height.

We kept as high as possible under the rock wall, over some very loose ground, and as soon as the ridge beyond the 'Coxcomb' looked feasible we edged up to the left to get on to it. To do this a patch of snow had to be crossed, but even at the late hour of midday it was in fair condition, a fact we noted with premature satisfaction. On the crest of the ridge we were once more on rock and at one o'clock we reckoned the height at 19,000 ft. This was gauged by taking a clinometer reading to the top of what was known as 'Longstaff's Col', a col on the rim of the Basin at the foot of the shoulder of East Nanda Devi. It is not a pass, or at least it was not then, because it had not yet been crossed, but in 1905 Dr Longstaff and his two guides, the Brocherels, had stood on this col and were the first to look down into the inner Sanctuary. To quote Dr Longstaff: 'Below us was an extraordinary chaos of wind-driven cloud, half veiling the glaciers which surround the southern base of Nanda Devi. Above was the vast southern face of the great peak, its two summits connected by a saddle of more than a mile in length. From this spot the mountain strangely resembles Ushba, and the likeness must be even more striking from the West. Directly from the col rose the southern ridge of the eastern peak by which we hoped to make the ascent.'

By now none of us were feeling very strong and it was time to look for a camp site, for there was nothing suitable in the immediate vicinity. While we were admiring the view or, less euphemistically, resting, Houston and Loomis went up about 300 ft. and reported there was a possible site. When we got to it, it appeared so uninviting that I went up still higher, hoping to find something better. But there was not the vaguest suggestion of a tent platform, the rock of uniform steepness sloped away to the névé of the glacier on the one side, on the south was a precipice, and the ridge in between was too narrow and broken even to climb, much less furnish a platform. It now began to snow, so we fell furiously to digging out and buiding up three platforms on the proposed site. At the end of an hour's hard work, we had three passable platforms, one big enough for the two-man bivouac tent and two for the larger 6 ft. × 7 ft. tents. This done, we stowed the loads under a convenient ledge and hurried back to the Base Camp at half-past four. The height of this Camp I was 19,200 ft.

At breakfast next morning what may have been a spontaneous and was certainly an almost unanimous desire for an off-day found expression. It happened to be a Sunday, so we may have felt that some recognition of this was due, or perhaps a mental itinerary had persuaded us that we had more time in hand than would be needed to complete the job. It was so tempting to divide the remaining 6000 ft. into three lifts of 2000, allot a couple of days to each and one day to get down, and so climb the mountain in a week. Poor Maurice Wilson, who tried to climb Everest alone and die on the glacier from exhaustion, had much the same notion; but for him the problem was even simpler, for he did not worry much about height and estimated his task in terms of distance—a mere seven miles from Rongbuk monastery to the top.

A fine, sunny morning made some of us regret the waste of a good day, but a wet afternoon made amends. It may have been a wise resolve physiologically, but tactically it was a mistake, because experience shows that there are usually enough involuntary rest-days due to weather without adding any voluntary ones. The time was spent pleasantly enough smoking too much, eating too much, and in too much group photography—the results of these alone, portraying as they do what looks like a blackguardly group of political refugees (politics according to taste), are ample condemnation of off-days. Loomis and Emmons relieved me of the catering for the day and I have grateful recollections of some inspired hominy cakes. The Sherpas had rigged up a very effective roof for the kitchen out of the bit of tarpaulin and the ponderous steel tent poles, which now almost justified their existence, but which, I am glad to say, were not to go any higher. We had three light aluminium poles for use on the mountain and, though they were fragile enough to look at, they stood up uncommonly well.

Early in the night the rain turned to snow and when we woke next morning there were six inches of snow at the camp, and the glacier below was white down to 14,000 ft. It was still snowing hard, so we sat tight and towards midday the wind got up and very soon a blizzard was blowing from the southwest. Conditions were rather miserable, the kitchen roof blew away at intervals or collapsed under the weight of snow, and even when up afforded little protection to the fire or to anyone working there. To add to our worries Kitar and Nuri were now on the sick list. Nuri had never recoverd from his attack at Pisgah and daily looked more fragile and more anxious; clearly we could strike him off the strength. Kitar had complained of his stomach at Pisgah, but after being dosed had said no more about it. I noticed he always took the lightest loads he could and we thought he was a bit of a 'lead-swinger', but in this we maligned him.

Meanwhile we lay in our tents thinking sorrowfully on sundials and their sententious advice about the passing moment and the lost day that never returns, and vowing with many oaths that we would go up to Camp I on the morrow, blizzard or no blizzard. It was still snowing and blowing in gusts when we turned out, but there were breaks in the flying scud and a brighter patch of light in the murky sky assured us that the sun had risen even if the cock had not crowed.

This day we meant to establish Camp I, but only ourselves were to sleep there, the Sherpas returning to the Base Camp and bringing up the final loads on the following day. The loads had to be dug out from under a canopy of snow and it was half-past nine before we began plodding heavily up to the ridge in the soft new snow. On the north side of the 'Coxcomb' the snow was deeper and we were forced to take a lower route, changing the lead every ten minutes. This route took us on to the névé of the glacier, where we had a sorry time floundering in soft snow, and were finally led into what appeared to be a bottomless pit. At this point there was some discussion whether we should keep down a little longer or at once strike up over the snow-covered rocks to the ridge. It seemed to me rather like debating the advisability of walking in the ditch or on the road, but the luckless man in the lead, although up to the neck in snow, still evinced a strange preference for the lower route. Pasang, however, who happened to be next, had no doubt about it and struck out boldly for the rocks, where the rest of us speedily followed. Our ruffled

15   The 1936 Nanda Devi team (minus Houston) at Raniket on their return:
(l to r) Peter Lloyd (UK), H. Adams Carter (US), W.F.Loomis (US), N.E.Odell (UK), Arthur Emmons (US); *(seated)* T.Graham Brown (UK) and H.W.Tilman (UK). *Photo: Salkeld archive.*

16   Nanda Devi and Nanda Devi East from Lamchir Col to the south. Longstaff's Col is the lowest point of the intervening ridge. *Photo: John Harvey*

Views of Nanda Devi:

17 (above) The summit slopes. The route follows the line between the snow slope and the mixed ground on the left.

18 (left) West Peak from the South Glacier. The route follows the obvious diagonal line.

19   Camp 1 (19,200ft/5853m) on the Nanda Devi climb in 1936.

20   In the gully at c.23,000ft. on Nanda Devi during the first ascent. 'We began to search the snow above us for the slightest break in the relentless angle of the slope.'

21 A view from the Nanda Devi South Ridge over Longstaff's Col to Nanda Kot.

22 H.W. Tilman
Pasang Kikuli
and Charles
Houston, at
Martoli after
their first crossing
of Longstaff's
Col at the end of
the 1936
expedition.

23 Thirty-nine years after their historic climb, Bill Tilman (left), Noel Odell (centre right) and Dr Charles Houston (right) were together again at the 1975 Alpine Club Medical symposium at Plas Y Brenin in North Wales. John Jackson, the PYB Director, is between Tilman and Odell.

24 Members of Maj. Gordon Osmaston's Nanda Devi survey team in the Sanctuary in 1936 including Tensing Norgay (centre) and Fazal Ellahi (second from right)

25 Dunagiri seen from the south-east from above the Rhamani Glacier. Pt.6135 is on the right. Th ridge attempted by Shipton, Angtharkay and Sen Tensing is in profile on the left. *Photo: Joe Tasker*

26 The view east from Dunagiri towards Changabang, Kalanka and Pt. 6957 on the left. The Baga Col is a breach in the linking ridge in the bottom left corner of the picture. *Photo: Joe Tasker*

27   Angtharkay (left), with Kusang and Pasang Bhutia, was a key figure in the 1934 trip and (with
Sen Tensing) equally effective on Shipton's 1936 survey expedition. This ebullient and resourceful
Sherpa sirdar, along with these partners and others (Tensing Norgay, Lhakpa Tensing, Rinsing) took
part in most of the Tilman/Shipton ventures of the 1930s, and then in postwar French expeditions.

28 29 30
Eric Shipton, dapper and charismatic, and the taciturn and down-to-earth Bill Tilman, formed one of the most effective mountain partnerships of their day – their reputation underscored by their prodigious literary output.

Pamela Freston (lower left, at Kalimpong c. 1935) played an important part in Shipton's life, not least as a skilled editor and overseer of his books and articles.*

Tilman, a fine writer, needed no such support, but Elizabeth "Betsy" Cowles (lower right), who he met during the 1950 Everest reconnaissance trip, became a valued friend.

* *Nanda Devi* was selected by the National Book League as one of a hundred modern books to represent literature at the Festival of Britain in 1951. Bip Pares, the illustrator of *Nanda Devi* and *Blank on the Map* should also be noted for her major contribution to their success.

feelings caused by this ignominy soon recovered on the better going afforded by the ridge, and by two o'clock we had reached our goal.

The snow had stopped by now and the wind died away, but the diminutive platform buried under snow and the complete absence of any drips of water from the rocks formed a very discouraging welcome. All hands fell to clearing away the snow, and at almost the first dig one of our two precious Bernina shovels went down the *khud*. These Berninas are light collapsible shovels of aluminium which are invaluable for digging tent platforms in snow. The business end of this one was improperly secured and at the first thrust came off the handle, went over the edge of the platform, and so down the snow slope to the glacier 500 ft. below. This was the second, but neither the last nor the most aggravating, occasion on which we learnt that the laws of gravity were much the same on Nanda Devi as elsewhere.

Owing to the accident of the ground, the three platforms were of necessity at considerable intervals apart, and to pass from one to the other was quite a climb. The job of cooking was assigned to the middle tent, of which Odell and myself were the unlucky occupants, on the specious pretext that it was most handy. Our system of allotting tents was a haphazard one and the only guiding principle was that of frequent changes. The object of this was to avoid any tendency to form cliques and it was beneficial in various ways. If a man knows that his martyrdom has only to be endured for a night or two running, he can tolerate good-humouredly the queerest little idiosyncrasies of his stable-companions. Some of us talked too much or too loudly, some did not talk enough, some smoked foul pipes, some ate raw onions, some *never* washed, some indulged in Cheyne-Stokes breathing, and one even indulged in Cheyne-Stokes snoring. I should explain that this form of respiration afflicts one at high altitudes and only occurs during unconsciousness. Short bursts of increasingly violent panting, as though the victim was suffocating, rise to a crescendo and are succeeded by complete stillness as if the man has died, although a quickly recurring spasm convinces the other occupants of the tent that this unfortunately is not so. The devastating effects of this sort of thing when combined with snoring can be imagined. But these singularities, which, if endured for too long, might lead to murder, were, by our system of musical chairs, matter only for frank criticism or even amusement.

The unfortunate necessity of cooking, from which we seem to have wandered, was on the mountain a very simple routine. All that it implied was boiling the porridge and beating up the dried milk in the morning, and in the evening boiling the pemmican. No more was allowed, and in the fullness of time (such is habit), no more was expected—I was going to say 'desired', but that perhaps would be putting it too strongly. It sounds simple enough, but the production of these sybaritic repasts needed first the presence of a Primus stove in the cook's tent. Moreover, this stove had to be lit and kept alight in the teeth of all the devils which seemed at once to take possession of it, causing it to splutter, smoke, lick the tent roof with a devouring flame, do everything in fact except burn. Perhaps I exaggerate, for all were not like this, the outbreaks were few, and with skilled and sympathetic handling need not occur at all. Still there the beastly thing was in the tent, room had to be made for it, patience exerted on it, the fingers burnt by it, the nostrils assailed by it, and its fumes swallowed. To have to do and suffer thus was excellent moral discipline, but it should only be taken in small doses and the stove should change tents as frequently as the personnel.

Cooking was only the penultimate duty of the cook; before this came the providing of water and after it the dishing out into seven expectant mugs—enamel ones that is. Here both skill and expedition were required, for if there was expedition and no skill the tent floor received the most liberal helping, and, if the converse held, the pemmican congealed before the other tents got their ration. Practice, as always, makes perfect, and it was astonishing what prodigies of pouring were performed from any height, at any angle, and, if need be, in the dark.

The provision of water was at Camp I a simple matter except on this first night when everything was under snow. Thereafter there was a useful drip from some nearby rocks and a cunning distribution of pots in the morning assured the evening supply. Higher up it was not so easy, and ice or hard snow had to be dug out in sufficient quantity. The melting of this takes longer than the boiling, and some judgment is needed to know what amount of water different types of snow will yield. The hapless cook lights his stove, puts the snow on to melt, and while this is doing takes off his boots and gets into his sleeping bag. He then discovers that a heaped saucepan of snow has yielded a teacupful of water, and perforce leaves his warm bag, puts on his boots, and collects more snow—not only in the saucepan but also in his imperfectly laced boots and socks. An attempt was made to enact that the tent doing the cooking should also distribute the food to the other tents, but this seemed to Odell and me (at that moment anyhow) a monstrous arrangement akin to sweated labour, or like making the condemned man dig his own grave.

Next morning was fine and cold but did not look promising. The party split up, three went down to the dump to help the Sherpas and were also commissioned to look for the shovel, Graham Brown and Houston were to prepare a fourth tent platform against the arrival of the Sherpas, and Odell and myself had the more interesting job of reconnoitring for the second camp. Immediately above us there appeared to be about 800 ft. of rock and snow ridge similar to that on which we were, and beyond was a steep snow arête, which continued for possibly 500 ft., before flattening out into a convenient snow saddle, the very place, we thought, for Camp II.

It was indeed the very place for a camp, but it was not Camp II that we put there but Camp III, and it was five days later before it was occupied.

How hopelessly out we were in these glib estimates, due to foreshortening, was apparent in a very short time, and henceforth we took very little on trust. For 700 or 800 ft. we mounted steadily, taking a line just below the crest of the ridge on the east side of it, for on the western it was precipitous. It was by no means similar to the ridge below, being decidedly steeper and very much looser. In fact when we came to carrying loads up here it became a nightmare owing to the danger from loose rocks, nor was it possible to escape the danger by keeping to the crest, so sharp and broken was it. If I am ever guilty of using the phrase 'firm as a rock' again, I shall think of this ridge and strike it out.

Above this horrible section the rocks were snow-covered and before going any farther we sat down for a long rest at what was subsequently known as the 'roping-up place', for from this point onwards a rope was essential. Both of us were feeling the effects of altitude here, though later in the day, when we got higher, we felt it less; perhaps we were taken out of ourselves by the more interesting and difficult climbing in the same way that a man will cease being sea-sick if the ship is sinking—having something better to think about. Between 19,000 ft. and 20,000 ft. seemed to be the critical height and both the old hands and the newcomers suffered from extreme lassitude, and one or two from headaches and slight nausea. Personally I was astonished at the speed with which those who had not been high before did acclimatise, and how comparatively mild their symptoms were. In 1935 four of us, crossing a pass of only 17,000 ft. from Sikkim into Tibet, suffered extremely, and although carrying no loads were quite incapable of keeping pace with our transport which, since it included some yaks, was not exactly devouring the ground. Such discrepancies are difficult to explain and a great deal has yet to be learnt about acclimatisation. Houston collected all the data he could to help in this object and persuaded most members of the party to submit to keeping a very detailed and indecently intimate record of their day-to-day symptoms and feelings. The keeping of such records in the cause of science is I suppose very praiseworthy, and since questions had to be answered and symptoms noted in that grim interval between awakening and getting out of one's sleeping bag, it showed amazing restraint and commendable determination in all who undertook the task. To be confronted morning after morning, at that unseasonable hour, with such questions as how one had slept, and what one at that moment desired, would compel most people, including the writer, to try to be funny at the expense of truth. Psycho-analysis, medical examinations, oxygen masks, *et hoc genus omne*, seem a far cry from mountaineering as understood by Whymper, Leslie Stephen, Mummery and the giants of the past.

The effects of the recent blizzard were felt on this upper section, because there was a lot of fresh snow which had to be cleared away before steps could be cut in the underlying harder snow or ice. For some way it was a straightforward upward traverse just below or sometimes on the crest of the ridge, but presently a double cornice warned us off the crest just when this course had become most desirable owing to the increasing angle of the snow slope.

On one pitch the snow beneath the cornice was so steep and deep that, instead of steps, a continuous track had to be scraped and stamped out, and at the farther end of this critical passage a hole had to be flogged through another cornice, crowning a short lateral rib, which crossed our line at right angles. Having successfully emulated the camel, we were rewarded by a good stance, where one man could anchor the party with an axe belay while the other essayed a traverse across some rotten rocks, covered with snow and verglas. Thanks to a loose rock, the leader here came unstuck and shot down some distance before being stopped by the rope secured round the second's axe driven deeply into the snow.

After this, in every sense *moving* incident, we regained for a short space the security of the ridge only to be driven off again by a cornice under which another long traverse had to be made. Early in the day our ambitions had been fixed on the snow saddle; at the roping-up place the snow arête leading to it would have contented us; and, as the difficulties increased, so our hopes receded down the ridge, until now we were aiming at what looked like a rock platform, only 100 ft. above us and still 300 ft. from the foot of the arête. Even this we were destined not to see.

This last traverse took longer than we expected, because once more a continuous track had to be beaten out while the overhang of the cornice did its best to shove us off. By the time we had finished this, snow was falling, and it was three o'clock, so we decided to call it a day. We were probably 1500 ft. above Camp I and, considering the route, it was clear that this would be a long enough carry when laden. The fact that in all the distance we had come there was no suitable place for a tent was disturbing, but we had strong hopes of the top of the rock bulge now just above us.

We got down at five o'clock to find the others back and four Sherpas ensconced in the fourth tent. No Bernina shovel had been found and another similar accident had occured. A full tin of tea, left on the platform outside one of the tents, had for some unexplained reason gone over the edge. The only witnesses to this tragedy were Graham Brown and Houston, who were working on another platform and suddenly noticed it rolling down the slope; and it was the more serious because, but for an ounce, this was all the tea we had left. I think that the only drink worth having on a mountain is one which will quench thirst, and that things like cocoa and patent drinks, which pretend to be food as well, are not worth their weight. After all, the bulk of the food, like pemmican and porridge, is slops and what is really wanted is something to eat, that is chew, and something to drink, not an anaemic mixture of the two. Even the Americans, traditionally hostile to tea and addicted to cocoa and kindred drinks, came round to this point of view and felt the deprivation as much as the tea-swilling British.

We were rather wet and miserable and by nightfall it was snowing hard, a state of affairs which gave us more concern on account of the lost tea than for its effect on the mountain; every flake that fell buried it deeper and lessened the already remote chances we had of finding it.

Lloyd and Carter were still feeling the altitude here and Kalu and Phuta were both sick, so they were detailed to go down and look for the tea. Four full-grown men poking about in the snow of a glacier for a 1 lb. tin of tea sounds like mountaineering with Alice in Wonderland, but it seemed natural enough at the time and it gives some measure of how we felt our loss. In a few days the Americans, who have not been brought up on tea, were talking about it as they might of whisky in the days of Prohibition, so that the hell of unfulfilled longing which the wretched Englishmen endured can well be imagined.

Five of us carrying 20 lb., and Pasang and Nima carrying 40 lb., set out to find Camp II. The 700 ft. up to the roping-up place were purgatorial, particularly for the leader, for the task of finding the best route and at the same time treading delicately, like Agag, to avoid launching great rocks on to those below was very wearing. The slightest mistake in placing a foot would inevitably send down a stone and a too vigorous use of the hands would have brought a large piece of the arête about one's ears. In places it was impossible to avoid crossing back above those behind, and the only thing to do was to wait until they were clear. I nearly bagged Odell this way, but he managed to duck and the rock went over his head.

At eleven o'clock it began snowing again. We climbed on two ropes of three and four, with a Sherpa in the middle of each, and by half-past one had reached almost to yesterday's highest point. The old steps were of great use, but all had to be cleared again of snow and, laden as we were, we moved with great caution, particularly on the traverse leading to the needle's eye, which was petrifying for the performer though probably amusing enough for the onlooker. At the thinnest part of the traverse a protruding ice bulge enforced the adoption of almost a crawl to get by, and, if the attitude was not sufficiently humble, the load jammed under the bulge, greatly to the embarrassment of its bearer and the diversion of the second man who, fortunately, at this critical juncture, had a secure axe belay in a niche beneath the cornice.

Just before the upper traverse there was perhaps room for a small bivouac tent, so, leaving the others there in case nothing better was found, Odell and I crossed the traverse to investigate the platform which we had failed to reach the previous day. The movement round the projecting nose of rock covered with snow of doubtful integrity was a delicate one, but we were rewarded by finding on top of the nose a place which with a little work could be made to hold one tent, possibly two. It was a slightly sloping snow-covered ledge measuring about 6 ft. x 20 ft. set in the angle of a sheer rock wall, which enclosed it on two sides. On the third side was the way by which we had come and the fourth fell away steeply to the glacier now nearly 2000 ft. below. At first sight it looked as though we had entered a cul-de-sac, but a little search disclosed a snow ledge outside the rock wall furnishing an exit almost as perfunctory as the entrance.

It was now late, so without bringing the others up we dumped our two loads there and all went down together. We got back to Camp I wet through and found Emmons had come up to see what was happening. When he went down he took with him Kalu, the great chest-thumping Kalu who had already had enough—perhaps he wanted to get back to somewhere where he could dig holes in the ground for a pipe. The all-important matter of finding a place for Camp II had been settled and we had learnt that at any rate two of the Sherpas were fairly safe climbers. Pasang was particularly steady and Nima too was good but a bit light-hearted in his management of the rope. On the whole therefore it had been a day of gains, but against this was Kalu's defection, Phuta's sickness, the weather, and failure to find the tea. I must have been feeling a bit hipped myself, a state of mind which in politer society than that of our own we would have called 'sanguinary-minded', for the last entry in my diary runs: 'Still snowing 7 p.m. and we still cooking.'

CHAPTER FOURTEEN

On the Mountain

OUR plan now was for two of us to occupy Camp II or the Gîte, as it was appropriately called, and on the following day, while those two went up higher to look for a Camp III, two Sherpas would join them at the Gîte. We assumed that a site for Camp III would be found on the snow saddle, and on the third day the Sherpas would assist in establishing the two Sahibs there while two more of us in turn occupied the Gîte.

It was a fine morning on the 14th, but we did not get away until 10 a.m. Graham Brown and Houston, who were going to sleep at Camp II, had to pack up the bivouac tent and their own gear and then someone dropped a mug down the *khud* and Houston very sportingly went down after it. The task looked hopeless in all the new snow, but he got it. Odell stayed in camp to catch up with his geological notes, but six of us started with Pasang and Nima.

At the roping-up place Carter went back as he had not yet acclimatised, and from there we climbed on three ropes, Lloyd and Nima, Pasang and myself, and Graham Brown, Houston, and Loomis. As usual the steps had to be cleared of snow and in places they were now not very reliable, but by cutting deep in they held sufficiently well. The passage round and up the projecting nose below the Gîte roused so much misgiving that we talked of putting a fixed rope there. But it was an awkward place to fix anything and in the end familiarity bred sufficient contempt for us to do without. A rope of two can move quicker than one of three, so Lloyd and I got there well ahead of the others and Pasang and Nima began making a platform; it now looked as though there would just be room for the bivouac tent and a big one. When they had finished I took them down on my rope, Lloyd waiting for the others, who had not yet arrived. By six o'clock it was snowing again.

The journey to Camp II, though now a daily routine, was never boring however unpleasant it might be in other ways. The unstable rocks of the lower half still lay in wait to punish any carelessness, and on the upper section the daily snow-fall made it at least look like a new ascent.

The next day all started except Phuta and, when we reached the roping-up place, we descried what looked like two flies crawling up the steep snow arête above the Gîte. These of course were Graham Brown and Houston, and we watched them anxiously, making ribald remarks about their rate of progress and their frequent halts. The fact that we were ourselves sitting down eating chocolate by no means lessened our enjoyment of this spectacle and certainly increased the flow of wit. We felt like dramatic critics eating their chocolates in the stalls, and sharpened the pencils of our wit accordingly.

It was a fine day for a change and the bright sun on the snow sapped our energy. We were up by 2 p.m. and having seen the tent pitched, for which there was just room enough, and Pasang and Nima safely established there, Lloyd and I went down, while Odell and Loomis waited to hear the news from above. An hour later Graham Brown and Houston got back to Camp II, and reported that there were a couple of hundred feet of difficult climbing before the snow arête was reached, that this was steep and long, but that a good site for a camp had been found where the arête merged into the broad saddle. They had felt the sun even more severely than we had.

We got down to Camp I at four o'clock and Phuta requested that he might go to the Base Camp that evening. It was no use keeping him, so I gave him a chit to Emmons and sent him down. There were now five of us at Camp I, two Sahibs and two Sherpas at Camp II, and Emmons, Kalu, and three Sherpas at the Base Camp.

Next day, the 16th, two more Sahibs had to occupy Camp II, and at half-past nine we all started, Odell and I carrying our personal kit and some odds and ends. Some student of human nature has remarked that 'no one can do an act that is not morally wrong for the last time without feelings of regret', but now I was doing the climb from Camp I to Camp II for the fifth and last time and can very positively refute that statement. Of course devout Hindus might say that in climbing Nanda Devi we *were* committing an immoral act and that would account satisfactorily for my absence of regret.

Before reaching the roping-up place, we were bothered by seeing two tents still standing at the Gîte and it looked as though no move was in progress. Later we made out somebody on the arête but could see only two instead of the four we expected. We puzzled our heads over this and made many wild conjectures. If Graham Brown and Houston were not moving up to Camp III there would be some congestion at the Gîte, but Odell and I were determined to sleep there, even if it meant four in a tent. We could not face yet another ascent from Camp I.

It was no use speculating, and as Odell was going slowly, and I was not unwilling to do the same, he and I went along together while the other three pushed on as fast as they could to find out what the matter was. We two continued in leisurely fashion, not arriving until three o'clock. Perhaps we were carrying heavier loads; Odell certainly was, for he was cluttered up with hypsometers, clinometers, and thermometers, and was so attached to certain favourite but unnecessary articles of clothing that his personal kit was a portentous affair—nor was Da Namgyal there to carry it as he should have been. I remember particularly a hideous yellow sweater, a relic of the War, which weighed more than the five Shetland woollies carried by us all; and at the highest camp he produced a hat which none of us had ever seen before and which, I suppose, had some attributes peculiarly fitting it for wear at 24,000 ft.

The mystery of the two tents was solved by a note and the presence of both Sherpas. Nima was sick and Pasang was completely snow-blind. The note told

us that they had gone up with food and kit and asked us to bring on the tent
and their sleeping bags. Loomis and Lloyd had already left with these when
we arrived and half-way up the snow arête they were met by Houston and
Graham Brown. For these four it was a hard day.

Houston's note went on to say that the necessary dope for alleviating snow-
blindness had been unaccountably left at Camp I, and suggested that strong
tea should be tried in the interim. Tea was at a premium, for we were
carefully conserving our solitary ounce for higher up, but we brewed some
and did what we could for Pasang, who was in considerable pain. He was lying
on his face in the tent and quite unable to open his eyes, but by forcing the lids
apart we managed to get some tea in. This treatment was continued until the
medicine arrived two days later, but had little effect; nor had the medicine
either for that matter, and, though we did not then suspect, Pasang was now
out of the hunt.

It was not easily understood how he had managed to get such a severe
attack. Yesterday had been very bright and sunny but no one noticed him
with his glasses off, nor were these any different from Nima's which were
perfectly efficient. While he was preparing the platform here, I noticed he was
working without glasses and it must have been then that his eyes were
affected, although the platform was in shadow and there was more rock than
snow. But a rarefied atmosphere makes the light more dangerous in this
respect and we read that on Everest in 1924 Norton was snow-blind merely
from the glare off rocks. In 1930 Shipton and I climbed Kilimanjaro (19,700
ft.), and on snow near the summit we both took off our glasses to see where
we were, for there was a thick mist and not a sign of the sun. Nevertheless that
same night we both went snow-blind and suffered great pain, but in twenty-
four hours it passed off without any treatment and this led me to think that
Pasang's would do the same.

When Lloyd and Loomis returned, we agreed that they should please
themselves whether they came up tomorrow with the little that was left at
Camp I to bring. They would not be able to sleep here because Odell and I
would still be in residence. Another tent, more food, and our own kits had to
be carried to Camp III before we could move up, and for reasons of
acclimatisation it was a sound plan to sleep two nights at a camp before going
on to the next.

When they had gone, we took stock of our surroundings. These consisted of
blank rock wall and thin air in equal proportions; there were about four feet
of terra firma between the two tents and one could walk, without a rope, for
about ten paces round the corner where the exit lay. All view of the ridge was
cut off and only a little of it immediately below the Gîte was visible, but to the
east a wide field of vision included East Nanda Devi, 'Longstaff's Col' now
well below us, a great crescent of fluted ice wall on the rim to the south of it,
and, beyond, the beautifully proportioned Nanda Kot. The height was about
20,400 ft.

Having brewed the tea for Pasang's eyes and drunk some ourselves, we
tried to instil some life into Nima, who seemed very lugubrious and
lethargic—in much the same frame of mind as a passenger in the last stages of

sea-sickness, who having prayed long and earnestly for the ship to sink has almost abandoned hope that it will. I think they had not eaten since they got there, so we made him light his stove and cook some pemmican, which the Sherpas relish far more than we do. They were in the roomy 6 ft. x 7 ft. tent while we occupied the small bivouac tent vacated by Graham Brown and Houston, who had taken up one of the larger ones. We graciously allowed the Sherpas to remain in the enjoyment of their luxurious quarters, but this generosity will not be counted unto us for righteousness because the atmosphere in their tent was such that no tent at all would have been preferable.

I forget the exact dimensions of our tent, but it was very long and narrow and the two occupants lay, literally, cheek by jowl—that is if the human face has a jowl; or is it confined to pigs? It was admirably suited to Odell, who is also long and a bit narrow, and I think this was the first night that he was able to lie at full length since he had left Ranikhet. On this expedition we were experimenting with air beds as insulation when lying on snow, instead of the usual rubber mats, half an inch thick and 3 ft. x 4 ft. The extra room they took up was very noticeable in a small tent and apart from that they were not altogether successful. Punctures were numerous and unless they amounted to bursts, as they sometimes did, they were not easy to locate; situated as we were, the method of plunging them into a bath and watching for bubbles was seldom practicable. If your bed did go flat, it was a serious matter because no protection at all was afforded, and the result was a cold and sleepless night. Again, if you blew them up too hard you rolled off, and if they were too soft you were in contact with the ground and therefore cold. The Sherpas used to blow them up as if they were blowing up a dying fire, with the result that one bounded about like a pea on a drum, and if two people sat on it when in that state the whole thing exploded. Pasang got a lot of amusement out of the operation of blowing up and deflating beds by making them produce discordant noises like ill-played bagpipes. Now that only two of the Sherpas were left, and those two incapable of raising even a zephyr, we had to blow our own up, and this process provided yet another example of the perfection of natural laws which can even legislate for the remote association of a mountaineer and an air bed; as we gained in altitude and lost breath, the beds required less air to fill them owing of course to the diminution of pressure.

There was a storm in the night but, packed as we were, it was easy to keep warm and difficult to keep cool. Pasang was still blind and very sorry for himself, but Nima was brighter and offered to come with us to Camp III. Odell and I took a tent and paraffin, and Nima 40 lb. of sugar. Care was required on a short stretch above the camp and an upward traverse on rather shaky snow took us on to the ridge. We left it again where it suddenly stood on end and got into trouble on the rocks which would, when climbed, bring us out above this steep bit which had so frightened us. Odell led over a steep ice-glazed traverse which Nima and I resolved mentally to have nothing to do with, and when he was securely placed we had ourselves more or less pulled up in a direct line.

We were now at the foot of the steep snow arête which was such a prominent feature from below, and we settled down to kicking steps up it very slowly and methodically, the steps made by our forerunners having vanished. It was a narrow ridge, but we were able to stick to the crest, or slightly on the Rishi side, which was now less steep than the east side, though both fell away sharply, and the upward angle was 40 or 45 degrees; it will be remembered that from Camp I to Camp II the route lay always on the east flank and that the Rishi side was a precipice. As might be expected after the persistent falls of the last week, there was a lot of fresh snow to kick through before solid footing was obtained, and when we reached the tent at Camp III Graham Brown told us exactly how many of these steps we had kicked out, he having counted them. As far as I remember, the figure was disappointingly small for we felt that it must be something astronomical, but in sober fact there were only about 700 ft. of snow ridge. Approaching the tent, the angle eased off and we found it pitched snugly under the shelter of a steep snow bank.

It was after midday, but Graham Brown and Houston were still in bed and evidently intended 'lying at earth' after their efforts of yesterday. Going back we rattled down in an hour, and this time reversed our upwards procedure by descending the very steep snow patch in order to avoid the rocks. Nobody had come up from below, Pasang was still blind, we both had slight headaches, it was snowing again, and there was a big sun halo; but all this was forgotten in the warm glow of self-righteousness induced by our virtuous activity.

Having thus acquired enough merit for the time being by working while others slept, we sat about next morning until Graham Brown and Houston came down from Camp III for more loads. We found it such a pleasant occupation that we sat about some more until the other three came up from Camp I. As soon as the first man's head appeared round the corner of the bulge below us, a shout went up to know if they had found the tea. They had no tea, but they brought the zinc-sulphate medicine and we now hoped that Pasang's recovery would be speedy; at present his eyes were as firmly closed as ever. Nima too had relapsed into his former state of misery, but even yet we did not despair of getting some useful work out of these two. There was still a load to come up from Camp I, so it was arranged that Carter and Nima should go down tomorrow for this and as much more food as they could carry.

At three o'clock four of us started back for Camp III, Odell and Houston on one rope, Graham Brown and myself on the other. We had the advantage of the steps made by them on the way down and, in spite of heavy loads, were up in two hours. Our tent platform was ready for us, so the others had not been so idle yesterday as we thought, and it was pleasant to have some room again, room outside as well as in. I was sorry we had not got a cat to swing.

As Odell and I lay that night with our cheeks and our jowls at a reasonable distance apart, we wondered happily whether the three below were suffocating in the bivouac tent or succumbing to asphyxiation in the overripe atmosphere of the Sherpas'.

We flattered ourselves that the height of this camp was about 21,500 ft. but, if it was, it seemed highly improbable that from here we could put a bivouac within striking distance of the summit. It postulated a carry of 2000 ft. at the very least, 2500 would be better, and on the difficult going below we had not done a carry of more than 1500. The climbing was likely to get harder rather than easier and, of course, the increasing altitude would slow us up progressively. Repeated trials with the hypsometer made things appear even more discouraging by giving Camp III a height of only 21,200 ft., and though we knew by now that this instrument was, to put it mildly, subject to error, we had perforce to accept the lower figure in making future plans.

The question of the height of our camps bothered us a lot and, quite early on, the hypsometer had earned for itself an opprobrious name of a like sound which may not be printed. For some reason or other we omitted to bring an aneroid barometer graduated for reading height; possibly our numerous scientists scorned an instrument which even the half-wits of the party could read. I remember in 1934 Shipton and I, having no scientific training, took with us an aneroid barometer out of an aeroplane. I think it cost ten shillings at one of those miscellaneous junk shops in Holborn. Our Sherpas conceived a great affection for it and called it 'Shaitan', probably because we consulted it so frequently. It worked very well until we dropped it. But this hypsometer, or boiling-point thermometer, while not giving us any very precise information, afforded everyone a lot of fun and the scientists food for thought. The results it gave were always interesting, sometimes amusing, and seldom accurate. For example, after several hours of exhausting climbing in what we foolishly thought was an upward direction, it was startling to learn that we had in reality descended a hundred feet from where we started. The learned scientists explained with bland assurance that such vagaries were to be expected, and were accounted for quite simply by the presence of a 'column of cold air', the unlearned oafs on the contrary thought that it must be something to do with 'hot air', and plenty of it.

But there is generally some use to be found for the most unlikely things, and so it was with the hypsometer. It had as part of its equipment a small bottle of methylated spirits, and when we ran out of solid methylated for priming the stoves, this came in very handy. Priming a stove with paraffin is both noisome and inefficient.

On the 19th Graham Brown and Houston went down again to Camp II for loads while Odell and I went to spy out the land higher up. At the point we had reached, our ridge had widened out into a great hog's-back, so wide that it was in reality the south face, though up the middle of this face a ridge was still discernible, and 1000 ft. higher up it again stood out prominently. We struck straight up the middle of the face over what we called the 'snow saddle', avoiding the steep bank above the camp by a short traverse to the left. The snow was in good condition and the angle of slope about 30 degrees for the first 700 ft., after which it began to steepen. Above this was a sort of glacis of snow-covered rock lying at an angle of 45 to 50 degrees. In the steep places outcrops of rock appeared through the snow. This broad glacis appeared to stretch upward for 1000 ft. until it narrowed again to a sharp ridge. On our immediate right was a forbidding gully, a trap for falling stones and ice, and beyond that the tremendous cirque which forms the connecting ridge between East Nanda Devi and Nanda Devi itself. Some two or three hundred yards to the left was a wide shallow depression, scarcely a gully, and on the far side of it the horizon was bounded by a very bold and steep ridge, probably the same which we had looked at from Pisgah.

We attacked the glacis in the centre and worked upwards and to the left, making for what looked like a slight ridge overlooking the shallow gully. As we mounted, the angle grew steeper and the climbing more difficult. At first a good covering of snow overlay the rocks, but presently this became thinner and the outcrops of rocks more numerous. For mountaineering as well as geological reasons we were keenly interested to reach the first of these outcrops, for the line we should take, and our progress, depended greatly upon its quality. We hoped that at this height it might have changed to something more honest than the treacherous rock of the lower ridge, and that the strata might lie in a more favourable direction. Technically it may have differed, but for a climber it was substantially the same crumbling yellow stuff upon which no reliance could be placed, and though the dip of the strata was now more in our favour, little comfort was to be derived from that on rock of such rottenness.

When we had climbed about 500 ft. from the foot of the glacis, it became apparent that the supposed ridge we were making for was no ridge at all. To go straight up was still possible, but with loads on it would be both difficult and dangerous, for nowhere was there enough snow for an anchorage with an axe, or any rock round which a rope could be belayed. We decided to traverse to the left and go for the shallow gully which appeared to offer a safe route on snow for at least 1000 ft. But shortly after putting this resolve into practice, we contrived to get ourselves into such a mess on the ice-glazed face of a rock outcrop that all our attention was concentrated on getting out of it, and instead of continuing the traverse to the left we were compelled to embark upon a long and tricky traverse in the opposite direction. By sticking wherever possible to snow, and avoiding any rock like the plague, we worried a way back down the glacis until we rejoined our earlier track.

A lower route was obviously the best line for the gully, but it was now too late for any more and we hurried back to camp, where we arrived in time to avoid the start of a blizzard. Two days had elapsed since the warning of the sun halo.

Lloyd and Loomis had come up here to sleep after only one night at Camp II in defiance of our self-imposed rule of two at each camp. No one, however, with experience of the Gîte would doubt their wisdom in making that camp an exception to the rule.

The results of our reconnaissance were mainly negative but not without value. It was clear that a route directly up the glacis should only be tried as a last desperate resort, and also that whichever way we went it was going to be a painfully long carry before a place where a tent could be pitched would be found. The conclusions were that further reconnaissance was needed, that the most promising line was the broad gully, and that in any case it would be advantageous to move the present camp to a new site at the foot of the glacis.

CHAPTER FIFTEEN

Alarms and Excursions

THE night was cold and windy and no one turned out until nine o'clock. Lloyd and Loomis started out to have a look at the way to the gully, and the rest of us went down to Camp II for loads. All the tracks down had to be remade after the blizzard and we had long ceased to expect any tracks to last for twenty-four hours. To anticipate, they did not last so long today, and when we returned in the afternoon all were once more obliterated.

We found Pasang still blind and Nima not well, and it was pretty clear that neither would be any use. Nima's single journey to Camp III, the highest reached by any of the porters, was but a dying kick. The almost total failure of the Sherpas is easily explained, for, as I have pointed out, we had to take the leavings of several other expeditions. The only two I expected to go high were Pasang and Kitar. Of the others three were past their best and one was too young and inexperienced. Pasang of course was unlucky to be struck down with snow-blindness, but it cannot be said that it was not his own fault. Kitar was a victim to disease.

The medicine seemed to be having little effect on Pasang's eyes, and Nima's cheery grin was a thing of the past. That they should both go down was now the best course, but this was not possible until Pasang could see something. Apart from their rather miserable mode of existence at the Gîte, I was anxious to have them safely down at the Base Camp before we lost touch with them entirely by going higher up the mountain. We left them there, alone now, in the big tent, having told them that two of us would come down again tomorrow, and we started back, Carter with us, taking the small bivouac tent. Carter had a note which he had found at Camp I telling us that Emmons had moved the Base Camp down to the foot of the scree slope and that he was busy with the plane table, but only Kalu was able to help him by carrying loads.

It was cold and windy when we reached Camp III in a flurry of snow. There was a halo round the sun and two mock[1] suns, and I have seldom seen a more ominous-looking sky. The report of the reconnoitring party was more cheering than the weather. Taking a line below and to the left of ours, they had reached a point from where they could see into and up the gully. They had not

1 Mock suns are coloured images of the sun which appear on either side of the sun and at the same altitude. They probably result from the intersection of two halos and are fairly common in high latitudes.

got into it, but they reported that it could be reached by a route which lay almost entirely on snow, and that the going up the near side of it looked straightforward enough. Like us, they had seen no promise of a camp site higher up, and it was agreed to move this camp to the top of the snow saddle and to press the attack by the gully.

It was a quiet night in spite of all the signs of approaching storm, but the morning of the 21st dawned dull, misty, and snowy. We had a late breakfast and spent the morning in one tent discussing ways and means. Now that the thing was to be put to the test, it was clear that some difficult decisions would have to be made, and the upshot of our talk was that the responsibility for these decisions was put upon the writer. The too frequent use of the word 'I' in this narrative will not have escaped the notice of the reader. The reason for this is that up to now I may have had most to say in our affairs; but that was merely through the accident of my being the only one who knew the country or the porters. We had no official leader, and managed very well without, until at this crisis the need was felt for some kind of figurehead.

After a cup of cocoa additional to our lunch which, by the way, was usually a slab of chocolate and nothing else, Lloyd, Carter, and I went down again to Camp II for more loads, and the others took a first instalment of loads up to what would presently be Camp IV.

Pasang and Nima still appeared to be immovable, but I told them that two of us would come down again tomorrow and see them safely over the worst of the route to Camp I. Until they were down they were merely a source of anxiety, and, after tomorrow, we expected to be out of reach. We climbed up again in one and a quarter hours and it was satisfactory to see that our time on the snow arête became faster, indicating that we were still acclimatising and not deteriorating. The other party had found a good camp site on the snow saddle near the foot of the glacis, and had dug out one tent platform.

The sunset was again threatening, with greasy-looking cigar-shaped clouds hanging low over East Nanda Devi, a greenish watery haze to the west, and, to the south, black banks of cumulus tinged with copper.

We woke to find the tent shaking and banging to the blasts of a fierce blizzard. The wind was coming out of the south-east, some snow was falling, but it was impossible to tell what was new snow and what was drift, for outside was nothing but a whirling cloud of driving snow. The three tents were close together and guyed to each other for mutual support. Six of us occupied the two big ones and Carter was by himself (a doubtful privilege under these conditions) in the small bivouac tent, pitched on the weather side. Odell, Lloyd, and I held the baby in the shape of the Primus stove, but it was conceivable that the inconvenience of fetching ice and breathing paraffin fumes was outweighed by the advantage of getting the food hot without having to fetch it. Going from the comparative warmth of the sleeping bag and the tent out into the blizzard was a breathtaking experience. Breathing was almost impossible facing the wind, and nothing could be handled without mittens, while the act of leaving or entering the tent by the small sleeve entrance required the quick co-operation of all, unless the inside was to be covered with a layer of snow.

There was nothing to be done but lie in our bags, with one eye on a book and the other on the furiously flapping fabric and the quivering tent pole. The pole was of very light aluminium and we were rather nervous about it, but it stood the strain well, as did the tents, for which we forgave them all our past discomforts. At five o'clock, when we cooked our evening pemmican, conditions were unchanged. The wind still maintained a steady roar with occasional gusts of gale force, and we discussed the advisability of sleeping with windproofs on in case the tent went in the night. However, we pinned our faith to the fabric and did not resort to these extreme measures.

Morning brought no change in these unpleasant conditions, and we wondered whether it was blowing as hard at the Gîte and how the Sherpas were faring. Anyhow, with the direction of the wind as it was, the rock wall would stop them being blown off their ledge.

The snow was being blown away as soon as it fell, and round our tent it had not accumulated to any great depth. The other big tent had not fared so well and there was a high bank of snow around it by morning. The pressure of this snow had reduced the space inside by half, so that the unfortunate residents were sleeping almost on top of each other. They had the consolation of knowing that their tent was now securely anchored. Carter too, in the bivouac, was experiencing trouble in keeping the snow-laden walls off his face.

Another weary day of inactivity and torpor passed, but towards evening the wind began to moderate and we were able to get outside, clear the accumulated snow away from the doors, and attend to the guys. Snow was still falling lightly and a leaden pall hid everything but the snow at our feet and three forlorn-looking tents.

Followed another cold and stormy night, but the morning of Monday the 24th dawned fine, calm and sunny. Had it been black as night, we would not have complained, for stillness was all we asked for after the battering of the last two days. The loss of this valuable time was disturbing, and though it may seem strange that two days in bed could be anything but beneficial, there was no doubt that the strain and the inaction had done us harm physically. Nor could we tell what effect the blizzard might have had on the snow of the upper slopes. It was imperative now to push on with all speed, and surely after such a snorter we might expect several days of fine weather.

These blizzards which we experienced, three of them lasting for thirty-six, twelve, and forty-eight hours respectively, all came from between east and south-east. Monsoon weather in the hills generally comes from between south and west, but these storms may have been deflected by the mountain. Such blizzards are more to be expected prior to the break of the monsoon, and during two previous monsoon periods in the Himalaya, one in Garhwal and one in the Everest region, I do not recollect one of any severity. This year the monsoon broke early and ended late, and was exceptionally severe in the United Provinces and Garhwal.

At nine o'clock Lloyd and I started out for Camp II in accordance with our promise to the Sherpas, the fufilment of which the blizzard had compelled us to postpone. We left to the others the cold work of breaking out the tents from their frozen covering and digging out the buried stores, preparatory to carrying one big tent and the bivouac to the new Camp IV site. Five of us were to sleep up there tonight in readiness for carrying up a bivouac for the first summit party next day.

The presence of a lot of powder snow made conditions on the arête bad, and we both felt weak and got progressively weaker as we descended. Arrived at the Gîte, we were surprised to find it empty; evidently the Sherpas had tired of waiting for us and left early. It was comforting to know that the tent had weathered the storm, that Pasang's eyes must be better, and that we ourselves had not to descend any father. Indeed, we were now in such a state of languor that our chief concern was how on earth we were going to get up again. We lolled about on the ledge, assailed by a violent thirst, feeling complete moral and physical wrecks; and it was evident that two days and nights in our sleeping bags had taken more out of us than a hard day's work.

The Sherpas had taken the stove and cooking pot with them, but there was some food here and we opened a tin with an ice-axe—not for the sake of the food but for the tin, in which to catch the elusive drips from the rock wall. We had to sleep at the higher camp that night, so at midday we summoned up all our resolution and, taking with us all the food that was left here, we crawled weakly away from the Gîte.

I should be ashamed to say how long it took us to get back to Camp III, but by the time we arrived we were feeling better and our strength was beginning to return. Graham Brown and Carter, who were spending the night here, came down from Camp IV just as we arrived and informed us that up there it was perishing cold. Carter thought his toes were slightly touched with frostbite.

Adding some more food to our loads, Lloyd and I went off once more and an hour of steady plodding brought us to the new camp. They had evidently started late that morning owing to the frozen tents, and, when we got up, the second tent was just being pitched. There was a bitter wind blowing and Loomis was inside attending to his feet, which also had been slightly affected by cold.

In spite of the cold, it was difficult to turn away from the astonishing picture painted by the fast-sinking sun. Nanda Kot still shone with dazzling purity like an opal, and beyond to the east was range upon range of the snow peaks of Nepal, looking like rollers breaking in white foam on a sunny sea. From the snow slope falling away out of sight at our feet, the eye swept across a great void till arrested by the castellated ivory wall of the Sanctuary, dominated by Trisul, up which the shadows were already stealing. And to the west was the dark chasm of the Rishi gorge, the clear-cut outline of the 'Curtain', and the blue-green swell of the foothills.

The height of Camp IV we estimated to be 21,800 ft., and with five of us here and food for nearly a fortnight we were in a strong position. If we could push a bivouac up another 2000 ft., the summit would be within reach, and, big 'if' though this was, the time had come to make the attempt. Of the five now at this camp, it was not difficult to decide which two should have the privilege of first shot. Odell was going very well and his experience, combined with Houston's energy, would make a strong pair. Assuming that we could place the bivouac high enough tomorrow, they were to have two days in which to make their attempt, and on the third day a second pair would take their place, whether they had been successful or not. The form shown tomorrow would indicate which two would have the second chance, and, provided the weather held, it might be possible to send up a third pair.

The 25th broke fine, but it was ten o'clock before we had made up our loads of 15 lb. each, which included food for two men for six days. During the blizzard, not very much snow had actually settled, and since then sufficient time had elapsed for this new snow to consolidate. We found it in good condition. After gaining some height by kicking steps, we approached the gully by a long traverse where steps had to be cut and great care exercised. The snow covering grew thinner and we came to an uncomfortable halt on the steep lip of a minor hollow, cutting us off from the main gully. This was the farthest point reached by Lloyd and Loomis, and they had seen that this difficult little gully could be avoided by working round the head of it, 200 ft. higher.

We sat here for a little, but it was no place for a long sojourn without prehensile trousers. There was not enough snow to afford a step, much less a seat, and the angle of the rock was such that mere friction was of no avail— boots, hands, and ice-axe were all needed to prevent the beginning of a long slither which would only end on the glacier 6000 ft. below. Turning up the slope, the next few feet were of the same precarious nature that Odell and I had experienced on the glacis, but this was as yet the only part of the route where we had to forsake the security of the snow for the uncertainty of the rock. Once over this, we settled down to a long steady grind, kicking and cutting our way up very steep snow, and having rounded the head of this minor hollow, we took a line up the true left bank of the broad gully.

We were climbing on two ropes, so by changing the leading rope and also the leading end of each rope, the work was divided among four. It was a beautiful day, but in our perverse way we were not content, and were captious enough to wish the sun obscured so that we could climb in more comfort. Nanda Kot, 22,500 ft., sank below us and we began to cast jealous eyes on Trisul, which still looked down upon us majestically from its height of 23,400 ft. Meantime we began to search the snow above us for the slightest break in the relentless angle of the slope which might afford a site for a tent. We were tempted momentarily by the broken outline of the skyline ridge away across the gully, but we decided it was too far off and the approach to it too steep.

As we gained height, the curve of the face to our right grew rounder and narrower and the central ridge was beginning to stand out again like the bridge of a Roman nose. We edged over towards it, thinking that the rocks might provide easier going than the snow, and aiming for the foot of a rock tower where there might be a platform. Knowing by now the sort of rock we might expect, it was curious that we should so think, but such was the distorting effect on our minds of five hours of laborious step-kicking. The change of course was for the worse and we had some awkward moments before we dragged ourselves to the foot of the tower, to find it sloping away as steeply as the rest of the mountain.

The time was now three o'clock and our height something over 23,000 ft., practically level with Trisul. Loomis had an attack of cramp, but when he had recovered we turned our attention to the rock tower at our backs, on top of which we hoped to find better things. Lloyd did a grand lead up a steep rock chimney with his load on and was able to give the rest of us some much needed moral and, in my case, physical encouragement with the rope. This took some time and it was four o'clock before we were all on top of the tower, where there was barely room for five of us to stand, much less pitch a tent. Looking up the ridge, it was impossible to say where such a place would be found, but it was sufficiently broken to offer considerable hope. Meantime three of us had to get back to Camp IV and at this time of the afternoon of a bright sunny day the snow would be at its worst. With the assent of all, it was decided to dump our loads here leaving Houston and Odell to shift for themselves. It seemed a selfish decision at the time and it seems so now; no doubt we could have cut it a bit finer and yet got down before dark, but it was likely that they would not have to go far before finding a bivouac, and, in any case, with sleeping bags and warm clothing they could not come to much harm.

We learned afterwards that they had an uncommonly busy evening. They had to climb another 150 ft. before even the most imaginative could discern the makings of a platform, and then they had to make two journeys up and down with the loads. It was dark before they were finally settled.

Oblivious of this activity and the curses which were being bestowed, rather unjustly, on us for our premature desertion, we climbed hastily but cautiously down, reaching the camp at sundown. There was no sign of Graham Brown and Carter, so we assumed they were having a day off at Camp III.

Discussing the results of this day's work, we decided the bivouac was about 23,500 ft., probably too low for an attempt on the summit, but as high as we could push it in the day. We thought they would probably move it higher tomorrow and make their bid on the following day. The closer view of the upper part of the mountain which we had obtained had not made it look any easier, and it was a puzzle to make out where exactly the peak lay. I began to fear we had not allowed them enough time, but now it was too late to alter plans.

Next day was fine, but mist shrouded the upper mountain from our anxious gaze. We felt slack, and took the morning off before going down to Camp III to give Graham Brown and Carter a hand with their loads. As their tent was the one which had been half-buried by the blizzard, it took them a long time to dig it out, so we returned before them and prepared a platform.

The 27th was to be for us at Camp IV another day of idleness. That at least was the plan, but the event was different, and for some of us it was a day of the greatest mental and physical stress that we had yet encountered.

I had been worrying all night over the waste of this day, trying to devise some scheme whereby the second pair could go up at once to the bivouac. The trouble was that a second tent was essential, and having seen something of the extraordinary difficulty of finding a site even for the small tent, to go up there on the slim chance of finding a site for the big one as well was incurring the risk of exhausting the party to no purpose. While we were having breakfast, debating this knotty point and wondering how far the summit party had got, Loomis disclosed the fact that all was not well with his feet, the toes being slightly frost-bitten, and that henceforward we should have to count him out. The loss of carrying power knocked the scheme for a second tent on the head and a few moments later we had something else to think about.

We had just decided they must be well on the way to the top when we were startled to hear Odell's familiar yodel, rather like the braying of an ass. It sounded so close that I thought they must be on the way down, having got the peak the previous day, but it suddenly dawned on us that he was trying to send an S.O.S. Carter, who had the loudest voice, went outside to try and open communications, and a few minutes later came back to the tent to announce that 'Charlie is killed'—Charlie being Houston. It was impossible to see anyone on the mountain, but he was certain he had heard correctly. As soon as we had pulled ourselves together, I stuffed some clothes and a bandage into a rucksack and Lloyd and I started off as fast as we could manage, to be followed later by Graham Brown and Carter with a hypodermic syringe.

It was a climb not easily forgotten—trying to go fast and realising that at this height it was impossible to hurry, wondering what we should find, and above all what we could do. The natural assumption was that there had been a fall, and that since they were sure to be roped, Odell was also hurt, and the chance of getting a helpless man down the mountain was too remote to bear thinking about. As if to confirm this assumption, we could get no answer to repeated calls on the way up.

Remembering our struggles yesterday on the ridge and in the chimney, we took a different line and tackled a band of steep rock directly above us, in between the gully and the ridge. It proved to be much worse than it looked and, when we had hauled ourselves panting on to the snow above, we vowed that the next time we would stick to the gully, which here narrowed and passed through a sort of cleft in the rock band.

The time was now about two o'clock, and traversing up and to the right over snow in the direction of the ridge, the little tent came in sight not thirty yards away. Instinctively we tried almost to break into a run, but it was no use, and we advanced step by step, at a maddening pace, not knowing what we should find in the tent, if indeed anything at all. The sight of an ice-axe was a tremendous relief; evidently Odell had managed to crawl back. But when another was seen, conjecture was at a loss. Then voices were heard talking quietly and next moment we were greeted with, 'Hullo, you blokes, have some tea.' 'Charlie is ill' was the message Odell had tried to convey!

Lloyd and I experienced a curious gamut of emotions; firstly and naturally, of profound relief, then, and I think not unnaturally, disgust at having suffered such unnecessary mental torture, and, of course, deep concern for Houston. While we swallowed tea, tea that reeked of pemmican but which I still remember with thankfulness, we heard what they had done and discussed what we were to do.

They had devoted yesterday to a reconnaissance. Following the ridge up they found, at a height of about 500 ft. above the bivouac, a flat snow platform capable of holding two tents comfortably. Beyond that the climbing became interesting and difficult, but they had reached the foot of a long and easy snow slope leading up to the final rock wall. Here they turned back, having decided to move the bivouac next day to the higher site. Both were going strongly, but early that night Houston became violently ill, and in the cramped quarters of the tent, perched insecurely on an inadequate platform above a steep slope, both had spent a sleepless and miserable night. Houston attributed his trouble to the bully beef which both had eaten; Odell was unaffected, but it is possible that a small portion was tainted and certainly the symptoms pointed to poisoning of some kind.

Houston was still very ill and very weak, but it was he who suggested what should be done, and showed us how evil might be turned to good. It was only possible for two people to stay up here, and his plan was that he should go down that afternoon and that I should stay up with Odell, and thus no time would have been lost. We demurred to this on the ground that he was not fit to move, but he was so insistent on the importance of not losing a day and so confident of being able to get down that we at last consented.

We all four roped up, with Houston in the middle, and started slowly down, taking frequent rests. We struck half-right across the snow and joined the gully above the rock band according to our earlier resolution, and there the two men anchored the party while Lloyd cut steps down the narrow cleft, which was very icy. Houston was steady enough in spite of his helpless state of weakness, and having safely negotiated this awkward bit, we kicked slowly down to the left and found our up-going tracks. Presently Graham Brown and Carter hove in sight, and I imagine their amazement at seeing four people coming down was as great as ours had been at the sight of the two ice-axes. When we met, Lloyd and Houston tied on to their rope and continued the descent, while Odell and I climbed slowly back to the bivouac.

This illness of Houston's was a miserable turn of fortune for him, robbing him as it did of the summit. Bad as he was, his generous determination to go down was of a piece with the rest of his actions.

CHAPTER SIXTEEN

The Top

SCENICALLY the position of the bivouac was very fine but residentially it was damnable. It was backed on two sides by rock, but on the others the snow slope fell away steeply, and the platform which had been scraped out in the snow was so narrow that the outer edge of the tent overhung for almost a foot, thus reducing considerably both the living space and any feeling one yet had of security. Necessity makes a man bold, and I concluded that necessity had pressed very hard that night when they lit on this spot for their bivouac. Odell, who had had no sleep the previous night, could have slept on a church spire, and, as I had Houston's sleeping bag and the extra clothing I had fortunately brought up, we both had a fair night. Odell, who was the oldest inhabitant and in the position of host, generously conceded to me the outer berth, overhanging space.

The weather on the 28th still held and without regret we packed up our belongings and made the first trip to the upper bivouac. The snow slope was steeper than any we had yet met but, at the early hour we started, the snow was good and in an hour we reached the spacious snow shelf which they had marked down. It was about 20 ft. × 20 ft., so that there was room to move about, but on either side of the ridge on which it stood the slope was precipitous. After a brief rest the increasing heat of the sun warned us to be on the move again and we hurried down for the remaining loads. The snow was softening rapidly under a hot sun nor was this deterioration confined only to the snow. We already knew, and it was to be impressed on us again, that at these altitudes a hot sun is a handicap not to be lightly assessed.

Guessing the height of this camp, aided by the absence of the hypsometer, we put it at about 24,000 ft. Trisul was well below us and even the top of East Nanda Devi (24,379 ft.) began to look less remote. The condition of the wide belt of snow which had to be crossed, the difficulties of the final wall, and the weather were so many large question marks, but we turned in that night full of hope, and determined to give ourselves every chance by an early start.

We were up at five o'clock to begin the grim business of cooking and the more revolting tasks of eating breakfast and getting dressed. That we were up is an exaggeration, we were merely awake, for all these fatigues are carried out from inside one's sleeping bag until it is no longer possible to defer the putting on of boots. One advantage a narrow tent has, that at lower altitudes is overlooked, is that the two sleeping bags are in such close proximity that boots which are rammed into the non-existent space between them generally survive the night without being frozen stiff. It worked admirably on this occasion so that we were spared the pangs of wrestling with frozen boots with cold fingers. Frozen boots are a serious matter and may cause much delay, and in order to mitigate this trouble we had, since the start, carefully refrained from oiling our boots. This notion might work well enough on Everest in pre-monsoon conditions where the snow is dry, but we fell between two stools, rejoicing in wet feet down below and frozen boots higher up.

By six o'clock we were ready, and shortly after we crawled outside, roped up, and started. It was bitterly cold, for the sun had not yet risen over the shoulder of East Nanda Devi and there was a thin wind from the west. What mugs we were to be fooling about on this infernal ridge at that hour of the morning! And what was the use of this ridiculous coil of rope, as stiff as a wire hawser, tying me for better or for worse to that dirty-looking ruffian in front! Such, in truth, were the reflections of at least one of us as we topped a snow boss behind the tent, and the tenuous nature of the ridge in front became glaringly obvious in the chill light of dawn. It was comforting to reflect that my companion in misery had already passed this way, and presently as the demands of the climbing became more insistent, grievances seemed less real, and that life was still worth living was a proposition that might conceivably be entertained.

This difficult ridge was about three hundred yards long, and though the general angle appeared slight it rose in a series of abrupt rock and snow steps. On the left was an almost vertical descent to a big ravine, bounded on the far side by the terrific grey cliffs that supported the broad snow shelf for which we were making. The right side also fell away steeply, being part of the great rock cirque running round to East Nanda Devi. The narrow ridge we were on formed a sort of causeway between the lower south face and the upper snow shelf.

One very important factor which, more than anything, tended to promote a happier frame of mind was that the soft crumbly rock had at last yielded to a hard rough schistose-quartzite which was a joy to handle; a change which could not fail to please us as mountaineers and, no doubt, to interest my companion as a geologist. That vile rock, schist is, I believe, the technical term, had endangered our heads and failed to support our feet from the foot of the scree to the last bivouac. It was a wonder our burning anathemas had not caused it to undergo a geological change under our very eyes— metamorphosed it, say, into plutonic rocks. But, as had been said by others, there is good in everything, and, on reflection, this very sameness was not without some saving grace because it meant that we were spared an accumulation of rock samples at every camp. A bag of assorted stones had already been left at the Glacier Camp, and I tremble to think what burdens we might have had to carry down the mountain had the rock been as variegated as our geologist, and indeed any right-minded geologist, would naturally desire.

Thanks to the earlier reconnaissance by him and Houston, Odell led over this ridge at a good pace and in an hour and a half we had reached the snow mound which marked the farthest point they had reached. It was a ridge on which we moved one at a time.

In front was a snow slope set at an angle of about 30 degrees and running right up to the foot of the rock wall, perhaps 600 or 700 ft. above us. To the west this wide snow terrace extended for nearly a quarter of a mile until it ended beneath that same skyline ridge, which below had formed the western boundary of the broad gully. On our right the shelf quickly steepened and merged into the steep rock face of the ridge between East Nanda Devi and our mountain. We were too close under the summit to see where it lay, but there was little doubt about the line we should take, because from a rapid survey there seemed to be only one place where a lodgement could be effected on the final wall. This was well to the west of our present position, where a snow rib crossed the terrace at right angles and, abutting against the wall, formed as it were a ramp.

We began the long snow trudge at eight o'clock and even at that early hour and after a cold night the snow was not good and soon became execrable. The sun was now well up. After it had been at work for a bit we were going in over our knees at every step, and in places where the slope was steeper it was not easy to make any upward progress at all. One foot would be lifted and driven hard into the snow and then, on attempting to rise on it, one simply sank down through the snow to the previous level. It was like trying to climb up cotton wool, and a good deal more exhausting, I imagine, than the treadmill. But, like the man on a walking tour in Ireland, who throughout a long day received the same reply of '20 miles' to his repeated inquiries as to the distance he was from his destination, we could at any rate say, 'Thank God, we were holding our own.'

The exertion was great and every step made good cost six to eight deep breaths. Our hopes of the summit grew faint, but there was no way but to plug on and see how far we could get. This we did, thinking only of the next step, taking our time, and resting frequently. It was at least some comfort that the track we were ploughing might assist a second party. On top of the hard work and the effect of altitude was the languor induced by a sun which beat down relentlessly on the dazzling snow, searing our lips and sapping the energy of mind and body. As an example of how far this mind-sapping process had gone, I need only mention that it was seriously suggested that we should seek the shade of a convenient rock which we were then near, lie up there until evening, and finish the climb in the dark!

It is noteworthy that whilst we were enjoying, or more correctly enduring, this remarkable spell of sunshine, the foothills south and west of the Basin experienced disastrous floods. As related in the first chapter, it was on this day that the Pindar river overflowed sweeping away some houses in the village of Tharali, while on the same day nineteen inches of rain fell at the hill station of Mussoorie west of Ranikhet.

We derived some encouragement from seeing East Nanda Devi sink below us and at one o'clock, rather to our surprise, we found ourselves on top of the snow rib moving at a snail's pace towards the foot of the rocks. There we had a long rest and tried to force some chocolate down our parched throats by eating snow at the same time. Though neither of us said so, I think both felt that now it would take a lot to stop us. There was a difficult piece of rock to climb; Odell led this and appeared to find it stimulating, but it provoked me to exclaim loudly upon its 'thinness'. Once over that, we were landed fairly on the final slope with the summit ridge a bare 300 ft. above us.

Presently we were confronted with the choice of a short but very steep snow gully and a longer but less drastic route to the left. We took the first and found the snow reasonably hard owing to the very steep angle at which it lay. After a severe struggle I drew myself out of it on to a long and gently sloping corridor, just below and parallel to the summit ridge. I sat down and drove the axe in deep to hold Odell as he finished the gully. He moved up to join me and I had just suggested the corridor as a promising line to take when there was a sudden hiss and, quicker than a thought, a slab of snow, about forty yards long, slid off the corridor and disappeared down the gully, peeling off a foot of snow as it went. At the lower limit of the avalanche, which was where we were sitting, it actually broke away for a depth of a foot all round my axe to which I was holding. At its upper limit, forty yards up the corridor, it broke away to a depth of three or four feet.

The corridor route had somehow lost its attractiveness, so we finished the climb by the ridge without further adventure.

The summit is not the exiguous and precarious spot that usually graces the top of so many Himalayan peaks, but a solid snow ridge nearly two hundred yards long and twenty yards broad. It is seldom that conditions on top of a high peak allow the climber the time or the opportunity to savour the immediate fruits of victory. Too often, when having first carefully probed the snow to make sure he is not standing on a cornice, the climber straightens up preparatory to savouring the situation to the full, he is met by a perishing wind and the interesting view of a cloud at close quarters, and with a muttered imprecation turns in his tracks and begins the descent. Far otherwise was it now. There were no cornices to worry about and room to unrope and walk about. The air was still, the sun shone, and the view was good if not so extensive as we had hoped.

Odell had brought a thermometer, and no doubt sighed for the hypsometer. From it we found that the air temperature was 20 degrees F., but in the absence of wind we could bask gratefully in the friendly rays of our late enemy the sun. It was difficult to realise that we were actually standing on top of the same peak which we had viewed two months ago from Ranikhet, and which had then appeared incredibly remote and inaccessible, and it gave us a curious feeling of exaltation to know that we were above every peak within hundreds of miles on either hand. Dhaulagiri, 1000 ft. higher, and two hundred miles away in Nepal, was our nearest rival. I believe we so far forgot ourselves as to shake hands on it.

After the first joy in victory came a feeling of sadness that the mountain had succumbed, that the proud head of the goddess was bowed.

At this late hour of the day there was too much cloud about for any distant views. The Nepal peaks were hidden and all the peaks on the rim, excepting only Trisul, whose majesty even our loftier view-point could not diminish. Far to the north through a vista of white cloud the sun was colouring to a warm brown the bare and bleak Tibetan plateau.

After three-quarters of an hour on that superb summit, a brief forty-five minutes into which was crowded the worth of many hours of glorious life, we dragged ourselves reluctantly away, taking with us a memory that can never fade and leaving behind 'thoughts beyond the reaches of our souls'.

If our thoughts were still treading on air, the short steep gully, swept by the avalanche bare of steps, soon brought us to earth. We kicked slowly down it, facing inwards and plunging an arm deep into the snow for support. Followed another exhausting drag across the snow, hindered rather than helped by the deep holes we had made coming up, and then a cold hour was spent moving cautiously, one at a time, down the ice and the benumbing rocks of the long ridge above the bivouac. We paused to watch a bird, a snow pigeon, cross our ridge and fly swiftly across the grey cliffs of the ravine beneath the snow terrace, like the spirit of Nanda Devi herself, forsaking the fastness which was no longer her own.

At six o'clock we reached the tent and brewed the first of many jorums of tea. After such a day nothing could have tasted better and our appreciation was enhanced by our long enforced abstinence. There was but a pinch left and we squandered it all recklessly, saving the leaves for the morning. Food was not even mentioned.

We paid for this debauch with a sleepless night, to which no doubt exhaustion and a still-excited imagination contributed. Each little incident of the climb was gone over again and again, and I remember, in the small hours when the spark of life burns lowest, the feeling which predominated over all was one of remorse at the fall of a giant. It is the same sort of contrition that one feels at the shooting of an elephant, for however thrilling and arduous the chase, however great has been the call upon skill, perseverance, and endurance, and however gratifying the weight of the ivory, when the great bulk crashes to the ground achievement seems to have been bought at the too high cost of sacrilege.

It was very cold next morning when we packed up and started down. Near the bottom of the gully we were met by Lloyd and Loomis, who were coming up to help us down and who were overjoyed when they heard that success had crowned the efforts of the whole party. Houston and Graham Brown had already gone down and we decided to stop the night at Camp IV. There were still three or four days' food left in hand but Loomis and Carter were both troubled with their feet, which must have been touched with frost the day Camp IV was occupied. Lloyd was going stronger than ever and it was much to be regretted that we could not make up a second party.

The weather, which during this crucial period had been so kind, now broke up and on the morning of the 31st it was blowing half a gale out of a clear sky. Lloyd, Loomis, and I started some time before the other two, all carrying heavy loads because we left nothing but the two big tents, some snow-shoes, and two pairs of crampons or ice-claws. The snow-shoes had been lugged up to assist us on soft snow and the crampons for use on hard snow, but the slopes were, of course, all too steep for snow-shoes, and the only time we might have used the crampons was now when they had been abandoned.

It was bitterly cold, and the snow on the arête was hard and dangerous—the mountain had not finished with us yet. We started to descend in the usual way, plunging the heel in at each step with a stiff leg. When one or two 'voluntaries' had been cut, we should have taken warning that the snow was not right for such tactics, but we were all pretty tired and in a hurry to get down, and it is in such circumstances that care is relaxed and the party comes to grief. Fortunately before this happened we had another warning which could not well be ignored. The leader's heels went from under him and he slid down the slope pulling the second man after him until checked by the rope belayed round the end man's axe, which fortunately held firm. We all felt rather ashamed of ourselves after this exhibition and abandoned that method in favour of the slower but safer one of cutting steps and moving one at a time, which should have been adopted at the start.

There was another slip, quickly checked, when one of the snow steps above the Gîte gave way, and we reached this camp in a chastened frame of mind and hoping that the mountain had now exhausted its spite. After a brief rest we pushed on, unroped gladly when we were off the snow, and picked our way with great caution down the unstable rocks to Camp I. On the way we noticed with concern that Odell and Carter were still high up on the arête and moving very slowly.

We found here Graham Brown and Pasang. The former's leg was troubling him, so he had spent the night here where there were still two tents, and Pasang had come up from below to take his load. We heard that Graham Brown and Houston too had narrowly escaped disaster on the previous day by the breaking of a step above the Gîte. Pasang had completely recovered his sight, but he was not yet his former bright self, for I think he felt keenly the disability which prevented him from helping his Sahibs at grips with the mountain.

It was now midday and after a drink of cocoa, which served only to bring home to us the loss we had suffered, we continued the descent. The cocoa so wrought upon Lloyd that, with a desperation born of thirst, he turned aside to prosecute a last and unsuccessful search for the tea. On the Coxcomb ridge I met Phuta going up to help Pasang and was shocked to hear that Kitar had died in the night. We got down to the new Base Camp at the foot of the scree at two o'clock and but for the melancholy news of Kitar's death there was nothing to mar our contentment. Twenty-one days had elapsed since we left.

CHAPTER SEVENTEEN

A New Pass

HOUSTON had almost recovered, Da Namgyal was there, still coughing, but obviously bursting to lay out Odell's pyjamas. He had brought with him six men from Lata, the mail, and one or two luxuries which had been scrapped at the Bridge Camp. Best of all, one of our old Mana men had come with them bringing a letter of greeting and a present from the Rawal of Badrinath—an enormous basket of apples, nuts, potatoes, and other vegetables, than which nothing, not excepting a tin of tea, could have been more acceptable. After living as we had been, any fresh food is the greatest luxury imaginable; many of our idle hours had been passed in devising the sort of meal for which each of us most longed, and in every imaginary menu fruit bulked large. We were deeply touched by this kindly and thoughtful act on the part of one who had already helped us in every way he could. Fortunately some of the party were able to visit Badrinath on the way back and thank our benefactor personally.

Not the least of our delights was that of being, if not on grass at any rate on the sort of soil which looked as if, with very little encouragement, it might grow grass, and that did in fact support some moss and scant herbage. To our starved senses it looked like an oasis and smelt divinely. Fresh water to drink in unstinted measure, a wood fire to look at, bare feet on warm earth, the cry of a marmot, such were the simple things which now gave us unbounded pleasure. Some averred that the air felt and tasted differently, and on the mountain they went so far as to claim that this difference could be felt on going down from Camp III to Camp II; but speaking personally, provided of course one sits still, I would not undertake to say whether the air I was breathing was that of 10,000 ft. or 20,000 ft.

While we were on the mountain Emmons had not been idle, having almost completed a plane-table survey of the South-East glacier and its tributaries. He had further made a valiant and almost successful attempt to reach the top of 'Longstaff's Col', accompanied only by the inexperienced Kalu. Kalu apparently had worked very well and was once more in the mood for chest-beating. In the midst of these activities he, Emmons, had had two sick men to look after, Kitar and Nuri. Kitar got steadily worse in spite of all that could be done for him in the way of medicines and special food, and on the night of the 30th he died. He was buried before we got down, and on his grave the Sherpas built a large cairn and fenced it about with a ring of stones. He sleeps amongst the mountains to which he had given of his best, to which his long record of service is eloquent testimony. He had probably served on more major expeditions than any other Sherpa living. Nuri was still with us, but more wasted and woebegone than ever, and so weak as to cause us some anxiety. The other porters had recovered, Pasang his sight and Nima his cheery grin.

By the evening it was snowing hard, but that did not prevent Emmons and Houston from preparing for us, and serving, a supper that put to shame any previous efforts. Odell and Carter had not yet arrived but, knowing our geologist by now, we were not unduly worried and thought they might be spending the night at Camp I. However, as darkness fell they came down the scree, soaked to the skin and dog-tired. It was too late now for the mountain to strike back.

September 1st was a day of luxurious idleness devoted to settling plans for our return. I was bent on attempting to force a new route out of the Basin by 'Longstaff's Col' and Houston was keen to come too, despite the fact that it was imperative for him to be in Ranikhet by the 13th, and no one could tell how long it would take us. Of the others, all were anxious to see Badrinath of which they had heard so much, and Emmons wanted another day or two in the Basin to complete his survey.

On the 2nd the various caravans got under way; first to leave was Nuri, carrying no load, for in his feeble state he wanted a long start. He was followed by Graham Brown, Lloyd, and Odell, with a most ambitious programme which entailed double-marching all the way—we called them the 'express'. Then Loomis and Carter pushed off with most of the porters carrying the surplus gear—they were the 'slow freight'. Emmons and Kalu then departed, bound for the other side of the glacier, after a moving display of chest-thumping by Kalu. If he got safely across the glacier he would have something to thump about, for his load was of staggering dimensions. Finally

Houston, Pasang, and I left about midday in a snow storm, travelling as light as possible and bound for a bivouac at the foot of the snow slope below the Pass.

The 'express' and the 'slow freight' seem to have changed rôles soon after starting, the 'express' having trouble with its feet. Ranikhet was reached in the reverse order to that of leaving the Basin, and some time behind schedule.

We three followed up the true right bank of the glacier and crossed it when it began to curve round at the foot of the Coxcomb ridge. We were armed with a plan, drawn by Emmons, showing us where he had made his bivouac, but we misled ourselves by assuming his progress was as slow as our own and, failing to find it, camped on snow, all in one tent, some way below it. The height was about 17,500 ft., the col is 19,200 ft., so we made preparations for a very early start. We took a gloomy view of our chances of getting over on account of the snow which had fallen that day and was still falling that night.

We were up at 3.30 a.m. and left at five on a fine morning, creeping along at the foot of a rock wall. The snow was soft, filling us with alarm and despondency, but once we were clear of the rocks it hardened up and soon we had to scrape out steps with our ice-axes, The slope steepened rapidly and we made for an outcrop of rock over to our right, where we thought we would be more comfortable and which would, when scaled, led us to the foot of a snow rib set at a slightly easier angle than the rest of the face. We had studied the approach to this col long and earnestly from our camps on the mountain in all conditions of light and shadow; always hoping for, but never receiving, some slight hint that it was not really as steep as it looked. Coming up last night we had caught a distorted glimpse of it through snow and swirling mists, when it looked ridiculously easy, but now, as every step brought us closer under it, our first impressions were not only confirmed but deepened.

After tentative essays to effect a lodgement on the rock bulge in two different places, we decided there was too much verglas on the rock for safety, and retreated stealthily to the snow. We climbed up till level with the top of the rocks and then began traversing across above the outcrop in order to gain the snow rib. The snow of the traverse was horribly deep and loose and, with no supporting snow below but only rock, conditions seemed ideal for an avalanche. It was with considerable misgiving that we crept slowly and cautiously across it, but the rib was temptingly close and the alternative route straight up the snow to our left was minatory in its steepness. The sun, which was now well over the wall above us, added to our anxiety, but the snow held, and once astride, literally astride, the rib we breathed more freely. For the first few feet of this the snow was rather worse than that which we had experienced near the top of Nanda Devi, and for every step up we sank down two. After tremendous exertions we struggled up a few feet and then began to find solid bottom. A prolonged bout of step-kicking landed us on top of the col at eleven o'clock.

For most of the way up the weather was clear and there was a magnificent view of our ridge on Nanda Devi seen in profile. I had brought a camera solely for the purpose of taking this invaluable picture, but it was stowed away in the bottom of my rucksack which was in turn part of a load, strapped to a carrying frame. Once we were fairly committed to the difficult part of the climb there was little inclination or opportunity for getting it out; but that is a feeble excuse and with a little trouble the thing could have been done—but I kept on putting off the evil moment. Now, of course, when we sat down exhausted on the top of the pass the whole mountain had disappeared in the mist. Had we been higher I might cite this as a fair sample of high-altitude mentality, but since we were only 19,000 ft. the less said about it the better. One lesson at least it teaches, which is not to carry your camera in a rucksack, and the corollary to that is a small, light camera.

Our field of view was restricted to within a hundred yards of where we sat, but we had looked at the pass and its neighbourhood so long and frequently that we knew, or thought we knew, the topography of it. We were on the eastern rim of the Basin at the foot of the long shoulder which runs up to East Nanda Devi. To the south the rim climbs for a thousand feet to form the fluted ice wall which towers above the main arm of the South-East glacier. From somewhere on this ice wall and outside the Basin, a ridge extends eastwards linking Nanda Kot with the Nanda Devi group. On this ridge, between Sanctuary wall and Nanda Kot, there is a pass, called Traill's Pass after the first Commissioner of Kumaon, whose administration lasted from 1815 to 1835. He was also the first to cross this pass in 1830, and it has been suggested that his object was not mountain exploration but to find a short cut between the Pindar valley and Milam which would be useful for commercial purposes. The pass is 17,700 ft. high, and whatever his object it was a very remarkable feat for one who was not a mountaineer and who lived almost before the dawn of mountaineering. Since then it has been crossed in 1855 by Adolph Schlagintweit as related in Chapter One, in 1861 by Colonel Edmund Smyth, and again in 1926 by a party which included Mr Hugh Ruttledge. The Pass leads to the Pindari glacier and from there to Ranikhet is a short and easy route, so it was attractive to us for that reason as well as for the few time which it had been crossed.

On the east side of the col, or what might now be truly be called the Pass, a slope of rock and snow, decidedly less steep than the Basin side, led down to the Milam valley. This was a known and suitable route for us to take, but we had not yet given up hope of finding and crossing Traill's Pass, although the heavy mist was a severe handicap. Our very distant surveys from high on Nanda Devi had led us to think that the ridge on which the Pass lay was not far from where we now sat, and we thought that by traversing to our right we might arrive somewhere in the vicinity of the Pass without losing much height—a consideration which in our then feeble state of mind and body seemed of paramount importance. We sat there for an hour waiting for a clearing in which we might see something of what lay between us and the Pass. No clearing came, so we began traversing blindly.

After we had been going for two hours on steep, soft, and rather unsafe snow, the mist was as thick as ever and we appeared to be getting nowhere except, possibly, into trouble. We gave up traversing and began casting about for a tent site, and in the process we were driven lower and lower down the slope. When there was still no sign of a suitable platform and it was getting late, we decided to go straight down to the glacier, although we knew that this probably meant the abandonment of Traill's Pass. We were all very tired and made a sorry job of the descent, getting into trouble in a long ice runnel which was like a water-course full of ice. I was in front of the others and, after one or two involuntary glissades, had half made up my mind to forsake the firm but dangerous going in the icy channel for the safe but laborious snow-plodding on the bank above. My mind was made up for me by a boulder which came spinning down and which I only just managed to dodge. With more haste than dignity I scrambled up the bank. We finally camped at about half-past five on what was almost a grass sward a few hundred feet above the Lwanl glacier. For once Pasang seemed to have had enough.

Talking things over that night we reluctantly gave up an attempt on the Pass and decided to go home via the Milam valley. Having lost so much height we were not in the right trim for facing a climb up again and, though the valley route might be longer, in the weather and snow conditions prevailing it was conceivable that once more the longest way round might be the shortest way home.

Next morning, lightened by the scrapping of the Primus stove and some paraffin, we descended to the glacier, crossed it to the north side and followed it down to below the snout. There was the usual stream, here only in its infancy, issuing from the glacier, but, mindful of the ways of these streams, I decided that we would do well to get on the Ranikhet side of it while we could. I therefore forded it without much difficulty, but Pasang, seeing a likely-looking line of country ahead and sniffing the fleshpots from afar, went off at score down the north bank where Houston, for his sins, followed him. Walking along our respective banks of the river we came soon to the grazing alp of Narspati which lies under the northern slopes of Nanda Kot. Looking back, the whole head of the valley was filled with the magnificent bulk of East Nanda Devi, seen with advantage from a fresh angle and no longer overshadowed by its namesake, which was now hidden away behind it. West of the glistening pile of Nanda Kot, with its familiar table-top, was the long low ridge which we should then have been crossing by Traill's Pass. It was much farther away from our pass than we had imagined nor did the Pass look by any means a walk-over.

There were here a few stone huts on both sides of the river, but on the north side there was also a well-marked path, along which I watched Pasang disappearing with envy. On my side the river lapped the foot of the moraine of a big glacier coming down from Nanda Kot, and soon I was blaspheming and boulder-hopping along this in a very evil frame of mind. Presently the going became so bad that I decided to climb 200 ft. up to the top of the moraine, where I thought I would find better going or even the path, which I was convinced must exist from the evidence of the stone huts. But this exhausting climb was to no purpose, I had merely exchanged boulder-hopping on a slope for boulder-hopping on the razor-backed moraine top, and my already sour temper grew worse as I thought how the other two must be enjoying my antics from the security of their path.

Having won clear of the boulders of the glacier I did find a sort of path and, hurrying along to catch up, I at length saw the others waiting for me on the opposite bank. It was impossible to carry on any conversation above the roar of the river, which was now a formidable torrent, but they were complacent enough to suggest by signs that I should try to cross it, at which I shook my head with terrific violence and signalled a counter suggestion that it was time they joined me. Then I remembered that Houston was carrying all our chocolate and by pointing to my mouth I got him to throw some over. We lunched amicably but distantly and then pursued our divided but parallel courses.

I could see what was happening on their steeply sloping bank much better than they could and, while my path steadily improved, I could see that there was trouble ahead for them in a series of big landslides, which could only be circumvented by using another path much higher up. They failed to spot this path and presently got spread-eagled on the almost vertical earth cliff left by the landslide. I gesticulated wildly to indicate that they must go up, but they seemed to think I was merely 'registering' enjoyment of their discomfiture, as perhaps I was, and paid no attention.

Finding themselves at last completely baffled they climbed wearily up and found the track, and we all started legging it for Martoli, the first village and the place where our respective paths would, in the fullness of time, unite. More trouble of the same sort awaited them round the next bend and, seeing this, I pushed on, leaving them to it, bent on vindicating my judgment by arriving before them, but never imagining it would be so thoroughly vindicated as it was.

While yet some three miles from Martoli and with no sign of my rivals on the other bank, I suddenly came upon a tributary river, and was dismayed to find the path turning off at right angles to follow up this side valley for one and a half miles, where it crossed the river by a bridge and then came back down the other side for a like distance, before once more following the main valley down to Martoli. This extra three miles was an unexpected blow for I imagined that they would soon be gloating over my receding back as I toiled up this side valley, getting farther from Martoli every minute. However, there was no help, though all was not yet lost and, putting on all steam, an hour and a half later I was back in the main valley, very much hotter in mind and body and scanning the opposite slopes eagerly for signs of my pursuers. There was nothing to be seen and it seemed hardly possible that they could be already out of sight ahead. I noticed that as it approached Martoli the opposing slope grew steeper and steeper, and below the village, which was perched high up on my side, the river flowed through a deep gorge—nor was there a bridge nor any sign of a path leading to a bridge.

Reflecting that this would give them something to think about, I pushed on and reached Martoli at three o'clock.

CHAPTER EIGHTEEN

The Bhotias of Martoli

MARTOLI is one of the main trade routes between India and Tibet and is the last village but one (which is Milam) on the Indian side of the border. Situated on a high spur between the Gori and Lwanl rivers, 11,000 ft. up, it is a bleak and desolate spot, surrounded by high hills and swept by piercing winds. It is occupied by a population of about two hundred Bhotias. 'Occupied' is the word rather than inhabited, because these people only come up here in the early summer with their sheep, and go down again in October to pass the winter at Munsiara and other villages lower down the Gori valley. All food has to be brought up, for nothing is grown there except a little mustard and potatoes; but the grazing is excellent, and juniper and rhododendron bushes supply fuel. The houses are solidly built of stone and roofed with heavy slate, and are usually in the form of a hollow square surrounding a flagged courtyard.

About these most interesting people, the Bhotias, and their trade with Tibet, much could be written, but I must attempt only a brief sketch. As has been said, the Bhotias are of Mongolian extraction and speak a dialect akin to Tibetan. Bhot or Bod is really the same word as Tibet, but the people of Garhwal and Almora seldom use either of these names when referring to the country north of them, but call it Hundes. They have been Hinduised to a certain extent and worship not only Tibetan deities but also the gods of the Hindu pantheon. But they are not very orthodox Hindus, and the caste system is interpreted as it suits them. In the matter of food they are quite ready to eat with Tibetans, which would be defilement to strict Hindus, but which is probably of advantage to the Bhotias in their trade relations; nor did the Garhwal Bhotias show much scruple about eating any of our foods. Of their character it can be said that they are cheerful, hardy, industrious (at least the women), honest, hospitable, charitable, and a thoroughly likeable people. Nor are they the wild uncivilised barbarians that is sometimes thought. Their houses are well built and have some pretence to architecture; they are shrewd traders, willing to be educated, and have produced such men as Rai Kishen Singh Bahadur, the famous Pandit 'A.K.' of the Indian Survey, and one or two others who have earned a name for themselves in the exploration and mapping of Tibet.

The Bhotias enjoy a monopoly of the trade with Tibet, which appears to be a lucrative one in spite of the many taxes imposed by the Tibetans. The route from Milam to Tibet involves the crossing of three passes between 17,000 and 18,000 ft., all of which have to be crossed in one day because there is no grazing in between. The two chief markets to which the Bhotias of this valley resort are Gyanema and Gartok. The latter is a journey of five days or ten when travelling with sheep. In the spring the local Tibetan official visits Milam and, having first assured himself that there is no epidemic disease in the Bhotia villages, he levies a general toll before declaring the passes open. Further taxes are paid in Tibet. At one time the Indian Government decreed that no taxes were to be paid to the Tibetans, but when the Tibetans replied by closing the passes, the Bhotias were so hard hit that at their request the decree was rescinded. Tibet produces very little grain and is largely dependent on imports from India; wheat, barley, rice, therefore, are the chief articles carried in by the Bhotias, but sugar, tobacco, brass, copper, and iron are also taken. In return they bring from Tibet wool, salt, borax, yaks' tails, ponies, and of these the wool is by far the most important. The figure of 400 tons of wool for the year 1907 is an impressive one when the route and the means of transport are considered. The Bhotia traders and their households come up to Milam and Martoli in the spring and establish depôts there, and in the course of the summer they make two or three journeys into Tibet. In the early autumn they begin sending their wool, salt, and borax to centres in the southern valleys, and by early November Milam and Martoli are once more deserted. Goats and sheep are the principal carriers, but yaks, jibbus, and mules are sometimes used. No fodder is carried for these, and in consequence the greater part of each day must be devoted to grazing. Marches are therefore short, seldom exceeding six or seven miles.

There is romance in trade and not least in this carried on in the grim defiles and over the stern passes of the Himalaya.

And now to continue the story of our strange antics on this the first day of our return to the habitations of man. I sat down beneath a low stone wall in the middle of the village to avoid the wind and to await the event. A crowd soon began to gather, as it would in an English village if someone dropped out of the skies, and a barrage of questions was fired at me. Their own knowledge of the country to the west stopped at the grazing alp of Narspati; beyond was hearsay, and they found it difficult to believe that anyone could have come over the icy barrier which lies west of this; if I *had* flown there they could not have been more surprised. When I had got it into their heads that we had come from Joshimath, climbing Nanda Devi on the way, they were profoundly impressed and showed an insatiable curiosity about our experiences on the mountain. Time and again they asked me if we had seen the goddess on top of the mountain, and when I was obliged to confess that we had noticed nothing but snow they seemed loath to believe it, and returned to the charge with suggestions that we must at any rate have seen the house in which the goddess dwelt. My boots, ice-axe, rope, clothes, face, and beard were all appraised and commented upon, fortunately in a language which I could not understand, and having thus provided them with considerable free instruction, entertainment, and amusement, I thought it was their turn and hinted that a little food and drink would not come amiss. Enormous thick chapatties, some blistering hot curry, and Tibetan tea, were soon forthcoming, and the clumsy way I handled the curry with my fingers amply repaid the donor.

A wet mist now blew up the valley and the whole party adjourned to a low, stone, windowless building, and the noise inside made it unnecessary for them to tell me it was the village school. Fifty diminutive Bhotia infants, boys and girls, were turned out, and the schoolmaster with one or two favourite pupils did the honours. He was a man of the world, and to impress upon me that at least one man in Martoli was not an ignorant savage he sent over to his house for a Thermos flask, of all things. It was full of very hot Tibetan tea, flavoured with red pepper, and at the moment I could not have too much to drink. But before I was allowed to start every man in the crowd had to stick his fingers down the mouth of it, not to enhance the flavour of the tea, as of course it did, but to assure himself that there was no deception about this modern miracle. While I was drinking, the favourite pupils were put through their paces, the most advanced had to write a sentence in Hindustani (in Roman characters I was relieved to find), and to this I had to write a suitable reply which the unfortunate scholar had then to read aloud for the edification of the audience. He passed the examination with far more credit than I did.

I found these mental exercises rather exhausting and welcomed a diversion in the shape of some 'chang' which one of my well-wishers brought along. This is a thin whitish beer made from barley and no Tibetan is ever far away from it. Just as we were settling down happily to some solemnish drinking a cry went up outside and we all trooped out to investigate. The excitement was caused by the strange spectacle of two men clinging like flies to the cliffs on the far side of the gorge. At first I thought it must be two enthusiasts of the Martoli Mountaineering Club, if such there was, enjoying a little practice on the local crags, but soon, in the failing light, I realised that it was Houston and Pasang looking for some means of reaching the haven where they would be, and, at almost the same moment, that they were not at all likely to find it. I was told that the bridge was a mile below the gorge and that they were way off the path to it. I suggested that someone should go over and show them the way, but it was obvious that nothing would be done, for it was now almost dark—besides there was a lot of beer left. We returned to the school.

When the party broke up I was not allowed to take up quarters on the earth floor of the school as I hoped. Under the guidance of the schoolmaster we stumbled in the dark through narrow lanes between house walls, colliding several times with what seemed to be the town band, a gang of youths who paraded the village after sundown, singing and beating a sort of tattoo on drums. Presently we turned through a narrow tunnel and emerged in a large courtyard about thirty yards square, and, stumbling first over a yak and then over some goats, I was led up a stone staircase and into a little room which seemed to be a kind of store. There were bales of wool, sheepskins, skins of bharal and musk deer, baskets of grain, and a couple of hand-dressed mill-stones. There was a primitive oil lamp and a carpet was spread on the floor, so I hung up my hat and took possession. Then the genial Bhotia who was my host arrived, bringing with him my supper of curry and rice and a few intimate friends to watch me dispatch it. This done I distributed tobacco and one of them produced some fiery home-made brandy. It had been too hard a day for me to shine socially and, when I nearly fell asleep where I sat, they took the hint and withdrew.

My host insisted on sleeping in the store with me, rather, I hope and believe, to ensure that nobody stole anything from me than that I should appropriate anything of his. He spent half the night measuring out rations of flour to one of his drovers who was going on a journey next day, and he was up before four to see the sheep loaded with their saddle bags. This activity did not disturb me, for I was too tired, nor did the bales of wool, which I had remarked with concern, discharge the clouds of fleas that I expected.

I was out at daylight next morning to have a look round but was not earlier than the women, who had already settled down to their endless task of weaving, seated round the courtyard at their twelve-foot lengths of cloth in the making, darting the shuttle through, and pressing the woof home with flat wooden staves. The spinning of thread for the weaving is done by the men and the children, who are never without a hank of wool on one wrist, which they spin into thread on wooden spindles, as naturally as breathing, and half-unconsciously like a woman knitting.

The village is, as I have said, on a high bluff in the angle between the main Gori river and the tributary Lwanl stream down which we had come. To the north the valley is open and grassy, and nine miles away is Milam, the last village on the road and a much more important one than Martoli. Walking out of the village that morning, towards the end of the spur, I could look down on to the bridge over the Lwanl 400 ft. below, and beyond it to the white ribbon of road leading up the valley to Milam, whose position was indicated by the shining Milam peak. Down this road and across the bridge came flock after flock of white sheep and goats, bringing their burdens of wool, salt, and borax, from distant Tibet. Some took the valley road below the village but many climbed the steep zigzag track up to Martoli, and as they gained the flat plateau on which the village stands they were met by the band of last night and escorted to their owner's house in triumph with tap of drum. The patient plodding yaks and the jostling sheep, many of them lame and all of them tired, seemed to take fresh heart; it was for all the world like a footsore regiment being played into billets after a long march.

There was no one to play the two weary, belated wanderers in. I spotted them on the far side of the river accompanied by a third man, evidently a guide. They came slowly up the hill, wading knee-deep amongst a sea of sheep, and when Pasang saw me sitting there, trying hard to suppress a malicious grin, he had the grace to look sheepish himself. Perhaps I have dwelt too long on this incident, but to me at the time it afforded more amusement than it may when set down on paper, because so often the boot is on the other leg—it is the Sherpa who hits off the best route and the Sahib who is the fool.

We all returned to my lodging, where we ate eggs and potatoes and Houston told of their adventures. They had left the track which they should have followed because it turned up the hill away from the river and the village, and they were further betrayed by the sight of a man coming down from Martoli towards the river, whom they rashly assumed to be making for a crossing place. By dusk they were deeply involved on the cliffs above the gorge where I had seen them, and when they had extricated themselves they had to go back up the valley for a good half mile before finding a camping place. In the morning they chanced upon a shepherd who took them to the bridge by a short cut.

While we were breakfasting a man, a girl, and a baby came into the courtyard, and while the man played on a drum with his hands, the baby being parked at his side, the girl danced and sang in a blood-curdling falsetto. She hardly moved off the flat stone on which she stood and expressed more with her hands and her body than with her feet. Occassionally she stopped to pass round the hat in the form of the shovel-shaped basket which is used for winnowing, but her performance impressed by its sustained effort more than by its beauty. However, it seemed to be appreciated by the weaving women, the idlers, and by a small party who, having slaughtered a sheep, were busy cutting it up alongside the man holding the drum and the baby. Nor did the sheep, goats, yaks, cows, and mules, sunning themselves on the warm stones of the courtyard, show any violent symptoms of dislike. Contributions of grain, rice, and bits of wool found their way into the basket and we, with mistaken generosity, added a four-anna piece. This was fatal, because the girl promptly took up a position close to Houston, who was foolishly sitting outside, and gyrated in front of him till he was dizzy and fled inside for refuge.

We did not want to leave the protection of our room until this dangerous dancing girl had gone, but she showed no signs of stopping and it was time to think of starting, although the hospitable Bhotias wanted us to stop and make another night of it. We tried to hire two porters to carry our loads, but no one would come for less than the outrageous rate of Rs 3 a day and, like the Mr Ramsbottom in the song 'Runcorn Ferry' who would 'sooner be drownded than done', we continued to carry our own packs. Then came the question of settling with the good people of Martoli for my board and lodging and the food we had bought, and in that I am afraid my host's trading instincts overcame his geniality; not in the amount asked, for that was only Rs 3, but in a little comedy that was acted for our benefit. Having nothing else, we tendered a five-rupee note, and after a prolonged absence our host returned with the sad news that there was no change in the village. We offered him a 120 ft. climbing rope in full settlement, but as this would not do we took back the five-rupee note. That worried him a lot and off he went again to return at last with one rupee. We were hard-hearted enough to refuse this, and the whole farce was re-enacted and that time one and a half rupees were forthcoming. It was a consummate piece of acting, but by now we had tumbled to it, so, pocketing our five rupees, we shouldered our packs, said goodbye and walked off, when of course he at once produced, quite unabashed, the two rupees change.

Turning our backs on Martoli and the mountains we marched down the valley towards the plains.

CHAPTER NINETEEN

Last Days

THE short, sweet grass of the Martoli spur was soon left behind and the road grew ever rougher as the towering walls of the valley closed in upon the river, so that soon we were marching through a wild and savage gorge out of which we were not to escape until the second day. The gorge of the Gori, or 'white' river, rivals the Rishi gorge in its stark and gloomy grandeur and surpasses it in length and continuity. For twenty miles there is scarcely any break in the precipitous nature of either bank of the river, and in this distance the fall is about 4000 ft. The river runs with such violence and rapidity that for many miles it is nothing but a series of cascades and rapids. The rough track is nowhere level, climbing up and down, crossing and recrossing the river as it avoids impassable rock faces and seeks a way over the many torrents that come leaping down the sides of the great gorge. At one point, thinking we had already seen the last of snow for many a month, we were astonished to find ourselves walking over a huge avalanche cone of hard, dirty snow. Considering the time of the year and the altitude of only about 9000 ft., the presence of this snow is a convincing witness to the little sunlight that reaches the bottom of this deep and narrow cleft, and the depth of the winter snowfall.

There were no villages in the gorge, indeed no habitations of any kind, and at five o'clock, in pouring rain, we found shelter in a big cave. There were already five travellers and drovers in it who occupied the best pitch, and who did not invite us to join them round their fire. However, when Pasang asked them for some tea one of them gave us a handful of the stalks they use as tea and refused indignantly to take any of our sugar in exchange. At dusk six more wayfarers arrived and, finding the ground floor occupied, took possession of a second storey reached by a difficult rock climb up a slab. We thought it was now time to put out a 'House Full' notice, but in this we were mistaken, for, after dark, five more men came in and found a niche for themselves in yet a third storey.

When we woke to another wet morning most of the hotel guests had already left, apparently without any breakfast, and by half-past five we were left in sole possession and with a feeling that we were disgracefully late risers. We regretted this laziness because we had planned to touch some of our fellow lodgers for some atta, to make the chapatties for which our hearts yearned. We breakfasted austerely off satu.

All that morning the gorge continued to amaze us with its ruggedness and the road by its makers' ingenuity. It was carried backwards and forwards across the river on spidery bridges, it was carried up slabs on wooden stairs, across cliff faces, on cunningly built stone revetments, and through tunnels carved out of solid rock. The gloominess and the severity of the scene, the rain and the eternal roar of the river, became oppressive, so that we were glad when the gorge at length opened out, and the track climbed up out of the valley to a gentler land of villages and fields.

We stopped at the village of Munsiari, where we were able to buy some flour and some rice, but we were worried about the state of our purse because we had only a few rupees, apart from a note for Rs 100, which was as valuable in these parts as waste paper. Even at this short distance from the mountains the peasants were as different from the frank, self-sufficient Bhotias of Martoli as chalk from cheese. We seemed to have nothing in common, and they displayed not the slightest interest or curiosity in us or our doings. And this, I think, without any implications of self-importance on our part, can only be attributed to the apathy of ignorance.

We were both by now terribly footsore and we learnt later that the rest of the party suffered in the same way. It may have been due to the cold and wet feet we frequently had on the mountain or to the wearing of several pairs of socks for a long period, and now that we had gone back to rubbers we felt like penitents condemned to walking in shoes full of peas or pebbles. In spite of this we sturdily refused to put on climbing boots again, even though this refusal meant an extra 5 lb. weight on our backs. Walking through hot valleys in heavy climbing boots is as incongruous as it is tiring, and for me it had become a point of honour to return to Ranikhet shod with the same rubbers in which I had started, although there was now little but the soles remaining.

Our loads, of which to relieve us we had not yet been able to hire a coolie, weighed us down and made us limp the more, but for all that it was difficult not to enjoy every minute of this march. The trees, the grass, the paddy fields, the birds; the streams in which we bathed and which, on one memorable occasion, provided us with a meal of fresh-caught fish.

The streams were not always so friendly, for one of them nearly cost Houston his passage which we were racing to catch. At a place of evil memory called Tejam, we camped in a field of wheat-stubble by a big river called the Ramganga, and it is difficult to say which were the most trying, the villagers or a small venomous fly known locally as 'mora'. The villagers adopted what we found on this march to be their usual *non-possumus* attitude in the matter of food, but an ex-soldier of the Kumaon Rifles came to the rescue with some rice and milk. In all our travels in Garhwal it was always the reservist, usually of the Garhwal or the Kumaon Rifles, who was the most willing to help and the ablest. While talking to him we learnt the unexpected news that the bridge over the river was down—had been down in fact for two years. There did not appear to be the remotest chance of fording it, but he told us that two miles up there was a ford. To offset our relief he was careful to add that it was a difficult ford and that sometimes the water was up to a man's neck. Provided it did not rain in the night, he thought we might get across and volunteered to come with us to lend a hand. After paying him for the rice and milk we had only one rupee left, and, as we should have to travel for at least two more days before there was any hope of changing our Rs 100 note, we could not afford to pay him for any services rendered and had to decline his offer.

From the colour of the river, a lovely turquoise, we judged it not to be a glacier-fed stream, but in this we were mistaken, for we found later that it rises under the southern slopes of Nanda Kot. A heavy thunderstorm up the valley soon changed the colour to mud and we were concerned to hear the thunder growling away for most of the night. It was raining in the morning, and when we set off at seven it got steadily worse. The path was ill-defined, but having made what we thought was a liberal two miles we began to look for the ford.

The path appeared to terminate at the water's edge at a place where the river momentarily slackened the pace of its current, and on the far side we thought we could make out a continuation of the path. Much against our wishes we concluded that this must be the ford, but it looked so uninviting that, before trying it, we went a bit farther up stream. We could see no path, so we sent Pasang on to try higher up while Houston and I went back to what we now feared was the ford. Linking hands we took to the water, but had not covered more than a few yards out of the necessary fifty before we were up to our waists and hard put to keep our feet on the bottom. We turned back, convinced that there must be some mistake, for the water there would be up to a giraffe's neck let alone a man's.

While we were in the water we saw two men striding along the path who beckoned to us to come back. They were going to the ford they said and advised us to follow, and on they went again at a furious pace. They were active, long-legged beggars, with a minimum of clothing, and they carried a little bundle of short bamboo sticks, and clutched in one hand a great bamboo pole about 8 ft. long. I assumed this must be a necessary item of equipment for crossing the ford, and thought dismally how singularly ill-provided we were for pole-jumping with ice-axes 3 ft. long. However, there was not much time for thought as we had practically to run to keep them in sight; I imagined that they were as nervous as we were that the heavy rain, which still persisted, would make the river unfordable, possibly for several days.

We picked up Pasang, and a mile farther up they turned down towards the river and began removing the little surplus apparel they had preparatory to business. It was a curious place and the obvious one for a ford, for the river ran over a bed of shingle flats perhaps 300 yards wide. The water flowed in four separate channels, divided by banks of shingle, and the crossing of the first two of these was so easy as to make us think that it was all over bar shouting. The sight of the third soon dispelled this impression, and we watched with anxiety while our long-legged and half-naked friends tackled it. It was not very deep, just over the knees, but the speed of the current made one gasp. Their technique was instructive but quite impossible for us to emulate with the heavy loads we had. They took a diagonal line down stream, not attempting to stem the current, and went as fast as they could, lifting the foot clear of the water at every bound. In a few moments they were safe on the far side, laughing at us as we advanced slowly and fearfully into midstream hand in hand. The effort required to maintain any footing was tremendous and it was difficult to keep the point of an ice-axe on the bottom to support one. Houston cast off from us and attempted to finish at speed, as they had done, but in the deepest part he lost his footing and I thought he was gone, but after rolling right over he struggled up again and reached the bank. Pasang and I were still ten yards from the shore and making very heavy weather of it, so I was mightily relieved when one of the bamboo merchants dashed in and caught me by the hand. We were soon over the rest, and I was so thankful to have the Ramganga behind us that I bestowed on our deliverers nearly all the tobacco I had left.

Travel in the Himalaya involves sooner or later the bridging or fording of rivers, and it is surprising what can be crossed with an axe, a few straight trees, and a good eye for a likely place for a bridge; and when fording, how great is the assistance obtained from a rope, an ice-axe, and the mutual support of two or more persons. In dangerous rivers it is advisable to carry the load so that it can easily be slipped off, for though a load helps to keep your feet on the bottom, once that footing is lost the same load would be a fatal handicap.

Two more days of hard going, getting daily more footsore, and we reached Kapkot in the valley of the Sarju river on the route to the Pindari glacier. This is a deservedly popular tourist route, well provided with dâk bungalows, the last of which is but a mile or two from the glacier snout. The one-horse village of Kapkot seemed in our eyes a wealthy metropolis, for there were several native shops and a big dâk bungalow pleasantly situated on a green lawn above the river, and shaded by an enormous banyan tree.

The caretaker of the bungalow was not much impressed by our appearance, and indeed if we were to be taken at our face value this was quite understandable. Very grudgingly he opened one of the rooms for us and began, metaphorically, to count his spoons; but when he asked where our coolies were, and we were obliged to confess that the faithful but dishevelled Pasang was the sole member of our suite, he seemed half inclined to shut it again. We had no cash at all now except for the Rs 100 note, and, large though Kapkot appeared to us, we doubted whether the combined population could find change for this amount. If this, as we expected, proved true, then our creditors would be asked to accompany us on the march until we were, as it were, solvent; nor did we allow this consideration to make us stint ourselves in the orders we gave to the caretaker for the provision of food. However, when we did produce the note as an earnest of good faith the eyes of the caretaker shone with a sudden geniality, and he hastened to assure us that change would be found. His former surliness was forgotten, he became profoundly respectful, and bustled about throwing open doors, setting chairs and tables, attending to our wants in every way he could.

Being now on the well-ordered Pindari glacier route it was from here on nothing but roses, roses, all the way. At the next halt Bageswar, the Rawal of the temple, a fine type of Indian gentleman of the old school, very dignified and erect in spite of his age, sent us with his customary generosity a present of

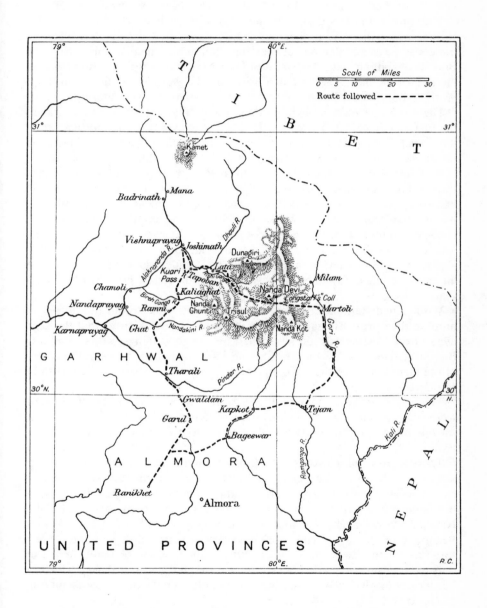

fruit; a party who were also stopping at the bungalow pressed upon us a loaf of bread and an enormous fish out of the Sarju river, while the khansama in charge of the bungalow served up a four-course dinner. I had been this way before and had promised Houston that at Bageswar we would get a five-course dinner, but this disappointment he generously overlooked.

Bageswar is not the prosperous market town that it once was when its traders acted as middlemen between the Bhotias and the plainsmen. Now the Bhotias deal direct with the banias of Haldwani, Tanakpur, and Ramnagar at the foot of the hills. The bazaar consists of solid well-built houses with shops on the ground floor, but it was sad to see so many of these shut up.

There is a very old temple here; the present building, which is by no means the first, is said to date back to A.D. 1450. It is over this that our benefactor the Rawal, Poona Sahib, presides, a man who throughout a long life has stood for unswerving loyalty to the British Raj under very difficult circumstances.

At Someswar we joined the road from Ranikhet to Garul which we had travelled over in a bus on the way out, and all that remained for us now was to find some conveyance. The *deus ex machina* soon appeared in the guise of a native chauffeur who was, he said, waiting here for his master who had disappeared into the blue and had not returned. At least that was the tale that was told to us, but we asked no questions and, for a consideration, we were wafted into Ranikhet in a high-powered, opulent-looking, new car. A kindness Pasang returned by being sick all over the rich upholstery of the back seat.

We reached Ranikhet on September 12th and took up our quarters once more in the Forest Bungalow, where we found, to our sorrow, that the keen edge of our desires was already dulled by the good things we had found at Bageswar. Houston left on the 13th and I sat down alone to await the arrival of the main body, for there were porters to pay off and various matters to be settled.

The first to arrive came in on the 19th and the last, I think, on the 21st, on which day, by the way, Houston, who was flying, was already in Paris. And, for one night only, the party was reunited before another and final dispersal took place.

There were several lessons to be learnt from this show, but of too technical a nature to be discussed here. We live in an age of mechanisation and, in recent years, it has become apparent that even mountaineering is in danger of becoming mechanised. It is therefore pleasing to record that in climbing Nanda Devi no mechanical aids were used—apart that is from the Apricot Brandy. Our solitary oxygen apparatus was fortunately drowned, pitons were forgotten at the Base, snow shoes and crampons were solemnly carried up only to be abandoned, and I hope it is clear that the glacier drill with which we burdened ourselves was a scientific instrument and not a device for facilitating glacier travel.

Another interesting point is that the age limit for high climbing, previously put at 35, seems to have expanded, for our party was of all ages from twenty-two to over fifty, but I do not want to imply that either of these extremes is the best. Porters for high camps were found to be not indispensable, and a certain amount of hard work and hard living on the march up did not incapacitate anyone for work on the mountain. Even stranger was the fact that men of two different nations could work together under trying conditons in complete harmony and without jealousy.

It was but a short three months that we had met, many of us as strangers, but inspired by a single hope and bound by common purpose. This purpose was only achieved by team-work, team-work the more remarkable on account of the two different nationalities; and though these two nations have a common origin they are for that reason more critical of each other's shortcomings—as relationship leads proverbially to ill-feeling. The Americans and ourselves do not always see eye to eye, but on those rare occasions when we come together to do a job of work, as, for example, in war or in the more serious matter of climbing a mountain, we seem to pull together very well.

Where each man pulled his weight each must share the credit; for, though it is natural for each man to have his own aspirations, it is in mountaineering, more than in most things, that we try to believe

> The game is more than the players of the game,
> And the ship is more than the crew.

SURVEYING AROUND NANDA DEVI IN 1936

Fazal Ellahi, the skilled Indian surveyor, at work at a station above the Rhamani Glacier in 1936. Changabang is in the background.

SURVEYING TRIPS AROUND NANDA DEVI IN 1936

by ERIC SHIPTON

A paper originally read before The Alpine Club, March 9, 1937 and later reproduced in *A.J.* 49. pp. 27-40 entitled "Survey in the Nanda Devi District".

MOUNTAINEERS will have been interested to learn that the Survey of India is now engaged on a new ½-inch map of the mountain regions of Kumaon and Garhwal. Previous surveys, as produced on the present ¼-inch sheets 53N and 62B, had been confined almost entirely to the populated and revenue-producing areas in or near to the great arterial valleys. Most of the glacier-covered country and the remoter valleys of these sheets are very sketchily drawn, in many places, indeed, so sketchily as to bear no resemblance whatever to the ground in question. Over much of the country, too, it has been found necessary to extend the primary triangulation. While engaged on this task in the Badrinath-Kedanath range, Major Osmaston found that the whole trunk of the Gangotri Glacier was, in fact, several miles west of the position allotted to it on the map. I hope that now at last we shall have a final solution to the topographical problems of this area which have excited so much discussion.

The usual method employed for hill surveys in India is plane-tabling by Indians, who are each responsible for a section of the area. These men work with remarkable speed and neatness, and, under the close supervision of their officers, they produce very good work. But in the high Himalaya they are faced by unusual difficulties, which they are not used to. Not being trained mountaineers they have great difficulty in moving their parties about in the glacier regions and in reaching suitable stations.

Owing to the peculiar difficulties presented by the country round Nanda Devi it was decided to depart from the usual practice and to send Major Osmaston, who is in charge of these mountain surveys, to carry out a photographic survey of the basin drained by the Rishi Ganga. As I had made a reconnaissance of the region in 1934,[1] the Survey Department invited me to accompany the party in order to assist Major Osmaston in the selection of suitable stations.

A Wild photo-theodolite and 100 plates were taken as well as a plane-table. I took with me the Watts-Leica photo-theodolite belonging to the R.G.S., partly

1 *A.J.* 47. 58-75.

to supplement the main survey, and partly in order to give a further test to this novel instrument. Six Sherpa porters were brought from Darjeeling, including Angtharkay. The name Sherpa has become almost generic for all porters engaged in Darjeeling. Actually one of these men, Gyalgen, came from two months' journey north of Lhasa.

We left Ranikhet on August 27, 1936. We had to take an unusual route to the Kuari Pass, as one of the bridges on the Wan route had been carried away by floods. We had terribly bad weather all the way to Joshimath. The rains reached their climax on the night of August 29 and our camp was flooded out. Later we heard that ten inches of rain had fallen in Mussoorie that night. Incidentally, the 29th was the day on which Nanda Devi was climbed!

We reached Joshimath on September 3 and left again on the 6th. On the 7th we camped at Lata, near the mouth of the Rishi Ganga. As we were sitting in camp a bearded and tattered figure appeared rushing down the steep path. This proved to be Peter Lloyd, the first of the returning Nanda Devi party. From him we heard of their splendid achievement. In my opinion the climbing of Nanda Devi is perhaps the finest mountaineering achievement which has yet been performed in the Himalaya; certainly it is the first of the really difficult Himalayan giants to be conquered. This expedition was a model of what such an expedition should be; the party was a team consisting exclusively of mountaineers; they avoided the great mistake which, to my mind, nearly all the major Himalayan expeditions since the war have made, and did not handicap themselves with a vast bulk of stores and superfluous personnel. Each man was prepared to carry loads up to any height, and indeed all were called upon to do so during the most arduous part of the climb; above all, they avoided newspaper publicity. I was delighted to hear that Tilman had been one of those to reach the summit. He had accomplished more than his share of the donkey work, having earlier in the year ascended the Rishi Nala and dumped provisions in the 'Basin' and then returned, all the way to Ranikhet, to organise the transport of the party. Later that evening Graham Brown turned up. The rest of the party we met on the cliff track to Durashi, except for Tilman and Houston who had crossed a very difficult pass to Milam— 'Longstaff's Col'.

The passage of the Rishi Gorge was now quite devoid of difficulty. There were cairns at every turn, a small but adequate path wound across the steep slopes and any rock steps were cleared of loose rock; above all, it was now not necessary to hunt for a way. The monsoon was still active and we had a lot of bad weather. However, when we reached the Basin on September 16 the days were gloriously fine and the nights clear and frosty. The rivers were already fast sinking to their low autumn level and they presented us with no difficulties.

IN THE NANDA DEVI BASIN

Osmaston decided to tackle the northern section of the Basin first. I was keen to examine the ridges and valleys leading from the main basin up to the peaks bounding the western flanks of the Rhamani and Bagini Glaciers, as we had not had the opportunity in 1934 of exploring this area. This I was able to do while Osmaston was mapping this part of the Basin. The peaks in this vicinity are mostly composed of a beautiful pale granite, and soar to around 21,000 ft. in clean curving lines, supported below by wonderfully carved ice flutings.

Tensing [Tenzing of Everest fame], one of our Sherpas, had developed some sort of fever in the Rishi Nala and every day for more than a fortnight he ran a very high temperature – often as much as 105°. Even when he had recovered he was no more than a passenger as the fever left him very weak and thin. Owing to this we kept on two of the Lata men who had accompanied us into the Basin. They worked splendidly and with a little training would be as good as the Sherpas. It is quite time that someone undertook the task of training these people of Garhwal as mountaineers. There is any amount of splendid material in the higher valleys. They have one tremendous disadvantage, however, and that is that their religion forbids them to eat either with Europeans or anything cooked or touched by Europeans or Indians of other castes. When a party is engaged in a long and difficult task, this taboo would produce an impossible situation. With the Sherpas, I am in the habit of eating out of the same dish and drinking out of the same mug, and no one loses caste or feels embarrassed. Later in the year when we were employing some Dotial porters and the party ran short of food, the Dotials, who had finished their own food, allowed themselves to become feeble with hunger rather than eat the rice which we had been carrying in our rucksacks. Angtharkay always becomes infuriated by this prejudice, and taunts the victims unmercifully.

We had a delicious camp by the lake at the junction of the two great glaciers of the Northern section. We had brought a goat we gave orders for it to be with us from Lata, and at this camp we executed. It was a sad business, as we had all become very attached to the animal. It had shared with us the fatigues of a long journey and the warmth and comfort of our caves and campfires. It had been no easy task getting it up the gorge, and Angtharkay, who had been its keeper and principal helper, was particularly distressed at the idea of killing it and had defended its life for some days with arguments for keeping it alive—the chief of these being that it might as well be made to carry its meat as far up the glacier as possible. That night, however, when eating fried liver and kidneys, he had no regrets. The execution itself was performed quickly by the two local men before the animal had time to bleat.

We crossed the Great North Glacier, which was a severe trial to poor Tensing, who was now so weak that he found difficulty in walking. His temperature was still alarmingly high in the evenings, and we were beginning to get very worried about him. However, in the large ablation valley on the other side of the glacier we made a base camp from which the remainder of the Northern section could be reached. After a week's rest at this camp the fever left him. Angtharkay, Ang Dawa and I set out to climb a fine triangulated peak (21,770 ft.) on the watershed overlooking the Milam Glacier. We camped at about 17,500 ft. in a subsidiary valley and started before dawn the following day (September 23). We climbed up a steep and quite difficult ice ridge, which involved a great deal of step cutting. The conditions were excellent, however, and the climb was pleasant and safe. Ang Dawa was quite the strongest of our six Sherpas; in fact, he used to entertain us in camp with feats of strength. In the Rishi Nala too he had displayed considerable skill on steep rocks and would run about over precipices without turning a hair. On this ice ridge it was very surprising to see him crack up. He could not adjust his movements to the ground he was on and was terrified on steep snow slopes. He became exhausted early in the climb and a few hundred feet from the summit gave up the struggle. This delayed us a good deal, and by the time Angtharkay and I had reached the top the Milam Glacier was filled with cloud and I did not get the view I had hoped for. We looked down on two gorge-like glacier valleys running eastward from the two cols on the watershed on either side of the peak. Lower down we could just discern their junction with the Milam Glacier. It would be possible to cross either of these two cols and so to reach the Milam Glacier from the Nanda Devi Basin; but it would be a difficult undertaking with the loads it would be necessary to carry.

Although the peak we had climbed is the highest on that part of the watershed, in common with most of the great peaks of the Nanda Devi Basin it has no name. With the new survey of the range a complete revision of the nomenclature of the district is being made. It is no easy task to decide on the most appropriate names for peaks and glaciers. Each group of villages has a different name for the same feature and they do not agree upon the names of even the great peaks which dominate the whole district. Thus all the peasants of the Dhaoli Valley, in the vicinity of the mouth of the Rishi Ganga, call Nanda Devi Nanda Ghunti, and have never even heard of the former name. The peak known to us as Dunagiri is called by these people Tolmai Pahar, and it is only in the vicinity of the village of Dunagiri in the Bagini valley that one hears the name Dunagiri used for the mountain. On the other hand, the shepherds of the Rishi call the glacier which flows down the Changabang into the Rishi Nala, the Bagini, whereas Bagini is the name given by the Dunagiri villagers for the great glacier in their valley; and so on. This state of affairs is found throughout the district—and indeed throughout all mountain districts I have travelled in, in Africa as well as the Himalaya. It is not surprising that it should be so. The peaks and glaciers are as yet of no economic value to the peasants, and to them only the grazing grounds, streams and forests are worth naming. Thus the most prominent peak standing above a grazing ground would simply take the name of that grazing ground as indicating roughly its direction when seen from afar, while the shepherds on the opposite side of the peak call it after their nearest grazing ground. In this way the traveller is confronted by several peaks known by the same name and several different names given to each of the peaks. It seems to me that the best solution is for the pioneer traveller to adopt the pleasantest sounding of the various names, for geographers to accept their suggestions, and for subsequent travellers to refrain from futile discussion. In the case of uninhabited areas, of course; such as the Nanda Devi Basin, none of the glaciers or lesser peaks has a local name and there are a great many 22,000 and 23,000 ft. peaks which, though triangulated, cannot be seen clearly from the inhabited valleys and thus remain unnamed. In these cases it is the duty of explorers to invent suitable names for all prominent features, and map producers should make an effort to adopt their suggestions.[2] A tremendous amount of confusion and misunderstanding is caused by procrastination in this matter. We have produced a list of names for peaks, glaciers, lakes, etc., of the Nanda Devi region, for official consideration when the map has been drawn.

TO SHIPTON'S COL

After accompanying Osmaston up the Great North Glacier (which, by the way, will be given a more suitable name in due course) [later called the Uttari Rishi Glacier], I returned to the lake, and from there went with Rinzing Bhutia up the Changabang Glacier. The moraine covering the greater part of the surface of the ice is made up of huge blocks of that remarkable white granite of which the cliffs of Changabang are composed. Halfway up we camped on the flat top of a glacier table. Except for the fact that the table might have collapsed, it made an excellent campsite. The weather turned bad, and that evening a good deal of snow fell. Starting before dawn the following day (September 27) we reached the head of the glacier which rises in a cirque of stupendous granite cliffs. We were making for a saddle at the foot of the southern ridge of Changabang which I hoped would offer a practicable route to the head of the Rhamani Glacier. A gully in the granite slabs led us to the crest of the col without much difficulty, and from there we looked down on to the great snowfield which Dr Longstaff had reached after crossing the Bagini Pass in 1907.[3] We were separated from it, however, by a vertical wall of rock whose smooth face was quite impossible to climb down. Although by now most of the peaks were covered by cloud, the view was quite magnificent and I sat for an hour fascinated by the gigantic white cliffs of Changabang.[4] The great snow dome of Dunagiri appeared now and then from across the Rhamani Glacier, but I did not get a view of the main mass of the mountain. We returned to our camp in the afternoon and thence, in heavily falling snow, down the glacier to the lake. We returned to the glacier junction camp the following day to find that Osmaston had been delayed by the bad weather and still had one more station to do in the northern section. He had been right lip to the head of the Great North Glacier and had completed the survey of that valley and its tributaries.

ATTEMPT ON DUNAGIRI

We descended the main glacier and crossed the rivers into the southern section. There I left Osmaston and went down the Rishi Gorge to Dibrughata with Angtharkay and Sen Tensing, reaching there on October 3. We left again on October 4 and on the evening of the 5th reached a high pasture in the ablation valley of the Rhamani Glacier. I was hoping to reconnoitre the South-West Ridge of Dunagiri and, if time permitted, to make an attempt to climb the peak. On the 6th we went up a side glacier and camped on its moraine at about 17,000

2 See pp. 106-7. 3 *A.J.* 24. 108-33. 4 *Ibid.*, illustration facing iii.

ft. The following day we managed to reach a col of nearly 20,000 ft. connecting the South-West Ridge of Dunagiri with a peak which on the old one-inch maps bore the strange name 'Niti No. 3'. On the northern side of the col the ground fell away with tremendous steepness to the Tolma glen and we found ourselves looking straight down to Surai Tota in the Dhaoli valley. We turned right-handed and followed a narrow icy crest towards Dunagiri. Sen Tensing succeeded in dropping his ice axe. We recovered it two days later, but its temporary loss produced a horrid feeling of insecurity for the whole party. Reaching a point where the ridge sweeps up with considerable steepness we pitched our tent under a great rock buttress. Later in the evening Angtharkay and I climbed several hundred feet further up the ridge to reconnoitre the route. We found that the going was over hard ice and that steps would have to be cut every foot of the way.

Our camp was in a superb position and commanded views from the great peaks of the Nanda Devi Basin and Trisul ranges to the mountains of Badrinath and Kamet. After a bitterly cold night we started before dawn, a very painful performance from which there, was no relief until the sun appeared. We had left Sen Tensing behind in camp and Angtharkay and I took the labour of step cutting in turns. It was very slow and tiring work, and when after some difficult climbing we reached the long, almost level ridge leading to the summit it was late in the day and we had not time to cut our way along the knife-edged crest to the top. The route, however, is quite feasible and, as far as I have been able to see, by far the best way of climbing this grand peak. We got to a point within a thousand feet of the top (23,184 ft).

CROSSING THE BAGINI PASS

We returned to the Rhamani Glacier and camped at its head below the col which Rinzing and I had reached from the Nanda Devi Basin. On October 10 we started to cross the Bagini Pass. I was a bit confused by the topography at the head of the glacier. The western face of Changabang falls with its characteristic sweep of white granite to a col some 2500 ft. below the summit. West of this the watershed ridge rises to a sharp conical peak, and further still falls again to a long, serrated granite ridge which, nearly a mile further on, abuts on to a peak 21,290 ft. of the great North-East Ridge of Dunagiri. Between this peak and Dunagiri itself is another low depression forming the watershed between the Rhamani and Dunagiri Glaciers; this one, however, is almost inaccessible from this side. I was by no means certain which of these cols was the Bagini Pass which Dr Longstaff had crossed in 1907, and as far as I know had not been crossed since. We chose the middle one and reached the crest of the serrated rock ridge at 12.30 on October 11, only to find that from where we stood there was no chance of descending on the northern side.

We spent the rest of the day moving ourselves and our loads along the knife-edged crest of the ridge before we could rope down into a gully from which a descent could be made. We were overtaken by dark when only 200-300 ft. down and had to construct a tiny platform on which to camp for the night. Early next morning we completed the descent of the rocks and ran down the snow-covered head of the Bagini Glacier. The valley we were in was bounded on the east by a most magnificent wall of peaks which form the north-west rim of the Nanda Devi Basin on which we had stood two years previously. From lower down we could look up a small side glacier to the col under the western face of Changabang. I was extremely glad that we had not tried that route, as it would have been almost impossible to descend from the col with our loads. The first crossing of the Bagini Pass must have been an anxious business, as apart from the difficulty of the climbing, Longstaff and his companions had no idea of where the pass would lead them, and even when they had negotiated the Rhamani valley they were still many days from habitation. We had none of these anxieties and thus our passage was vastly easier.

DOWN THE BAGINI GLACIER

The Sherpas were eager to reach fuel before nightfall and we sped down the glacier without halting anywhere. Every step of the way was vastly interesting to me, and I spent an absorbing day fitting in the topography of the Bagini Glacier with our explorations of two years previously. We had magnificent views of the huge unnamed peaks of the Garhwal-Kumaon watershed. Immediately north of these peaks is the Girthi river which makes such a strange intrusion into this line of elevation. The sun had long set before we reached the first juniper on the southern side of the glacier, and we were lucky enough to find a stream running down the ablation valley and soft turf on which to camp. The excitement of reaching juniper after some time on the higher glaciers never loses its force. In spite of the hardihood of this plant it is peculiarly sensitive to its position and at higher altitudes never grows on slopes with a northern aspect. For some miles that evening we had seen it growing on the opposite side of the glacier in tantalising profusion, and it was not until the lateral moraine on our side became sufficiently large to produce a fertile south-facing slope that we came across any. The reverse is the case with rhododendron and birch, and at lower altitudes the aspect of one's camp is indicated by the different effect these woods have upon the food.

Next morning below the snout of the glacier we found a blaze of autumn colours. The bare, almost feathery branches of the birch woods contrasted deliciously with the brilliant green of rhododendron and juniper, and the whole valley was interlaced with vivid patches of red, flame, and copper. The glades were filled with long wavy grass, the colour of ripe corn in the morning sunlight. In place of the raging torrents of muddy water which issue from Himalayan glaciers throughout the summer we found sparkling crystal streams. The air too had a sparkle of frost, enhancing the beauty of a myriad autumn tints. Early in the day we reached the village of Dunagiri, where we found all the population busily engaged in reaping their crops and storing the grain for the winter. The houses were decorated with huge yellow marrows and cucumbers. The whole valley seemed steeped in sunshine and the rich colourful ripeness of autumn harvest.

The remainder of the day was spent basking in the sun outside one of the houses, chatting with the villagers who, to celebrate our arrival, indulged in a half-holiday. We were besieged with questions about our doings and the reasons for them; to these we gave the usual unsatisfactory answers, in return for which we received much interesting information about the valley and its people. It appears that in the autumn all the inhabitants descend as far as Karnaprayng and even further with their flocks, and the whole valley is deserted. All the farm produce is stored in the village for consumption the following summer. This winter exodus takes place by slow degrees and was already in progress. The Sherpas spent a happy day trading old tins for food, and after some hours of hard bargaining had obtained, without spending a single *pice*, enough to keep us supplied for a week. The children in these villages are made to work from a very early age. In the evening I watched some tiny mites supervising with extraordinary skill the herding of enormous flocks into pens. There were innumerable lambs, each of which had to be placed beside its mother. The children worked until long after nightfall, settling the disputes and attending the bleated complaints of the sheep.

DUNAGIRI FROM THE NORTH

The following day I went up with Sen Tensing to investigate the so-called Dunagiri Glacier and to reconnoitre the northern approaches of the peak. The glacier terminates in an immense wall of moraine-debris which has been thrust into the birch forest high up the side of the main valley a mile or so below the snout of the Nagini Glacier. It is very much alive and appears at the present time to be advancing; though in former ages it must have flowed far down into the main Bagini valley. It rises, not at the foot of the peak of Dunagiri as I had expected, but in a rocky cirque culminating in a peak 21,290 ft., whose acquaintance I had made on the opposite side. The North Face of Dunagiri itself was half hidden from view by this cirque, but from what I saw I should say that any route on this side would be a great deal more difficult than that which we had reconnoitred a week before. The best approach to the foot of the North Face would probably be up the Nala, which joins the Dhaoli about 3 miles below Jumagwar. I do not know whether anyone has been up this nala.

TO JOSIMATH

I regretted leaving our friends of the Bagini valley and their charming village; their hospitality and kindness matched their beautiful surroundings. Further down the valley the autumn tints were even lovelier than they had been near the glacier. I spent nine months in the Himalaya last year and at no time did I see such a wealth of lovely things as during that October; even flowers were not wholly lacking, and occasionally in some well-watered glen we would come across drifts of primulae defying the rule of the seasons. In my opinion there is no better time to travel in Garhwal than the autumn; the days are cool, the nights not too cold, snow conditions are good (except high up on north facing slopes) and the weather is usually fine. An added advantage is that, with the newly reaped crops, it is very easy to live off the country. In the forest we came upon several small encampments of peasants, busily engaged in collecting the stones of wild apricots, from the kernels of which they make oil. Further down, the Bagini torrent enters the main Dhaoli valley through a fine canyon, which is not the least impressive feature of the very beautiful valley down which we had come. Two more marches took us to Joshimath, where we rested for two days. I had been there only a couple of hours when Professor Arnold Heim arrived with Dr August Gassner, and I was delighted to be able to spend the two days in their company. They had just completed a tremendous season of geological work in the vicinity of the Almora-Tibet frontier.[5]

I left Joshimath with the two Sherpas and three Mana porters on October 18. Halfway to Tapoban I met Osmaston returning from his work in the Nanda Devi Basin. The excellent weather of the last three weeks had enabled him to complete the survey of the southern section a great deal sooner than we had expected and he had been supported in the Rishi Nala by Fasal Ellahi [Fasil Eligh in the original account], probably the most competent of his plane-tablers. Ellahi had surveyed the Trisuli Nala at a remarkable speed, averaging nearly five square miles a day, which is fast going for such difficult country. He was now working in the Rhamani Nala and, later, completed the mapping of the lower part of the Rishi Gorge.

THE TRISUL/NANDA GHUNTI BASIN

Only one section of the Outer Basin remained; this was the valley running north from glaciers between Trisul and Nanda Ghunti. It had been decided, therefore, that I should make a survey of this area with the Watts-Leica photo-theodolite, with the dual object of rounding off the Nanda Devi survey and of trying out this instrument in an independent survey. Osmaston went off up to Badrinath with the object of inspecting his surveyors in that district. Most unfortunately one of his camp officers had died in the Arwa valley, and although Captain Crone had gone up to deal with the situation, a lot of reorganisation was required.

We camped our first night out of Joshimath at Rini, which is situated at the mouth of the Rishi Nala. The following day we enlisted the help of a local man to show us the best way to the highest pastures in a valley we were making for, and to help me in naming some of the prominent features. Dr Longstaff has referred to this valley as the Rinti Nala, though the name used by the people of this district is more like Ronti. We followed the main gorge for a bit by a path which has been very cleverly engineered by the peasants, but soon the going became difficult and we turned right-handed and climbed up over steep,

5 *Die Alpen*, 1937, pp. 81-5, well illustrated.

heavily forested slopes past another tiny village basking happily in its rich, self-contained isolation. Higher up, the Rini man introduced us to a variety of wild fruits which grew in the forest, some of which were new to the Sherpas. The commonest of these resembled a crab apple on the outside, though its internal construction and taste were more like those of a persimmon. All through the forest there was a wonderful profusion of autumn colours. Every few yards we put up some Monal pheasants, which sailed over our heads, screeching noisily. During the two days we were going through this forest we must have seen nearly a hundred of these birds. Even in this remote valley they were very wild and very rarely gave us a chance to get near to them.

We entered the Ronti valley several thousand feet above its floor and on October 20 camped in a cave high up on the side of the nala commanding a magnificent view of the surrounding country. The lower section of the valley in which we found ourselves is bounded on the east by huge precipices culminating in a line of jagged aiguilles; but the western slopes are gentle, well wooded and frequented by shepherds from the villages in the neighbourhood of Rini. Their grazing ground was pointed out to me by the Rini man, who called it Chamba Kharak. This part of the valley is enclosed by a great ice-covered wall which forms the east ridge of a peak 19,893 ft. Round the eastern end of this wall the valley runs up through a narrow gorge to a large glacier basin forming its upper section. Through this gorge we could see the tongue of the glacier protruding. There has been a good deal of confusion regarding this peak, 19,893 ft., and its 20,700 ft. southern neighbour which is such a prominent feature seen from Ranikhet and Almora. The present map labels the former Nanda Ghunti and the latter Nandakna. Dr Longstaff, however, has always referred to the higher peak as Nanda Ghunti, and certainly that is what it is called by the inhabitants of the valleys to the south-west of the range. We found that the Rini villagers refer to the northerly peak as Ronti, and I hope that these two names will be adopted on the new map.

One of the Mana porters had been with Tilman's party and entertained us in the evenings by voluble descriptions of their adventures in the Rishi gorge during the monsoon. I was amused to find that these men had nicknamed Tilman 'Balu Sahib' (Balu meaning a bear) owing to the speed with which he moves over steep forested ground. On reaching the Ronti Nala I discharged the local men and set to work with the two Sherpas on the survey. But the weather broke and we were confined to our cave for three days. A good deal of snow fell and it began to look as if winter conditions would prevent any further work. Also I was afraid that our food supply would run too short to allow us to attempt to cross the pass across the watershed. However, we had brought another sheep with us and occupied ourselves concocting fancy meat dishes. The morning of October 24 was fine, and by starting before dawn we managed to reach a high spur in time to take a round of angles and photographs before the mists rose out of the valleys and swamped the view. The dawn views were magnificent and showed nearly all the great peaks of this section of the range like islands washed by an ocean of flame-coloured cloud. In the afternoon we humped our heavy loads over to Chamba Kharak, from which I was able to do another station. We repeated this procedure every day until five stations had been completed in the lower section of the nala. Owing to the fact that the view was invariably obscured by 9 a.m. it was difficult to put the stations sufficiently high, and we had to do twice as many as would have been otherwise necessary. The great advantage of this method of photo-survey over plane-tabling is the very short time that it is necessary to occupy a station. Plane-tabling in the conditions we were experiencing would have been almost impossible. The photo-theodolite which I was using weighs a total of 18 lbs., including its stand and cases; also it is extremely simple and convenient to use, and if it is found possible to plot with sufficient accuracy from the tiny photographs, it will bring photographic survey within the scope of even the most lightly equipped parties. Moreover, the use of roll films instead of plates makes it a great deal easier to bring back one's results intact. The film is held flat while being exposed by means of a pressure glass in the back of the camera.

On the afternoon of October 27, in a heavy snowstorm, we made our way through the bottle-necked gorge lying between the lower and the upper section of the Ronti Nala. We were climbing on the moraine-covered ice of the glacier, which squeezes itself through the gorge. Our great difficulty was to find any water, as at this time of the year all the glacier pools are hard-frozen day and night and we could not afford the fuel necessary to melt ice at this stage, being now above the limits of juniper. I was surprised to find Monal pheasants far up the glacier. Up here they seemed extraordinarily reluctant to embark on their gliding downward flight and we got so close to them as to tempt the Sherpas to chase them with a fusilade of stones. Although the Sherpas threw with amazing accuracy, the birds seemed to have a cunning knack of hopping over the missiles, and we failed to replenish our larder in this way.

Fortunately the next day the weather became finer and we were able to make the best use of the short time in the upper glacier basin. We found it to be divided into three sections. First, there was a large ice-stream coming down from the saddle between Nanda Ghunti and Nandakna. This saddle must lead to the head waters of the Bireh Ganga. I was very tempted to visit it, but could not spare the time. Next there is a small tributary glacier rising under the West Ridge of Nandakna; at the head of this is the saddle reached by Longstaff and Ruttledge from the other side. Thirdly, what is probably the main glacier flows under the ice-terraced cliffs of the North Ridge of Trisul. Although the upper part of this was out of sight, I decided, when the survey was finished, to look for a way across the watershed in this direction. It proved to be the right line and we encountered no difficulties whatever. Our last camp and station were on the saddle itself and commanded glorious views on both sides of the range. The glaciers on the southern side are very small and we were soon back in heavily forested country. In the upper part of the Nandagini we saw large herds of game. Near the entrance to the Nandagini gorge, where we camped, we found signs of the visit of the surveyor who had been working in this area. In spite of this we found it quite difficult to follow his track in the jungle. Sen Tensing became separated from us, and Angtharkay and I retraced our steps for a long way in search of him. Instead of him we found a good path, which we concluded he must have been following. It was not until late in the evening that we discovered him, however. He had not struck the path and had been struggling alone, some hundreds of feet below it. Angtharkay and I told him, untruthfully, that we had visited a village in the afternoon and had been sitting there imbibing milk and baked potatoes. Angtharkay told him to go back to get food for himself from the mythical village. However, I thought that was carrying the joke too far and stopped him.

From Sutol we crossed the Wan Pass to Gwaldam; and later from Wan we crossed into the valley of what, on the existing map, is called the Kurumtoli Glacier, which Dr Longstaff explored in 1905, He calls it the Keil Glacier. In this region I did several photographic stations, which were intended to supplement the work of the plane-tabler who had not had time to complete his work in this part.

On my way to Bombay I went to Dehra Dun, where I met Osmaston and Captain Crone, whom I had met previously at Joshimath. Osmaston's photographs had come out well, except for a certain amount of fogging round the edges. Crone calibrated the camera I had been using and appeared to think that there would be no difficulty in plotting the data I had brought back. He is working on it now and I am anxiously awaiting his report on the work of this very handy little instrument.

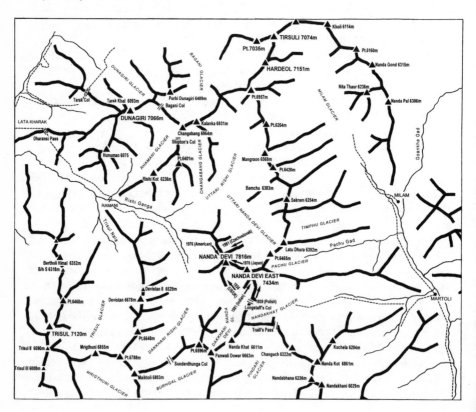

EXPEDITIONS AND ASCENTS
ON NANDA DEVI

*Note: Expedition members only noted. Most parties were enlarged by
porters, sherpa high-altitude porters/climbers, liaison officers etc.*

1934 Nanda Devi. South Ridge attempt. Eric Shipton and H.W.Tilman advanced 3000ft
/914m up the most likely looking ascent route (September). First ascent of Maiktoli (Shipton,
Angtharkay, Kusang). First traverse of Sunderdhunga Col (Tilman, Shipton, Angtharkay, Kusang
and Pasang). Nanda Devi by Eric Shipton (Hodder and Stoughton, London. 1936)

1936 Nanda Devi. South Ridge. First ascent by Noel Odell and H.W.Tilman (29 August),
members of an eight-strong Anglo-American party led by T.Graham Brown and Charles Houston.
Kitar died in Base Camp. Longstaff's Col traversed by Tilman, Houston and Pasang Kikuli.
The Ascent of Nanda Devi by H.W.Tilman (Cambridge University Press, London; Macmillan, New York. 1937)

1939 Nanda Devi East. South Ridge. First ascent by Jakob Bujak and Janusz Klarner
(2 July), members of a four-strong Polish expedition led by Dr Adam Karpinski. This is the
ridge that rises from Longstaff's Col. The party approached from the east. On 19 July Karpinski
and Stefan Bernadzikiewicz were killed during an attempt on Tirsuli. AJ 51, p327

1951 Nanda Devi and **Nanda Devi East** South Ridge. Second ascent by Roger Duplat
and Gilbert Vignes (29 June), members of an eight-strong French expedition led by Duplat. The
pair were last seen moving steadily upwards a short distance below the summit. Their plan
was to attempt the long ridge-traverse to Nanda Devi East. This peak was climbed by Louis
Dubost and Tenzing Norgay (second ascent – using the Polish South Ridge route) on 6 July
in the process of searching for signs of Duplat and Vignes.
A Kiss to High Heaven by J-J Languepin (William Kimber, London. 1956)

1957 Nanda Devi South Ridge attempt. An Indian expedition led by Nandu Jayal reached
a point 500ft / 152m below the summit. Mountain World 1964-5, p53

1961 Nanda Devi South Ridge attempt. An Indian expedition led by Gurdial Singh. Later
Devistan (first ascent) and Maiktoli (second) were climbed. A.J 66, p390; Mountain World 1964-5, p53

1964 Nanda Devi. South Ridge. Third ascent by Nawang Gombu and Dawa Norbu (20
June), members of an eight-strong Indian expedition led by Maj. N Kumar. First ascent of
Devistan 2 by Capt B.P.Singh and three others (24 June) – a day's climb of nearly 6000ft
/1829m matching Longstaff's celebrated Trisul ascent in 1907! Mountain World 1964-5, pp52-56

1964 Nanda Devi East South Ridge attempt. An Indian expedition led by M.S.Kohli
abandoned the route after mid June storms and when a sherpa fell 3000ft /914m and luckily
sustained only broken bones. Alpen 1964, p140; Mountain World 1964-65, p53

1965-1968 Nanda Devi. South Ridge. Fourth ascent. American and Indian Everest climbers and others reportedly involved in a joint mission to place a nuclear-powered device on the summit to monitor Chinese missile tests etc. in Sinkiang. The meteorologists in the 1964 Indian expedition may have been a preliminary to this? Though the CIA and American Government were involved, it seems that on the Indian side only the Army participated and the Prime Minister (Indira Ghandi) was not informed. The device was carried to 22,000ft / 6707m and secured but on return (1966) was found to have been swept away by avalanche necessitating further (unsuccessful) expeditions to locate and remove it. There is concern that at some point it will emerge from the ice and pollute the Rishi Ganga which eventually feeds the Ganges. Later a similar device was installed on Nanda Kot – soon made redundant by improved satellites. This event was not formally recorded in the mountaineering press as the participants are believed to be "sworn" to secrecy under the relevant national laws. These events may have led to the embargo on foreign expeditions visiting the Inner Sanctuary in the following years and also the more recent restrictions. One climber is believed to have soloed the peak during the 1966 visit and others are believed to have suffered (and even died) from radiation poisoning. Anecdotal reports plus: *Berkeley Barb* Vol 4, Issue 95 – "USAF Mystery Mission"; *Seattle Post Intelligencer*, 5 May 1974 – "Filling in the Blanks on the CIA" by Jack Anderson; *Outside*, May 1978 – "The Nanda Devi Caper" by Howard Kohn.

1970 Nanda Devi East. South Ridge attempt. An Indian expedition led by Nandlal Purohit. reached Camp 3 before bad weather intervened. *AAJ* 1971, p444

1975 Nanda Devi and **Nanda Devi East.** South Ridge. Fifth ascent by Jean Coudray, Raymond Renaud (14 June), Balwant Sandhu and Prem Chand (16 June), members of a thirteen-strong Indo/French expedition (including eight ENSA Instructors). Nanda Devi East was climbed by Yves Pollet Villard, Walter Cecchinel and Dorjee Lathoo (16 June). An attempt to link both peaks (using fixed ropes) was aborted when the monsoon broke. *AAJ* 1976, pp523-524

1976 Nanda Devi East and **Nanda Devi** First traverse. Sixth ascent. Yoshinori Hasegawa and Kazushige Takami traversed from East to Main peak on 13/14 June, supported by Yazuo Kato and Masafumi Teramoto – members of a twenty-one-strong Indo/Japanese party. Four camps were established on the South Ridges of each peak during May and early June. From the highest Nanda Devi camp (23,635ft / 7205m) Kato, Teramoto, Minoru Kobayashi and Nawang Phenjo traversed horizontally across the South Face to establish a camp where Nanda Devi's steep East Ridge joins the level linking arête. While the others retired Kato and Teramoto awaited Hasegawa and Takami who were traversing the linking ridge (from their camp near the summit of Nanda Devi East). The main difficulties were at the lowest point of the traverse (in parts overhanging and knife-edged) which took five hours to pass. The Ridge Camp was reached in mid-afternoon. Kato and Teramoto then retired (with some difficulty) to their Nanda Devi South Ridge camp. Both pairs met at the summit in mid-afternoon the next day having climbed the South and East Ridges. All four climbers then descended the South Ridge. *AAJ* 1977 pp 244, 248.

1976 Nanda Devi. North-West Face / North Buttress. Seventh ascent. This hard new route was completed on 1 September by John Roskelley, Jim States and Lou Reichardt, members of a twelve-strong Indo/American expedition led by Willi Unsoeld and H.Adams Carter. During another attempt Ms Nanda Devi Unsoeld, the co-leader's daughter died of an altitude aggravated illness. *AAJ* 1977, pp1-29; *Nanda Devi: The Tragic Expedition* by John Roskelley (Stackpole, Harrisburg. 1987)

1977 Nanda Devi. South Face. Eighth ascent by Eric Roberts, Gil Harder (21 June), Len Smith and Stuart Jones (22 June), members of a twelve-strong Anglo-American party led by Roberts. *AAJ* 1978, pp599-600

1977 Nanda Devi. North-West Face / North Ridge attempt. A seventeen-strong Indo/ Japanese party led by Tokichiro Morita turned back 3500ft / 1067m from summit. Morita and Naoto Haniu (both ill) and Toyokaza Muranishi (head injury) evacuated by helicopter on 15 and 28 Sept. This venture was (implicity) criticised for campsite litter. *AAJ* 1978, p600; *AAJ* 1979, p281

1978 Nanda Devi. South Ridge. Ninth ascent by David Hambly, David McClung, William Fryberger, Bruce Byers, Steve Casebold and Glenn Brindiero (21 June), members of an eight-strong American team. Capt S.S.Dhillon (liaison officer) fell and was killed below Camp 2. The expedition spokesman Michael Clarke later criticised the Japanese and Czechoslovak teams on the mountain at this time for leaving campsites in a polluted state. *AAJ* 1979, pp280-281

1978 Nanda Devi North-West (Rishi) Spur attempt. A seventeen-strong Czechoslovak expedition led by Vladimir Starcala aborted its seige-style bid (with many fixed ropes) on this complex ridge on 20 June when monsoon snow made progress on the crumbling rock towers very difficult. This expedition was later (implicitly) criticised for campsite litter. *AAJ* 1979, p281

1978 Nanda Devi East South Ridge attempt. An eight-strong Japanese expedition led by Mitsuharo Nishimoto reached 500ft / 152m below the summit on 14 June. *AAJ* 1979, p283

1978 Nanda Devi North Face / North-East Pillar (Spur) attempt. Between 15 and 22 September Terry King and Paul Lloyd (British) made an alpine-style bid to climb the left-hand of the three North Face ridges, hoping to traverse the mountain and descend the South Ridge. At 22,500ft / 6860m unstable snow on a very complex ridge prompted a retreat. No further attempt was possible as at Base Camp they were arrested and taken to Josimath by Border Police for questioning about possible espionage. *Mountain* 61, pp34; *AAJ* 1979, pp282-283

1978 Nanda Devi East South-West Ridge ascent. A six-strong British expedition led by David Hopkins. David Challis and Andrew Wielochowshi completed the South-West Ridge to its junction with the South Ridge but turned back 800ft / 244m below the summit on 23 September. Plans to traverse (alpine-style) from East to Main Peak were aborted after Ben Beattie fell and was killed while descending from a bivouac. Both this and the aforementioned King/Lloyd expedition experienced official complications attending the mid-summer press revelations about the 1965-1968 CIA/Indian Army activities in the Sanctuary. *AAJ* 1979, pp283-284

1980 Nanda Devi. South Ridge attempt. Two members of a twenty-four strong Indian Army (Engineers) expedition led by Capt. Jai Bahuguna failed 300ft / 91m below the summit on 11 June. A porter was drowned on the approach march. *AAJ* 1981, p274

1981 Nanda Devi. North Face / North-East Pillar (Spur). Tenth ascent. This fourth new route on the mountain was climbed by Otokar Srovnal, Bohumil Kadlcik, Leos Horka, Ludvik Palecek, Kamil Karafa (16 September), Josef Rakoncaj and Leopold Sulovsky (19 September) members of a thirteen-strong Czechoslovak team led by Vlastimil Smida. Having attempted the North-West (Rishi) Spur in 1978 the same group shifted their objective to the difficult spur tackled by the Lloyd/King party in 1978. In a climb reminiscent of the British Annapurna South Face route, fixed-rope was used to establish three camps, the highest at 23,625ft / 7202m. From here they pushed on in semi-alpine-style (ropes fixed on the final headwall), with snow hole bivouacs, to complete a difficult route. AAJ 1982, pp77-78

1981 Nanda Devi. South Ridge ascent. Ms Rekha Sharma, Ms Chandra Prabha Aitwal, Ms Harshawanti Bisht – first female ascents – Rattan Singha, Dorji Lhatoo, and Sonam Paljor reached the summit on 19 September and two days later it was climbed by Nandial Purohit – all members of an eleven-strong Indian party led by Balwant Sandhu. AAJ 1982, p241

1981 Nanda Devi and **Nanda Devi East** South Ridge and South-West Ridge ascents. An Indian Army (Paratroops) expedition led by Maj. Kiran I. Kumar was active on both peaks. The South-West Ridge of East Peak was climbed (four camps) to the summit for the first time on 4 October by Capt. Premjit Lal and Phu Dorjee but both fell and were killed on the descent. Four other members climbed the route on 7 October and five more on 9 October but of this group Havildar Daya Chan slipped and fell to his death on the descent. The South Ridge of Main Peak was climbed on 12 October by Gyarsi Ram, Wangdu Tsering and Duhsera Kami but in two seperate incidents Ram and Lakha Singh slipped and were killed – a total of five deaths, raising questions about expedition competence in basic alpine skills? AAJ 1982, p242

1982 Nanda Devi South Ridge attempt. A six-strong Australian expedition led by Michael Rheinberger failed at 24,000ft / 7317m because of high winds. AAJ 1983, p250

1982 Inner Sanctuary closed to allow area to "recover" from expedition pollution etc.

1989 Nanda Devi East. South Ridge attempt. A thirteen-strong Indo/Polish expedition (Ldrs. Jan Kwaiton, S.P.Chamoli) failed at 21,000ft / 6402m on 30 September. AAJ 190, p257

1991 Nanda Devi East South Ridge ascents. A twenty-eight-strong Indo/Ukrainian expedition led by S.Bhattacharjee. Matislav Gorbenko and Vladislav Terzeol succeeded (21 September) and on three further bids twelve more climbers reached the summit. AAJ 1992, p230.

1993 Nanda Devi South Ridge ascent. An Indian ecological expedition led by Lt.Col.V. K.Bhatt, comprising twenty-five climbers, ten eco-scientists, five foresters, two doctors, two nurses and a camera crew visited the Inner Sanctuary to assess the recovery, check flora and fauna and clean up garbage (over one ton removed). The normal route was climbed on 15 May by Maj. Amin Naik, Capt. Anand Swaroop, G.K.Sharma, Lance Havilidar Didar Singh, and Naik S.P.Bhatt. The presence of a strong medical team on this trip suggests that finding the nuclear device may have been on the agenda – the continued restrictions on access to the Sanctuary implies the failure of this aim? AAJ 1994, p228

1993 Nanda Devi East South Ridge ascent. S.D Thomas and six others, members of an Indian expedition led by S.C.Negi, summitted on 5 October. AAJ 1994, p228

1994 Nanda Devi East South Ridge ascents and attempts. A Catalan group led by Ferran Garcia succeeded on 27 June and Roger Payne (UK) and Ms Julie-Ann Clyma (NZ) made an alpine-style ascent on 6 October (first female ascent); a Basque party led by Montxo Lopez de Ipina and an Indo/US party both failed in their attempts. *AAJ* 1995, p259

1995 Nanda Devi East South Ridge attempt. A twelve-strong Czech expedition led by Josef Umerala reached a height of 23,288ft / 7100m in mid May. Miroslav Rychlik fell 656ft /200m to his death when a fixed-rope broke. *AAJ* 1996, p252

1996 Nanda Devi East. South Ridge ascent. Four members (including two sherpas) of a Korean expedition led by Jeong Jeon-Mo succeeded on 1 September. *AAJ* 1997, p278

Summary At present Nanda Devi has four routes (the South, East and N.W.Face / N.Buttress and the N.Face/N.E. Pillar) and Nanda Devi East has one – the South Ridge (with a variation approach up the South-West Ridge). Following the Vignes/Duplat traverse bid in 1951, alpine-style attempts have been few and it seems only two have been successful (the unnamed climber in 1966 – though he may have had support camps – and the Payne/Clyma East Peak ascent in 1994, though the 1939 Polish ascent of East Peak was clearly very frugal). Spurs on the north and west of Main Peak remain unclimbed but the most obvious challenges are the "Eigerish" North-West Face of Main Peak and the equally daunting North Faces of Main and East Peaks. Alpine-style ascents of the existing routes also remain, notably the Traverse, which resembles a high-altitude Bezingi Traverse, albeit more serious with few escape routes. The continued restriction on Inner Sanctuary access may persist until the "nuclear-device question" has been resolved.

Nanda Devi Early Ascensionists (those who took part in the first ten ascents)

Noel Odell (1936)	Yazuo Kato (1976)	David McClung (1978)
H.W.Tilman (1936)	Masafumi Teramoto (1976)	William Fryberger (1978)
Roger Duplat (1951) •	Yoshinori Hasegawa (1976)	Bruce Byers (1978)
Gilbert Vignes (1951) •	Kazushige Takami (1976)	Steve Casebold (1978)
Nawang Gombu (1964)	John Roskelley (1976)	Glenn Brindiero (1978)
Dawa Norbu (1964)	Louis Reichardt (1976)	Otokar Srovnal (1981)
Un-named (1966)	Jim States (1976)	Bohumil Kadlcik (1981)
Jean Coudray (1975)	Eric Roberts (1977)	Leos Horka (1981)
Raymond Renaud (1975)	Gil Harder (1977)	Ludvik Palecek (1981)
Balwant Sandhu (1975)	Len Smith (1977)	Kamil Karafa (1981)
Prem Chand (1975)	Stuart Jones (1977)	Josef Rakoncaj (1981)
	David Hambly (1978)	Leopold Sulovsky (1981)

Expedition fatalities: Nanda Devi and Nanda Devi East (from accident • or illness +)

Kitar (1936) +	Ben Beattie (1978) •	Gyarsi Ram (1981) •
Roger Duplat (1951) •	Unnamed porter (1980) •	Capt. Lakha Singh (1981) •
Gilbert Vignes (1951) •	Capt. Premjit Lal (1981) •	Miroslav Rychlik (1995) •
Ms Nanda Devi Unsoeld (1976) +	Phu Dorjee (1981) •	
Capt. S.S.Dhillon (1978) •	Havildar Daya Chan (1981) •	

INDEX